Encountering
the Book of Isaiah

Encountering the Book of Isaiah

A Historical and Theological Survey

Bryan E. Beyer

Baker Academic

Grand Rapids, Michigan

© 2007 by Bryan E. Beyer

Published by Baker Academic
a division of Baker Publishing Group
P.O. Box 6287, Grand Rapids, MI 49516-6287
www.bakeracademic.com

Printed in the United States of America

Library of Congress Cataloging-in-Publication Data

Beyer, Bryan.
    Encountering the book of Isaiah : a historical and theological survey / Bryan E.
Beyer.
        p.   cm. — (Encountering biblical studies)
    Includes bibliographical references and indexes.
    ISBN 10: 0-8010-2645-8 (pbk.)
    ISBN 978-0-8010-2645-4 (pbk.)
    1. Bible. O.T. Isaiah—Textbooks. I. Title.
    BS1515.55.B49 2007
    224'.1061—dc22   2007012918

To Mom and Dad,
with deep gratitude for
your immeasurable contribution
in shaping my life
to follow Jesus.

Proverbs 6:20–22

Contents in Brief

Contents

Contents

Contents

Preface

I love fishing; in fact, I'm totally hooked! (Pun intended.) I have two uncles whose enthusiasm for fishing spilled over into my childhood, and now I have a son who has caught my enthusiasm.

Learning to fish is a process. At the beginning level, the focus is often simply on acquiring a taste for fish. Or perhaps novices learn the mechanics of reeling in a fish after more experienced anglers prepare the rod and reel, cast the line, and maybe even hook the fish for them.

At the intermediate level, the responsibility begins to shift. Those who have mastered the basics now work on the mechanics of baiting the hook or choosing a lure, casting it, and setting the hook when a fish strikes. However, as at the beginning level, they still often draw on the knowledge of more experienced anglers.

At the advanced level, the responsibility has shifted even more. Those fishing have a good idea where the fish are and apply their knowledge to select the correct tackle to maximize their chances of catching fish.

The parallels between fishing and Bible study become clear when we stop to consider the various levels of skill required. The beginning level of fishing corresponds to the Bible survey course, in which the instructor provides information for the students to digest. The goal is to cover a basic amount of content and to instill in students an enthusiasm for studying the Bible.

The intermediate level of fishing corresponds to hermeneutics and exegesis courses. Here students learn about Bible study tools and how to use them effectively. Nonetheless, they continue to lean on their instructor's guidance.

The advanced level of fishing parallels upper-division college and graduate-level courses. In such courses, the instructor "turns students loose" to apply the tools they have acquired to do their own biblical and research projects. Through such work, students develop their skills and learn to do independent biblical research.

This book was written for serious students of the Bible. It assumes a completion of Bible survey courses as well as a working knowledge of the principles of hermeneutics and exegesis. I hope advanced college students and graduate students will find it challenging and useful.

You will need to apply the tools and skills you have learned along the way as you dig for meaning in the book of Isaiah. I hope you will experience the joy that comes with discovering truth for yourself and wrestling with its implications for your life.

As this project goes to press, I realize I have many to thank for their contributions. I am grateful to my colleagues at Baker Publishing Group for their assistance along the way and for the collegial work and encouragement of former editor Jim Weaver and current editor Brian Bolger. Thank you, gentlemen!

I also had the privilege of having Eugene H. Merrill, Distinguished Professor of Old Testament at Dallas Theological Seminary, serve as my editor. I am blessed and the book is richer because of his interaction with the manuscript. I have also appreciated Dr. Merrill's encouragement along the way when the task seemed unending.

Columbia International University granted me a study leave during fall 2003 so I could devote more attention to the project. I am grateful to serve at an institution where the focus is "preparing world Christians to know Christ and to make him known." I am especially grateful for the assistance and encouragement of former CIU provost Ralph E. Enlow Jr.

I also wish to thank the many CIU students who have taken my Isaiah course. I have gained much from their enthusiasm, and their sharp questions and insights have helped me focus my thoughts. Many have also assured me they have prayed regularly for my completion of this work, and their support has meant a lot.

Many thanks go to Amanda Thomas for her careful work in helping me prepare the manuscript. I am grateful for her eye for detail and for her suggestions, but mostly for her passion to see the Lord's work advance.

I also wish to thank my graduate research assistant Jason Conrad for his timely assistance as I came down the "home stretch" on the manuscript. Sue Mitchell also assisted in the preparation of the manuscript's final copy.

My wife, Yvonne, has faithfully stood by me through this project and has supported me with her love, her encouragement, and her prayers. Our life together continues to be a wondrous celebration.

Finally, I owe a great debt of gratitude to my parents, Ronald and Irene Beyer, who modeled Christian marriage for me for over forty-seven years until my mother's unexpected passing on August 27, 2000. In the spring of 1998, I even had the joy of having both Mom and Dad in my Isaiah course! I am deeply grateful for their contribution to my life, and it is with much love and appreciation that I dedicate this book to them.

Dad, thank you for faithfully loving Mom to the end. Thanks for spending so much time with me as I was growing up and for encouraging me to follow the Lord wherever he directed. I'm grateful for our continuing deep relationship.

Mom, my earliest memories are of you telling me about Jesus. In doing so, you helped lay the foundation for my life. You loved me then, and I know you love me still.

To the Student

Encountering the book of Isaiah in a systematic way for the first time is an exciting experience. It can also be overwhelming because there is so much to learn. You need to learn not only the content of the book but also important background information about the world in which the writer of the book lived.

The purpose of this textbook is to make that encounter less daunting. To accomplish this, several learning aids have been incorporated into the text. You should familiarize yourself with these aids by reading the following introductory material.

Sidebars

Sidebars isolate contemporary issues of concern and show how the book of Isaiah speaks to these pressing ethical and theological issues.

Chapter Outlines

At the beginning of each chapter is a brief outline of the chapter's contents. *Study Suggestion*: Before reading the chapter, take a few minutes to read the outline. Think of it as a road map, and remember that it is easier to reach your destination if you know where you are going.

Chapter Objectives

A brief list of objectives appears at the beginning of each chapter. These present the tasks you should be able to perform after reading the chapter. *Study Suggestions*: Read the objectives carefully before beginning to read the text. As you read the text, keep these objectives in mind and take notes to help you remember what you have read. After reading the chapter, return to the objectives and see if you can perform the tasks.

Key Terms and Glossary

Key terms have been identified throughout the text by the use of **boldface** type. This will alert you to important words or phrases you may not be familiar with. Definitions of these words can be found at the end of the book in an alphabetical glossary. *Study Suggestion*: When you encounter a key term in the text, stop and read the definition before continuing through the chapter.

Study Questions

A few discussion questions have been provided at the end of each chapter, and these can be used to review for examinations. *Study Suggestion*: Write suitable answers to the study questions in preparation for tests.

Further Reading

A helpful bibliography for supplementary reading is presented at the end of the book. *Study Suggestion*: Use this list to explore areas of special interest.

Visual Aids

A host of illustrations has been included in this textbook. Each illustration has been carefully selected and is intended to make the text not only more aesthetically pleasing but also more easily mastered.

May your encounter of the book of Isaiah be an exciting adventure!

Abbreviations

Old Testament

Genesis	Gn
Exodus	Ex
Leviticus	Lv
Numbers	Nm
Deuteronomy	Dt
Joshua	Jos
Judges	Jgs
Ruth	Ru
1 Samuel	1 Sm
2 Samuel	2 Sm
1 Kings	1 Kgs
2 Kings	2 Kgs
1 Chronicles	1 Chr
2 Chronicles	2 Chr
Ezra	Ezr
Nehemiah	Neh
Esther	Est
Job	Jb
Psalms	Ps(s)
Proverbs	Prv
Ecclesiastes	Eccl
Song of Songs	Sg (Song)
Isaiah	Is
Jeremiah	Jer
Lamentations	Lam
Ezekiel	Ez
Daniel	Dn
Hosea	Hos
Joel	Jl
Amos	Am
Obadiah	Ob
Jonah	Jon
Micah	Mi
Nahum	Na
Habakkuk	Hb
Zephaniah	Zep
Haggai	Hg
Zechariah	Zec
Malachi	Mal

New Testament

Matthew	Mt
Mark	Mk
Luke	Lk
John	Jn
Acts of the Apostles	Acts
Romans	Rom
1 Corinthians	1 Cor
2 Corinthians	2 Cor
Galatians	Gal
Ephesians	Eph
Philippians	Phil
Colossians	Col
1 Thessalonians	1 Thes
2 Thessalonians	2 Thes
1 Timothy	1 Tm
2 Timothy	2 Tm
Titus	Ti
Philemon	Phlm
Hebrews	Heb
James	Jas
1 Peter	1 Pt
2 Peter	2 Pt
1 John	1 Jn
2 John	2 Jn
3 John	3 Jn
Jude	Jude
Revelation	Rv

1 Who Was Isaiah, and What Do We Know about Him and His Book?

Outline

Objectives

After reading this chapter, you should be able to

1. List the basic facts regarding Isaiah's personal life.
2. Summarize the historical setting in which Isaiah ministered.
3. Describe the major features and themes of Isaiah's message.

theophoric

The year was 740 BC. Uzziah (also known as Azariah), Judah's great king, had died after a fifty-two-year reign. Uzziah became king at age sixteen following his father Amaziah's assassination. He had accomplished many great works on behalf of his people, defeating enemies, solidifying Judah's borders, and enhancing Jerusalem's defense.

Uzziah had begun well spiritually too. Late in his reign, however, he became proud and tried to burn incense in the temple—a task reserved for the priests—and God struck him with leprosy for his sin. Uzziah's son Jotham served as co-regent of the kingdom of Judah during the last eleven years of Uzziah's life. Now Uzziah had died; what would happen to Judah?

The death of a king and the accession of a new king was often a perilous time for a kingdom. Enemies might choose such a time to attack the kingdom, forcing the new monarch to prove his power immediately. New policies might affect government, taxes, the economy, and life in general. Citizens often became uneasy as they wondered how life might change under new leadership.

However, this time of uncertainty for God's people was not a time of uncertainty for God. The sovereign Lord of history knew exactly what he was doing. He was preparing a messenger—a prophet—to bring his message to a people who desperately needed to hear it. Isaiah was that prophet.

Isaiah the Man

Who exactly was the prophet Isaiah, and what do we know about him? His name means "Yahweh saves" and is related to the names Joshua and Hosea (see sidebar 1.1). The Bible reveals virtually nothing about Isaiah's family of origin. Isaiah 1:1 says he was the son of Amoz, but we know nothing about Amoz—except, of course, that he was Isaiah's father! Other scriptural references to Amoz—twelve more in all[1]—provide no additional information.

Rabbinic sources suggest Isaiah may have come from royal lineage.[2] He may have been the cousin of King Uzziah (or Azariah), who ruled as Judah's king from 792 to 740 BC.[3] Some scholars have suggested such a relationship might explain why Isaiah apparently had regular access to Judah's kings (Is 7:3–17; 37:6–7, 21–35). On the other hand, other prophets, such as Nathan, also enjoyed access to the court (2 Sm 7:2–17; 12:1–15; 1 Kgs 1:22–27). Kings might have had many reasons to consult prophets on a regular basis.

The book of Isaiah reveals Isaiah had at least two sons. One was Shear-Jashub, whose name means "a remnant will return." Shear-Jashub appears in Isaiah 7:3, accompanying his father to an important meeting with Ahaz, Judah's king, who was trying to determine how to deal with an impending threat from an Israelite-Syrian coalition (7:1–2). No doubt Isaiah brought his son to the meeting as a living object lesson to encourage the wavering king to take heart.

Isaiah's second son was Maher-Shalal-Hash-Baz, whose name means "swift is the plunder, speedy is the prey." His prophetic birth and naming appear in Isaiah 8:1–4 as a sign of Judah's deliverance from the above-mentioned Israelite-Syrian coalition. Isaiah declared that before the child learned to cry out, "Mommy! Daddy!" the coalition's threat would have disappeared.

The text does not mention Isaiah's wife by name. Isaiah may in fact have had two wives if the prophecies of Immanuel and Maher-Shalal-Hash-Baz have a relationship to each other. If one takes the view that the names Immanuel (7:14) and Maher-Shalal-Hash-Baz (8:1–4) refer to the same child, that the Hebrew word 'almah in 7:14 means "virgin," and that the "prophetess" of 8:3 is Isaiah's wife, then Shear-Jashub (7:3), who was present for Isaiah's meeting with Ahaz, must have had a differ-

Sidebar 1.1
Theophoric Personal Names in the Bible

Ancient Near Eastern names often included a divine name in them. Parents tended to give their children names that honored a deity they worshiped. In polytheistic societies, **theophoric** (god-bearing) personal names often provide insight into which deities are most popular with the general population.

In the Old Testament, two divine names are by far the most common. One is the name Yahweh, the other is *'el*, translated "God."

The divine name Yahweh usually appears in the shortened form *-yahu* at the end of a name or *Yeho-* at the beginning of a name. Each name contains the Lord's name plus a descriptor highlighting one of his qualities. Consider the following examples:

English Form	Hebrew Form	Meaning
Isaiah	*yisha'yahu*	Yahweh saves
Jeremiah	*yirmeyahu*	Yahweh is exalted
Hananiah	*hananyahu*	Yahweh is gracious
Hezekiah	*yehizqiyahu*	Yahweh is my strength
Jehoahaz	*yeho'ahaz*	Yahweh has seized
Jehoiakim	*yehoyaqim*	Yahweh will establish
Jehoshaphat	*yehoshaphat*	Yahweh has judged
Uzziah	*'uzziyahu*	Yahweh is my might
Zechariah	*zekaryahu*	Yahweh remembers
Zedekiah	*tsidqiyahu*	Yahweh is my righteousness

The Hebrew word *'el*, which means "god" or "God," also commonly occurs in personal names. As with the names that contain the name Yahweh, those that contain *'el* also include a descriptor highlighting a divine quality or action. Again, consider the following examples:

English Form	Hebrew Form	Meaning
Daniel	*dani'el*	God has judged (or perhaps "God is my judge")
Eleazar	*'eli'azar*	My God has helped
Elijah	*'eliyahu*	My God is Yahweh (note the combination of both Yahweh and *'el*)
Elimelech	*'elimelech*	My God is king
Elkanah	*'elqanah*	God has acquired
Ezekiel	*yehizqi'el*	God is my strength
Immanuel	*immanu'el*	God is with us
Ishmael	*yishma'el*	God has heard
Joel	*yo'el*	Yahweh is God ("Jo" is probably a shortened form of "yeho-"; see the preceding chart)
Nathaniel	*netani'el*	God has given

ent mother. (Further discussion of these issues occurs in chap. 5.)

Rabbinic tradition suggests Isaiah died a martyr's death during the reign of King Manasseh, Hezekiah's son.[4] According to the tradition, Isaiah was placed between two boards and sawn in two. Perhaps the writer of the book of Hebrews knew this tradition and was alluding to the prophet in his list of heroes of the faith (Heb 11:37).

Like other prophets, Isaiah possessed a heart devoted to God and a strong sense of calling. His dramatic encounter with the Lord, the Heavenly King (6:1–8), laid a foundation for his prophetic ministry. Isaiah's im-

passioned messages revealed his own zeal for God as the prophet-messenger spoke the words God had given him.

Isaiah also possessed great courage and conviction. He is not known—as is the prophet Ezekiel—for his many symbolic prophetic actions, but he did lay aside his garments for three years as a sign of impending judgment against Egypt (20:1–6). Isaiah also interacted with kings Ahaz and Hezekiah, and his words suggest a confident air that comes from a clear sense of calling (7:4–16; 37:6–7, 21–35). Isaiah knew his God and knew what his God had called him to do.

Isaiah's world
(Courtesy of
Tim Dowley
Associates Ltd.)

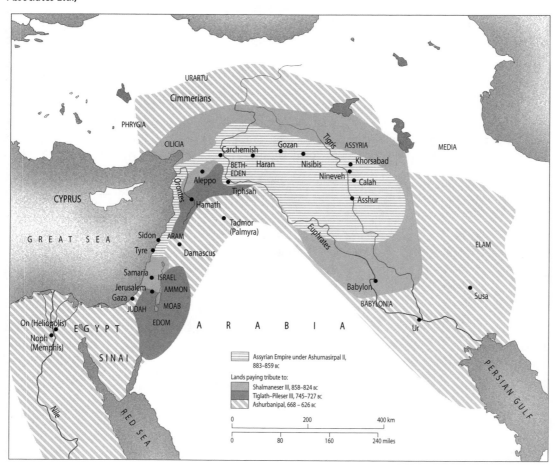

Sidebar 1.2
Chronology of the Hebrew Kings

The chronology of the Hebrew kings has challenged many a Bible student. The books of 1 and 2 Kings alternately shift between the northern and the southern kingdoms, and many kings of Israel and Judah have similar or identical names. Furthermore, when students attempt to lay out a chronology for these kings, they find it difficult to align the years in which the kings reigned. Is there a solution to the many apparent discrepancies in the numbers?

In the early 1940s, Edwin R. Thiele wrote his doctoral dissertation on the problem of the chronology of the kings of Israel and Judah. How could they all fit? Thiele approached his task assuming the numbers made sense to the biblical writers. As he investigated, he began to make discoveries that helped solve the chronological problems that appear in Kings and Chronicles.

First, Thiele noted that the northern and southern kingdoms used the expression "first year" in different ways. Sometimes ancient chronologists would call the period between a king's accession and his coronation his first year, whether it was two days or eleven months. On other occasions, the expression "first year" might designate what we would consider the first year. Thus, a "short year" could confuse the chronology.

Second, Thiele suggested that in Israel the king's coronation occurred in the spring, whereas in Judah the ceremony occurred in the fall. Scholars could account for variations of a year or less in this way.

Third, Thiele found significant cases of overlapping reigns or co-regencies (see also sidebar 1.3). Uzziah and Jotham, for example, overlapped for eleven years due to Uzziah's leprosy late in his reign (2 Chr 26:16–21). Thus, though the Bible correctly asserts that Jotham reigned sixteen years, he reigned only five by himself.

Thiele found that by applying the principles he suggested, virtually all the chronological difficulties in the lists of the kings of Israel and Judah could be resolved.

Thiele's conclusions, presented in his *Chronology of the Hebrew Kings* and *Mysterious Numbers of the Hebrew Kings*, are still fundamental to solving the problems of royal chronology in Kings and Chronicles, and scholars continue to build on his works.

Isaiah's Times

Isaiah 1:1 mentions four Judean kings whose reigns overlapped Isaiah's prophetic ministry: Uzziah, Jotham, Ahaz, and Hezekiah. The following is a brief summary of the kings who reigned during Isaiah's ministry, including Manasseh, who is not mentioned in Isaiah 1:1. (See also sidebars 1.2 and 1.3 regarding the chronology and heritage of Israel's and Judah's kings.)

Uzziah (2 Kgs 15:1–7; 2 Chr 26:1–23)

The writers of Kings and Chronicles evaluated Judah's kings as alternately good or evil, in contrast to the northern kingdom of Israel, all of whose kings were evil. Uzziah, also known as Azariah, was all in all a good king.

Uzziah assumed Judah's throne at age sixteen and reigned fifty-two years, some as co-regent with his father Amaziah. He enjoyed military victories over the Philistines in the regions of Gath and Ashdod and also received tribute from the Ammonites to the east. The king fortified Jerusalem, enhancing its security, and boasted a strong army of well-trained soldiers. He also cultivated the land to get the most out of his agricultural and pastoral holdings.

Despite his success and power, Uzziah did not finish his reign well. Early in his reign, Uzziah had followed the

Following in His Father's Footsteps? The Heritage of Judah's Kings

Nineteen kings ruled Judah from the division of the kingdom until its fall to Nebuchadnezzar in 587 BC. The following list presents kings, their reigns, their evaluation, and some general observations. The chronology is based on Thiele's *Mysterious Numbers of the Hebrew Kings*.

KING	REIGN*	EVALUATION
Rehoboam	930–913	Evil
Abijam	913–910	Evil
Asa	910–869	Good
Jehoshaphat	872–848	Good
Jehoram	848–841	Evil
Ahaziah	841	Evil
Athaliah	841–835	Evil (ruled as queen between Ahaziah and Jehoash/Joash)
Jehoash/Joash	835–796	Good
Amaziah	796–767	Good
Azariah/Uzziah	792–740	Good
Jotham	750–732	Good
Ahaz	735–715	Evil
Hezekiah	729–686	Good
Manasseh	696–642	Evil
Amon	642–640	Evil
Josiah	640–609	Good
Jehoahaz	609	Evil
Jehoiakim	608–598	Evil
Jehoiachin	598–597	Evil
Zedekiah	597–587	Evil

*All dates are BC.

Observations

1. Eight kings received an evaluation of "good," while eleven kings and one queen, Athaliah, received an evaluation of "evil."
2. A generally stable period under good spiritual leadership prevailed from Asa through Jotham, except for about fifteen years that encompassed the reigns of Jehoram, Ahaziah, and Athaliah. The Bible records that some of Judah's good kings had serious struggles during this time but prevailed as they sought the Lord.
3. After Hezekiah, six of Judah's last seven kings were evil. Josiah's spiritual reforms were insufficient to pull the nation out of its downward spiritual spiral.
4. No discernible pattern exists regarding the kings' spirituality. Each king had to decide for himself whether to follow the Lord.

The legacy of Judah's kings is both encouraging and sobering. The Lord can take people who do not have a godly heritage (e.g., Hezekiah, Josiah) and use them greatly for his service as they surrender their lives to him. At the same time, having a godly heritage (e.g., Ahaz, Manasseh) does not guarantee a life of faithfulness or one filled with God's blessing. One must choose personally whether to follow the Lord.

The Hinnom Valley, where Ahaz and Manasseh carried out many of their idolatrous practices. (Courtesy of Jim Yancey)

co-regency

Lord faithfully (2 Chr 26:5). But late in his reign, the king became proud and tried to usurp the priests' duties and burn incense to the Lord in the temple. God struck Uzziah with leprosy, and the king remained a leper to the day he died. Jotham, the crown prince, reigned eleven of his sixteen years as co-regent with his leprous father.[5]

Jotham (2 Kgs 15:32–38; 2 Chr 27:1–9)

Jotham was a good king overall, reigning for eleven of his sixteen years in a **co-regency** with his father, Uzziah. Spiritually, he followed the Lord as his father had done, though the people by and large did not follow his example. He also subdued the Ammonites, receiving tribute from them, and strengthened Judah's hill country by establishing fortifications and lookout towers.

Meanwhile, in Assyria Tiglath-Pileser III had become king and was contemplating westward expansion. Israel's king Pekah and Syria's king Rezin formed a coalition against Assyria and began to assert pressure on Judah to join the coalition or face invasion. Jotham's son and successor, Ahaz, would have to face the full measure of this pressure.

Ahaz (2 Kgs 16:1–20; 2 Chr 28:1–27)

The biblical writers portray Ahaz as an evil and idolatrous king. Ahaz promoted Baal worship alongside the worship of the Lord and also reinstituted and practiced the abominable custom of child sacrifice in the Hinnom Valley on Jerusalem's southern edge. In response, the Lord brought judgment against Ahaz through the Syrians and the Israelites, who on separate occasions raided Judah and inflicted heavy casualties. Only God's gracious intervention through the prophet Oded prevented Judah's judgment from being even worse. Edomite and Philistine raids also plagued Ahaz's reign.

Ahaz also faced a Syrian-Israelite coalition as it braced itself for war against Tiglath-Pileser III, king of Assyria. Syria and Israel wanted Judah's support against Assyria to ensure they would not be caught between Judah and Assyria if both these kingdoms decided to attack them at once. Judah's king faced a crucial decision: should he join the coalition or stand on God's promise to protect David's line (2 Sm 7:12–16)?

Isaiah met Ahaz and urged him to stand on God's promise (Is 7:1–9), but the king refused. Instead, Ahaz appealed to Tiglath-Pileser III for help, thus giving Assyria even more incentive to push westward. Tiglath-Pileser responded by defeating Damascus, annexing Israel, and imposing vassal status on Judah.

Hezekiah (2 Kgs 18:1–20:21; 2 Chr 29:1–32:33)

Hezekiah followed his spiritually wayward father, Ahaz, to Judah's throne, but in contrast to his father, he determined to follow the Lord. He took steps to eradicate idolatry from the land and promoted Yahwism to an extent Judah had not witnessed for some time. Hezekiah ordered the cleansing of the temple in Jerusalem and consecrated the people to serve God. He also oversaw the reestablishment of regular offerings to provide for the priests and Levites.

During Hezekiah's reign, the northern kingdom of Israel fell to the Assyrian empire (see sidebar 1.4). Hezekiah reached out to the Israelites who remained in the land and invited them to Jerusalem to celebrate Passover. Many came, and a time of spiritual healing occurred.

Hezekiah rebelled against Sennacherib, king of Assyria, then realized his error, quickly capitulated, and offered terms of peace. But when Sennacherib refused and demanded Jerusalem's surrender and exile, Hezekiah again turned to the Lord for deliverance. The Lord responded, striking the Assyrian army with a plague and delivering his people again. In the face of foreign oppression, Hezekiah possessed the faith and courage to do what his father, Ahaz, had refused to do: trust in the Lord and his promises.

Manasseh (2 Kgs 21:1–18; 2 Chr 33:1–20)

Hezekiah had undone much of the spiritual harm of his father, Ahaz. However, Hezekiah's son Manasseh again reversed the trend and sent Judah into a downward spiral from which it would not recover.

Manasseh reestablished Baal worship throughout Judah and ordered the construction of idolatrous altars on the temple grounds. He also promoted and practiced divination and sorcery and reinstituted child sacrifice in the Hinnom Valley. And as stated earlier, Manasseh may also have put Isaiah to death. Indeed, God's people paid a heavy spiritual price during Manasseh's reign.

Manasseh's evil continued throughout his fifty-five-year reign, except for a brief period when he sought the Lord after the Assyrians captured him. The Lord restored Manasseh to his throne, but Manasseh was unable to undo the spiritual damage he had brought to Judah.

Sidebar 1.4
The Capture of Samaria

Second Kings 17:1–6 records Samaria's fall to the Assyrian army in 722 BC and credits the conquest to Shalmaneser, king of Assyria. In the Assyrian royal annals, Sargon II, who succeeded his father, Shalmaneser, to the throne about this time, took credit for the victory. Likely Sargon finished what Shalmaneser began, or perhaps Sargon took credit for victories he won as general before he became king. The following is a description in Sargon's words:

> I besieged and conquered Samaria, led away as plunder 27,290 inhabitants of it. I formed from among them a contingent of 50 chariots and made remaining (inhabitants) assume their (social) positions. I installed over them an officer of mine and imposed upon them the tribute of the former king. . . . I conquered and sacked the towns Shinuhtu and Samaria, and all Israel [literally "Omri-land"].

Adapted from Ancient Near Eastern Texts Relating to the Old Testament *(hereafter* ANET), ed. J. B. Pritchard. 3rd ed. (Princeton: Princeton University Press, 1969), 284–85.

forthtelling

foretelling

Authorship and Date of the Book

Who wrote the book of Isaiah and when? Evangelical scholars have traditionally ascribed authorship of the entire book to Isaiah of Jerusalem, the eighth-century prophet. Some have suggested the book came directly from his hand or through a scribe Isaiah employed to prepare the manuscript. Others have surmised that perhaps shortly after Isaiah's death, his disciples collected his writings and sayings and established them in the book we now call the book of Isaiah.

Since the late nineteenth century, however, many scholars have questioned the traditional view. They have suggested some of the material in chapters 1–39 and all the material from chapters 40–66 did not originate with Isaiah. Naturally, questions about authorship affect questions about date of composition. Since the heart of the issue centers around the dramatic shift in the book's perspective beginning with chapter 40, we will reserve discussion of this topic until later in the text.

Dating Isaiah's Ministry: Does Isaiah 6 Describe Isaiah's Call?

Most interpreters understand Isaiah 6:1–8 as describing Isaiah's call. They point out the grandiose nature of the vision Isaiah experienced, as well as the prophet's confession of utter uncleanness in the presence of God's holiness. Then, following his cleansing by the seraph, Isaiah quickly responded to Yahweh's invitation to take his message to his people. Such an experience was more likely Isaiah's initiation into prophetic ministry than

a confirming vision after years of prophetic service.

If, indeed, Isaiah 6 describes Isaiah's call, then the text also dates the beginning of Isaiah's ministry. Isaiah 6:1 places Isaiah's vision in the year King Uzziah died. The text does not clarify whether Isaiah received his vision prior to or following Uzziah's death, so an approximation of 740–739 BC adequately covers either possibility. Assuming Isaiah's death occurred early in Manasseh's reign, 740–690 BC appears the likely range for his prophetic ministry.

Isaiah's Message

Isaiah's sixty-six chapters cover a wide range of topics and contain a variety of prophetic features. Isaiah uttered words that had primary application for his own generation (**forthtelling**), but he also predicted a great day God would bring about (**foretelling**). His message focused on Judah but was global in its scope. Moreover, Isaiah returned to certain key themes again and again as he proclaimed the Lord's unchanging purpose for his people.

Forthtelling

Isaiah delivered most of his prophetic utterances first and foremost for his own generation. They faced terrible judgment because of their sin, and he tried to warn them. They needed to repent and turn to God in faith.

Bible interpreters often refer to this kind of prophecy as forthtelling. The prophet decried the evil of his day and warned his hearers of the awful consequences they would face if they persisted in their evil. Of course, Isaiah's words still apply today when we encounter situations parallel to those of Isaiah's day.

Foretelling

Isaiah also spoke of the distant future and the great kingdom God was kingdom

Great
Commission

remnant

preparing. His messages announced restoration of God's people to their land, peace and prosperity, victory over their enemies, and a special covenant relationship with the Lord through his anointed servant.

Bible interpreters often refer to this type of prophecy as foretelling. Even though Isaiah's generation would not live to see the fulfillment of these words, the people could draw encouragement for their present situation because the prophet assured them that one day God would establish his **kingdom** forever.

Focus on Judah

Isaiah's ministry focused largely on Judah. Isaiah 1:1 begins, "The vision concerning Judah and Jerusalem that Isaiah son of Amoz saw." The prophet's opening indictment (1:2–26) denounced the wickedness God saw among his people, even in Jerusalem! Many early references in Isaiah's book highlight Judah and Jerusalem as the focus of God's attention (2:1; 3:1, 8; 5:3). Isaiah spoke about other nations too, but Judah received a significant share of his prophetic attention.

Even today, although God hates sin wherever he finds it, he especially wants his people free of it. When God's people live by God's commands, they bring honor to him and also blessing to themselves.

Global in Scope

Isaiah may have focused many of his pronouncements on Judah and Jerusalem, but his vision extended far beyond Judah's borders. God was calling everyone everywhere to serve him.

Isaiah saw a day when all nations would stream to Jerusalem to learn of God and his ways (2:1–4). He also prophesied God's warnings of judgment to the nations of the ancient world (chaps. 13–23). God was no less sovereign over them just because they did not acknowledge him.

Isaiah called all nations to turn to the Lord and be saved, because one day, every knee would bow to God

(45:22–23). He promised foreigners a noble place in God's kingdom if they proved themselves faithful (56:6–7). In fact, Isaiah said that God cared for them so much he would send his messengers to reach them (66:19). Isaiah's words anticipate the **Great Commission** proclaimed by the risen Jesus as he sent forth his disciples to make more disciples throughout all the world (Mt 28:18–20).

Isaiah's Major Themes

The book of Isaiah addresses many issues. Nonetheless, certain themes appear repeatedly. Five of the most significant themes are the remnant, the sovereignty of God, the servant, the Holy One of Israel, and the Messiah. A concordance and/or computer software program can greatly enhance the student's study of these themes.

Remnant

The two Hebrew words often translated "**remnant**" (*she'ar* and *she'erit*) literally mean "remainder," "rest," or "residue." The concept sometimes occurs in contexts where it has this basic meaning and refers to various objects. It describes the sparse number of trees that remain after the Lord's judgment (Is 10:19), as well as the wood left over after the craftsman finishes carving his idol (44:17). It denotes the money left over after financing temple refurbishing (2 Chr 24:14), the portion of a city under a general's control (1 Chr 11:9), and a group of people who remain after God's judgment (Is 16:14; 17:3; Am 5:15).

However, in other contexts, "remnant" denotes a faithful remainder, a group God has chosen, people who are looking to God to work his will in and through them (Is 37:4, 32). They return to the Lord and experience the fullness of his salvation when others do not (Is 10:21–22; Mi 2:12). The remnant concept carries into the New Testament as well (Rom 9:27; 11:5). God is still seeking a faithful remnant that will follow him no matter what the cost.

sovereignty
of God

servant

Holy One
of Israel

Messiah

The Sovereignty of God

The concept of the **sovereignty of God** occurs regularly throughout Isaiah. In fact, those who read the Bible find this concept assumed on every page of Scripture. God is the sovereign Lord of the universe, and as Sovereign, he is actively at work in the world, guiding all history in accordance with his grand purpose.

The theme of God's sovereignty appears in Isaiah's words "the LORD has spoken" (1:2), proclaiming the Lord as ruler of the heavens and earth. When the ruler speaks, the matter is settled.

Isaiah 13–23 declares another astounding truth: God's sovereignty does not end at the borders of Israel and Judah. God is Lord of all nations, whether or not they recognize him. Isaiah clearly grasped the implications of this truth even though he focused his ministry on Judah and Jerusalem. Many people from many nations will recognize God's sovereignty one day, while others never will, but God nonetheless remains sovereign (10:5–7; 37:24–26).

Servant

The term "**servant**" (Heb. *'ebed*) occurs almost eight hundred times in the Old Testament and of those occurrences, thirty-nine appear in Isaiah. The terms "servant" and "slave" are synonymous, though "servant" carries a gentler connotation in our society. Servants are slaves to their master. They have no rights, and their duty consists totally of doing their master's will.

In Isaiah, the term "servant" occasionally describes God's people as a group (41:8; 54:17) but usually denotes individuals who fully follow God's will and serve his people faithfully (22:20; 42:1; 52:13). As they do so, they completely fulfill God's will for their lives.

The New Testament Greek word *doulos* has the same semantic range as *'ebed* and uses the concept in the same way. It occurs 122 times. The apostle Paul described himself as a "servant of Christ" (Rom 1:1) and exhorted the church at Rome to lay hold of the full implications of their slavery to God (Rom 6:16–23). Indeed, he argued that slavery to God and his righteousness grants people the highest freedom life offers—freedom to become all God has created us to be.

The Holy One of Israel

The expression "**Holy One of Israel**" occurs thirty-one times in the Old Testament, and twenty-five of those references appear in Isaiah.[6] The words of the seraphim, "Holy, holy, holy is the LORD Almighty . . ." (Is 6:3), profoundly affected Isaiah's thinking and theology. God stood utterly apart from his creation, including his people. His holy nature clashed with his people's sin. Yet he loved them, desired fellowship with them, and called to them through the law of Moses, as well as through Isaiah and other prophets.

The expression "Holy One of Israel" occurs in both judgmental and redemptive contexts. The Holy One of Israel has experienced rejection from his people, who have resisted his sovereign purposes (Is 1:4; 5:19, 24). He also will judge nations who oppose him (37:23). But the Holy One of Israel also stands as Israel's Savior (43:3) and Redeemer (43:14), who delivers them from exile and establishes his kingdom (see sidebar 1.5).

Messiah

The word "**Messiah**" comes from the Hebrew *mashiach*, which means "anointed one." Kings, priests, and prophets all experienced God's anointing, which symbolized God setting them apart for special service (Lv 4:3; 1 Sm 10:1; 2 Kgs 9:3).

The term *mashiach* and the corresponding verbal form *mashach* occur only twice in Isaiah (45:1; 61:1 respectively). One of the most interesting usages appears in 45:1, where Cyrus, king of Persia, is so designated. We do not know to what extent Cyrus understood his mandate from the Lord (Ezr 1:1), but the Bible is clear that God

Sidebar 1.5
The Expression "Holy One of Israel" in Isaiah

A **concordance** is a tool for Bible study. Students can look up a key word and find in one place all the biblical occurrences of that word. Electronic concordances now available provide the opportunity to search whole phrases or even grammatical constructions in the original languages.

The following list presents all the occurrences of the expression "Holy One of Israel" in Isaiah. Look them up in your Bible, and as you do, note the contexts in which Isaiah uses the expression. Does "Holy One of Israel" tend to emphasize God's judgment, his salvation, or both? Why do you think Isaiah used this term instead of "Holy One of Judah"?

Uses of "Holy One of Israel" in Isaiah

1:4	30:11, 12, 15	47:4
5:19, 24	31:1	48:17
10:20	37:23	49:7
12:6	41:14, 16, 20	54:5
17:7	43:3, 14	55:5
29:19	45:11	60:9, 14

concordance

set him apart for a special work: to bring his people back to their land.

The Messiah is God's chosen instrument to bring about his kingdom. Even though the word does not occur regularly in Isaiah, the concept of messiah lies beneath the surface of many prophetic utterances (9:6–7; 11:1–10; 32:1–4; 42:1–4; 52:13–53:12). God's chosen instrument works faithfully to bring about God's earthly and heavenly kingdoms.

Though many prophets, priests, and kings carried the title *mashiach* in Old Testament times, the New Testament points to Jesus, God's Son, as the ultimate Messiah (Gk. *Christos*). As we will see, many of Isaiah's prophetic utterances point to this Jesus.

Key Terms

concordance	kingdom
co-regency	Messiah
foretelling	remnant
forthtelling	servant
Great Commission	sovereignty of God
Holy One of Israel	theophoric

Study Questions

1. What do we know about Isaiah's background?

2. Summarize the basic characteristics of Isaiah's world, including the kings whose reigns he overlapped.

3. Describe the difference between forth-telling and foretelling.

4. Highlight briefly Isaiah's five major themes.

2 Isaiah's Opening Words to God's People

Isaiah 1:2–31

Outline

- **God's Witnesses against the People (1:2–3)**
- **God's Description of the People (1:4–9)**
  The People (1:4–6)
  The Land (1:7–9)
- **God's Indictment of the People (1:10–15)**
  The Situation (1:10–14)
  The Result (1:15)
- **God's Solution for the People (1:16–20)**
  God's Commands (1:16–17)
  God's Promises (1:18–20)
- **God's Lament over the People (1:21–26)**
  Jerusalem's Sinful Condition (1:21–23)
  Jerusalem's Coming Purge (1:24–26)
- **God's Promise to His People (1:27–31)**
  Blessing to the Repentant (1:27)
  Judgment to Transgressors (1:28–31)

Objectives

After reading this chapter, you should be able to

1. Explain the relationship of chapter 1 to the rest of Isaiah's message.
2. Describe specific details of Judah's sin.
3. Articulate Isaiah's remedy for Judah's sin problem.

Have you ever noticed how news items in a newspaper follow a standard format? Typically, everything the reader really needs to know appears in the first sentence. Who, what, when, where, why, and how—if those things are important, they appear in that first sentence. Other items in the story may be important, but that first line usually summarizes everything that follows.

Isaiah 1 functions in a similar way for the book of Isaiah. The chapter lays a solid foundation for the rest of Isaiah's message by including important themes the prophet develops in the next sixty-five chapters.

Isaiah 1:1 gives no date for the delivery or composition of chapter 1, though scholars have proposed various suggestions.[1] Perhaps it includes the first words Isaiah prophesied to God's people. Perhaps God gave them to him later as a summary of all he had prophesied. Either way, the chapter prepares readers well for the prophetic words that lie ahead.

God's Witnesses against the People (1:2–3)

Sounding much like a prosecuting attorney, God called heaven and earth as witnesses against his people. Why heaven and earth? Because they had seen everything Judah had done. And why should heaven and earth listen? Because the Lord was speaking. The sovereign God of the universe commanded the attention of all his creation.

God then spoke: "I reared children and brought them up" (1:2). God was describing his tender care of the nation of Israel from its birth. He had cared for his people every step of the way—during Abraham's life, during his people's slavery in Egypt, and through the wilderness wanderings. He had brought them into the land triumphantly, a land he had promised their ancestors cen-

turies earlier. When the people failed him, he continued to act graciously toward them. In response to their cries for a king, he gave them a king. But no matter what God did for his people, little seemed to change their rebellious attitude.

God illustrated the people's rebellion by comparing them with common animals. Oxen and donkeys learned respect for and dependence on their human masters. But the people of Israel—led through the centuries by God's sovereign hand—didn't seem to understand the first thing about following him. Nonetheless, God continued to love them; notice how he referred to them as "my people" (1:3).

God's Description of the People (1:4–9)

God the prosecutor then continued to build his case. Now that his witnesses were in place, he began to describe in more detail the sin of his wayward people.

The People (1:4–6)

The Hebrew word translated "ah" at the beginning of verse 4 can also be translated "alas." The Lord lamented the sinful condition into which his people had fallen.

Have you ever tried to run or move quickly while carrying a heavy burden? When we carry something heavy, we cannot move as fast as we can when we are carrying nothing. God's people carried the heavy load of their own sin. Isaiah described them as "loaded with guilt" (1:4). Israel's sinfulness was like a burden, prohibiting the nation from becoming all it could be in God's purpose. Even today, sin keeps people from achieving God's highest purpose.

Israel's sin had continued over many generations. The Hebrew word translated "brood" (1:4) literally means "seed" or "offspring." Israel's ancestors had strayed from God's ways, and their children followed in their footsteps. The sin problem had compounded over the generations, and God's people were having a hard time breaking the cycle. In today's families, sin can also carry its effect across generational lines, but the power of God remains available to those who seek it to break sin's hold.

Why had the people become so immersed in their sin? Because they had turned their backs on the Lord. The expression "Holy One of Israel" (1:4) occurs twenty-five times in Isaiah as a designation for the Lord. God's character displayed infinite holiness, and he called his people to uphold his holy standard (see sidebar 1.5).

Isaiah then described the pitiful condition of God's people, using the metaphor of a human body. He described the body as totally sick, covered with wounds, bruises, and welts. Perhaps the wounds were marks of God's loving discipline. God had struck the people to get their attention, but they had refused to acknowledge his discipline (see Am 4:6–11). Or perhaps God had simply allowed the nation to experience the sad consequences of its sinful actions. In effect, the wounds had been self-inflicted, and Israel would only get worse until the nation turned back to God.

The Land (1:7–9)

Isaiah then described how Israel's sin had affected the land. God had allowed and sometimes brought sad consequences in an effort to turn his people back to him, just as he said he would (Lv 26:14–29). But the land lay desolate, with fields devoured by enemy and famine. Perhaps the people saw drought, nomadic raiding parties that looted their crops, and foreign nations that invaded them as flukes of history, but Isaiah saw them as God's instruments of judgment against his wayward people.

The expression "**daughter of Zion**" often occurs in Isaiah as a metaphor to describe the population (10:32; 16:1;

37:22; 52:2; 62:11). Isaiah used three similes to describe the daughter of Zion's desperate situation. First, she was as a shelter in a vineyard and a hut in a field of melons (1:8). Such a hut provided a place out of the sun and wind. A watchman often could stay there and protect the field or vineyard from wild animals. But these structures provided no protection at all from an invading army. That wasn't their purpose.

Second, Isaiah described the daughter of Zion as "a city under siege" (1:8). An invading army typically surrounded the city to cut off any hope of assistance or escape. A besieged city needed to have access to water, because invaders were certain to try to cut off its water supply.[2] When King Hezekiah prepared to face Sennacherib's army, he ordered a tunnel dug from the Gihon Spring near Jerusalem's wall to the Pool of Siloam further inside the wall (2 Chr 32:30).

But third, as isolated as the people were, Isaiah said they would have been far worse apart from God's grace. Their fate would have become as that of **Sodom and Gomorrah**, two cities God destroyed for their wickedness during the days of Abraham (Gn 19:24–25).

Sometimes when we face difficult circumstances, we are tempted to blame God or to think he is no longer listening. However, the Lord knows our every circumstance. Usually when we stop to reflect, we can think of many blessings remaining in our lives.

God's Indictment of the People (1:10–15)

The heavenly prosecuting attorney now took his case to the next step. He had called his witnesses—heaven and earth—into the courtroom (1:2–3). He had described his people's sinful condition and the sad consequences that befell both them and the land because of it (1:4–9). In the next section, the Lord

View of the Dead Sea from Masada. Scholars have usually identified the southern edge of the Dead Sea as the area formerly occupied by Sodom and Gomorrah. (Courtesy of Chris Miller)

would bring an indictment against his people in which he challenged the value of their responses to him. Perhaps they thought they were appeasing his wrath or even pleasing him, but Isaiah assured them this was not the case.

The Situation (1:10–14)

Isaiah's words must have shocked the people, for he had described them as Sodom and Gomorrah. Why would the prophet associate them with those names? Perhaps someone even challenged him: "Isaiah, this is *Jerusalem*, not Sodom and Gomorrah!" Isaiah no doubt would have replied that God was having a hard time telling the difference between the cities. The prophet used strong words against his people, but he did so to get their attention so they would turn back to God. He had no desire to condemn them for their sin only to leave them in it. Christians today need to remember that God hates their sins, but he also loves them and wants to rescue them from sin.

The people were certainly already surprised that Isaiah had referred to Jerusalem as Sodom and Gomorrah, but now Isaiah really must have confused them. He maintained that God was

sick of their sacrifices and wanted no more of them. In fact, he considered them absolutely worthless. They were not the blessing he had intended them to be, but rather, they had become a burden.

The book of Leviticus describes in detail all the sacrifices and festivals God desired his people to observe (Lv 1:1–7:38; 23:1–44; see sidebar 2.1). Had God now changed his mind? He wanted no more burnt offerings and took no pleasure in sacrifices. In fact, he called Israel's appearance before him the "trampling" of his courts (1:12). He counted their offerings meaningless, as he did all their assemblies. Moreover, God went further than that: he *hated* them (1:14). Why?

The Result (1:15)

Verse 15 indicates the reason for God's displeasure. The people had committed great sin against one another. Isaiah's reference to their bloody hands means not the blood of sacrifices but the blood of their fellow Israelites that they had shed.[3] The people lived lives filled with sin and injustice and then turned to God with their prayers and sacrifices. God wanted none of it. It was as if he would hide his eyes and

sacrificial
system

Sidebar 2.1
The Place of the Sacrificial System in Israel's Faith

Isaiah 1:11–15 appears at first to read like an utter denunciation of Israel's **sacrificial system**. Among the many offerings and festivals God prescribed, these offerings, described in Leviticus 1–7, played a key role.

1. Burnt Offering (Lv 1)

This was the typical Hebrew offering, dominant throughout Old Testament history, and probably the oldest form of atonement sacrifice. The term describes an "offering of ascent," or an offering that goes up to the deity. The animal was completely burned on the altar, its smoke rising toward heaven. A male animal without blemish was required. Various animals were used according to the worshiper's financial means.

2. Grain Offering (Lv 2)

This offering may have originally been a gift, since the term often means "gift." In Levitical regulations, the grain offering carried an expiating sense and was also linked to the agricultural seasons. Some scholars believe it may also have served as a less-expensive burnt offering for those who could not afford an animal.

3. Peace Offering (Lv 3)

The peace offering was a celebrative offering consumed by both the priest and the worshiper. It could be offered for general thanksgiving, in fulfillment of a vow, or freely by the worshiper for no reason in particular.

4. Sin Offering (Lv 4:1–5:13)

The sin offering was expiatory for offenses against God. It emphasized the act of purification and served for cleansing from ceremonial defilement, deception, misappropriation, and seduction. The details of the sacrifice varied depending on the class of the one offering it (priest, congregation, ruler, individual).

5. Guilt Offering (Lv 5:14–6:7)

The guilt offering was a subcategory of the sin offering. It was expiatory but devoted to restitution and reparation. It often related to the profaning of sacred items and violations of a social nature.

Isaiah was not condemning the sacrificial system per se in his words to Judah. Rather, he decried the emptiness of sacrifices offered apart from genuine repentance marked by faithful obedience to God's commands. Ritual apart from a change in attitude was worthless.

Adapted from Bill T. Arnold and Bryan E. Beyer, Encountering the Old Testament: A Christian Survey *(Grand Rapids: Baker Academic, 1999), 120.*

cover his ears whenever they called to him.

God's strong words indicate the importance of a proper attitude toward him. Merely attending worship services does not make one a Christian. The Bible affirms that genuinely Christian faith comes from a personal relation-

Artist's impression of priests making a burnt offering on the altar. Isaiah denounced the people for bringing their sacrifices apart from attitudes of genuine repentance. (Courtesy of Tim Dowley Associates Ltd.)

ship with Jesus Christ (Rom 3:21–22). When believers depend on the Holy Spirit's power, they are able to serve God faithfully, and he makes them more like Jesus (2 Cor 3:18; Eph 2:10).

God's Solution for the People (1:16–20)

God's words to the people now took an interesting twist. Up to this point, he had functioned as a prosecuting attorney, calling his witnesses into court, describing the people's basic sinful state, and bringing indictments against them for their wickedness. But now God Almighty became their advocate, their encourager. He told them it didn't have to be this way. God had, in fact, provided a solution for the people if they would only listen and follow it. God gave the

people certain commands to follow and promised blessing if they did.

God's Commands (1:16–17)

Verses 16–17 contain nine imperatives. The first six stress the basic heart decisions the people would have to make. They needed to choose to cleanse themselves from their wicked ways. Doing that involved washing, but it also involved getting out of the filth of their sin. Once they had washed and cleansed themselves of their evil deeds, they would be able to see clearly to choose between right and wrong. God encouraged them to "seek justice" (1:17) when they reached that point. The last three imperatives in verse 17 describe specific actions the people could take to follow through on their decisions to refuse evil and choose good. The words translated "encourage the oppressed" also can be translated "rebuke the oppressor." If the first is correct, Isaiah was calling the people to stand alongside

lament

social justice

and support those who felt the oppression of society. If the second is correct, Isaiah was calling his listeners to challenge the wickedness of their day.

The second and third imperatives focus on the fatherless and widows, who often became the focus of oppression because they did not have the power or means to fight back against a corrupt system (Ex 22:23–24; Dt 24:17). Even today, one sign of a person's true character is the way he or she treats people who either cannot possibly repay them or who cannot fight back (see sidebar 2.2).

God's Promises (1:18–20)

The Lord called his people to personal dialogue with him. They should understand the wonderful blessing he planned to bring them if they would only listen. He would wash away their sins, and they would eat of the land's bounty. But if they refused and continued to resist him, the sword would eat them. The words "eat" (1:19) and "devoured" (1:20) translate the same Hebrew word and thus constitute a wordplay in the Hebrew. In Isaiah 1:2, the Lord called heaven and earth to pay attention because the Sovereign was speaking. Now, that same Sovereign called his people to heed his promises.

God's Lament over the People (1:21–26)

Biblical **lament** often begins with the word "how" (2 Sm 1:19; Lam 1:1). What

---

Sidebar 2.2
The Prophets and Social Justice

Isaiah 1:21–26 denounces social injustice. Indeed, for the prophets, a proper relationship with God demanded that God's people treat others fairly. What about today? Are issues such as feeding the poor, providing shelter for the homeless, working for civil rights for all, and fighting abortion part of the gospel? Should Christians care about **social justice**?

The gospel message centers on Jesus Christ and his death, burial, and resurrection. Through repentance and faith, we can receive his offer of salvation. The Holy Spirit then begins to work in us to make us more like Jesus (Rom 8:29).

The Bible teaches that social justice should be a natural product of our relationship with God. Consider the examples below:

- The law of Moses insists on fair treatment of foreigners, widows, and orphans (Ex 22:21–24).
- The prophets speak of God's concern for social justice and demand fair and compassionate treatment of underprivileged people and/or those who have no advocate to speak for them (Is 1:21–26; 58:6–7; Am 2:6–7).
- The early church sends famine relief to Jerusalem on more than one occasion (Acts 11:27–30; 1 Cor 16:1–3).
- James, the Lord's brother, encourages Christians to put their faith into action and help those in need (Jas 2:14–26).

As the Holy Spirit makes Christians more like Jesus, we learn to share God's concerns. Christians today should work to bring about social justice in our society.

Adapted from Bill T. Arnold and Bryan E. Beyer, Encountering the Old Testament: A Christian Survey *(Grand Rapids: Baker Academic, 1999), 446.*

typically follows then is a statement of great contrast. In 2 Samuel 1, the mighty warriors have fallen in battle. In Lamentations 1, a formerly rich and populous city lies desolate and deserted. And here in Isaiah, Isaiah writes of how Jerusalem has experienced utter moral collapse.

Jerusalem's Sinful Condition (1:21–23)

Notice the moral extremes Isaiah described for his audience. The once faithful city had become like a harlot, a woman faithful to no one. The city once full of righteousness now only had room for murderers.

So often a society's direction is directly linked with its leaders, and Jerusalem was no exception. Its rulers loved bribes and did not judge criminals but associated with them. Isaiah had encouraged his people to defend the helpless, but the rulers brushed them aside.

Jerusalem's Coming Purge (1:24–26)

God again identified himself in the most sovereign of terms: he was "the Lord, the LORD Almighty, the Mighty One of Israel" (1:24). He would bring vengeance on his foes and judge sin wherever he found it. He would remove their impurities and restore their leaders as in earlier days when the city experienced faithful leadership.

Isaiah used an image from metallurgy to drive home his point. Metal

---

Key Terms

daughter of Zion

lament

redeem

sacrificial system

social justice

Sodom and Gomorrah

---

workers removed a metal's impurities by heating it until it was molten. Typically impurities of lighter weight would come to the surface and be removed by the metal worker. When the metal worker could look into the molten metal and see his image reflected, the metal was pure. What a picture of God's work in people's lives! Isaiah had described the city as having fallen from the state of faithfulness and righteousness (1:21). But God promised a day in which the city would again lay claim to the name "City of Righteousness, the Faithful City" (1:26). God wanted to restore his people, just as he wants to restore people today.

God's Promise to His People (1:27–31)

Before he died, Moses set before Israel words of blessing and words of curse (Dt 28:1–68; 30:19–20). If Israel demonstrated its faithfulness by obeying God's commands, blessings would follow; if people showed their lack of faith by disobedience and rebellion, judgment would follow. God had laid before them both choices in Isaiah 1:18–20. In the chapter's closing verses, he did so again.

Study Questions

1. How does Isaiah 1 prepare the reader for the rest of Isaiah's message?

2. Why did Isaiah suggest God was not pleased with the people's sacrifices when the law of Moses had commanded them?

redeem

Blessing to the Repentant (1:27)

Isaiah prophesied Zion's redemption. The word "**redeem**" means to buy back or to restore from a fallen state. But God's plan included more than simply buying his people back. He wanted to restore their moral character so that it displayed justice and righteousness. Today God's desire is not only to redeem people but also to make them into his image again (Col 3:10). Notice too how God's offer of redemption was linked to repentance. God was not promising blanket redemption for all the nation regardless of how individuals responded to his grace. He wanted to see genuine repentance, to which he would respond with grace and restoration.

Judgment to Transgressors (1:28–31)

Isaiah also warned of the impending disaster looming just ahead for rebels and sinners. They would be broken, and they would perish. They would experience great shame at their pagan practices when the light of God's holiness shined on them. The fire of their judgment would burn forever.

The Christian faith—like the message of Isaiah 1—calls us to embrace one of two options. We can experience a personal relationship with God by faith, along with all the blessings that relationship includes. Or we can choose to reject God's ways—either intentionally or by neglect—and miss everything he has to offer. Isaiah warned his people, and the Bible warns us, that God has left us no other choice.

3 God's Call to Live in Light of the Future

Isaiah 2:1–5:30

Outline

- **The Coming Blessing (2:1–4)**
  The Lord's Temple
  God's People
  The Lord's Peace
- **Judgment Speeches (2:5–4:6)**
  Call to Recognize God's Ways (2:5–21)
  Judgment against the Leaders (2:22–3:15)
  Judgment against the Women (3:16–4:1)
  God's Day of Restoration (4:2–6)
    The Branch
    The Lord's Cleansing and Protection
- **Song of the Vineyard (5:1–7)**
- **Six Woes against the Nation (5:8–30)**
  Oppressive Landowners (5:8–10)
  Pursuers of Drunken Revelry (5:11–17)
  God Testers (5:18–19)
  The Morally Twisted (5:20)
  The Self-Exalted (5:21)
  The Immoral Opportunists (5:22–23)
  The Conclusion: Vengeance (5:24–30)

Objectives

After reading this chapter, you should be able to

1. Describe the role of the nations in the future day of blessing Isaiah described (2:1–4).
2. Explain the importance of a society having good leaders.
3. Articulate the particular sins of which Judah's citizens were guilty.

City of David

Great leaders find ways to get their followers to accomplish tasks the followers never thought possible. Great coaches do this all the time. Many teams have won games against better teams because the coach convinced the players they could win. The coach may have described the glory of victory, the potential shame of losing, or a particular strategy for wearing down the opponent. The team members still had to play the game and win the victory, but the coach had already placed the notion of success in their minds.

The prophets also used various strategies throughout the Old Testament as they sought to turn God's people back to him. Sometimes they exhorted their audience with great promises of God's blessing; at other times, they warned them of the peril of disobedience. Throughout they described God's desired response and his "game plan" for reconciliation with him.

In Isaiah 2–5, the prophet Isaiah utilized all these strategies. He began by describing an incredible day of blessing God would bring to pass (2:1–4). He then described Judah's wickedness and called the people to recognize God's ways (2:5–21). He chastised the leaders for their moral failures and their exploitation of those who could not defend themselves (2:22–3:15). He spoke against proud women who dressed and acted provocatively and told them that God would humble them (3:16–4:1). He described a great day of restoration and salvation that God would bring to his people (4:2–6). He used the symbolic language of a vineyard to describe God's care for his people (5:1–7). Finally, he described God's judgment against six categories of people who opposed his ways (5:8–30).

The Coming Blessing (2:1–4)

Isaiah 2:1 introduces the chapter much as Isaiah 1:1 introduced the book.

Whereas 1:1 clearly forms an introduction to the entire book, the prophetic passage to which 2:1 refers is not as clear. Perhaps the introduction only highlights 2:1–4, or perhaps it covers the text through chapter 4 or some part of these three chapters.[1]

The coming blessing of "the last days" involves three aspects: the Lord's temple, God's people, and the Lord's peace.

The Lord's Temple

During Isaiah's ministry, Solomon's temple adorned Jerusalem's skyline. King Solomon (970–931 BC) had expanded the **City of David** northward to include the threshing floor of Araunah the Jebusite (2 Sm 24:18–25) and selected that spot to build the temple (2 Chr 3:1). Isaiah emphasized God's temple as providing special blessing in the latter days.

The Hebrew word translated "chief" (NIV, NASB) is *r'osh*, which can also mean "head" and encompasses the same semantic range as the English word "head." *R'osh* may describe a human head or denote someone who leads a delegation (Jos 24:1). Probably Isaiah meant that Zion will stand as first in rank among the world's mountains, though the parallel expression "will be raised above the hills" may suggest Zion's special elevation among Jerusalem's many surrounding hills. Peoples of many nations will recognize its prominence as the recipient of God's blessing.

God's People

Isaiah described a day in which God's people would assume a new dimension. The Hebrew verb translated "stream" (*nahar*) parallels the noun *nahar*, "river," and provides a beautiful word picture. As the nations stream to Jerusalem to worship God, the seemingly unending lines of people will resemble mighty, rushing streams. Since water would have to run uphill to reach Jerusalem's 2,500-foot elevation, Isaiah's language seems to indicate an

Gentiles

millennium

especially powerful surge of people toward God's holy city.

The Hebrew word translated "nations" is *goyim*, which is translated in the Septuagint as *ethnē*, the Greek word commonly translated "**Gentiles**" in the New Testament. In contrast to Isaiah's day, when God's covenant purpose focused primarily, though not exclusively, on Israel, Isaiah foretold a day when people from all ethnic groups would receive God's special favor.

Isaiah's radical idea—that Gentiles would become part of God's people—anticipated the apostle Paul's statement that Jesus abolished the walls between Jew and Gentile so all could receive reconciliation to the Father (Eph 2:14–16). Many in Judah probably struggled to believe the amazing concept Isaiah described, just as many people struggle to believe it today.

The peoples of the world would stream to Jerusalem for one purpose: to learn God's ways so they could walk in them. Over the generations, people came to Jerusalem again and again to conquer it, to loot its treasure, to humble its people. But in that day, they would come to learn. They would come to learn of God. And they would come to learn his ways so that they could live in faithful obedience to him.

Isaiah described Jerusalem as a major focal point of faith, the hub from which the word of God would go forth. Indeed, after Jesus rose from the grave and before he ascended into heaven, he gave his disciples instruction to serve as his witnesses to the whole world, beginning with Jerusalem (Acts 1:8). But did Isaiah see more than the launch of the Great Commission (Mt 28:18–20)? Did he anticipate an even greater day?

Today, Jerusalem stands as the center of three religious faiths: Christianity, Judaism, and Islam. The city curiously blends old and new, ancient tradition and modern technology. Jerusalem's Old City, with its well-known sixteenth-century stone wall, narrow streets, and markets, contrasts sharply with western Jerusalem's modern buildings and twenty-first-century look. Political, social, and religious tensions continue to exist throughout the land. Isaiah's words provide hope for Jerusalem's future. One day—and every day is one day closer—Jerusalem's people will again experience unity.

The Lord's Peace

Verse 4 announced the Lord's direct hand in governing his people in the great day Isaiah described. Throughout its history, Israel had experienced many examples of bad leadership. But this would occur no longer; rather, Yahweh's judgment would carry the day among all nations and peoples.

Isaiah also described the result of God's leadership. Instruments of war would become useful agricultural tools. The land of Israel lent itself especially well to two types of livelihood, pastoral and agricultural. Most citizens either raised flocks and herds or farmed the land. The prophet's description of people converting their swords to plowshares and spears to pruning hooks communicated to them a day when war would cease, and thus people would no longer need military weapons.

Such notions must have spoken powerfully to a people whose neighbors were usually hostile to them. Not only would they no longer experience war, but they also wouldn't even have to train for war (literally "learn war") ever again, because the possibility for war would end under the Lord's rule.

Some Christians understand Isaiah's words to mean Jesus Christ will return one day to bring this present age to an end and establish an earthly kingdom. They believe Jesus will come on the clouds, return to Jerusalem triumphantly, establish his administration, and usher in lasting peace for a thousand year period known as the **millennium**. Others believe Isaiah's words will find fulfillment in Christ's heavenly kingdom after God judges the world and brings in a new heaven and a new earth. Both agree that under the reign of the King of kings, peace such as the world has never known will flood forth.[2]

The Hebrew word *shalom*, often translated "peace," describes a wholeness that pervades an individual's life or a society. When a person or a society experiences the fullness of all God intends for his creation, that person or society experiences God's *shalom*. Isaiah described such a day, though he didn't use the word *shalom* in this passage.

The words of Isaiah 2:1–4 also appear almost verbatim in Micah 4:1–4. Isaiah and Micah were contemporaries, and God privileged them to see the same glorious day. Interestingly, Isaiah's words have also found their way into modern society. The United Nations building in New York City has a stone engraving outside that bears Isaiah's description of nations beating their swords into plowshares and their spears into pruning hooks and ceasing to learn war. Today, nations work hard to bring about peace on earth, and many times their efforts produce good results. Ultimately, however, lasting peace of the deepest and most thorough kind will occur only when Jesus returns.

Judgment Speeches (2:5–4:6)

Isaiah's judgment speeches of 2:5–4:6 feature four aspects: a call to recognize God's ways, a judgment of Judah's leaders, a judgment against Judah's women, and a description of God's day of restoration (see sidebar 3.1).

Call to Recognize God's Ways (2:5–21)

Isaiah called the people to recognize God's ways. Knowing God was the implied first step in turning back to him, and knowing his ways was the second

---

Sidebar 3.1
Sin in the Lives of God's People

The good news of the gospel is that salvation is the free gift of God received by faith (Eph 2:8–9). Christians understand that Christ's sacrifice on their behalf provides the basis for forgiveness (Rom 3:24–25). Becoming a Christian does not include working to become a better person; rather, it means beginning a personal relationship with the living Lord of the universe.

Because of the gospel's emphasis on God's grace, Christians may think their sins are unimportant. After all, they might reason, Christ has paid their penalty and God has forgiven them. Does God really care about how they live their lives?

People in the apostle Paul's day sometimes reasoned along similar lines. If forgiving an "average sinner" demonstrated God's grace to the world, perhaps forgiving a terribly wicked sinner would demonstrate it even more (Rom 3:8; 6:1).

Paul insisted such thinking was ridiculous (Rom 6:2–11). The eternal life that Jesus's death and resurrection provided began at the moment one became his follower. To be sure, at Jesus's second coming believers will receive their resurrection bodies and be free from sin once and for all (1 Jn 3:2). However, the Holy Spirit's power within believers provides them strength to experience consistent victory over temptation. Sin does not have to and should not control Christians (Rom 6:14). Rather, God calls his children to live godly lives as evidence to the world of his work within them (Mt 5:15–16).

At the same time, God's grace patiently works within the lives of Christians who struggle with sin. The certainty of forgiveness when believers confess their sin (1 Jn 1:9) provides great assurance, though it should never be taken as an excuse to sin and receive forgiveness later. God has called us to be like Jesus, our perfect example (1 Pt 2:21–24).

day of the Lord

step. Walking in his ways was the third step, the desired outcome.

Isaiah described the Lord's ways as "the light of the LORD" (2:5). Light reveals things. Light can reveal a path. It can also reveal danger. It can even reveal dirtiness. In every case, light clarifies the situation so that a person can take appropriate action. The psalmist described God's word as a lamp to his feet and a light to his path (Ps 119:105). It brought proper clarity so that he could see a circumstance or situation for what it was and take appropriate action. God's way was always best.

Isaiah warned his people that the day of the Lord was coming (2:6–21). The expression "**day of the Lord**" occurs commonly in the prophets and in the New Testament. It includes three aspects, though each aspect does not appear every time the expression occurs: the judging of unbelievers, the cleansing of God's people, and the salvation of God's people (see sidebar 7.1).

Isaiah condemned his people's abandonment of the Lord. They had replaced proper worship of God with pagan practices. They had lusted after financial gain and filled their lives with material things that could offer them no lasting value. Even today, many people try in vain to find lasting satisfaction and fulfillment in the accumulation of wealth and in various non-Christian spiritual pursuits (see sidebar 3.2).

The prophet described a day when humanity, despite its supposedly great stature, would tremble in humility and fear before God's majesty as he displayed his power in judgment. The cedars of Lebanon to the north, the oaks of Bashan in Transjordan, "towering mountains" and "high hills" (2:13–14) would be humbled; how much more so God's people. People would see God for who he was in that day.

A fresh view of God's power would bring sweeping changes. Idolatry would cease as people realized the shame of their sin and the powerlessness of their idols. People would seek in vain for protection from God's display of power.

They would discard their idols any way they could, burying them in the ground or casting them into caves. A mighty display of God's majesty would quickly reveal humanity's smallness. How could mere mortals stand in the face of such a God?

Judgment against the Leaders (2:22–3:15)

Verse 22 serves as a bridge between the previous section and the next. In both sections, God's majesty and power reveal humanity's smallness. Isaiah challenged the people to place their ultimate trust in the Lord.

Of course, the Scriptures encourage believers to submit to leaders and show them proper respect (Rom 13:1–7; Heb 13:17). Nonetheless, ultimate allegiance must be to the Lord, not to human leadership. People sometimes experience great disappointment when they place more faith in humans than they do in God.

God vowed to strip away all human leadership from Jerusalem and Judah (3:1–7). He would cut off food, water, and other supplies. He would eliminate all kinds of leadership: military, political, spiritual, and social. The ensuing chaos would lead to desperate searches for leaders, with the result that unqualified people would be pressured to assume leadership roles. Society would desperately try to replace its fallen leaders but would find no one suitable.

Isaiah placed the blame squarely where it lay: on Jerusalem and Judah (3:8–15). Their leaders were not ashamed of their sins and would receive just recompense for their wickedness. They led people away from the Lord and further into sin. Those in power abused the poor, "grinding the faces of the poor" (3:15) into the ground with oppressive measures.

Judgment against the Women (3:16–4:1)

Isaiah next highlighted a sinful tendency among the women of Zion.

51

Real Meaning in Life (2:6–8)

Isaiah decried his people's abandonment of the Lord to pursue other potential sources of meaning. Consider the list from Isaiah 2:6–8:

Verse	Potential source of meaning
6	Superstitions (placing faith in untruth)
	Divination (seeking to discern the will of God or of pagan gods through false means)
	Alliance with foreign nations (placing faith in other nations)
7	Silver and gold, treasures (trusting in material things for security)
	Chariots and horses (trusting in military strength for security)
8	Idolatry (substituting the worship of other gods or things for the worship of the one true God)

Many people in the twenty-first century seek meaning for life in these same places:

Superstitions: Some people carry a rabbit's foot or other item "for good luck." Some even wear gold or silver crosses as jewelry for protection or blessing.

Divination: Some people seek guidance through the future by dabbling in astrology, horoscopes, and/or occult practices.

Alliances: Some people put their trust in human relationships. Political leaders may feel themselves secure because they have developed a network of allies, but those allies may or may not prove loyal. On a personal level, people may seek security in their trust of particular leaders—even church leaders. They then experience great disillusionment when those leaders fail them. People who marry merely for status or money also often fall into this category.

Material things: The Bible does not condemn material things, nor does it condemn those who have much. At the same time, Jesus warned that having great riches could hinder a close relationship with God (Mt 19:23–24). Ironically, material things do not pose a threat to finding life's real meaning because they are innately evil. Rather, they pose a threat because they provide some level of satisfaction—for a time, perhaps, but never forever. Thus, people may more easily believe they can provide lasting satisfaction.

Military strength: A nation can think itself invincible and become proud and arrogant. The Bible records such thinking on the part of Assyria, Babylon, Egypt, and many other, smaller kingdoms. Such arrogance can lead to forgetting the Lord, the true source of strength. It may also lead to other sins to which people fall victim when they begin to think themselves spiritually invincible.

Idolatry: The attitudes and behaviors mentioned above can have an idolatrous aspect, but many people today also try to find meaning in other religions and their gods and/or their code of conduct. Others suggest, "What's true for you may not be true for me. If my way of thinking works for me, then it's true for me."

The book of Ecclesiastes explores various possible roads to ultimate meaning in life. In the end, it concludes:

> Fear God and keep his commandments,
>   for this is the whole duty of man.
> For God will bring every deed into
>   judgment,
>   including every hidden thing,
>   whether it is good or evil. (Eccl 12:13b–14)

Christians should find their ultimate fulfillment in fulfilling God's purpose for their lives (Phil 3:12–14).

branch

David

They dressed and walked in such a way as to draw undue attention from men. They practiced "walking along with outstretched necks, flirting with their eyes, tripping along with mincing steps" (3:16) to gain the attention of potential suitors. The language suggests they accented everything sensual about themselves.

Isaiah did not condemn the women for prostitution; rather, he condemned them for behaving improperly. They consumed themselves with presenting a certain image before the men of their society. God's response would strike at the heart of their problem. They focused on their external adornment and beauty, so he would take it all away. They would lose their soft skin, their flowing hair, their many ornaments and apparel. Who would want them then? Moreover, the Lord would slay in battle the men they desired to attract. Their obsession with attracting men would become worse than ever as they realized how few men remained (4:1).

The Lord often works in his children today in the same way. He knows what we value more than we value him, and he is able to take it away to drive us back to him.

God's Day of Restoration (4:2–6)

The expression "in that day" (4:2) does not necessarily mean a particular day Isaiah had described previously. Rather, it denotes the general period of time in which God would fulfill all the words he had spoken through Isaiah. The Hebrew word *yom* (day) often denotes more than a literal twenty-four-hour period and in prophetic language commonly describes a general period of unspecified length (Is 2:12, 20; 7:18; 11:10; 22:5).

The Branch

Isaiah's use of the term "**branch**" in 4:2 (Heb. *tsemach*) is his first such usage in the book, though other prophets would develop the branch concept more thoroughly (Jer 23:5–6; 33:15–16; Zec 3:8; 6:9–13; see sidebar

3.3). The Branch of the Lord ultimately refers to Jesus, the righteous Branch of **David**, who will execute justice and righteousness on earth and bring harmony between king and priesthood. Here, the prophet merely alludes to the concept of the branch, but later he raises it again (11:1), albeit with a different Hebrew word (*netser*). The branch will be exalted to a position of prominence "in that day."[3]

The Lord's Cleansing and Protection

Isaiah said the land and its people would experience renewed vitality. The day of the Lord would cleanse and purge the sin among God's people. It would remove the sin of the women mentioned in 3:16–4:1 and cleanse Jerusalem's bloodstains caused by oppression and injustice. Fire commonly occurs in Scripture as an instrument of cleansing and purification (Mal 3:2–3; Mt 3:11–12; 1 Cor 3:13–15).

Isaiah then used imagery from Israel's past to highlight the great day God had in store. The "cloud of smoke" and "glow of flaming fire" recalled the days of Israel's journey through the wilderness, when the Lord guided them with fire and cloud (Ex 40:36–38). God's loving care was revealed as he watched over his people even when they wandered in the wilderness for their sin (Is 48:21). Isaiah envisioned another such day when God would intimately care for and lead his people again.

The Hebrew word translated "shelter" in 4:6 (*sukkah*) recalled the festival of *sukkot*, the Feast of Tabernacles, when the people of Israel commemorated living in booths or temporary shelters in the wilderness as God led them along (Lv 23:33–43). The Feast of Tabernacles occurred in the fall, after the new year (*rosh hashanah*) and the Day of Atonement (*yom kippur*) and reminded the people of God's faithfulness to them in the wilderness. If God so cared for his people as he disciplined them in the wilderness, imagine how he would care for them in the day of restoration.

Sidebar 3.3
The Branch (4:2)

The prophets Isaiah, Jeremiah, and Zechariah all make use of the branch motif to describe Israel's future leader.

Isaiah introduces the concept in 4:2: "In that day the Branch of the Lord will be glorious." The context describes a day of restored relationship between God and his people but says nothing about the branch's identity.

Isaiah 11:1 describes the branch as coming "from the stump of Jesse," a clear reference to David's line (1 Sm 16:1, 11–13). He is empowered by God's Spirit to bring in an era of universal peace and righteousness, a kingdom over which he personally will rule (Is 11:2–9). He will stand as a banner for his people as the Lord regathers his own from the ends of the earth (11:10–16).

Jeremiah 23:5–6 and 33:15–16 are quite similar in proclaiming a righteous Branch of David whom God will raise up as king and name "the Lord Our Righteousness." Peace and security will prevail during his days. Jeremiah 33:17–18 adds the detail that kingship and priesthood will both feature strong leadership in that day.

Zechariah 3:8 describes the "servant branch" God will raise up in the coming days as he performs a great work among his people. Zechariah 6:12–15 climaxes the branch motif by describing the Branch as the one who will build God's temple, rule as a priest, and bring harmony between kingship and priesthood.

The New Testament proclaims this prophetic theme's fulfillment in Christ, hailing from the line of David (Mt 1:1), serving as our great high priest (Heb 9:11–12), and ruling as King of kings and Lord of lords (Rv 19:16).

The Hebrew word translated "branch" is typically *tsemach*, though the synonym *netser* also occurs.

Song of the Vineyard (5:1–7)

Isaiah now introduced a new prophetic genre, a song. Isaiah sang a song to the Lord that concerned the Lord's vineyard. The prophet's approach suggests he was now telling a parable through music.

Isaiah's careful attention to detail emphasized God's careful attention to his vineyard.[4] The Lord tilled the soil and removed its stones. He planted a vine there and took steps to assure its growth. He built a watchtower in the vineyard to provide shelter for the one tending it and to enable him to watch for animals that might raid the early fruit. In anticipation of the harvest, the Lord prepared a winepress to process the grapes. But after all of God's tender care, the vineyard produced only bad fruit.

The Lord could have done nothing more for his vineyard; the problem must reside in the quality of the vine. Therefore, God determined he would destroy the vineyard, breaking down its wall, exposing it to the elements, and cutting off its rain.

Isaiah identified the vineyard: Israel was the vineyard, and Judah his delightful garden. How had God cared for them as he cared for his vineyard? He had prepared the land for his people's coming and driven out peoples before them. He had led them through the wilderness by the pillar of fire and the pillar of cloud. He had provided food and water for their journey and graciously forgiven their stubborn rebellion again and again. He had done so much for them, and yet they had turned rebellious.

Watchman's hut in a vineyard (Isaiah 5:2; Courtesy of HolyLand Photos.org)

paronomasia

Therefore, God said, he would expose them to judgment. Isaiah's song of the vineyard expands Isaiah's words in 1:8, where the prophet said God had left his people as unprotected as a watchman's hut in a vineyard.

Isaiah employed **paronomasia**,[5] a play on words, in 5:7. God looked for justice (Heb. *mishpat*) in his people, but he found bloodshed (Heb. *mispach*); he looked for righteousness (Heb. *tsedeqah*), but instead he heard a cry of distress (Heb. *tse'aqah*). Two pairs of Hebrew words that sound very much alike meant something *very* different!

Six Woes against the Nation (5:8–30)

Six times in Isaiah 5:8–30, Isaiah used the introductory exclamation "Woe!" In doing so, he decried the sin of six groups of people: oppressive landowners, pursuers of drunken revelry, God testers, the morally twisted, the self-exalted, and immoral opportunists. God had seen their sin, and God would deal with them.

Oppressive Landowners (5:8–10)

Isaiah first denounced oppressive landowners who displayed misguided ambition. They added house to house and field to field, until their estates grew so vast that no one lived near them. They enjoyed the process of accumulation so much that they did not know when to stop.

God's judgment against these landowners involved reducing the effective yields of their fields. They would then have to work much harder than others merely to bring in the same amount of crops. Great homes would stand desolate as owners went bankrupt and walked away from their estates.

Ambition is wrong when its aim is merely to further our own selfish interests. Our focus becomes our next goal rather than pleasing the Lord. At the same time, the Bible encourages us to make the most of our lives in the Lord's service (1 Cor 12:31).

Pursuers of Drunken Revelry (5:11–17)

Isaiah's second woe focused on those who pursued drunken revelry. His allusion to the people who "rise early in the morning" and "stay up late at night" to pursue their drinking and partying emphasized the all-consuming nature of their pursuits. They furnished their parties and banquets with the finest music and wine they could obtain but cared little if anything for the Lord's work among them.

The people's obsession with wine created misguided priorities. It clouded their judgment so they didn't consider how they might serve the Lord; after all, they were too busy getting ready for the next party. Therefore, Isaiah said, they would "go into exile for lack of understanding" (5:13).

The day of God's judgment would take the drunken revelers totally by surprise. They had preoccupied themselves with things that didn't have lasting importance or value. They would understand too late the foolishness of their ways.

God Testers (5:18–19)

Isaiah then focused on those who put the Lord to the test. The prophet described them as pulling their sin and wickedness along behind them, all the while sarcastically calling for God to show himself in their daily experience.

Those who tested God assumed they knew exactly how God would act. Consequently, they cynically called on him to "hasten his work" (5:19) so that they might see and know it. They looked for him to fit into their conception of how he would act in a given situation.

The God testers' sin lay precisely in their faulty assumption about God's character. They did *not* know precisely how the Lord would act in every situation. What they perceived as God's slowness to act against them was in fact his patience toward them as he gave them time to repent (2 Pt 3:9).

Isaiah did not describe the God testers' judgment. Rather, he pointed out their evil and left the matter of judgment in God's hands. But his categorical "Woe!" against them (5:18) clearly anticipated God's action against them.

The Morally Twisted (5:20)

The morally twisted of Isaiah's day made their own rules and established their own standards of morality. Isaiah described them as substituting evil for good, darkness for light, and bitter for sweet (see sidebar 3.4).

The morally twisted people's sin went deeper than merely committing evil practices. They had convinced themselves (and probably tried to convince others) that their practices were actually good. They stood guilty of taking all that was evil and calling it good. Further, they commended it in themselves and in others (Rom 1:32). Their sin was much greater than the sin of those who sinned out of ignorance.

The Self-Exalted (5:21)

Isaiah also pronounced woe to the self-exalted. Wisdom and cleverness were not wrong in and of themselves, but the words "in their own eyes" and "in their own sight" clarify the issue. The self-exalted had a high opinion of themselves—an opinion the Lord did not share. They may have thought themselves wise, but in God's sight, they were fools.

The Immoral Opportunists (5:22–23)

Isaiah's sixth woe was directed against immoral opportunists. At first, Isaiah's words sound as if he were speaking against the drunken revelers again with his reference to wine and strong drink (5:22; cf. 5:11–12). But in light of the actual offenses listed, we should probably understand the drinking as part of a general meeting or party atmosphere in which the opportunists made their evil plans with one another.

The immoral opportunists acquitted the guilty and denied justice to the innocent. Their motivation lay not in what was right but in what was profitable. They saw the opportunity for an evil action, knew they had the power to get away with it, and made their decision on that basis. By contrast, God's law

Sidebar 3.4
New Names for Old Sins (5:20)

Isaiah pronounced woe against those who substituted evil for good. Many in our society have done the same thing by substituting more attractive names for practices the Bible calls evil. Consider the following examples; the more accurate descriptions follow in parentheses. Can you think of other similar terms?

Affair (fornication, adultery, illicit sex)
Alternate lifestyle (living together, homosexuality)
Abortion (killing of unborn babies)
Becoming a man or becoming a woman (giving away one's virginity)
Sexually active (promiscuous, sexually immoral)
Pro-choice (accepting of abortion)
Adult entertainment (pornography, strip clubs)
Adult videos (pornographic videos)
New Age philosophy (old lies of Eastern philosophy)

Many have also tried to belittle Christians while justifying their own sinful behavior by giving less attractive names to practices the Bible commends. Again, the more accurate expression follows in parentheses. Can you think of other similar terms?

Chicken (afraid; usually used to challenge someone who is unwilling to go along with the group's sin)
Old-fashioned (adhering to traditional standards of morality)
Prudish (adhering to traditional standards of sexual morality)
Rigid, inflexible, intolerant, bigoted (sticking to one's convictions, especially on moral issues)

Adapted from Bill T. Arnold and Bryan E. Beyer, Encountering the Old Testament: A Christian Survey *(Grand Rapids: Baker Academic, 1999), 357.*

proclaimed a justice based on truth, not on one's economic, political, or social standing (Ex 23:2, 6–8; Lv 19:15).

The Conclusion: Vengeance (5:24–30)

Isaiah drew his judgment speeches to a close with a powerful description of God's vengeance. Straw and dry grass wouldn't last long amid flames, and those who opposed God wouldn't last long against his judgment.

Judah's sin began with a rejection of God's word (5:24). When the people decided they no longer wanted to live by God's standard for justice and righteousness, they began to decay into all sorts of wickedness. The Hebrew words

Key Terms

branch

City of David

David

day of the Lord

Gentiles

millennium

paronomasia

Study Questions

1. Identify and summarize at least three passages in Isaiah 2:1–5:30 where the prophet denounced bad leaders. How did bad leadership typically impact society?

2. How do Isaiah's words in 2:5–4:1 apply to twenty-first-century life? Identify the modern parallels.

3. How does Isaiah's song of the vineyard (5:1–7) parallel Jesus's parable of the vineyard owner (Mt 21:33–44)?

for "rejected" and "spurned" (*ma'as* and *na'ats*, respectively) emphasize a conscious decision to depart from God's standards. Judah had not drifted into sin but had turned from God to run to it.

God's judgment would bring devastation; Isaiah described corpses lying in the streets as the mountains shook. Yet this did not satisfy God's fury. The expression "Yet for all this, his anger is not turned away, his hand is still upraised" occurs again in 9:12, 17, 21, and 10:4 to denote God's persistent anger even amid terrible judgments. Isaiah's words emphasize how seriously God takes sin, whether he finds it among unbelievers or among his people (see sidebar 3.1).

God would assemble an army from distant lands to invade his people (5:26–29). They would come without hesitation, well prepared to do the job God had called them to do. Later, Isaiah would describe Assyria as the rod of God's anger against his people (10:5). Nations that did not know God nonetheless served his grand purpose.

As the army descended on Judah, it brought darkness and gloom to the land. The day of God's judgment was at hand, and none could stop it.

4 Isaiah's Call to Prophetic Ministry

Isaiah 6:1–13

Outline

Objectives

After reading this chapter, you should be able to

1. Summarize the basic details of Isaiah's vision and call.
2. Discuss Isaiah's first prophetic message (6:9–13) and its use in the New Testament.

In 740 BC, the year King Uzziah died, the prophet Isaiah experienced an awe-inspiring encounter with the Lord God. The Holy One of Israel revealed his glory, and Isaiah struggled to deal with the implications. God's splendor and majesty stood in stark contrast to the prophet's uncleanness. God's holiness revealed the depths of Isaiah's own iniquity and sin. How could he stand before such a God, much less serve him?

Throughout the centuries, people have struggled with the question of how a holy God can allow sinners to come into his presence. Many people answer the question by either lessening God's holiness or minimizing humanity's sinfulness, but the Bible does neither. Instead, it asserts that God's holiness requires him to judge sin wherever he finds it. He must deal with sin, even when that sin lies in his own people. The answer Isaiah received changed his life, just as it changes everyone who dares to receive God's commission.

Does Isaiah 6 Describe Isaiah's Call to Prophetic Ministry?

Does Isaiah 6 recount Isaiah's "prophetic call"? Most interpreters believe so.[1] They argue that such a powerful experience as Isaiah described could not have come subsequent to his call. Second, the comprehensive nature of Isaiah's experience—including Isaiah's fear and confession of sin, as well as God's cleansing of his sin—suggest an initial experience, not a later one. Third, the general summary nature of the message Isaiah received suggests to many that the message typifies the focus of Isaiah's later messages.

Other scholars have understood Isaiah 6 differently. They argue that if Isaiah 6 truly described Isaiah's call,

Isaiah would have placed this in chapter 1, right up front. As to the argument concerning the depth of Isaiah's response, they suggest that since Isaiah was still a sinner even after his initial call, it would not have been surprising if he responded as he did every time God met him. Isaiah 6:1–8 thus represents more a commissioning to a task than a general call to prophetic ministry.[2]

As you study Isaiah 6, consider these arguments and decide for yourself what you think about the vision and its relationship to Isaiah's call.

Isaiah's Vision (6:1–8)

Five of the sixteen prophetic books contain accounts of visions God gave his prophets. Isaiah, Ezekiel, Daniel, Amos, and Zechariah all recorded their visions as part of the books that bear their names. Obadiah (1) and Nahum (1:1) also used the term "vision" to describe their encounters with God, though their books do not contain visions per se.

In each prophetic vision, the Lord revealed something about himself. Sometimes, as here, he revealed something about his character and majesty. At other times, he used visions to reveal a great work he was going to do (Dn 8:1–27; Zec 2:1–5). Those who experienced these visions often participated actively in them, conversing with God or another heavenly being (Am 7:1–9; Zec 5:1–4).

Where Did Isaiah's Vision Occur?

Did Isaiah have his vision in Solomon's temple? The Hebrew word *hekal* (6:1) can mean either "temple" or "palace," and the context would seem to indicate the former meaning because it later mentions the altar (6:6). Indeed, all modern translations render the word *hekal* in 6:1 as "temple."

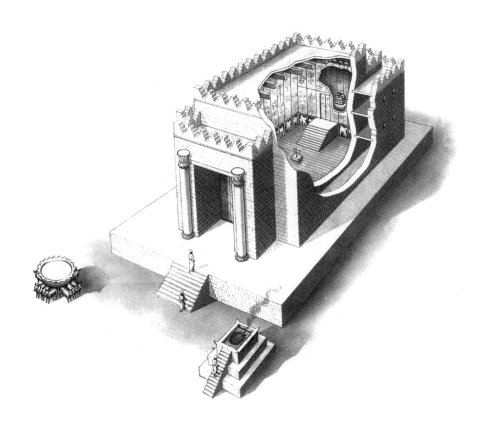

A reconstruction of Solomon's temple, the temple of Isaiah's day (Courtesy of Tim Dowley Associates Ltd.)

On the other hand, thrones typically appeared not in temples but in palaces. In Isaiah's vision, Yahweh the king sat enthroned among his attending seraphim. If the setting was the temple, where in the temple was he sitting? The most holy place, or "holy of holies," would seem likely, but then how would Isaiah have seen him? Only the high priest ventured behind the curtain, and even then, only once a year (Lv 16:15–17). In fact, King Uzziah had lived the last eleven years of his life stricken with leprosy because he entered the temple and tried to usurp the priestly duties (2 Chr 26:16–21). Would Isaiah have ventured into the temple with such a vivid scene so fresh in his memory?

Questions and issues such as these have led many interpreters to conclude Isaiah saw God's heavenly throne room, not the inside of Solomon's temple.[3] God was surrounded by his heavenly court, and his grandeur displayed itself. Such an understanding makes the scene Isaiah described—seraphim flying around the throne, the antiphonal praise to the Lord, the thresholds shaking from their voices, and the house filling with smoke—even more awe inspiring. All heaven shook before the heavenly King.

Isaiah's vision comprised four aspects: Isaiah saw the Lord's glory, Isaiah confessed his uncleanness, Isaiah received God's cleansing, and Isaiah responded to God's call.

Isaiah Sees the Lord's Glory (6:1–4)

Isaiah's vision occurred in the year of the death of King Uzziah. As such, it no doubt provided Isaiah and Judah a sense of confidence at a time of uncertainty. Regardless of who would next occupy Judah's throne, God still sat on heaven's throne.

seraph

Isaiah's statement, "I saw the Lord," presents the heart of his vision. Everything else that followed was simply commentary on this amazing truth. The expression "high and lifted up" may refer grammatically either to God or to his throne but probably describes the Lord. Later, the same two Hebrew words would describe the Lord's servant in 52:13.

Isaiah's reference to the train of the Lord's robe further highlighted the Lord's majesty. The train filled the entire room. The impressiveness of the train pointed to the great stature of the One who wore it.

The word "**seraph**" comes from the Hebrew word *saraph*, which means "to burn." The term denotes the bright, fiery appearance of the winged beings that attended the Lord. Perhaps they reflected the dazzling countenance of the One they served. Christians are called to reflect Christ's image today, though in a different way than the seraphs did (2 Cor 3:18).

The Bible nowhere else mentions six-winged seraphs, though other writers had visions of dazzling heavenly beings (Ez 1:4–14; Dn 10:4–6; Rv 4:6–11). The seraphs covered their faces to avoid beholding the full glory of God. "Feet" may be a euphemism for genitals and refer to the seraphs' modesty, though not all scholars agree with this interpretation. Covering the entire body was the general practice of decency in the ancient Near East, but especially in the presence of monarchs, covering the feet and bowing the head were tokens of reverence.

The seraphs joined their voices in antiphonal declaration of God's holiness. The temple shook from their voices as they cried, "Holy, holy, holy is the Lord Almighty; the whole earth is full of his glory." The threefold repetition of the word "holy" emphasizes the superlative degree to which God manifested this characteristic. He displayed his glory throughout his creation; earth's best testified to his greatness. The book of Psalms regularly echoes the theme of

God's glory abundantly revealing itself in creation (Pss 8:1; 19:1–6; 24:1–3).

The seraphs' calling must have been virtually deafening as it resounded through the structure. Isaiah's common designation of the Lord as the "Holy One of Israel" certainly must have found its origin in Isaiah's vision experience. The presence of smoke added to the eeriness of Isaiah's vision but also recalled the smoke of the incense that filled the earthly temple (Ex 30:34–38). Perhaps the smoke also paralleled the cloud, representing God's presence, that led Israel through the wilderness (Ex 40:36–38).

Isaiah Confesses His Sin (6:5)

Isaiah responded to this great vision of God's majesty as so many others who experienced God's presence did—with great fear (Ex 3:6; Rv 1:17). The Hebrew expression translated "Woe is me!" emphasizes Isaiah's feeling of utter ruin (see sidebar 4.1).

The vision of God's glory thus had a twofold result. It revealed the depths of God's majesty and splendor, but it also revealed the depths of Isaiah's uncleanness. He felt as if he couldn't go on.

Isaiah confessed that he, a man of unclean lips, lived among a people with the same fault (6:5). Lips shape speech, and speech reveals what lies in one's heart and mind. The prophet stood as a sinner in the midst of a sinful nation; neither he nor the people of Judah could stand before this holy God.

Isaiah cried, "My eyes have seen the King, the LORD of hosts!" (6:5 NASB). People coming into the king's presence naturally would dress themselves with the finest clothes they had. They would want to make as good an impression as possible. But Isaiah knew he had nothing with which to impress his heavenly Sovereign. The King of kings knew him for what he was, and he also knew the people of Judah for what they were. Their sinfulness contrasted sharply with his holiness, just as their lowly estate contrasted sharply with his regal majesty.

theophany

The clash of God's holiness with Isaiah's uncleanness brings the reader to a powerful tension point in the call narrative. How could a holy God establish a relationship with this soon-to-be prophet? He could not unless he dealt with the problem of Isaiah's sin. Indeed, it is precisely this issue that lies at the heart of the Christian faith today (Rom 3:21–26; see sidebar 4.2).

Isaiah Receives God's Cleansing (6:6–7)

The Lord's messenger, no doubt acting at the Lord's direction, took immediate action in the face of Isaiah's despair (6:6). He flew to Isaiah carrying a coal he had taken from the altar. The earthly temple had two altars—an altar for burnt offerings, which stood outside the temple in the courtyard, and an altar for incense, which stood in the temple inside the holy place. If Isaiah's vision occurred inside Solomon's temple, then the incense altar is probably intended. If Isaiah's vision occurred in heaven's throne room, as has been suggested, the exact nature of the altar would remain unclear. Perhaps the altar for burnt offerings was intended since it was the place where sacrifices were burned.

Ultimately, an altar was always a place of sacrifice, a place of offering. God used an image Isaiah would understand to minister to him and meet his spiritual need.

The Hebrew of verse 7 literally begins, "And he touched against my mouth." Did the actual coal touch Isaiah's lips? Did the seraph touch the tongs or the hand that held the tongs against Isaiah's lips? The text does not concern itself with such details, leaving us only to observe the solemnity of the moment. The Hebrew masculine form *zeh* (this) in verse 7 grammatically refers to the tongs rather than to the coal (Heb. *ritspah*, a feminine noun), but we should probably not make too much of this distinction.

The seraph then described the significance of his act: "your guilt is taken

---

Sidebar 4.1
Human Reactions to Theophanies in Scripture

The term **"theophany"** describes an appearance of God to human beings. In such appearances, God or his messenger typically takes human form temporarily to interact with people. These accounts further emphasize God's desire to reach people with knowledge of him.

In one sense, we might say the incarnation of Jesus Christ was the ultimate theophany, though his incarnation was a permanent taking on of humanity. Theologians usually do not use the term to describe Christ's incarnation.

People responded to theophanies in different ways. In many cases, they responded with fear and awe. Sometimes, they feared death. Still others felt their own sin in the presence of a holy God. The following table relates how many responded.

Name	Reference	Occasion	Response
Hagar	Genesis 16:7–14	Commands Hagar to return to Sarah; promises her great posterity.	Dialogues with angel; expresses surprise she saw God and lived.
Abraham	Genesis 18:1–33	Announce birth of Isaac; reveal fate of Sodom.	Humility, hospitality; dialogue with God over Sodom.
Moses	Exodus 3:1–4:17	Appears to Moses in burning bush; commands him to lead Israel from Egypt.	Fears, hides his face; tries to convince God he's not the right man for the job.

Name	Reference	Occasion	Response
Joshua	Joshua 5:13–15	Encourages Joshua as he prepares to fight Jericho.	Approaches cautiously; humbles himself after he knows who it is; speaks humbly.
Gideon	Judges 6:11–24, 36–40	Encourages Gideon to fight Midian.	Responds in unbelief; cannot believe God has chosen him; fears death after seeing angel "face to face"; asks God to prove himself with a fleece.
Samson's parents	Judges 13:1–23	Announces Samson's birth and coming work.	Woman tells her husband, Manoah; Manoah prays, angel appears again; Manoah fears death after seeing angel's power, but wife reassures him.
Isaiah	Isaiah 6:1–8	God's glory displayed in temple.	Isaiah confesses his uncleanness; volunteers for prophetic service after angel cleanses him.
Nebuchad-nezzar	Daniel 3:24–30	Sees angel of the Lord protecting Shadrach, Meshach, and Abednego in fiery furnace.	Treats Shadrach, Meshach, and Abednego well; issues decree that no one should speak against their God.
Daniel	Daniel 8:15–27	Gabriel informs Daniel of the meaning of the vision Daniel has just seen.	Fear and humility; exhaustion and sickness following vision.
Daniel	Daniel 9:20–27	Gabriel informs Daniel of seventy periods of seven God has decreed.	Response not given.
Daniel	Daniel 10–12	Heavenly being informs Daniel of future events prior to and including end times.	Daniel's friends fear and run; Daniel loses strength, falls to ground as though asleep; strengthened by messenger to stand, does so; Daniel inquires further at end of vision and is told the vision will pertain to a future generation.
Zechariah (prophet)	Zechariah 1–6	God's work for his people's future described in eight night visions.	Zechariah records what he sees and the conversations he has (no indication of emotional state).
Zechariah (father of John the Baptist)	Luke 1:8–23	Gabriel appears to announce impending birth of son (John the Baptist) to Zechariah and his wife, Elizabeth.	Initial fear, followed by unbelief (asks for a sign so he'll know the truth of the message).
Mary	Luke 1:26–38	Gabriel appears to announce Mary will give birth to the Messiah.	Initial fear; asks how God will do this work in her; responds in faith and surrender.
John	Revelation 1:9–20	Glorified Christ appears to announce his message to the seven churches of Asia Minor.	Falls down as dead.
John	Revelation 4:1–22:17 (intermittent)	Provide John further insight into God's plan for the ages (may be more part of larger vision than theophanies proper).	Records accounts of conversations, but no hint of emotional state; at end (22:8–9), tries to worship the angel but is rebuked.

Sidebar 4.2
God's Holiness and Humanity's Sinfulness Meet in the Gospel

The book of Leviticus calls God's people to holiness. A key verse is Leviticus 19:2—"You shall be holy, for I the Lord your God am holy" (NASB). To be holy is to stand totally separate from sin. Thus God is holy, but we, as sinful people, are not.

The book of 1 John teaches that God is love (1 Jn 4:8). God's love for us is as infinite as his holiness. These truths present a tension in God's being: How can a holy God allow sinners to come into his presence? It would seem God's love would move him to accept us, while his holiness would move him to reject us.

In Romans 3:21–26, the apostle Paul boldly proclaims the solution: the sacrifice of Christ has paid sin's price. He wrote:

> But now a righteousness from God, apart from law, has been made known, to which the Law and the Prophets testify. This righteousness from God comes through faith in Jesus Christ to all who believe. There is no difference, for all have sinned and fall short of the glory of God, and are justified freely by his grace through the redemption that came by Christ Jesus. God presented him as a sacrifice of atonement, through faith in his blood. He did this to demonstrate his justice, because in his forbearance he had left the sins committed beforehand unpunished—he did it to demonstrate his justice at the present time, so as to be just and the one who justifies those who have faith in Jesus.

God's holy character is satisfied by the atoning sacrifice of his Son; sin's awful price was paid in full, Paul says, by Christ's death. God thus extends his infinite love to humanity by sending his Son to secure the salvation of all who place their faith in him.

---

away and your sin atoned for" (6:7). Through an act of God's messenger, God cleansed Isaiah from his uncleanness. Notice that the seraph said nothing about Judah's sin but only spoke of Isaiah's. God's people had not yet come to realize their need for divine cleansing. Only with the end of the Babylonian exile would Judah receive God's restoration (40:2).

Isaiah Responds to God's Call (6:8)

Isaiah leaped at the sound of God's call. As God called to his court, "Whom shall I send? And who will go for us?" a cleansed Isaiah stood ready to respond. He had confessed his sin and experienced God's cleansing. He now could serve the Lord. Note that Isaiah responded to God's request even before Isaiah knew what task God would give him.

The Bible consistently puts confession and cleansing *before* worship and service. We likewise must come to an understanding of our deep spiritual failure and need, and experience the grace of God's cleansing before we can serve him effectively.

Isaiah's eager response set the stage for his first prophetic message. What would God give him to tell Judah?

Isaiah's First Prophetic Message (6:9–13)

Isaiah's Commission (6:9)

The undoubtedly excited prophet now received his simple commission from heaven: "Go and tell this people. . . ." The Lord then put before Isaiah a simple five-verse message. To some degree this initial prophecy presented the overall basic thrust of Isaiah's message to Judah.

The Prophecy Itself

Most of the Old Testament prophets focused primarily on their own generation, though their messages were also applicable to future generations. Isaiah's first message to Judah was largely negative and focused on the nation's desperate situation.

Isaiah's initial words (6:9) must have sounded paradoxical or even contradictory to his hearers. Why would God command them to keep looking, but never understand? Why would he ask them to keep seeing, but never come to know? The prophet instructed his people to continue to listen intently to God's truth but assured them it would not reach their hearts. Was this some sort of "reverse psychology" intended to goad them into repentance?

God then actually instructed Isaiah to make sure Judah did not understand (6:10). The prophet was to make the nation's heart calloused, make its ears heavy, and smear over its eyes. As such, the nation would prove unreceptive to God's message. What kind of words were those? Would the prophet's message actually harden people's hearts rather than open them?

The Lord's instruction contained within it the idea that the people of Judah were not ready to respond fully to God's message. Any repentance at this point would prove superficial at best and would give the impression that the Lord required only half-hearted allegiance. He was not ready to heal and restore them yet, for they had deep spiritual lessons to learn. Once they learned these lessons, they would find his arms open to them.

Isaiah asked the Lord how long the situation of spiritual blindness would continue (6:11). The Lord responded that only a time of complete devastation would awaken the nation. Cities and land would lie desolate; homes would sit uninhabited. Survivors would experience exile (6:12), and signs

of God's judgment would appear at every turn.

Nonetheless, Isaiah's initial message contained a kernel of hope (6:13). A sacred portion of Judah would remain, and from it God would rebuild his people. Dreadful circumstances would come first, but afterward God's restoration.

Isaiah 6:9–10 in the New Testament

All four **Gospels** (Mt 13:14–15; Mk 4:12; Lk 8:10; Jn 12:40) cite Isaiah 6:9–10 or a portion of it. Acts 28:26–27 also cites the verses. The **Synoptic Gospels** (Matthew, Mark, and Luke) use the verses in similar fashion and apply them to the same historical context, while in John and Acts, the verses address a different situation. The citations in Matthew and Acts exactly match the Septuagint (see sidebar 4.3).

Matthew 13:14–15 provides the clearest and most complete account of the events surrounding Jesus's citation of Isaiah 6:9–10. After Jesus related the parable of the sower to the crowds along the Sea of Galilee, his disciples asked him privately why he spoke to the crowds in parables. Jesus explained that the disciples had been privileged to know the mysteries of the kingdom, but the multitudes had not. Consequently, Jesus spoke to them in parables.

Verse 12 seems particularly instructive to Jesus's meaning. Jesus prefaced his citation of Isaiah 6:9–10 by saying, "For whoever has, to him more shall be given, and he will have an abundance; but whoever does not have, even what he has shall be taken away from him" (Mt 13:12 NASB).

Jesus appears to indicate that the disciples enjoyed a special privilege by virtue of Jesus's call on their lives that the general population did not. The disciples might hear Jesus's words explained again and again, while others did not. Jesus's parables challenged his listeners to listen carefully, and those with "ears to hear," that is, those who genuinely sought the truth, would find

Sidebar 4.3
Isaiah 6:9–10 in the New Testament

Reference	Nature of Citation	Historical Context	Application
Matthew 13:14–15 (clearest, most complete text of the Synoptics)	Cites vv. 9–10 verbatim; follows the Septuagint; matches Acts 28 exactly.	Following parable of the sower; disciples ask why Jesus speaks to crowds in parables.	Isaiah text is fulfilled in the multitude's unbelief; it has been given to the disciples to know the mysteries of the kingdom, to others it has not. That is why Jesus speaks in parables. Verse 12 seems key here: "whoever has will be given more."
Mark 4:12	General allusion, not a direct quote.	Following parable of the sower; disciples are asking about the parables.	Jesus alludes to Isaiah's words but doesn't specifically cite prophetic fulfillment. Says it has been given to the disciples to know the mysteries of the kingdom, and "those on the outside" hear parables.
Luke 8:10	General allusion, not a direct quote.	Following parable of the sower; disciples ask about the parable's interpretation.	Jesus alludes to Isaiah's words, but doesn't specifically cite prophetic fulfillment. Says it has been given to the disciples to know the mysteries of the kingdom, and "the rest" hear parables.
John 12:40	Verse 10 only, but in third person (sustainable by repointing the Hebrew text; heart and eyes only, nothing about the ears).	Following Palm Sunday entry; Jesus had performed many signs, but the general population did not believe in him.	Isaiah's words fulfilled in the unbelief of the general population. John adds (v. 41) that Isaiah said these things because he saw Jesus's glory.
Acts 28:26–27	Cites vv. 9–10 verbatim; follows the Septuagint; matches Matthew 13 exactly.	Paul has arrived in Rome, and an audience has gathered at an appointed time to hear his message; many refuse to believe.	Paul says their unbelief is fulfillment of Isaiah's words. Therefore, he is taking the message to the Gentiles.

it and would receive more. The others fulfill Isaiah's words through their unbelief or disinterest.

Mark 4:12 and Luke 8:10 describe the same historical context as Matthew 13:14–15 and are similar in their use of Isaiah's words. Both give only a general summary statement of Jesus's words, as well as a general allusion to Isaiah's words. However, the basic meaning remains the same: the disciples are privileged to know the kingdom's mysteries, but the rest hear parables.

John 12:40 applies Isaiah's words to Jesus's ministry during the last week of his earthly ministry. Jesus's triumphal entry had already occurred (12:12–19), and Jesus had foretold his death (12:31–33). John explains to his readers that although Jesus had performed many miracles, many people did not believe in him.

John cites two Isaianic texts: 53:1 and 6:10. The use of 53:1 seems to parallel closely Isaiah's intended meaning, namely, that the question functions rhetorically, to highlight the amazing general rejection of the Servant and his message (53:2–3).

When John cited Isaiah 6:10, he gave a different rendering. In John's rendering, the Lord plays a more active role in blinding the eyes and hardening the hearts of those who refuse to believe. Interestingly, the rendering can also be supported by the Hebrew text if one alters the vowels, which were not part of the original Hebrew manuscripts. John suggests that Isaiah's words were fulfilled in the unbelief of the general population. John adds (Jn 12:41) that Isaiah said these things because he saw Jesus's coming glory.

Acts 28:26–27 cites Isaiah 6:9–10 verbatim. The text carefully follows the Septuagint and thus also exactly matches Matthew 13. Paul had arrived in Rome and had engaged in dialogue with some of the local Jewish leaders, who asked to hear more about his ideas (Acts 28:17–22). They set a time to discuss his ideas further, and a large number gathered (Acts 28:23).

Paul's presentation seems to have received only a modest positive response, while the rest of his audience refused to believe. Paul contended that just as their ancestors had fulfilled Isaiah's words by their unbelief, so his unbelieving hearers were fulfilling Isaiah's words by their unbelief. Consequently, Paul asserted, the gospel would now go to the Gentiles (Acts 28:28).

Paul's words stand as particularly instructive in that they suggest a multiple fulfillment of Isaiah's words. In Isaiah's day, many rejected his teaching, and his words were fulfilled. Isaiah's words came true again around AD 61, when the Jewish leaders rejected Paul's message. And of course, Jesus's words in the Gospels suggest that those who heard him also fulfilled Isaiah's words.

The combined testimony of the New Testament usage of Isaiah 6:9–10, then, suggests two important truths. First, Jesus's parables served a dual purpose. Those who had "ears to hear" and applied his teaching received more light. Those who rejected his message gained no use from the little they had.

Second, in each generation down through the centuries, people exist who hear God's truth and reject it. When they do, they fulfill Isaiah's words again. But others hear it, accept it, and thus receive more.

5 The Signs of Immanuel and Maher-Shalal-Hash-Baz

Isaiah 7:1–8:22

Outline

- **The Sign of Immanuel (7:1–16)**
  The Historical Setting (7:1–9)
  The Sign Offered, Refused, and Given
  (7:10–16)
- **Interpretations**
  The Meaning of 'Almah
  Conclusion: Isaiah 7:14 and the New
  Testament
- **The Coming Assyrian Invasion
  (7:17–8:22)**
  The Destruction of the Land (7:17–25)
  The Birth of Maher-Shalal-Hash-Baz
  (8:1–4)
  The Judgment of the People (8:5–22)

Objectives

**After reading this chapter, you should be
able to**

1. Summarize the key people and events
   related to the Syro-Ephraimite War,
   including Isaiah's Immanuel prophecy.
2. Discuss the various interpretations of
   Isaiah 7:14 in relationship to the New
   Testament.

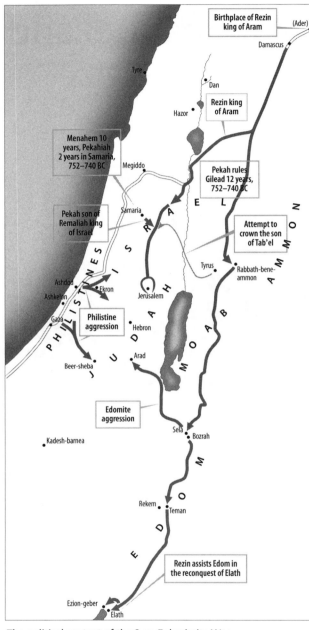

The following labels appear on the map:

Birthplace of Rezin king of Aram (Ader)

Damascus

Tyre

Dan

Hazor

Rezin king of Aram

Menahem 10 years, Pekahiah 2 years in Samaria, 752–740 BC

Megiddo

Pekah rules Gilead 12 years, 752–740 BC

Samaria

Pekah son of Remaliah king of Israel

Attempt to crown the son of Tab'el

Tyrus

Rabbath-bene-ammon

Ashdod

Ekron

Jerusalem

Ashkelon

Gaza

Philistine aggression

Hebron

Beer-sheba

Arad

Edomite aggression

Sela

Bozrah

Kadesh-barnea

Rekem

Teman

Rezin assists Edom in the reconquest of Elath

Ezion-geber

Elath

The political context of the Syro-Ephraimite War

Immanuel

Syro-Ephrai-mite War

Tiglath-Pileser III

The Sign of Immanuel (7:1–16)

The **Immanuel** passage stands as one of the most famous passages in the book of Isaiah. Anyone familiar with the Gospel writer Matthew's account

of Jesus's birth knows of Matthew's reference to Isaiah's prophecy. Matthew declared that Isaiah's prediction of a coming individual named Immanuel found its ultimate fulfillment in Jesus of Nazareth.

Many would recognize the Immanuel prophecy as coming from Isaiah, and probably many would also know the name means "God is with us." However, most people would not know the historical context from which Isaiah's words came. As we will see, Isaiah's words reflect a time when the people of Judah desperately needed to understand God was with them.

The Historical Setting (7:1–9)

The Immanuel passage's historical setting reflects a time of national crisis for Judah. Israel and Syria marched southward and threatened Judah's borders. What would King Ahaz of Judah do? This impending conflict is known as the **Syro-Ephraimite War**.

The Syro-Ephraimite War occurred in 735–734 BC.[1] The key figures included **Tiglath-Pileser III**, king of Assyria; Rezin, king of Syria; Pekah, king of Israel; and Ahaz, king of Judah. Second Kings 16 and 2 Chronicles 28 present the larger picture to which Isaiah 7 only alludes (see sidebar 5.1).

In 745 BC, Tiglath-Pileser III ascended Assyria's throne. He suppressed the revolts that accompanied any change in power and began to reestablish Assyria as the dominant force in the ancient world.[2] The Assyrian empire also flourished during the reigns of succeeding kings Shalmaneser V (726–722 BC), Sargon II (721–705 BC),[3] Sennacherib (704–681 BC; cf. Is 36–37), and Esarhaddon (680–668 BC; cf. Ezr 4:2), after whose reign Assyria began a period of decline from which it would not recover.

In Syro-Palestine, smaller nations such as Syria and Israel watched Assyria nervously. What if Assyria pushed westward and incorporated them into its empire? The prospect of loss of independence prompted two perpetual enemies—Israel and Syria—to join forces against their eastern threat. Kings Pekah and Rezin formed an alliance in the hope of repelling Assyrian expansion.

However, the Syria-Israel alliance had one potential flaw. Judah lay to the south, under the control of King Ahaz. If Ahaz joined them, all would be well. But if Ahaz joined Assyria, Syria and Israel would find themselves caught between hostile forces. They could not risk Ahaz siding with Assyria, so they advanced on Judah to "persuade" Ahaz to join their coalition.

Isaiah 7:1 presents the reader with the "headline": Israel and Syria came against Jerusalem, but they did not prevail. Why not? For the answer, the reader must continue.

Sidebar 5.1
The Syro-Ephraimite War— A Summary

Date	735–734 BC
Key figures	Tiglath-Pileser III, king of Assyria
	Rezin, king of Syria
	Pekah, king of Israel
	Ahaz, king of Judah
	Isaiah, prophet of God in Judah
Issue	Rise of Assyria forces smaller kingdoms to decide between joining forces and fighting Assyria or becoming vassal states; Israel and Syria decide to join forces and fight; Judah hesitates to join the coalition, so Israel and Syria move to attack Judah.
Isaiah's role	Encourages Ahaz to trust in the Lord rather than join the coalition or join Assyria.
Ahaz's decision	Appeals to Tiglath-Pileser III and becomes his vassal.
Results	Tiglath-Pileser III pushes westward, conquers Damascus (732 BC), kills Rezin; annexes Israel; Hoshea conspires against Pekah and kills him; Hoshea becomes vassal to Assyria.

Isaiah 7:2 reports the royal court's fearful reaction to the news: "Syria has encamped in Ephraim." Judah had good reason to fear. Right below Ephraim lay the tribal territory of Benjamin, and if Israel and Syria took the Central Benjamin Plateau, Judah would lose an important access to the international coastal highway to the west. Furthermore, the Judeans' enemies would be standing virtually on Judah's doorstep, only a few miles from Jerusalem.

In this context, then, Isaiah went at God's direction to meet Ahaz (7:3). Isaiah took along his son Shear-Jashub, whose name means "a remnant will return." God's instruction to bring the boy indicates that the Lord intended to bring Ahaz an optimistic message. Though the text gives specific information as to the location of the meeting—"at the aquaduct of the Upper Pool, on the road to the Washerman's Field"—archaeologists have not identified the specific place to which Isaiah referred.[4] A generation later, when Hezekiah also faced an Assyrian threat, his delegation and the Assyrian delegation would meet at the same place (36:2).

The prophet's message to Ahaz was clear and direct. Rezin and Pekah were like two smoldering firebrands, not producing much heat and soon to go out. God had established their places of sovereignty; Rezin ruled Syria and Pekah ruled Israel. They would not receive more.

Isaiah's challenge to Ahaz and the royal house (7:9; the Hebrew verb forms are second-person plural) contains a significant word play. The Hebrew word 'aman, from which the word "amen" is derived, appears twice in two different Hebrew forms. Its basic meaning is "to be confirmed." Literally, Isaiah told Ahaz that if the royal house would not believe (i.e., cause to be confirmed in their hearts) the message Isaiah brought, then the royal house would not remain established (or confirmed) over Judah.

What reason would Ahaz have to believe Isaiah? He might have believed

Sidebar 5.2
Living by Faith in Difficult Circumstances

Ahaz's struggle between standing on Isaiah's words and appealing to Assyria illustrates one of life's most significant areas of tension: God's promises versus earthly circumstances. In the end, Ahaz lacked the faith to trust in God's promise and instead appealed to Assyria for rescue. Ironically, the Bible records how Ahaz's predecessor, Jehoshaphat, did have such faith (2 Chr 20:1–30), as did Hezekiah, Ahaz's son (2 Kgs 19:14–19), when enemy forces threatened.

Throughout the ages, God has called people to believe in his promise over and against earthly circumstances. Consider these other examples from the biblical record:

Reference	Situation	God's Promise	Earthly Circumstance
Genesis 12, 15, 17, 18	Abraham and Sarah wait for a descendant.	God will make Abraham a great nation and give him a son by Sarah.	Abraham and Sarah are already seventy-five and sixty-five years old, respectively, when God first makes the promise, then must wait twenty-four more years before Sarah conceives.
Numbers 13–14	Israel is preparing to enter the promised land.	God has promised the land to Israel and will give it to them.	The cities are well fortified, and the land's inhabitants are larger and stronger than the Israelites.
Luke 1	God sends the angel Gabriel to Zechariah in Jerusalem.	Zechariah's wife, Elizabeth, will conceive in her old age and bear a son (John the Baptist).	Zechariah and Elizabeth have no children and are well past normal childbearing years.
John 20	Jesus's disciples are telling Thomas they have seen Jesus alive from the dead.	Jesus has told his disciples he would be crucified but would rise again on the third day.	Dead people stay dead, and Thomas knows Jesus had died.

Abraham needed to wait twenty-five years before God fulfilled his word to him. Nevertheless, despite sometimes struggling to believe (Gn 17:17–18), Abraham chose to trust God's promise (Rom 4:18–21).

Moses sent twelve spies into Canaan (Nm 13:1–20). All of them saw the same rugged terrain, the same fortified cities, the same giant peoples. Joshua and Caleb, however, trusted God's promise and encouraged Israel to do the same (Nm 14:6–9), but their pleas fell on unbelieving ears. God sent Israel to wander in the wilderness forty years until the unbelieving generation died (Nm 14:22–23, 33–34).

When Gabriel announced to Zechariah the priest that Zechariah's wife Elizabeth would conceive a son who would be the forerunner of the Messiah, Zechariah struggled to believe and asked for a sign so he would know for sure it would happen (Lk 1:18). He did receive a sign, but the sign gave testimony to Zechariah's lack of faith.

Thomas struggled to believe his fellow disciples when they assured him they had seen Jesus alive from the dead. After all, as much as he may have wanted to believe, Thomas knew dead men stay dead. However, Thomas didn't refuse to believe; rather, he determined what he would need as proof of Jesus's resurrection (Jn 20:25). When Thomas saw Jesus and was convinced it was indeed Jesus, he did not persist in unbelief but responded in faith (Jn 20:28).

Today, Christians sometimes worry over the basics of life when Jesus has promised they will have these things if they seek first God's kingdom and righteousness (Mt 6:33). They think God has forgotten them when he has promised never to leave them (Heb 13:5). Or they may assume they have no useful place in God's service when God has assured them they have spiritual gifts to be used for his glory (1 Cor 12:4–11). In each of these situations and in others, God calls his children to trust his promises over their earthly circumstances.

merely because Isaiah was a prophet, but he had an even greater reason as well: his own heritage. Ahaz—like all of Judah's kings—was descended from King David.

Second Samuel 7 records the incredible promise God had made to David: "When . . . you lie down with your fathers, I will raise up your descendant after you. . . . He shall build a house for My name, and I will establish the throne of his kingdom forever. . . . When he commits iniquity, I will correct him . . . but My lovingkindness shall not depart from him, . . . your throne shall be established forever" (2 Sm 7:12–16 NASB).

The promise of God's continued protection and sovereign care over David's descendants powerfully affected David's life. Even as David lay dying, he reminded Solomon that if Solomon and his descendants were faithful, they would never lack a man on Israel's throne (1 Kgs 2:3–4).

Ahaz was a descendant of David and, as such, an heir to this promise. Isaiah might have paraphrased his message thus: "Ahaz, your circumstances may look bad right now, but 250 years ago, God addressed future problems like this in his promise to your ancestor David. Go back and read it, and you'll see. If you choose to have courage and take by faith what God has already said instead of worrying about what your circumstances suggest might be happening, God will preserve you on your throne" (see sidebar 5.2).

The Sign Offered, Refused, and Given (7:10–16)

The words "spoke again" (7:10 NASB) suggest a possible change of venue. Based on Isaiah's reference to the house of David (7:13), the prophet's audience may have been those of the royal court. Isaiah now expanded on his original challenge to Ahaz (7:9).

The Sign Offered and Refused (7:10–13)

The Lord sometimes provided his people signs and wonders to demonstrate his power and the truth of what he said (Ex 3:1–4; 4:1–9; Lk 1:18–20; 2:12). In 2 Kings 20:8–10, Isaiah offered Hezekiah the chance to choose one of two options. However, Isaiah 7:10 records the only place in the Bible where a prophet offered a human being the opportunity to name the sign. God in his grace reached out in a special way to a king of Judah struggling to believe Judah would experience God's deliverance.

However, Ahaz refused to name a sign, attempting to hide behind false piety (7:12). Of course, he would not have been putting the Lord to the test in an improper way, for the Lord had given him authority to name the sign. Ahaz had probably already decided he would appeal to Assyria for help against the Syrian-Israelite coalition (2 Kgs 16:7). He did not want to risk his kingdom on a God he could not see. Instead, he determined to put his trust in an alliance with Assyria, a choice that ultimately would spell doom for the northern kingdom.

Isaiah challenged the entire house of David present that day (7:13). Note particularly the shift in his words from "your God" (7:11) to "my God" (7:13). The prophet was suggesting that by its unbelief, the house of David had shown itself unfit for a relationship with the living God.

The Lord's Sign: The Birth of Immanuel (7:14–16)

Isaiah announced that God remained determined to have Judah's stubborn leadership believe. Therefore, he himself would provide them a sign whether or not Ahaz chose one.

One of the difficulties is that Isaiah 7:14 may be translated differently depending on how one reads the Hebrew. The first question is how we understand the Hebrew word 'almah. Does it mean "virgin" or "young woman"?

Second, how should we translate the Hebrew word *harah*? Does it mean "will conceive" or "is pregnant"? Third, how should we understand the Hebrew word *yoledet*? Does it mean "will bear" or "is about to bear"?

Scholars have studied these alternate renderings of the three words and suggested three possible translations: (1) "The virgin will conceive and bear a son" (many modern translations);[5] (2) "The young woman will conceive and bear a son" (some modern translations);[6] and (3) "The young woman is pregnant and about to bear a son."[7] Other renderings are possible, of course, given the potential combination of meanings, but these three reflect the major views. We will consider each possibility in the following section.

One very clear aspect of the passage concerns the name of the child, Immanuel. *Immanu* means "with us" and *El* means "God," so Immanuel means "God is with us." Would the situation have appeared as though God were with Judah? Not at all; the Syrians were encamped at Ephraim. Nonetheless, Isaiah asserted, God was with his people. Immanuel's birth would somehow serve as a sign of Judah's deliverance.

Matthew 1:22 says when Jesus was born, "All this took place to fulfill what the Lord had said through the prophet: 'The virgin [Gk. *parthenos*] will be with child and will give birth to a son, and they will call him Immanuel.'" How should the New Testament affect our interpretation of the Old Testament? Put another way, how should Matthew's understanding of Isaiah 7:14 influence our interpretation of what Isaiah originally intended?

The New Testament record is quite clear, both in Matthew 1 and in Luke 1, regarding the nature of Jesus's birth. Mary was a virgin at the time she conceived Jesus by the power of the Holy Spirit and remained so until Jesus's birth. For some interpreters, this settles the issue. They conclude Isaiah meant only to speak of Jesus the Messiah's virgin birth. Others, however, see the issue differently.

The Greek word *pleroo* is commonly translated "fulfill" in the New Testament. In some cases (e.g., Mt 12:17–21 and Is 42:1–4), the verb indicates a direct fulfillment of a prediction Isaiah made. In other cases, it suggests rather a sort of "fillfullment," that is, a "filling full" or secondary fulfillment in some sense of an Old Testament prophecy (e.g., Mt 2:15 and Hos 11:1). Thus understanding the full range of meaning of *pleroo* is important to our understanding of Isaiah's words (see sidebar 5.3).

Such words and their meanings form the heart of the issue in Isaiah 7. There is no doubt in Matthew 1 and Luke 1 that Mary was a virgin when the angel Gabriel came to her. There is also no doubt that Mary remained a virgin until the time of Jesus's birth. So our understanding of the original meaning of Isaiah 7 does not necessarily affect what we believe about the manner of Jesus's conception and birth or his sinless nature.

The question, rather, concerns Isaiah 7. Is it only a prediction, finding its fulfillment seven hundred years later when Mary conceives Jesus? Or do Isaiah's words have a similar but different meaning in their original context, a meaning then taken to its ultimate fulfillment (or "fillfullment") in Jesus's conception and birth? And if so, what did they mean in Isaiah's day when he spoke them and Ahaz and others of David's house heard them?

Interpretations

This section will survey the basic interpretations evangelicals have given to these questions and enable students to wrestle with the evidence themselves and draw their own conclusions. A key issue is the meaning of the word *'almah*.

Sidebar 5.3
"Filled Full" Prophecies—The New Testament Writers' Use of the Old Testament

The New Testament writers saw all the Old Testament as pointing to Jesus Christ. The law of Moses, the prophets, and the writings all bore witness to his life and work (Lk 24:44).

With regard to Jesus and prophecy, the New Testament writers viewed Jesus's life and work as doing one of three things. First, Jesus *directly fulfilled* the prophetic word. That is, prophets predicted certain things about his life that came true as they said it would. Consider a few famous examples from Isaiah:

Old Testament Prophecy	New Testament Fulfillment
Isaiah 11:1: Messiah from root of Jesse, the line of David.	Matthew 1:1: Jesus the Messiah from the line of David.
Isaiah 42:1–4: Servant of the Lord quietly brings about God's kingdom.	Matthew 12:18–21: Jesus quietly brings in God's kingdom.
Isaiah 52:13–53:12: Servant of the Lord suffers, dies for the people's sin, ultimately triumphs.	Jesus suffers and dies on a cross for the world's sin but rises from the grave triumphant.
Isaiah 61:1–3: Spirit of the Lord anoints God's servant to proclaim God's coming kingdom.	Luke 4:16–21: Jesus announces his fulfillment of these words in Nazareth.

Second, Jesus *secondarily fulfilled* the prophetic word. That is, some prophecies had their immediate application in another person or event but later were fulfilled in him. Isaiah 7:14 may be such an example. The sign of Immanuel may have seen a fulfillment in Ahaz's day, but Jesus was the secondary and ultimate fulfillment of the "God is with us" prophecy.

Third, Jesus *filled full* the prophetic word. That is, the New Testament writers saw events in Jesus's life and work as paralleling concepts of which the prophets had spoken and hence "filling them full" of meaning.

For example, Hosea 11:1 clearly describes Israel's exodus from Egypt and is really a statement of historical fact, not a prediction. But when Joseph and Mary brought Jesus out of Egypt, the Gospel writer Matthew saw in it Hosea 11:1 all over again (Mt 2:15). God was bringing his son out of Egypt again, but this time, it wasn't his firstborn son Israel; it was his one and only Son Jesus.

Likewise, Matthew's suggestion that Jesus's living in Nazareth fulfilled prophecy (Mt 2:23: "He will be called a Nazarene") was merely pointing out the amazing "divine coincidence" that the Branch of David grew up in *Branchville* (the literal meaning of Nazareth; see discussion in chap. 6). Even where Jesus lived had its roots in the words of the prophets!

We do not know to what extent the New Testament writers distinguished carefully between *directly fulfilled*, *secondarily fulfilled*, and *filled full* prophetic words. What appears obvious is that as they looked at Jesus and at the Old Testament, they had no doubt that Jesus was the one who fulfilled the Old Testament promise.

The Meaning of '*Almah*

'*almah*

The word '*almah* also occurs in Genesis 24:43, Exodus 2:8, Song of Songs 1:3 and 6:8, Psalm 68:25, and Proverbs 30:19. Genesis 24:16 specifically says Rebekah (the woman described in Gn 24:43) was a virgin (Heb. *betulah*), thus suggesting '*almah* may have had a broader semantic range, at least in the patriarchal period. The other usages are inconclusive and appear to denote young women in general, without specific reference to whether they are virgins. Further, in the two usages of the masculine form '*elem*

(1 Sm 17:56; 20:22), the term denotes a young boy or young man, but the issue of virginity is irrelevant to the contexts in which they appear.

A key question in Isaiah 7:14 as it relates to the word 'almah is whether the word *can* mean "virgin" or denote a woman who is a virgin. We may answer this question affirmatively based on the existing evidence. But *must* the word mean "virgin"? The evidence appears uncertain. The term 'almah may denote a woman who is a virgin, but the usages suggest it may also denote a young woman, irrespective of sexual status.

Nonetheless, we must still attempt to understand this text's relationship to the text of the New Testament. Do Isaiah's words find their fulfillment only in Jesus's birth, or do they have another related meaning in their original context? Three interpretations have been advanced.

View 1: Isaiah's Words Find Their Fulfillment Only in Jesus

Some scholars have argued that Isaiah 7:14 finds its fulfillment solely in the virgin birth of Jesus.[8] In effect, when Isaiah gave his prophecy to Ahaz, he was saying, "Ahaz, you don't want to pick a sign, so the Lord will, and he will do something truly amazing. A *virgin* is going to conceive and bear a son. If that isn't amazing, Ahaz, I don't know what is. Further, the virgin will name that son 'Immanuel.' You don't believe God is with us, Ahaz, but he is, and he will prove it through this amazing sign."

Proponents of this view usually cite evidence from the Septuagint, the early Greek translation of the Old Testament. In the Septuagint translation of Isaiah 7:14, the word *parthenos* is used for 'almah. This word clearly means "virgin" and is the term Matthew uses. Perhaps the Septuagint provides early testimony to the meaning Isaiah intended.

On the other hand, some have argued the Septuagint writers did not always use the most accurate word available in various contexts.[9] Thus, in our context, perhaps a Greek word that means

"young woman" would have been more accurate for Isaiah's context.

View 1 suggests the sign is the virgin birth of Jesus, and that indeed, by the time of Jesus's birth, the kings of Syria and Israel were gone, just as Isaiah had said (7:16). But some scholars have pointed out the possible weakness of such a view. The weakness lies in the gap of over seven centuries between Isaiah's prophecy and its fulfillment.

If view 1 is correct, Isaiah was basically saying, "God is going to do a great work among us, and this will be a sign for you: a virgin will bear a son!" However, if the prophecy was not fulfilled for over seven hundred years, what value did the sign have for Ahaz or Isaiah's other hearers? The sign seems to lose its impact for Ahaz and his generation. Perhaps one may argue that since Ahaz refused to believe, God delayed the fulfillment of Isaiah's prophecy until the first century AD.[10]

View 2: The Prophecies of Isaiah 7 and 8 Are Linked

Some scholars have linked the prophecies of chapters 7 and 8, the births of Immanuel and **Maher-Shalal-Hash-Baz**, citing similarities in the two accounts.[11] In both chapters, the birth of a son occurs, and before the son is very old, the kings of Israel and Syria will be gone. The two texts record different perspectives on the same birth; the first is a pronouncement to a faithless royal house, the second is an announcement of hope to a desperate people.

The sign of 7:14, then, is not the manner of birth but the naming of the child. At a time when all hope appears gone, the names "God is with us" (Immanuel) and "Swift is the plunder, speedy is the prey" (Maher-Shalal-Hash-Baz) are given as a sign that God has not forsaken his people. The translation "virgin" is maintained for 7:14 but is almost incidental to the passage, for the woman conceives in the usual manner in 8:3.

According to this view, in 7:14 Isaiah was speaking of his betrothed, who would soon become his wife. This forces us to the conclusion that this was a second wife, since Isaiah already had a son (Shear-Jashub, 7:3). On the other hand, if we understand the word *'almah* to mean "young woman," this difficulty disappears.

Opponents of this view usually cite two difficulties. First, they question whether the naming of a child is sufficiently unusual to be deemed a "sign." Second, the timing of the two kings' defeat is different in the two prophecies, for children learn to say parents' names (8:3) earlier than they learn to distinguish right from wrong (7:16).

Those who hold this view usually attempt to minimize the differences between the two prophecies. Perhaps the expression "refuse evil and choose good" (7:16 NASB) designates a fairly young age of two to three years old, not necessarily bar mitzvah age (thirteen for boys, twelve for girls). Further, a biblical sign is not always something miraculous. Sometimes it designates something unusual that is "elevated" to sign status because it has been announced beforehand (Ex 3:12; 1 Sm 2:34; Is 37:30). Nonetheless, the opponents of this view raise valid questions.

View 3: The Woman Is Already Pregnant

View 3 translates Isaiah 7:14 as follows: "The young woman is pregnant and about to bear a son." As stated above, this translation is also possibly a correct rendering of the Hebrew text. According to this view, the woman is already pregnant and about to give birth. The identity of the woman is unimportant; perhaps Isaiah pointed to a woman present that day. This view finds no necessary link with the birth of Maher-Shalal-Hash-Baz in 8:1–4; the two births describe different events, albeit with related applications.[12]

In this understanding, Isaiah's words to Ahaz have the following impact: "Look, Ahaz! [And perhaps here the prophet points to a nearby pregnant woman.] The woman is pregnant and about to give birth, and she's going to name her son Immanuel. You, O king, a member of the royal house of David,

don't have the faith to believe that God can deliver Judah, but she does."

As with view 2, the sign is not the manner of the birth but the naming of the child, elevated to sign status because of its extreme unlikeliness in such perilous times.

Opponents of this view usually challenge it on two grounds.[13] First, does the word *'almah* only mean "young woman," or does it need to be rendered "virgin" in light of the link with Jesus's birth? Second, is the naming of a child unusual enough to be called a sign?

In response, proponents point to the lack of clarity regarding the word *'almah* and the many places in Scripture where a sign is something unusual, not necessarily miraculous, along the lines of the arguments for view 2.

Conclusion: Isaiah 7:14 and the New Testament

Any time the New Testament says an Old Testament passage is somehow fulfilled in the New Testament, we need to respect that assertion. Indeed, all three views presented here do so. Matthew 1 and Luke 1 are clear on the birth and nature of Jesus and do not contradict Isaiah. However, some evangelicals believe that in its original context, Isaiah 7:14 designates something other than merely Jesus's birth over seven hundred years later. If so, they nonetheless understand Matthew 1:22 as a secondary fulfillment, indeed as the grandest fulfillment, of Isaiah 7:14, and the fullest expression of the concept that God is with us. Again, students are encouraged to wrestle with the views, study the evidence, and draw their own conclusions.

The Coming Assyrian Invasion (7:17–8:22)

Following the Immanuel prophecy, Isaiah's focus quickly shifted back to what would happen in Judah. In the next section, Isaiah's message focused on three elements: the destruction of the land (7:17–25), the birth of Maher-Shalal-Hash-Baz (8:1–4), and the judgment of the people (8:5–22).

The Destruction of the Land (7:17–25)

Assyria, the very nation Ahaz sought as an ally, would become Judah's greatest adversary (7:17). Isaiah used metaphors from nature to highlight the magnitude of the coming destruction (7:18–19). Swarms of flies and bees would not be welcome in any society. Isaiah's mention of Egypt and Assyria reflects well the historical situation. As Egypt and Assyria vied for control of Syro-Palestine, smaller nations such as Judah often found themselves caught in the middle of a much larger struggle.

The prophet also described the oppressive conditions to come (7:20–25). Shaving the hair off one's body probably described the humiliating degree of Assyrian oppression (2 Sm 10:4–5; cf. Is 50:6). The number of livestock would drop significantly as food sources for animals became briars and thorns. Such prophetic threats would speak powerfully to a society whose economy was based primarily on agriculture and pastoralism.

The Birth of Maher-Shalal-Hash-Baz (8:1–4)

Isaiah gathered witnesses for his next announcement (8:1–2). Witnesses commonly served to confirm the legality of transactions, and other prophets also made use of them (Jer 32:10–15). The witnesses verified the writing of the Hebrew words *maher shalal hash baz*—"swift is the plunder, speedy is the prey"—on a large tablet.

We should understand Isaiah's comment that he "approached the prophetess" (8:3 NASB) as a euphemism for sexual relations. The woman gave birth to a son, whose name became Maher-Shalal-Hash-Baz in accordance with the writing on the tablet. The name signified the short time remaining before Assyria

would subdue Israel and Syria, thus eliminating the threat to Ahaz (7:2).

As stated earlier in the discussion of 7:14, commentators generally assume "the prophetess" is a designation for Isaiah's wife, but they disagree over the nature of the title. Some suggest she may have herself exercised the prophetic office, while others contend the name means something along the lines of "Mrs. Isaiah."

Isaiah asserted that before the child was old enough to call for his parents, Assyria would defeat Israel and Syria (8:4). His words proved true: Tiglath-Pileser III conquered Damascus in 732 BC and killed Rezin. He also annexed Israel into his empire and received tribute from **Hoshea**, Israel's last king, who later rebelled against Assyria's next king, Shalmaneser V (2 Kgs 16:9; 17:3–4). It was the beginning of the end for the northern kingdom.

The relationship of the Maher-Shalal-Hash-Baz passage to the Immanuel passage was discussed earlier in this chapter. The sign of Maher-Shalal-Hash-Baz appears as yet another indication of God's offer to bring deliverance—an offer Ahaz determined to ignore in his desire to partner with Assyria (2 Kgs 16:7–18).

The Judgment of the People (8:5–22)

Isaiah continued to decry the people's sin of putting their faith in other nations instead of in the Lord (8:5–6). The expression "gently flowing waters of Shiloah" may refer to one of the conduits the people had built off the **Gihon Spring**, Jerusalem's main water supply.[14] Others have suggested it is a poetic reference to the Lord's gentle care (Jer 2:13).[15] Assuming the prophecy comes from Ahaz's time, it cannot refer to the Pool of Siloam, which Hezekiah's workers constructed a generation later (2 Chr 32:30).

These gentle waters stood in stark contrast to the "strong and abundant waters of the Euphrates," a reference to the Assyrian empire (8:7–8 NASB). Isaiah's assertion that Immanuel (7:14;

The zodiac signs on the synagogue floor of Hammath Tiberias in Galilee, although later than Isaiah's time, illustrate the syncretism prevalent in Galilee. Isaiah 8:19–20 instructed God's people to consult the word of God, not the stars, as their true foundation for life. (Courtesy of Todd Bolen/Bible Places.com)

8:8) would see the day of Assyria's dominance warned Judah what would happen if Ahaz rejected Isaiah's challenge (7:9).

Isaiah's message extended to people everywhere (8:9–18). God was with Judah, despite the plans others might make. The Lord called his prophet to stand strong in the face of people who wanted to devise their own plans and who feared what other nations might do to them (8:11). They should fear the Lord, for he would protect and care for them. The Lord instructed Isaiah to record the prophetic word as a testimony for those who would stand firm in their faith (8:16–18). One day, they would see Isaiah's words come true.

Study Questions

1. Describe the factors that led to the Syro-Ephraimite War. Include key people and events. What was the final outcome?

2. Summarize the evangelical interpretations of Isaiah's Immanuel prophecy. Based on your personal study of the issue, which interpretation do you believe is most likely correct? Defend your answer.

3. Explain the difference between various types of prophetic fulfillment (direct fulfillment, secondary fulfillment, "fillfullment").

Key Terms

'almah

Gihon Spring

Hoshea

Immanuel

Maher-Shalal-Hash-Baz

Syro-Ephraimite War

Tiglath-Pileser III

Sidebar 5.4
Religious Pluralism and God's Truth (8:19–20)

We live in a world where many people believe all religious claims have equal value. The prevailing attitude is often "All religions have the same basic goal in mind; just find something that works for you." People pray to God, but they also try Eastern meditation techniques. They read their Bible, but they also read their horoscope. Others wear a cross as jewelry, not as a testimony to their faith, but more as a good-luck charm.

Isaiah also faced much religious pluralism in his day. People tried to tap the spiritual realm through many different means to obtain direction for life.

In Isaiah 8:19–20, the prophet denounced those of his day who consulted mediums and spiritists for spiritual insight. They needed to consult their God rather than following means that would only result in their ruin. And what was the chief means by which they should inquire of him? Through his written word.

The Hebrew word translated "law" (8:20) is *torah*, the familiar term that is more accurately rendered "teaching" or "instruction." The word "testimony" (*te'udah*) is related to a Hebrew root that means "to bear witness." *Torah* and *te'udah* thus emphasize different aspects of God's written word. It is teaching and instruction for life that bears witness to God's righteous character and demands. It is true and trustworthy because God is its source. Spiritual insights gained by means that God's written word had condemned were always suspect and revealed a lack of spiritual discernment in the people's minds.

Over and against today's culture, the Bible asserts that objective truth can be known. Just as importantly, the Bible asserts that the truth contained in its pages can change lives. Psalm 119 describes how God's word helps us stay pure (v. 9), helps us avoid sin (v. 11), opens our eyes to greater spiritual insight (v. 18), lights our life's path (v. 105), and enables us to see God's righteousness and the rightness of his ways ever more clearly (vv. 137–44). Truth shapes our attitudes, our feelings, and our behavior, and as we choose to embrace it, it provides a solid foundation for life.

Jesus himself directed his listeners to truth, telling them it would set them free (Jn 8:32). He directed them to the Old Testament's witness of him (Jn 5:39), but he himself also claimed to be the full embodiment of truth (Jn 14:6). He thus provided life's ultimate foundation for those who follow him.

All religious claims may be heard in a free society, but not all are equally true. Followers of Jesus must discern God's truth from the world's error and live accordingly.

Some looked to other nations for assistance, while others looked to the ways of mediums and spiritists (8:19). Isaiah insisted such speculation would prove worthless; the people should consult the living God and his living word (8:19–20; see sidebar 5.4). Their judgment would reveal they had made the wrong choice.

Indeed, for the biblical writers, life often presented God's people the choice to live either by faith in God's promises or by faith in one's circumstances. One generation later, Ahaz's son would face that same choice when Assyria returned to Judah (Is 36–37).

6 God's Kingdom Will Surpass All Earthly Kingdoms

Isaiah 9:1–12:6

Outline

- **Description of the Messianic Era (9:1–7)**

  The Restoration of the Nation, Especially the North (9:1–5)

  The Means of Restoration: The Birth and Rule of the Messiah (9:6–7)

- **Judgment against Israel (9:8–10:4)**

  Judgment by Other Nations (9:8–12)

  Judgment against Israel's Leaders (9:13–17)

  Judgment by Famine and Natural Disasters (9:18–21)

  Judgment against All Society (10:1–4)

- **Judgment against Assyria (10:5–34)**

  God's Judgment of Assyria's Arrogance (10:5–19)

  Israel's Ultimate Victory over Assyria (10:20–34)

- **Further Description of the Messianic Era (11:1–16)**

- **Song of Thanksgiving and Praise (12:1–6)**

- **Concluding Thoughts from Isaiah 1–12**

Objectives

After reading this chapter, you should be able to

1. Summarize key details of Isaiah's prophecies of the Messianic kingdom contained in Isaiah 9–12.
2. Explain Assyria's role as an instrument of judgment against Israel and Judah.

Isaiah 9–12 spends a significant amount of time stressing God's coming kingdom. However, in the middle of these chapters, the prophet announced God's coming judgment on Israel and Assyria. Israel had mocked God and his ways, despising his law and covenant, and had responded to God's redemptive efforts with further contempt and scorn. Assyria had functioned as God's instrument against Israel but had never understood this amazing truth. Assyria was too busy establishing its own greatness.

Isaiah announced an incredible coming day. Galilee would experience the light of God's special presence, and David's descendant would establish God's kingdom. As he did, a celebration such as the world had never known would begin. God's kingdom would surpass *all* earthly kingdoms.

Description of the Messianic Era (9:1–7)

As Isaiah began his discourse, he announced relief and blessing for those who had experienced past gloom and anguish (9:1). Those who had long endured without God's favor now would experience it in a way they never would have imagined.

The Restoration of the Nation, Especially the North (9:1–5)

Isaiah contrasted the times of coming prophetic fulfillment with former and perhaps current reality (9:1–2). In earlier times, the territory in the direction of Zebulun and Naphtali received no special favor from God. However, in the days to come, God would make the area much more important. The people who walked in relative spiritual darkness would see a great light.

It is preferable to translate the Hebrew of Isaiah 9:1 (8:23 in the **Masoretic Text**) as "toward the land of Zebulun and toward the land of Naphtali" rather than "the land of Zebulun and the land of Naphtali." The former provides a more general description of the land skirting the north and west shores of the Sea of Galilee.

Isaiah cited three important geographical references in 9:1: "the way of the sea," "the other side of the Jordan," and "Galilee of the Gentiles."

The Sea of Galilee region, where most of Jesus's public ministry took place (9:1–2; courtesy of Chris Miller)

The northwest corner of the Sea of Galilee looking north. The international highway thus ran right through the area where Jesus did much of his public ministry. (Courtesy of Todd Bolen/Bible Places.com)

way of the sea

Via Maris

Vulgate

Decapolis

The Way of the Sea

The **way of the sea**, called *Via Maris* in the Latin **Vulgate**, designated the ancient highway system that ran from the Levant to Egypt, following the Mediterranean coastline as much as possible. In later times, it designated the entire Galilean network of roads.[1] The highway came from the north above Caesarea Philippi, cut down past Capernaum, around the northwestern shore of the Sea of Galilee and through the Arbel Pass, around Mount Tabor, and into the Jezreel Valley past Megiddo.

The way of the sea provided passage for caravans and other travelers who had to journey through Galilee going south on their way to Egypt or going north to Anatolia, Syria, or Mesopotamia. Consequently, many foreign influences and ideas were transported on this road, a fact that at least partly explains the northern kingdom of Israel's earlier tendency to lapse into idolatry.

The Other Side of the Jordan

East of the Jordan River above and below the Sea of Galilee lay the **Decapolis**, a region under the control of first the Seleucid rulers and later the Romans.[2] Despite the non-Jewish ethnic makeup of this area, Isaiah said that they too would receive God's favor.

People living in this area centuries after Isaiah would see Jesus cast demons from a man and into a herd of swine, which rushed down and drowned themselves in the lake (Lk 8:32–33).

Galilee of the Gentiles

Where was the focus of God's prophetic work? Most of the biblical prophets ministered in Judah to the south and in the surrounding regions. Prophets such as Isaiah and Micah focused on Judah, though their messages were broader. Hosea, Amos, and Jonah all prophesied in the northern kingdom, and we know Jonah hailed from Gath Hepher in Zebulun's territory (Jos 19:13; 2 Kgs 14:25). However, we do not know if Hosea and Amos penetrated all the way to northern Galilee with their messages.

Galilee's intricate road system that linked the Levant with Egypt meant more interaction between Jews and Gentiles, along with the accompanying influx of foreign influences. Hence, the expression **Galilee of the Gentiles** accurately reflected both the ethnic and to some extent the spiritual realities of the region.

God's people to the north found themselves naturally more open to foreign influences because the road system required people who wished to travel between Egypt and the Levant to pass through Galilee. The land's rugged topography forced them to do so. By contrast, Judah lay off the major highway routes, so travelers typically did not go through Judah unless they had business there.

The Greek and Roman influence on Galilee in Jesus's day prompted the Pharisees' sarcastic comment to Nicodemus (Jn 7:52). With so much pagan influence, what spiritual good could come from that region? Nonetheless, Isaiah announced, "The people who walk in darkness will see a great light" (9:2 NASB).

The Gospel of Matthew records Jesus's settlement in the fishing village of Capernaum, an international community along the northern shore of the Sea of Galilee (Mt 4:13). His presence there, accompanied by his subsequent ministry in the surrounding region, fulfilled Isaiah's words (Mt 4:14–16). People in that region lived in the area where Jesus conducted most of his public ministry and performed most of his recorded miracles. The Gospel writer John also testified to Jesus as God's light (Jn 1:9; 8:12).

Isaiah described the joy that would fill the people as God multiplied their nation (9:3–5). He would ease their burdens and remove their oppression. But Isaiah's audience could not have imagined the magnitude of God's blessing the coming kingdom would bring, just as we cannot.

The Means of Restoration: The Birth and Rule of the Messiah (9:6–7)

Isaiah announced the birth of a baby boy. Notice the words "to us" that occur

twice in this verse. The child's significance extended beyond his immediate family to God's people in general. He was given to the nation as God's special gift.

The magnitude of the child's significance then emerges: the government will rest on his shoulders. The northern kingdom of Israel had experienced a long line of kings who failed to turn Israel back toward the Lord. Would this king prove different? The four names Isaiah gave for the child indeed indicated he would be.

Wonderful Counselor

The first name Isaiah announced for the child was "Wonderful Counselor." The masoretic scribes understood these two words as representing one name, though both words could stand by themselves. The Hebrew word *pele'* (wonderful) commonly denotes a quality associated with the divine realm. It occurs in Judges 13:18, where the angel of the Lord had appeared to Manoah and his wife and announced Samson's birth. Manoah and his wife asked his name, but the angel replied, "Why do you ask my name, seeing it is *pele'*?"[3] The angel apparently assumed this couple should recognize his heavenly origin.

The word *pele'* and derivative forms such as *niphla'ot* (wonders) often designate God's mighty acts. References in the Psalms, for example, to God's wonders (Ps 136:4) typically use the word *niphla'ot*. The amazing things God can do, particularly those things totally beyond our ability and comprehension, comprise his *niphla'ot*.

The child Isaiah announced would thus possess counseling and advising ability far beyond ordinary men. His ability would surpass people such as Ahithophel, counselor to David and Absalom, whose counsel was "like that of one who inquires of God" (2 Sm 16:23). He would render decisions with the very wisdom of God (1 Kgs 3:28).

Mighty God

The second name Isaiah announced for the child was "Mighty God."

"Mighty God" is a strange name for a child, in that it appears to ascribe deity to the child. The translation "God is a warrior" is theoretically possible but unlikely in view of the parallelism with the other three names. The name appears nowhere else in Scripture.

Many Old Testament names contain the Lord's name in the shortened form -*yahu*. Isaiah's name (Heb. *Yisha'yahu*) means "Yahweh has saved." Jeremiah means "Yahweh is exalted," Uzziah means "Yahweh is my strength," and Hananiah means "Yahweh is gracious." Each name contains the Lord's name plus a descriptor that highlights one of his qualities.

The Hebrew word '*el*, which means "god" or "God," also commonly occurs in personal names. Elimelech means "my God is king," Elijah means "Yahweh is my God," Eleazar means "God has helped," and Elkanah means "God has acquired." As with the names that contain -*yahu*, those that contain '*el* consist of the word "God" plus a descriptor that highlights a divine quality or action (see sidebar 1.1).

Isaiah's designation of the child's second name as "Mighty God" again linked the child with the divine realm. The expression "Mighty God" also occurs in 10:21, where it refers to the Lord. David used the Hebrew word translated "mighty" (*gibbor*) to describe the Lord's might as he went forth on behalf of his people (Ps 24:8).[4]

Eternal Father

The third name Isaiah announced for the child was "Eternal Father" or "Everlasting Father." We may also understand the Hebrew as "Father of eternity" or "Father of the ages." In the first two renderings, the emphasis is on the Father's eternal or everlasting nature. In the third and fourth renderings, the term "Father" indicates his control over eternity and time itself.

As with the first two names, the name appears to ascribe an eternal quality to the child. This child, born into time, somehow transcended and oversaw time.

Prince of Peace

The fourth name Isaiah announced for the child was "Prince of Peace." We might have expected the title "King of Peace" in light of the third name, because the word "prince" emphasizes sonship rather than fatherhood. Thus, the text links these two concepts in this one person.

Isaiah 2:1–4 describes how the Messiah will not only bring God's people together but also will bring God's *shalom*, God's wholeness and completeness, to society. *Shalom* indicates more than merely an absence of war and hostility; it suggests a society whose every aspect is in harmony with God's purpose. *Shalom* is life as it was intended to be.

Isaiah again highlighted in verse 7 the peace this child would bring. He linked his rule with King David, under whom Israel achieved its greatest territorial expansion and peace at every border. Justice and righteousness would prevail as pillars of this lasting kingdom.

The last line of verse 7—"the zeal of the LORD of hosts will accomplish this"—denotes two important truths. First, this kingdom will come about directly because of God's doing. Human effort alone will not bring it. Second, God is eager to establish this kingdom. His *zeal* will accomplish it, and everyone will recognize his special work.

Isaiah's words about this child ruling forever from David's throne foreshadow the angel Gabriel's words to Mary seven centuries later (Lk 1:32–33). Jesus would reestablish the glory of David's throne and more.

Indeed, Christian interpreters have long identified Jesus as the focus of Isaiah's prophecy. Jesus is the Wonderful Counselor, our source of heavenly wisdom (1 Cor 1:30). He is the Mighty God, who possesses divine power (Col 1:16–17). He is an Everlasting Father, who rules forever as Lord of time (Heb 1:10–11). And he is the Prince of Peace, who rules as God's Son and brings lasting peace, not only in this life (Rom 5:1) but in his coming kingdom.

Judgment against Israel (9:8–10:4)

Isaiah 9:8–10:4 describes the anger God felt at Israel's pride and arrogance. He had taken drastic measures against the people to get their attention, but they had largely ignored them. A key statement in this section is "Yet for all this, his anger is not turned away, his hand is still upraised" which occurs four times (9:12, 17, 21; 10:4). The people had ignored God's judgment, so he took it to another level. The concept parallels Leviticus 26:14–39 and Deuteronomy 28:15–68, where Moses described the awful progressive consequences that would befall God's people if they were unwilling to follow him.

Judgment by Other Nations (9:8–12)

The people answered God's judgments with confident pride. They could rebuild whatever God had torn down; in fact, they believed they could rebuild even better. In response, God sent the Syrians from the east and the Philistines from the west to threaten Israel's territory. But Israel failed to learn its spiritual lesson, so God's punishment continued.

Judgment against Israel's Leaders (9:13–17)

The people's refusal to turn back to the Lord led to his cutting off "head and tail" from Israelite society (9:14). The leaders provided some stability to society, although they led the people astray spiritually. Their lack of spiritual discipline filtered down to the common people, who mimicked the leaders' godless ways. But still Israel failed to learn its spiritual lesson, so God's punishment continued.

Judgment by Famine and Natural Disasters (9:18–21)

Israel's wickedness burned the land like fire (9:18), so the Lord responded with the fire of judgment. As these disasters befell God's people, they did not know what to do. They fell upon one another, fighting over what little remained. Even Manasseh and Ephraim—the two closely related half tribes descended from Joseph—went after each other. But Israel still failed to turn back to God, so judgment continued.

Judgment against All Society (10:1–4)

Isaiah announced God's displeasure with those who lived by evil principles (10:1). Justice meant nothing to them, so the weak and powerless of society—often the orphans and widows (1:17)—lost their rights. God's final answer was devastation that would come "from afar" (10:3). All the people could do was prepare for their inevitable doom. And who was the nation that would bring this awful judgment? It was Assyria.

Judgment against Assyria (10:5–34)

Isaiah had prophesied earlier of Assyria and its impending expansion westward to threaten Israel (7:17; 8:7).[5] Indeed, Assyria's imminent threat had pushed King Rezin of Syria and King Pekah of Israel to establish a coalition against Tiglath-Pileser III (745–727 BC), the king who reestablished the Assyrian empire.

Assyria would certainly figure in Israel's future, defeating Samaria in 722 BC and deporting Israel's people. However, Assyria nonetheless remained merely an instrument in the hands of a sovereign God. As Isaiah shifted his attention to describing the Assyrian kingdom, he focused on two aspects: God's judgment of Assyria's arrogance and Israel's ultimate victory over Assyria.

God's Judgment of Assyria's Arrogance (10:5–19)

Assyria had established itself as the dominant kingdom in the ancient world when Isaiah uttered this prophecy. Ironically, the prophet used a woe oracle to describe this nation.

Isaiah described Assyria as the rod (Heb. *shebet*) of God's anger and the one in whose hands was the club (Heb. *matteh*) of God's wrath (10:5). Rods and clubs (or staffs) had a variety of uses in ancient times, but here they probably designate weapons. Another possibility—perhaps suggested by 10:24—is that they designate a taskmaster's instruments to be used on slaves. The two words commonly occur together in Isaiah in a variety of contexts.[6]

The Lord had a high purpose for Assyria: Assyria was his instrument of judgment against his people. The great empire would plunder Israel and Judah, leaving little of value. How ironic that Isaiah should describe his own people as "godless" (10:6) when Assyria worshiped hundreds of deities! Over a century later, the prophet Habakkuk also struggled with the concept that God would use another pagan nation—Babylon—to judge his own people (Hb 1:13–17).

Nonetheless, Isaiah announced woe against Assyria. The Assyrians did not recognize their role in God's sovereign plan. Rather, they exalted themselves and boasted of their apparent greatness as they wreaked destruction on everyone in their path.

Isaiah paraphrased Assyria's boastful attitude (10:7–11). Assyria considered its commanders on a par with kings of smaller nations (10:8). Verses 9–11 have much in common with the words the Assyrian field commander mockingly proclaimed to Hezekiah's delegation (36:18–20; 37:11–13).

The Assyrian field commander whom King Sennacherib would later send against Hezekiah (36:2) tried to weaken Judean morale by describing Assyria's past victories. Here Isaiah became Assyria's mouthpiece, choosing Syrian cities and city-states Assyria had conquered to create a similar image in his hearers' minds.

Isaiah began in northern Syria and worked his way southward. Calno (or Calneh) had fallen to Assyria in 738 BC, and Carchemish, after holding out through Assyria's initial expansion, fell in 717 BC. Hamath fell in 720 BC, the same year Arpad fell, although Assyria had also conquered the latter in 738 BC. Damascus fell in 732 BC (2 Kgs 16:7–9), after which Tiglath-Pileser III also annexed much of Israel, leaving Hoshea as his vassal over the rest of the nation around 730 BC (2 Kgs 17:3).[7] By presenting the Assyrian victories in geographical order from north to south, Isaiah painted a picture of an unstoppable Assyrian advance.

The mention of Samaria as a conquered foe (10:11) may be anticipating the Assyrian victory of 722 BC.[8] But it is also quite possible Samaria had already fallen and that Judah is the real focus of Isaiah's prophecy.[9] In this understanding, Isaiah's use of Samaria in Assyria's list of vanquished foes would prove all the more frightening to God's people. God had already judged the northern kingdom, and he would not spare Judah if the nation did not repent.

However, when God's purpose for Assyria was complete, he would deal with Assyria's pride (10:12). Assyria credited its own great strength and wisdom for its accomplishments. It saw itself as the mighty conqueror that had subdued the world's kings and plundered their treasures (10:13–14). But Isaiah's rhetorical questions (10:15) clarified the situation—Assyria was merely an instrument in the hands of almighty God.

Isaiah prophesied that God would punish the Assyrians thoroughly (10:16–19). All they had amassed would disappear "in a single day" (10:17). So great would be the devastation of Assyria's forests that a child could count the few number of trees remaining.

Israel's Ultimate Victory over Assyria (10:20–34)

Assyria's fall would prove catastrophic for the Assyrians, but God's people would rejoice. Isaiah described the day of victory they would experience as the Lord went forth to fight for them.

Isaiah first described the remnant that would return to the land after the Lord's destruction of his enemies (10:20–22). Through their subjugation to Assyria, they would come to understand the value of their relationship with the Lord and turn to rely on him again. Nonetheless, they would first experience severe consequences for their sin. The people once great in number would see only a remnant return to inhabit the land. They would only become numerous again after they had learned how much their sin had cost them.

In light of these incredible promises of Assyria's ultimate defeat and God's ultimate victory, Isaiah encouraged his audience not to fear. God's wrath would soon turn from the Judeans to the Assyrians, and Judah would lay aside Assyria's yoke of oppression (10:24–27).

Isaiah described a day when all would appear lost for Judah as the Assyrian army marched through the territory of Benjamin, conquering its cities and moving ever nearer to Jerusalem (10:28–32). As they moved closer to Judah's capital, the population would become increasingly desperate. But in that day, God would fight for his people, and Assyria's destruction would be compared to the clearing of the forest. Isaiah's words likely predicted Assyria's defeat during the days of Hezekiah (chaps. 36–37).

Further Description of the Messianic Era (11:1–16)

Isaiah would revisit the theme of Assyria's defeat later in his book. He now returned to a theme he had begun to describe earlier: a wonderful kingdom God was preparing for his own. He shared this vision with his hearers to encourage them in the face of whatever came their way. They could find strength to live faithful lives in the present day in light of the glorious future that awaited them.

As he described this marvelous coming age, Isaiah again introduced the

View of modern Bethlehem from the east (Courtesy of Jim Yancey)

concept of God's Messiah—his anointed one—who would play a special role in ushering in the coming kingdom. As he described the Messiah's person and role, Isaiah focused on three aspects: the Messiah himself, the peace the Messiah would bring, and the people God would gather.

The Messiah Himself (11:1–5)

Isaiah had earlier described a "holy seed" that would remain as a "stump" in the land after God's judgment swept through (6:13). Using different Hebrew terms but similar imagery, Isaiah described a new work the Lord would begin in the land.

Isaiah 11:1 identifies the source of this new work: the line of Jesse, resident of Bethlehem, father of King David (1 Sm 16:1, 10–13). The Hebrew term for "branch" (*netser*) is related to the name of the town Nazareth (Heb. *natseret*), the place of Jesus's boyhood, and probably explains the Gospel writer Matthew's cryptic reference in Matthew 2:23 (see sidebar 6.1).

The reference to Jesse's line as opposed to David's line makes an important distinction. Isaiah was not announcing the coming of David's successor; he was announcing the coming of another David.[10] Other prophetic passages also support this concept (Jer 30:9; Ez 34:23–24; Hos 3:5).

The Spirit of the Lord came upon David from the time the prophet Samuel anointed him (1 Sm 16:13). Likewise, the Spirit would now rest on this new David to empower him to fulfill God's purpose.

Isaiah described the qualities the Spirit's presence would bring: wisdom, understanding, counsel, power,

---

Sidebar 6.1
Isaiah 11:1, Matthew 2:23, and the Branch

The Gospel writer Matthew sought to show his Jewish readers that Jesus was the promised Messiah, the anointed one announced by the prophets to usher in God's everlasting kingdom. Consequently, we often read in Matthew comments similar to "and so the words of the prophet were fulfilled." Matthew frequently linked something Jesus said or did with the prophetic word.

Describing Joseph and Mary bringing Jesus out of Egypt, Matthew writes, "When [Joseph] heard that Archelaus was reigning over Judea in place of his father, he was afraid to go there. And being warned by God in a dream, he departed for the regions of Galilee, and came and resided in a city called Nazareth, so that what was spoken through the prophets might be fulfilled: 'He shall be called a Nazarene'" (Mt 2:22–23). Yet, one searches in vain for the expression "He shall be called a Nazarene" anywhere in the prophets. What was in Matthew's mind when he made a connection between Jesus's place of residence and the fulfillment of prophecy?

The answer probably lies in the similarity between the Hebrew words for "branch" and "Nazareth." The Hebrew word used for "branch" in Isaiah 11:1 is *netser*, whereas the Hebrew word for "Nazareth" is *natseret*. One could thus understand "Nazareth" to mean "Branchville" or "Branchtown."

In effect, Matthew is saying, "Look how amazingly God fulfills his word. In the Old Testament, he promised that the branch of David—the Messiah—would come to rule. And when he did, just look where this branch lived: in Branchville! Even the place that the Messiah lives fulfills God's word through his prophets!"

According to this view, Matthew is not saying Jesus's settlement in Nazareth is something that specifically fulfills a prediction Isaiah made. Rather, he is calling his readers to marvel at the subtle details God has ordained in his redemptive plan. Such details would remind them of God's sovereign guidance of human history and emphasize the uniqueness of God's Son Jesus.

knowledge, and fear of the Lord (11:2). Wisdom, understanding, knowledge, and fear of the Lord appear in Proverbs 1:1–7 as foundational qualities of the life that pleases the Lord. One who displayed these qualities would be able to apply counsel and power appropriately in any given situation. Israel and Judah had never seen a leader who would embody these qualities so completely.

The concept of the fear of the Lord appears again in verse 3a, perhaps as a summative comment. The new David's fear and reverence for the Lord shaped all that he was, and everything else flowed from that relationship. His wisdom and discernment enabled him to get beyond what he saw and heard to the heart of a matter and to rule with true justice, righteousness, and faithfulness (11:3–5). Further, he understood that ruling well encompassed both encouraging all that was good and suppressing evil in all its forms.

The Peace the Messiah Will Bring (11:6–10)

Once Isaiah finished describing the person of the Messiah, he shifted to describing the societal transformation that would occur under his leadership. Society would experience true *shalom* (though Isaiah did not use the word here) as every aspect of existence came into perfect harmony.

Harmony in nature would result as animals that previously had been enemies with one another and even with human beings would come together in peace. The concept of young children either leading wild animals or playing among them (11:6, 8) further emphasizes the peaceful nature of the time. The knowledge of the Lord modeled by the Messiah would permeate the land and its people (11:10).

Some scholars have seen in such imagery the concept of a return to paradise, though the book of Genesis does not fully develop the images Isaiah portrays.[11] (See also Is 65:25.) Indeed,

some have suggested the entire flow of redemptive history is back to Eden, returning to paradise lost. Of course, the description of the new Jerusalem in the book of Revelation (Rv 21:1–22:5) describes a greater reality than the Garden of Eden. Rather than returning to Eden, Isaiah pointed his audience to a new work that God was preparing especially for them, a work beyond their wildest dreams.

In that day, the root of Jesse would become a rallying point, a signal banner (Heb. *nes*) for all peoples (11:10). Isaiah saw a day when the people of God would include people from every land, every ethnic background, who would seek him out (Heb. *darash*) for counsel and instruction. The prophet had already seen it (2:2–4), and he would return to this theme again and again (42:6; 45:22–23; 49:6; 66:18–23).

The People God Will Gather (11:11–16)

Israel's history was filled with battles. These battles were sometimes border skirmishes, while at other times they were major conflicts with other nations. One outcome of these battles was the displacement of Israelite prisoners of war to other parts of the ancient world.

Isaiah prophesied the return of the remnant that had suffered displacement (11:11–12). The reference to the Lord extending his hand "a second time" probably links this action with his work on behalf of his people during the days of the exodus.[12] He would again take steps to bring his people home.

The reader might naturally expect to see three nations mentioned specifically—Egypt, Assyria, and Babylon—and they are. Indeed, at the time of Isaiah's prophecy, the first two of these had already figured prominently in Israel's history, and the third would soon. But God's gathering of his people would prove much more thorough. His hand would reach to Cush in Africa, to Elam east of Babylon, to Hamath in Syria, and even to the "islands of the sea" visited by the seafaring and slave-trading Phoenicians (Am 1:9).

Isaiah also saw a reunification of God's people in his description of Judah and Ephraim (11:13). By Isaiah's time, the term "Ephraim" designated the part of the northern kingdom that remained under Israelite rule, albeit under vassal status with Assyria (7:2, 5, 8–9, 17). A reunited people would together subdue their neighboring enemies.

Finally, God's hand again would intervene in a miraculous way (11:15–16). His drying up the Nile and parting the Euphrates evoked memories of the exodus and the Jordan crossing (Ex 14:21–22; Jos 3:15–17). His creation of safe passage for his people scattered in Assyria would pave the way for their return home.

Thus, Isaiah 11 describes the person of the Messiah, the lasting peace he will bring, and God's great gathering of people to bring them home. In that day, the people will have much reason to rejoice. This fact leads us to the next section, a song of thanksgiving and praise.

Song of Thanksgiving and Praise (12:1–6)

Isaiah 12's song of thanksgiving and praise touched all aspects of Israelite society. Verses 1–2 focus on the individual response to the Lord's redemptive work, and the subject (v. 1, "you will say") is masculine singular. In verses 3–5, the verbs are plural, as the entire community joins in praising God and proclaiming his goodness. Finally, the verbs in verse 6 are feminine singular, perhaps a reference to the people of God as his bride.

Verses 1–2 describe the joy and trust redeemed sinners know because of God's great work on their behalf. God was angry, but his anger was now turned aside and he comforted his own. Because God is the source of salvation, his people may trust and not fear.

Verse 3 describes the people joyously drawing water from springs of salvation. Spring water provided the freshest

The powerful giant spring at Dan constitutes some of the main headwaters of the Jordan River. (Courtesy of Bryan E. Beyer)

Sidebar 6.2
Water Sources in Bible Times

Isaiah 12:3 describes God's people joyously drawing water from wells of salvation. Clearly, Isaiah's language is metaphorical. In the day of God's coming kingdom, his people will drink in his salvation, which will prove more abundantly refreshing than water to a thirsty person.

Water was a precious commodity in biblical times, just as it is today. Of course, people's homes did not feature running water as most do today. Consequently, people had to gather it from one of three sources: a spring, a well, or a cistern.

Springs provided the best source of water since the water continually bubbled up and renewed itself. The Bible sometimes uses the expression "living water" to describe springs (Jer 2:13; Jn 7:38). The Gihon Spring was Jerusalem's main water source, thus requiring the king of Judah to protect it at all costs (2 Chr 32:30).

Wells yielded good-quality water from underground pools. Since water was precious and the digging of a well represented a significant investment of time and energy, well ownership was sometimes the occasion for disputes and quarrels (Gn 21:25–31; 26:18–22; Ex 2:16–17). The expression "living water" was also sometimes used in reference to well water (Gn 26:19); the expression occurs in the Hebrew text, but is variously translated.

Cisterns collected rainwater so people would have at least something to drink during extremely dry seasons. Houses and even cities had channels that directed rainwater into these large reservoirs. Early limestone cisterns lost water due to leakage, but after about 1300 BC, people began to plaster the walls, which resulted in improved water preservation.

The biblical writers saw water's life-sustaining power as illustrating deeper spiritual principles. Jeremiah 2:13 described the false gods Judah worshiped as broken cisterns, worthless and unprofitable. In contrast, the Lord was his people's "fountain of living waters" (NASB) if they would only come and drink from his life-giving goodness. As David thirsted for water in the Judean wilderness, he affirmed that God's lovingkindness was better than life itself (Ps 63:1–3). The Lord invited the spiritually thirsty to come to him and drink (Is 55:1), and Jesus also promised that the one who would drink from him would never thirst again (Jn 4:13–14).

water, as opposed to wells, which provided access to underground pools, and cisterns, which merely collected rainwater. God's provision for his people continued, and since they knew his care for them, even the most basic tasks became reason for celebration.

The people proclaimed God's greatness, announcing it even to the peoples from which God had rescued them (12:4–5). They exalted him as they praised him for his *'alilot* (what he has done). This Hebrew term elsewhere denotes God's great works on behalf of his people (Pss 66:5; 77:11–12). How could his people keep silent about such things?

The command in verse 6 is literally addressed to the "people of Zion."

Isaiah's use of the Hebrew feminine forms alludes to Zion as an exuberant woman—perhaps the bride of the Holy One of Israel—as she celebrates all he is to her. The Holy One of Israel, the almighty God, now dwells personally with his people. Shout it out! Let everyone know!

Concluding Thoughts from Isaiah 1–12

Isaiah 1–12 contains many truths that readers may want to apply to their own lives. Indeed, the text tells us much

Study Questions

1. Explain the strategic significance of Galilee's location along the ancient highway routes.

2. List the names of the special child born (9:6–7) and explain their significance.

3. Summarize Assyria's role as an instrument of judgment against God's people during Isaiah's ministry.

4. Recount the key features of Isaiah's description of the messianic era established by the root of Jesse (11:1–16).

Key Terms

Decapolis

Galilee of the Gentiles

Masoretic Text

Via Maris

Vulgate

way of the sea

about who God is, who we are, and what God expects of us. As we conclude this section of the book, let us focus our attention on three such applications.

First, God's discipline should lead to repentance. Isaiah 9:8–10:4 describes God's disciplinary action against his people. He sometimes took drastic measures, but he did so in love, looking for their repentance. The Lord still uses difficult circumstances to bring people to repentance.

Second, people should remain sensitive to God's leading. Isaiah describes a world superpower—Assyria—whom God used as his instrument of judgment against his people. But the Assyrians proudly went about their conquests totally ignorant of their role in his sovereign purpose. By contrast, the root of Jesse delighted in the fear of the Lord, and that close relationship with God enabled him to rule effectively. The Lord continues to work through yielded hearts today.

Third, God is ushering in an exciting era. Isaiah 2 describes God's temple, God's people, and God's peace. Isaiah 9 places the Messiah on David's throne and bestows on him marvelous names. Isaiah 11 announces the coming of the root of Jesse—another David—and the age of peace and righteousness he will bring.

7 Oracles against the Nations

Isaiah 13:1–23:18

Outline

Objectives

After reading this chapter, you should be able to

1. Highlight the implications of God's sovereignty over all nations.
2. Identify the major nations and kingdoms Isaiah singled out for judgment in chapters 13–23.

Why Oracles against Other Nations?

Up to this point in Isaiah, the prophet has focused his attention largely on his own people. Although he mentioned all nations streaming to Mount Zion and rallying to the root of Jesse (2:1–4; 11:10) and discussed Assyria as the rod of God's anger (10:5–34), most of his pronouncements centered around God's work in Israel and Judah.

Why would Isaiah now take eleven consecutive chapters to turn to God's work in other nations of the earth? Two reasons stand out. First, the nations represented a challenge to the messianic kingdom. True, Isaiah had announced this wonderful era, but would earthly nations and their gods stand by and let it happen? Second, the nations represented a challenge to God's sovereignty. Ancient Near Eastern societies worshiped thousands of deities; dare Isaiah presume Yahweh reigned supreme above them all?

Challenges to the Messianic Kingdom

The preceding two chapters of this book described Isaiah 7–12 and the amazing prophecies there. Immanuel would be born as a sign of deliverance. The Messiah would take the government upon himself, and he would bear amazing names: Wonderful Counselor, Mighty God, Eternal Father, Prince of Peace. He would rule with justice and righteousness on David's throne. The root of Jesse—another like King David—would arise and bring a kingdom of peace such as the world had never seen. All nations would experience the best of what God had to offer as they rallied to him.

The Challenge of Earthly Kingdoms

But how could all this happen? After all, Assyria was the dominant power, and

Babylon and Egypt were stronger than either Israel or Judah. Many neighbors of Israel and Judah, small as they were, often posed considerable threats. The concept of a messianic kingdom must have sounded great, but what about all these nations? Surely they wouldn't allow it to happen, would they?

Isaiah 13–23 answered this challenge to God's establishment of a messianic kingdom. Isaiah's oracles against the nations announced that Yahweh was sovereign over the nations whether or not they recognized it. One day, they all would bow to him, and when they did, that would open the door to the messianic kingdom.

The Challenge of Other Gods

What about the gods of the other nations? The Assyrians worshiped the god Ashur, and their rulers boasted of the great victories he had won for them.[1] Babylon's chief god was Bel, called Marduk in earlier times. The Syrians had Adad, the Moabites Chemosh, the Ammonites Milcom, the Philistines Dagan, the Phoenicians Baal. And, of course, these nations worshiped many other deities as well. Hundreds and sometimes thousands of gods and goddesses formed their pantheons.

Isaiah's oracles against the nations also answer the challenge of rival deities. Yahweh not only reigned supreme over all earthly rulers; he reigned supreme over the universe. His acts of judgment against other nations would prove their gods powerless.

Challenges to God's Sovereignty

Beyond the challenges to the messianic kingdom lie the challenges to God's sovereignty. Yahweh is a god whose power Assyria had recognized during the days of Jonah (Jon 3:4–9), and Babylon would recognize his power during the ministry of Daniel (Dn 2:46–47; 3:28–29; 4:1–2, 34–37). But did Yahweh really reign supreme over the universe? Could he really do what his prophet proclaimed?

Isaiah's oracles against the nations do more than announce Israel and Judah's coming restoration in the messianic kingdom. More than that, they proclaim the ultimate victory of God. Yahweh's people share in the victory, but the victory brings glory to him first and foremost. All the world will bow in allegiance, not to God's people, but to him. Isaiah 13–23 focuses our attention on the work of the One who will not share his glory with another.

Babylon (13:1–14:23)

Why Begin with Babylon?

We might have expected Isaiah to begin his oracles against the nations with a judgment against Assyria. After all, Assyria was the dominant power during Isaiah's ministry. Or perhaps Isaiah would save Assyria for last as the climax to God's judgments. Isaiah did neither. Instead, he began his oracles with a judgment against Babylon.[2]

Why would Isaiah start with Babylon? At the time of this prophecy, Assyria under Tiglath-Pileser III (745–727 BC) was flexing its muscles and beginning its westward expansion. Smaller nations such as Syria, Israel, and Judah were getting nervous and trying to decide what to do (7:1–9). Babylon was not their concern.

Perhaps Isaiah began with Babylon because he understood Babylon's eventual place in Judah's history. Though Assyria would threaten Judah more than once, Assyria would never prevail. But Babylon would; the Babylonians would invade Judah, defeat and destroy Jerusalem, and take its people into exile. Ultimately, Babylon was the enemy about whom Judah first needed to hear prophetic words of judgment.

Babylon's Destruction (13:1–22)

Isaiah focused on three issues concerning Babylon's destruction. First, Babylon's destruction would come as the work of many nations. Nations would form a coalition to bring Babylon down. Those who had suffered under Babylonian rule would have the joy of participating in ending it.

Second, Babylon's destruction revealed the day of the Lord. The Lord would judge evil wherever he found it, and he had found much in Babylon's kingdom. Nations would participate in Babylon's downfall, but ultimately,

The dragon image of the god Marduk; from the Ishtar Gate, Babylon. (Courtesy of HolyLand Photos.org)

Babylon's downfall came through the working of the sovereign Lord.

Third, Babylon's destruction would be accompanied by a taunt song directed against Babylon's ruler. Babylon's pride had led its rulers to think they would rule forever. The day of judgment would correct that mistaken notion.

The Work of Many Nations

Isaiah described the armies that would gather against Babylon. The Hebrew word for "banner" (*nes*) that appears in 11:10 occurs again in 13:2. The signal flag indicated the rallying point for those going against Babylon. The commands in verse 2 are in the plural form, indicating a call for everyone to participate in inviting others to join the battle. The nations and peoples responded to the divine invitation to join in Babylon's day of doom.

The nations responded quickly (13:4–5). The sound of their din carried a great distance as they massed for battle. Isaiah's use of the terms "faraway lands" and "ends of the heavens" highlight again the interplay between the sovereign God and his human instruments. Forces in the spiritual realm shaped earthly events.

The Day of the Lord

The expression "day of the Lord" (Heb. *yom YHWH*; see sidebar 7.1) and its close parallels occur commonly in the prophetic literature and also in the New Testament. The *yom YHWH* describes not a twenty-four-hour day but rather a period of time in which God

---

Sidebar 7.1
The Day of the Lord Theme in Isaiah

The expression "day of the Lord" occurs sixteen times in the Old Testament, though related expressions (e.g., "day of reckoning," "day of vengeance") also seem to indicate the same phenomenon. The day of the Lord denotes a period of history that features one or more of three aspects:

1. God's judgment against unbelievers;
2. the cleansing and purging of God's people; and
3. the salvation of God's people.

The following table summarizes the usages of these expressions in the book of Isaiah (NASB):

Verse	Expression	Meaning (See List Above)
2:12	"day of reckoning"	2
10:3	"day of punishment"	2
13:6	"day of the Lord"	1 (Babylon)
13:9	"day of the Lord"	1 (Babylon)
34:8	"day of vengeance"	1 (Edom)
49:8	"day of salvation"	3
61:2	"day of vengeance" ("vengeance" may here mean "balancing the scales")	1, 3
63:4	"day of vengeance"	1 (Edom, possibly others)

As is apparent, all three aspects of the day of the Lord motif appear in Isaiah. The New Testament writers also spoke of the day of the Lord in these ways, proclaiming the day's ultimate fulfillment in Jesus's second coming (Phil 1:6; 2 Thes 2:1–10).

Medes

Cyrus

works his purposes in a particularly distinctive way in the heavens and on earth. The day of the Lord includes three elements, though different elements are stressed in various usages: God's judgment against unbelievers, the cleansing and purging of God's people, and the salvation of God's people.

In Isaiah 13, the *yom YHWH* highlights especially God's judgment against Babylon. The emphasis on the day's imminence parallels other prophetic passages (Ez 30:3; Zep 1:7). The warning "it will come like destruction from the Almighty" occurs in virtually identical form in Joel 1:15. Isaiah used the expression to describe God's judgment against unbelieving Babylon. Joel, writing around 500 BC,[3] utilized it to describe a locust plague God was using to turn his people to repentance.

Fear would grip the Babylonian people (13:7–8). Terror and anguish would surround them, and they would have no better chance of escape than a woman in labor had of escaping childbirth. They could only exchange looks of helplessness as the judgment advanced. The Hebrew verbs add emphasis in that each occurs at the end of its respective phrase and therefore in its pausal form.[4] The reader or speaker would naturally pause on each verb, thus adding dramatic effect:

> Because of this, all hands *will go limp*,
>> every man's heart *will melt.*
> Terror *will seize them,*
>> pain and anguish *will grip them;*
>> like a woman in labor *they will writhe.*
> At each other *they will look (in astonishment),*
>> their faces aflame.
>
> (my translation)

God's judgment would be not arbitrary but directed against sinners (13:9). Apocalyptic language described the heavens themselves as participating in the judgment, withholding their light. Spiritual darkness would meet physical and emotional darkness. The world shook under God's wrath, and he brought an end to humanity's pride and arrogance (13:11–13).

The switch to the Hebrew *tebel* meaning "world" (13:11) instead of the usual *erets* "land, earth" suggests God's wider judgment. The Lord focused on Babylon but would judge sinners wherever he found them. The hopelessness of the situation appears in 13:14–16, where the Babylonians find themselves without protection or a leader and will suffer the atrocities common to ancient warfare (Ps 137:9; Hos 13:16; Zec 14:2).

Isaiah identified the **Medes** as a primary instrument of judgment (13:17–18). The Medes lived in the region below the Caspian Sea, north of the Zagros Mountains and Elam and east of Assyria. They would participate in the coalition with Babylonians, Scythians, and others that defeated Nineveh in 612 BC and ended the Assyrian empire. King **Cyrus** of Persia subdued the Medes in 550 BC and incorporated them into the Persian kingdom, though significant Median influence appears to have remained (Dn 5:31; 9:1).[5]

Isaiah compared Babylon's final overthrow to that of Sodom and Gomorrah—absolute and final. The land would be fit not even for shepherds and nomads but only for wild animals—a judgment Isaiah declared elsewhere for Edom (13:20–22; 34:13–15).

Babylon's judgment did not come immediately with the fall of the Babylonian empire, but it did come. Cyrus, who conquered Babylon in 539 BC, took the city without a fight and allowed it to continue as a provincial capital. The city's influence continued into the Persian and Greek periods, but by AD 200 it had passed into oblivion. Its ruins remained virtually undisturbed until the nineteenth century, when new interest in archaeology led to its discovery.

The Taunt Song against Babylon's King (14:1–23)

Good News for Judah (14:1–2)

Babylon's downfall was bad news for Babylon but good news for all those it had oppressed. Isaiah described the new work the Lord would do among his people in that day. He would settle them in their land again, and foreigners would come and live with them in peace. Those who had oppressed them would find themselves subjected to the Israelites.

Details of the Taunt (14:3–23)

Isaiah recited the taunt Israel would sing against its former oppressor. The word "you" in 14:3–4 is in the singular, describing an act of the nation as a whole.

The prophet gave credit where credit was due: "The LORD has broken the rod of the wicked, the scepter of the rulers" (14:5). The two Hebrew words translated "rod" and "scepter" (*matteh* and *shebet*, respectively) are the same words with which Isaiah described Assyrian domination (10:5). The sovereign Lord installed rulers and also had the power to remove them.

Isaiah's reference to the trees of Lebanon rejoicing (14:8) alludes to the regular boasts of Assyrian and Babylonian kings that they cut down the trees of Lebanon as they advanced into Syria.[6]

Isaiah also described Sheol ("the grave") stirring to meet Babylon's fallen king (14:9). One by one, other fallen leaders of empires past would rise to join the taunt, for Babylon had finally become as weak as they (14:10–11).

The prophet highlighted the extreme humiliation of the deposed monarch (14:12–17). The king had been—at least in his own eyes—like the morning star, like one who exalted his throne among the stars. But now he was thrust down to the depths of Sheol. So great was his humiliation that those who saw him asked with amazement if he truly was the king who had reigned so mightily on earth.

The king of Babylon would experience no great honor in his death, in contrast to his famous predecessors (14:18–20). The Lord would cut off any memory of him and his descendants and lay waste to his land (14:21–23).

The Object of the Taunt: To Whom Does the Expression "King of Babylon" Refer?

The identity of the "morning star, son of the dawn" in Isaiah 14:12–14 has been the focus of much discussion among Christians. The language seems to many so grandiose and the boasts of the ruler so arrogant that some have concluded the text actually has Satan in view or perhaps the Antichrist of the last days.[7] They argue that no earthly ruler would speak *so* pompously. What hermeneutical issues should shape our interpretation? How might we support such a view?

First, we should examine the context to determine if there is any indication as to the identity of the ruler. Indeed, we discover that verse 4 clearly identifies "the king of Babylon" as the object of the taunt.

Second, we should ask if the New Testament alludes to this passage, because sometimes the New Testament sheds further light on an Old Testament passage (Jl 2:28–32; Acts 2:16–21). If the passage has a secondary fulfillment in Satan, for example, we might hope to find some reference to it here. However, no such parallel exists. The closest reference is probably Luke 10:18, where Jesus describes seeing Satan fall as lightning from heaven, but this is far from a direct quotation or allusion.

The New Testament does, however, speak of Babylon in eschatological terms. The book of Revelation describes Babylon as the head of the world's abominations, as the kingdom that receives its final judgment just prior to Jesus's second coming (Rv 17:5; 18:1–3; 19:1–3). Perhaps this parallel suffices for us to recognize in Isaiah 14:12–14 a secondary fulfillment. However, John does not cite Isaiah directly.

Mesha stela

Third, we should ask if anything else in the text demands a secondary fulfillment. Here some argue that the boastful, pompous, arrogant attitude of Babylon's ruler far surpasses the capacity of mortal kings. Would a ruler actually claim to "ascend above the tops of the clouds" and make himself "like the Most High"? In other words, does taking the text at face value, namely, taking the reference in 14:4 to the king of Babylon as determinative, entail more difficulty than suggesting a secondary fulfillment?

On the other hand, we do know from their own inscriptions that Assyrian and Babylonian kings often described themselves in grandiose terms. Assyrian inscriptions in particular use language quite similar to what Isaiah ascribes to their kings (10:13–14; 37:24–25).[8]

In summary, the evidence appears to suggest Isaiah 14:12–14 found its fulfillment in the king of Babylon. The context suggests the king of Babylon is in view, the New Testament contains no direct allusion to the passage, and Near Eastern kings sometimes did boast extravagantly of their accomplishments. Perhaps further evidence will shed new light on the issue.

Assyria (14:24–27)

Interestingly, after two chapters of prophetic words against Babylon, Isaiah took just four verses to pronounce Assyria's judgment.[9] Perhaps he did so because he had already dealt with Assyria (10:5–34) and would again later (36:1–37:38). In fact, 14:25 may allude to Sennacherib's judgment in chapters 36–37.

The sovereign Lord (Heb. *YHWH tseba'ot*, "Yahweh of hosts") had established his purpose, and none would thwart it. His plans reached to the end of the earth, and Assyria would not stand in his way.

Philistia (14:28–32)

The Philistines rejoiced in the year Ahaz died and Hezekiah became king.[10] The transition of kings often provided a convenient opportunity for subject and/or neighboring peoples to revolt or attack. Doing so would force the new king to prove himself immediately, often while he was still dealing with transitional issues. Further, Hezekiah was just twenty-five years old when he began his reign (2 Kgs 18:2), though Ahaz, whom the Philistines apparently feared, was merely twenty when he had begun to reign (2 Kgs 16:2).

The year was either 715 BC or 727 BC, depending on the chronology one assumes for Hezekiah's reign.[11] Isaiah warned the Philistines that bigger trouble lay ahead for them. The Judeans had exchanged earthly kings, but their heavenly king remained on his throne.

Isaiah warned of a greater enemy from the north, almost certainly Assyria (14:31). Indeed, the Philistines experienced Assyrian wrath several times. Tiglath-Pileser III conquered Gath in 734 BC, Sargon II conquered Ashkelon and Gath in 720 BC, and then returned in 711 BC to crush Ashkelon again. Sennacherib's invasion of Judah in 701 BC also affected the Philistines, and their major cities again suffered defeat.[12]

Moab (15:1–16:14)

Moab lay along the eastern coast of the Dead Sea, south of the tribe of Reuben's territory.[13] The Moabites descended from Lot, Abraham's nephew (Gn 19:37). Saul and David subdued them (1 Sm 14:47; 2 Sm 8:2), but during the days of the divided kingdom, Moab generally remained independent of Israelite or Judean control. Some battles did occur, as both the Bible (2 Kgs 3:4–27; 2 Chr 20:1–26) and the **Mesha stela** mention (see sidebar 7.2).

Sidebar 7.2
The Mesha Stela

In the mid-ninth century BC, Mesha, king of Moab (2 Kgs 3:4–5), commemorated the accomplishments of his reign in a monumental inscription that contained approximately thirty-five lines of text. The text was written in the Moabite language (a Canaanite dialect closely related to Hebrew) on a basalt block three feet high and two feet wide.[14] It reads:

> I am Mesha, the son of Kemosh-yatti, the king of Moab, the Dibonite.
> My father was king over Moab for thirty years,
> and I was king after my father.
>
> And I made this high-place for Kemosh in Karchoh,
> . . .
> because he has delivered me from all kings,
> and because he has made me look down on all my enemies.
>
> Omri was the king of Israel,
> and he oppressed Moab for many days,
> for Kemosh was angry with his land.
> And his son succeeded him,
> and he said—he too—
> "I will oppress Moab!"
> In my days did he say [so],
> but I looked down on him and on his house,
> and Israel has gone to ruin, yes, it has gone to ruin for ever!
>
> And Omri had taken possession of the whole land of Medeba,
> and he lived there in his days and half the days of his son, forty years,
> but Kemosh restored it in my days.

Adapted from *Context of Scripture* (hereafter *COS*), ed. William W. Hallo and K. Lawson Younger Jr., 3 vols. (Leiden: Brill, 1997–2002), 2:137.

Isaiah gave no date for his oracle. The allusions to seeking protection from Judah (16:1–4a) suggest a time of Assyrian invasion, when a country might naturally request assistance from a neighbor, but the pinpointing of a particular Assyrian incursion remains impossible.

Lament over Moab's Condition (15:1–9)

Moab's mourning extended throughout its land. The expression "in a night" (15:1) emphasizes the suddenness of Moab's destruction. Ar was located on Moab's northern border, but its exact location is unknown. Kir probably designates Kir Hareseth, Moab's ancient capital, located seventeen miles south of the Arnon and eleven miles east of the Dead Sea.

Dibon (15:2) also served as a capital of Moab, though Joshua had allotted it to Reuben (Jos 13:9, 17). Nebo sat southwest of Heshbon; it had belonged to Reuben until King Mesha captured it for Moab around 850 BC. Medeba's position along the King's Highway, a major north-south highway in Transjordan, made it a strategic city. Throughout history it often changed hands, a fact to which both the Bible and the Mesha stela attest (Nm 21:24, 26, 30; Jos 13:9, 16).

Verses 4–9 took Isaiah's hearers through various sites of Moab; the exact locations of some of these sites remain unknown to archaeologists. Heshbon was the capital of Sihon, king of the Amorites, whom Israel defeated during the days of Moses (Nm 21:26). Jahaz was the site of the Israelites' victory over Sihon (Nm 21:23–24). We may assume Isaiah's choice of the particular sites he mentioned portrayed for his hearers a picture of all Moab in wailing and lament.

Moab's Coming Judgment (16:1–14)

In chapter 15, Isaiah described the countrywide wailing and lament Moab would experience. In chapter 16, he stressed two elements: Moab's desperate plea for help and a lament on behalf of Moab.

Moab's Desperate Plea for Help (16:1–5)

As Assyria became stronger, many smaller nations in Syro-Palestine saw their days of independence as potentially short lived. They often sought alliances with Egypt or with other small nations to protect themselves. The alliance of Israel and Syria (7:1–9) was one such example.

Isaiah described Moab's seeking assistance from Jerusalem (16:1–4a). The Moabites sent lambs (the Hebrew literally reads "lamb") as tribute, hoping the Judeans would shelter Moabite refugees, including a great number of women, who especially feared the horrors of enemy conquest. We do not know if most actually sent the tribute or if Isaiah described it as Moab's only hope.

Isaiah described the ultimate outcome of the current chaos (16:4b–5). The oppression would not last forever, and David's throne would be graciously reestablished. Although David had subdued Moab during his reign, Isaiah clearly intended this promise as comfort to the Moabites, perhaps because of David's connection with Moab through Ruth, his great grandmother (Ru 4:17). But would Moab embrace such comfort? Would Moab have the courage to say by its going to Zion that its only hope lay there?

Lament for Moab (16:6–14)

The Moabites did not embrace the solution Isaiah offered them. Their pride and arrogance (16:6) precluded humbling themselves in such a way. However, their trust in their own abilities and resources would fail miserably.

Again, Isaiah listed cities of Moab that mourned the nation's imminent doom (16:7–9). Nothing would remain of Moab's agriculture, army, or rulers. As the prophet viewed the scene through his prophetic lens, he offered his own pain: "My heart laments for Moab" (16:11).

Moab's time was drawing to a close. Isaiah promised that within three years, Moab's splendor would disappear (16:14). We cannot date this judgment with precision since the Assyrian kings Tiglath-Pileser III, Sargon II, Sennacherib, and Esarhaddon all claim victories over Moab.[15]

Damascus and Israel (17:1–14)

The linkage of Damascus and Israel in Isaiah 17 strongly suggests the time of the Syro-Ephraimite War (735–734 BC; see Is 7:1–9 discussion) as the date of the prophecy. Isaiah warned of an impending day of reckoning for both nations.

Judgment against Damascus (17:1–3)

Isaiah described the judgment of Damascus; the great city would become a heap of ruins. Little would remain of its former splendor.[16]

Tiglath-Pileser III's response to Ahaz's gift (2 Kgs 16:7–8) was swift. He captured Damascus and killed Rezin, its king (2 Kgs 16:9). The city became ruins as Isaiah said. As with many other events of Isaiah's day, parallel accounts exist in the Assyrian royal inscriptions.[17]

Judgment against Israel (17:4–14)

Isaiah used agricultural imagery to describe Israel's devastation (17:4–6). Just as little remained in the Valley of Rephaim southwest of Jerusalem after the harvest, so little would remain to glean in Israel after the harvest of God's judgment. Tiglath-Pileser III's annexing of much of Israel's territory and placing Hoshea on Israel's throne[18] fulfilled Isaiah's words.

Verses 7–8 describe a turning of the remnant to the Lord. They would forsake all the trappings of false religious faith and follow him. But would their allegiance come too late? Isaiah's following these verses with verses 10–14 strongly suggests so. They had put their hope in military alliances rather than in the Holy One of Israel, and now they would learn the folly of having done so.

The coming desolation is described in verses 9–11. Cities will sit deserted; harvests will yield nothing. Disease and incurable pain will become commonplace.

Isaiah described the nations' uproar in the face of the Assyrian threat (14:12–14). The advance of such an empire would naturally lead nations to assess their current positions and develop a strategy for survival. Should they surrender to Assyria or try to join other nations against Assyria? Isaiah's words depicted the futility of placing one's hope in any earthly power.

Cush and Egypt (18:1–20:6)

Isaiah no doubt intermingled his words regarding Cush and Egypt be-cause of the historical situation at the time of his prophecy. The late eighth century BC was a period of Egyptian decline, when Cushite leaders were able to assume control of Egypt.

Cush (18:1–6)

Cush is often translated "Ethiopia," but such a translation is a bit misleading.[19] Modern Ethiopia lies farther to the southeast. The term "Cush" properly designated Nubia, an area upstream (south) of Egypt beyond the Nile's first cataract. Archaeological excavations there have yielded the remains of an impressive civilization.

Egypt generally controlled Cush during periods of Egyptian strength, but during a period of Egyptian decline in the late eighth century BC, Nubian leaders were able to establish supremacy. In 715 BC, they seized control of Egypt and established the Twenty-fifth Dynasty. They reigned until 663 BC, when the Assyrians invaded Egypt and defeated them. It appears Tirhakah, a ruler of this dynasty, tried to render assistance to Hezekiah during the days of Sennacherib's invasion (37:9).

Isaiah described Cush as "the land of whirring wings" (18:1), a reference to the swarms of flying insects that reside in the area. The Cushites sent their envoys down the Nile northward in their papyrus ships (18:2). Once they reached Upper (Northern) Egypt, they could disembark and access one of the highways leading into Judah.

Isaiah's reference to the sending of messengers (18:2–3) denotes the political situation. When the Nubians established themselves over Egypt, they sent messengers into Palestine, pledging assistance in the struggle against Assyria. Presumably they had reached Judah with their offer of support, and Isaiah sent them home with a different message. True security would lie not in an international alliance but in trust in Yahweh.

Isaiah intended his proclamation of God's work for all the inhabited world (18:3, Heb. *tebel*; see discussion of 13:11).

Images of Egypt, both ancient and modern (Courtesy of Jim Yancey and Todd Bolen/ BiblePlaces .com)

Earthly leaders fluttered to and fro with their attempts at diplomacy, but the sovereign Yahweh guided history's events. He would judge the nations and bring them low.

However, some would see the time of judgment as the time of submission (18:7). They had anticipated this day (18:3) and now brought a gift of homage.

Egypt (19:1–25)

During the time of Isaiah's prophecy against Egypt, the Egyptians were experiencing a period of subservience to their Ethiopian rulers. A day would come when they would be free from them; nonetheless, they would not escape God's plan for them.

Judgment against Egypt and Its Leaders (19:1–15)

First, Isaiah described the confusion the Lord would bring against the Egyp-

tians (19:1–4). The prophet described not only the fear and panic the people would experience but also used anthropomorphic language to emphasize the powerlessness of Egypt's gods as its idols trembled (cf. 46:1 and Ex 12:12). The "cruel master" (19:4) may be Pi-ankhi, the Ethiopian ruler who founded the Twenty-fifth Dynasty. Egypt had proven itself a cruel master to Israel; the Lord would now turn the tables on Egypt. Egypt would have nowhere to turn except to its powerless idols (19:3).

Second, Isaiah described the drying up of the Nile—clearly disastrous to a nation whose very life depended on the river and its annual flooding (19:4–10). The effects of this catastrophe gradually permeated the entire society. Plants died, fields withered, fishermen despaired, workers who spun flax lost their jobs, and the economy floundered.

Third, Isaiah depicted the hopelessness and confusion that would strike Egypt's leaders (19:11–15). What could they do? Their wisdom could not overcome the devastating effects of the drought. The scene brings to mind images of the exodus period, when the Egyptians' best efforts could not stop God's judgments against them.

Egypt's Submission and Restoration (19:16–25)

Isaiah 19:16–25 may be divided into five shorter sections, each one beginning with the expression "in that day" (19:16–17, 18, 19–22, 23, 24–25). These five sections describe an amazing future Yahweh was preparing for Egypt.

First (19:16–17), Egypt would lose all heart and shudder in fear at what befell it. God's blessing of Judah would become a source of fear to the Egyptians.

Second (19:18), five of Egypt's cities would speak Hebrew as their language of choice.[20] The identity of the cities is not given; presumably, Isaiah intended five leading cities. Nonetheless, the idea of the nationalistic Egyptians speaking anything but their own language must have astounded Isaiah's hearers. Isaiah also said the Egyptians would swear allegiance to the Lord. He continued to develop this even more astounding thought in the next verses.

Third (19:19–22), worship of Yahweh would expand at his initiative. Isaiah's reference to an "altar to the LORD in Egypt" was not intended judgmentally, as a violation of God's prohibition of worship outside Jerusalem (Dt 12:1–7). Rather, it testified to a redemptive work he was performing with a new people.

The language of verse 20 recalls Israel crying out because of its oppressors during the days of Egyptian enslavement. But in this coming day, God would rescue Egypt from its oppressors. He would reveal himself to them in a way he never had before, and they would come to know him and bring offerings to him (19:21–22). The divine judgment would prove redemptive.

Fourth (19:23), Assyria would join Egypt in worshiping the Lord. The irony lay in the fact of the bitter animosity that existed between the two nations. How could they worship together, let alone worship the one true God? Further, both Egypt and Assyria had brutally oppressed God's people during the course of history; would they actually find God's grace and favor? Isaiah's reference to a "highway from Egypt to Assyria" hints at a special work of God that would bring this about (cf. 11:16; 35:8; 40:3).

Fifth (19:24–25), Isaiah described a day when Egypt, Assyria, and Israel would all worship the Lord together. Incredible blessing would ensue as God reconciled bitter enemies to one another and to him. The terms "my people" and "my handiwork" applied to Israel elsewhere, but here Isaiah applied them to Egypt and Assyria, respectively. Isaiah could have chosen no stranger allies than these three nations.

As astounding as Isaiah's words were, they powerfully anticipated the New Testament proclamation of the reconciliation power of the gospel. The apostle Paul declared that Jesus Christ, through the blood of his cross, broke down the barriers between Jew and Gentile and reconciled the two groups to each other, that he might present them as one group to his Father (Eph 2:14–16).

Isaiah's Sign against Egypt and Cush (20:1–6)

Sargon II (721–705 BC), king of Assyria, had come against the Philistine city of Ashdod and captured it in 711 BC. The expression "at that time" (20:2) probably designates more the general period than the exact date. Nonetheless, Isaiah used the event as a springboard to a powerful object lesson for Judah.

Isaiah obeyed God's command to go about "stripped and barefoot" (20:2). Some scholars believe the Hebrew expression refers to Isaiah's complete nakedness, whereas others believe it signifies removal of outer garments. The significance of the prophetic sign was to mimic those whom Assyria would lead into exile from Egypt and Cush (20:3–4).

The mention of Cush relates to its control of Egypt during this time (cf. discussion of 18:1–7). "Those who trusted in Cush and boasted in Egypt" (20:5) are likely the Judeans who were hoping these nations would rescue them from Assyria.

Babylon, Edom, and Arabia (21:1–17)

Chapter 21 contains three oracles. The first addresses Babylon, a nation Isaiah has already condemned (13:1–14:23) and that would receive much more attention later (chaps. 43, 46–48). The second oracle addresses Edom, a nation to which Isaiah's prophetic words would later return (34:5–6; 63:1). The third oracle addresses Arabia, mentioned only here in Isaiah, except as an ethnic designation ("Arab," 13:20).

Babylon (21:1–10)

The expression "Desert by the Sea" (Heb. *midbar yam*) appears nowhere else in the Old Testament. Some scholars have associated it with the Negev ("southland," 21:1), while others see in it a cryptic reference to the region of lower Mesopotamia.[21] The references to Elam and Media (21:2) make it clear Babylon's judgment is in view. Isaiah himself recoiled at the spectacle of Babylon's devastation (21:3–4).

Judah's watchman manned his post intently (21:6–8). Suddenly, a charioteer arrived with the news: Babylon had fallen! (21:9). The repetition of the words "fallen" and "shattered" stressed Babylon's total destruction, a destruction that would comfort those who currently felt the weight of national oppression (21:10). Their oppression would not last forever.

Edom (21:11–12)

Isaiah 21:11 contains a textual variant. The Masoretic Text reads "an oracle of Dumah," while some other manuscripts read "an oracle of Edom." The reference to Seir (21:11) suggests Isaiah intended Edom here, as does perhaps the fact that Dumah was a son of Ishmael (Gn 25:14). The Hebrew word *dumah* means silence and may be an intentional wordplay in light of the silence that follows in the oracle.

The watchman's answer to his questioner (21:12) seems somewhat cryptic. The question supposes expectation, but the answer indicates that morning and night follow each other, with little else happening. The prophecy parallels other examples of quiet preceding a work of God (Zec 1:11; Rv 8:1). Edom's time was coming, but not yet.

Arabia (21:13–17)

Arabia would suffer along with the many others who suffered during the days of Assyrian expansion. The Dedanites were an Arabian tribe, whereas Tema was an oasis on a major caravan route passing through Arabia. Isaiah called the Dedanites and the citizens of Tema to assist refugees who fled the oncoming army (21:13–15), though their assistance would prove to no avail.

Kedar (21:16) designated a region occupied by a tribe of the same name. Isaiah foretold its destruction within a year. Most scholars see these prophetic words as fulfilled in the late eighth century BC. Kedar paid Tiglath-Pileser III tribute in 738 BC, and Sargon II, Sennacherib, and Ashurbanipal also recorded victories in this region.[22]

Jerusalem (22:1–25)

Isaiah earlier had inserted the northern kingdom of Israel into his prophetic oracles against the nations (17:4–14). He now inserted the southern kingdom of Judah and Jerusalem its capital. Both the northern and the southern kingdoms had abandoned their relationship with the Lord, and both would see God's judgment before they saw blessing.

Tombs along the Kidron Valley. Perhaps Shebna intended to have a lasting monument such as this for his name. (Courtesy of Jim Yancey)

Jerusalem's Siege (22:1–14)

The enigmatic expression "Valley of Vision" (22:1) is clarified by 22:8–9. Jerusalem's siege is intended. Isaiah mocked those who went to the rooftops to mourn (22:1–2). Had they not realized judgment was coming?

The day of the Lord (22:5) would focus on his own people. The sovereign Lord of Hosts was as concerned about cleansing and purging his own people of their sin as he was about judging the sin of those who opposed him. Yahweh would deal with sin wherever he found it. Elam and Kir (22:6) probably appear here as allies of Assyria. Perhaps the judgments described refer to Sennacherib's invasion during the days of Hezekiah, when divine intervention alone spared Jerusalem (36:1–37:38).

Verses 9–11 appear to describe the building of Hezekiah's tunnel that carried water from the Gihon Spring to the Pool of Siloam (2 Chr 32:3–4, 30). Hezekiah ordered the tunnel built to ensure a water supply for Jerusalem in the event of Assyrian attack.

Hezekiah's strategy must have seemed wise to his subjects, but Isaiah shared a different perspective. Had not God chosen Jerusalem with its vul-nerable water supply? Would he not therefore protect it now as he always had? The people celebrated their self-sufficiency (22:13), but actually, they were headed for disaster.

Shebna and Eliakim (22:15–25)

The prophets often addressed their words to the leadership of society because leaders typically set the course for the nation. Faithful leaders brought renewal, while evil leaders brought ruin. Shebna and Eliakim provide two examples of the consequences of bad and good leadership, respectively.

Shebna: Leadership for His Own Gain

Shebna served as a palace official. The term "steward" (Heb. *soken*) emphasizes that Shebna's role was to faithfully oversee what did not belong to him. His title "in charge of the palace" (Heb. *'al habbayit*, "over the house") describes one of high authority (1 Kgs 4:6).

Shebna, however, was using his office for his own gain. He carved a massive tomb for himself—probably in the Kidron Valley—so that after he died, others would remember him as a great man (22:16). God, however, saw it otherwise.

He would depose Shebna and bring on him a shameful end (22:17–19).

Eliakim: Leadership to Serve Others

Isaiah announced that God would raise up Eliakim as Shebna's replacement (22:20). If the Shebna and Eliakim mentioned in 36:3 are the same two men, then Eliakim's promotion and Shebna's demotion had occurred by the time of Sennacherib's invasion. Eliakim's servant attitude would enable him to utilize the authority of such a position appropriately. He would be a servant of God and a father to his people. He would lead with compassionate authority and provide stability "like a peg into a firm place" (22:23).

Sadly, Eliakim would not last either (22:24–25). People would turn to him for more and more, and he could not sustain such a load. Isaiah's words stand as a warning: even servants of God have their limits. Ultimately the people needed to find their security in the Lord, not in Eliakim or any other earthly leader.

Tyre (23:1–18)

Tyre was a Phoenician city located on the Mediterranean coast.[23] Joshua originally allotted it to the tribe of Asher (Jos 19:29), but Asher apparently never

Study Questions

1. Who are the major nations Isaiah identified as about to receive God's judgment? What wrongs had they committed?

2. What hermeneutical issues should shape our interpretation of Isaiah's prophecies against nations?

3. What evidence of God's sovereign control over nations do you see today?

Key Terms

Cyrus

Medes

Mesha stela

claimed it. Along with Sidon, Tyre provided important support to the Phoenician economy as a leading merchant and port city. People came to Tyre to trade by land and by sea.

Tyre had become a significant city of wealth, a city where not only goods but also ideas were freely exchanged. Nonetheless, the Lord of Hosts was lord of Tyre as well, and his prophet announced Tyre's coming destruction.

Call to Lament (23:1–7)

Prophetic oracles of judgment normally called on the objects of judgment (peoples or lands) to mourn and wail. In addition, they often called on others to mourn. Friends and business associates who also stood to lose needed to wail and lament as well.

Isaiah told the ships of Tarshish (probably Spain) to wail over Tyre's loss (23:1). The Sidonians too were to join the sad refrain (23:2). The great marketplace of nations had gone bankrupt (23:3). Egypt and others would join the mourners who realized the magnitude of Tyre's downfall—the city had been in business since ancient times (23:4–7).

Tyre's Judgment and Future (23:8–18)

Verses 8–9 clarify the situation. Did all of this happen by chance? Was this catastrophe merely Tyre's bad luck? Not at all; rather, the Lord of Hosts had again worked his purpose.

Isaiah had called Tarshish to mourn; now he turned Tarshish loose to gain even more economically (23:10–12). God had determined Tyre's destruction, and its fall would have implications for Canaan as well as for the entire Mediterranean coastal region. Tarshish still mourned, however, despite its potential gains (23:14). Who would have believed Tyre would ever fall?

Isaiah said Tyre would be forgotten for seventy years (23:15). Scholars debate the meaning of this reference because it is difficult to translate 23:13 with precision. Some understand Assyria as the instrument of judgment. In that case, the period would run from 701–630 BC, from the time of Sennacherib's invasion of Syro-Palestine to the period of Assyrian decline.[24] Others understand Babylon as the conqueror of Tyre and associate the seventy years with the seventy years of exile Jeremiah predicted for Judah (Jer 25:12).[25]

After seventy years, Tyre would resume her harlotrous ways (23:15–18). The ironic image is that of an elderly prostitute who now tries to reclaim her former livelihood. A second ironic twist is that somehow, this harlot's wages end up supporting not Tyre and her lovers but those who dwell in God's presence. The text does not clarify whether this implies some kind of spiritual turning for Tyre.

Tyre's Ultimate Fate

Both Assyria and Babylon fought and received tribute from Tyre at various times. Nonetheless, the city survived until the days of Alexander the Great (356–323 BC).

By the time of Alexander, most of the city sat on an island just off the coast. The people thought they could hold out against Alexander, but they grossly underestimated his determination. The city fell in 332 BC, when Alexander destroyed it.

Concluding Thoughts from Isaiah 13–23

Isaiah's oracles against the nations announced the fact that Yahweh, God of Israel and Judah, was in fact God of the world. Other nations might or might not recognize his sovereignty, but that did not matter. He would bring their judgment in the times he had appointed. He controlled the universe, a theme Isaiah would now develop in chapters 24–27.

At the same time, Isaiah's oracles demonstrate the extent of God's grace. They describe God reaching out redemptively to many who ignored or rejected him. In doing so, they set the stage for the fullness of God's revelation concerning the nations in the New Testament.

8 The "Little Apocalypse"

Isaiah 24:1–27:13

Outline

- **The Earth's Destruction (24:1–23)**
  General Aspects of the Destruction (24:1–6)
  Specific Aspects of the Destruction (24:7–23)
- **God's Victory over His Enemies (25:1–12)**
  Praise to God (25:1–5)
  Description of God's Restoration and Blessings (25:6–12)
- **Judah's Song of Deliverance (26:1–21)**
  Judah's Praise (26:1–6)
  Judah's Prayer (26:7–21)
- **Israel's Coming Salvation (27:1–13)**
  The Destruction of Evil (27:1)
  Israel's Position as God's Vineyard (27:2–6)
  The Purpose behind God's Judgment (27:7–11)
  The Returning Remnant (27:12–13)
- **Concluding Thoughts from Isaiah 24–27**
  God Is in Control
  God's Sovereignty Includes Judgment and Restoration
  God Calls Us to Peace
  Great Days Are Coming!

Objectives

After reading this chapter, you should be able to

1. Recognize and identify elements of apocalyptic writing in Isaiah 24–27.
2. Summarize Isaiah's description of God's judgment of the earth.
3. Highlight key aspects of Isaiah's description of God's deliverance and salvation.

Have you ever read the book of Revelation, the last book of the New Testament? If you have, you know it reads like no other book of the Bible. It uses images such as visions of heaven and earth, angels with bowls of wrath, the sun growing dark, stars falling from the sky, and the heavens rolling back like a scroll to describe God's intervention in human history prior to the establishment of his everlasting kingdom. This type of writing—known as **apocalyptic**, based on the Greek word *apokalypsis*, which means "revelation" or "revealing"—was quite common during Christianity's early period.

As you study Isaiah 24–27, you'll find many images that remind you of the book of Revelation. The book of Revelation also used or adapted some of these apocalyptic images from Isaiah. For these reasons, many scholars have labeled Isaiah 24–27 "the little apocalypse."

In Isaiah 13–23, the prophet's oracles against the nations proclaimed God's sovereignty to the ends of the earth. He was Lord of all nations, whether or not they realized it. Therefore, he was Lord of the whole earth. Just how far did his sovereignty extend?

Chapters 24–27 form a fitting conclusion to chapters 13–23. God is not only Lord of all nations; he is Lord of the entire universe. The great day of the Lord will bring the earth's destruction and victory over his enemies. But with that day will also come God's final victory on behalf of his people.

The Earth's Destruction (24:1–23)

Isaiah had earlier described the final judgment and destruction of many nations. God would bring them down, and they would not rise again. Now he described God's laying hold of the earth and shaking it violently. Who could withstand his judgment?

General Aspects of the Destruction (24:1–6)

"The earth will be destroyed!" This was the first piece of news Isaiah announced. The prophet articulated three general aspects of the destruction: the Lord is in charge, the Lord does not play favorites, and the Lord judges thoroughly.

The Lord Is in Charge (24:1)

Isaiah described the actions of Yahweh, the one in charge of the destruction. The Hebrew words translated "lay waste" (Heb. *boqeq*) and "devastate" (Heb. *boleq*) are **onomatopoeic**, that is, they sound like the meaning they describe. In this case, they mimic cracking sounds such as rocks breaking or trees snapping.

The word translated "scatter" (Heb. *puts*) is the same word used in Genesis 11:8 to describe God scattering the people who sought to build the tower of Babel. This time, however, the scattering would be of much greater magnitude.

Yahweh, who was Lord of the nations, was also Lord of the earth and universe. He consequently took the whole earth and shook it as he began the day of judgment.

The Lord Doesn't Play Favorites (24:2)

Isaiah assured his hearers that the Lord would play no favorites; the Judge of the universe would show no partiality! He described all the classes of society that would face his wrath. Religious office would not matter; social status would not matter; economic status would not matter.

Privileged places or exalted ranks in society mattered nothing to the sovereign Lord. He would judge sin wherever he found it. A faith relationship with the Lord was all that mattered, but Isaiah would address that point later (24:14).

guilt

The Lord Judges Thoroughly (24:3–6)

The Hebrew verbs Isaiah used in 24:3 emphasized the thorough nature of the earth's destruction. The clause "the LORD has spoken this word" assured the prophet's hearers of the event's absolute certainty. The sovereign King had spoken.

Isaiah described the whole world as languishing and withering (24:4). It did so because of its inhabitants' sin, which defiled it (24:5). They had transgressed God's instructions and broken the "everlasting covenant." Some interpreters believe this expression refers to the Mosaic covenant, but this interpretation seems unlikely. The sin of the whole world is in view, and therefore, it appears much more likely Isaiah was alluding to God's covenant with Noah and its accompanying moral requirement for all nations (Gn 9:16).[1]

Guilt in the Bible is always a condition, never merely a feeling. Humanity's sin had polluted the earth ever since the first sin (Gn 3:17), and now humanity would pay the price for its evil (Is 24:6).

Specific Aspects of the Destruction (24:7–23)

Isaiah now shifted from articulating general aspects of the earth's destruction to highlighting specific aspects of its destruction. What conditions would people encounter as God brought judgment? Isaiah proclaimed three. First, many people would experience gloom and despair. Second, God's people would give him glory. Third, the earth would face universal upheaval.

Gloom and Despair (24:7–13)

Isaiah described a time of gloom and despair. As agriculture failed, so would the people's spirit. Celebrations would cease; musical instruments would fall silent (24:7–9).

The Hebrew word translated "ruined" (24:10) is *tohu*, the word used in Genesis 1:2 to describe the state of the earth before God began to form it. No

word could better describe the emptiness and chaos that reigned. People barred their doors to outsiders, while the city gate lay shattered (24:12), thus exposing the city to attack.

Isaiah returned to imagery similar to what he had used earlier to describe Israel's judgment (24:13; cf. 17:5–6). Little remained in the fields after the harvest, and little would remain after God's harvest of judgment.

Glory to God (24:14–16a)

At this point, Isaiah's prophecy took an unexpected turn. Everything the prophet had said thus far in this oracle described the awful conditions surrounding God's judgment. Yet, in the day of this judgment would come celebration and praise. How could this be?

Giving glory to God was possible precisely because God's judgment proved his faithfulness. God was gracious, but he also hated sin and had promised to judge it one day. As he did so and all who opposed him suffered under his hand, his children saw his faithfulness in his mighty acts and praised him.

The proclamation of God's majesty began in the west and flooded eastward. It moved to the islands of the sea and finally to the ends of the earth. God had his faithful people all over the world, a fact to which Isaiah had testified earlier (2:3–4; 11:10–12). Now those people were celebrating him.

Universal Upheaval (24:16b–23)

The celebration of God's people (24:14–16a) stood in stark contrast to the universal upheaval the prophet described. Treachery continued, but it would not carry the day. God would bring people's wickedness back on their own heads. No escape was possible (24:18).

The expression "floodgates of the heavens" (24:18) would have reminded Isaiah's hearers of Genesis 7:11, where a similar expression described the beginning of the great flood. Indeed, this final judgment would prove just

113

as inescapable. The intensive Hebrew verbs of 24:19–20[2] and the accompanying images vividly portray the earth's last moments, when after receiving the full measure of God's wrath, it would stagger briefly, then fall, never to rise again.

Isaiah's concluding words in the chapter painted a sweeping picture of God gathering the forces that opposed him from heaven and earth (24:21–22). The time had come for both spiritual and earthly realms to pay their dues. Isaiah's description of the darkening of the sun and the moon (24:23) foreshadows imagery in the book of Revelation. The day of judgment brings the darkening of the sun and the moon (Rv 6:12), but the day of salvation renders the sun and moon unnecessary in the face of God's dazzling glory (Rv 21:23).

God's Victory over His Enemies (25:1–12)

As chapter 25 begins, the Lord's reign has begun. The last word of 24:23—"gloriously"—sets the tone for what follows. As God's people see his glory, they will bring their praise to him.

Praise to God (25:1–5)

Verses 1–5 comprise a personal declaration of praise. The speaker, who speaks in the first-person singular, must be the nation God has redeemed. The remnant speaks with one voice and announces praise to the Lord for two reasons: the Lord has demonstrated his faithfulness, and the Lord has protected his people.

God Has Demonstrated His Faithfulness (25:1–3)

Praise comes because God has demonstrated his faithfulness. He has worked wonders in perfect accord with his plan. The words "perfect faithfulness" translate the Hebrew words 'emunah 'omen. Both words come from the same root and are related to the word "amen," which means "it is so." God's people could certainly count on him. The Hebrew word pele', which earlier described the "Wonderful" Counselor of 9:6, now occurs again to describe God's amazing work (25:1).

God had worked two wonders in particular for which his people praised him. First, he had devastated the earth. Even in the judgment of the earth, his people saw his faithfulness to his promises. He had said he would judge sin, and he did.

Second, the Lord turned people to himself. He had said he would save his people, and now he had. He delivered them from their enemies in such a way that all could see his power. As he displayed his power, some turned to him. People of all nations experienced blessing as God fulfilled his promise to Abraham to bless the nations through him (Gn 12:1–3).

God Has Protected His People (25:4–5)

Isaiah described people praising God for his protection. He provided special defense for the poor and the needy—people the law of Moses instructed the Israelites to remember and treat fairly. The references to "storm" and "heat" (25:4) appear to designate more the storm and heat of oppression by those who would take advantage of the weak. God would rescue his own and silence the oppressors.

Description of God's Restoration and Blessings (25:6–12)

The rest of chapter 25 describes details of the exciting era Isaiah said the Lord would usher in. This time of God's restoration and blessings includes three aspects. First, God will establish fellowship with his people. Second, God will comfort his people. Third, God will remove his people's enemies.

God Will Establish Fellowship with His People (25:6–7)

Isaiah described the intimate fellowship the Lord would establish with his people. The reference to Yahweh as "the LORD almighty" or "LORD of hosts" stresses God's power and ability to make it happen. The Lord would prepare a banquet for his people such as the world had never seen. Many interpreters link Isaiah's vision with the apostle John's vision of the wedding supper of the Lamb (Rv 19:6–9).

The Lord would also clear away obstacles to fellowship. He would remove the shroud or sheet that lay over the nations. The apostle Paul used similar language to describe people's inability to understand truly and fully a relationship with God during this life (1 Cor 13:12; 2 Cor 3:14–16). Fellowship with God at its core embodies sharing, not merely of food, but of all we are. God's coming kingdom will feature intimate fellowship with God beyond anything possible in this life (2 Cor 5:1–9).

God Will Comfort His People (25:8–9)

Isaiah next depicted the comfort God would bring his people. First, he would swallow up death forever. Death was something that brought sorrow and grief and, of course, loss of fellowship and relationship. But Isaiah promised that death itself would die and exert no more power in God's coming kingdom.

Second, the Lord would comfort his people by wiping tears of sorrow from all faces. Not only would he comfort the grieving, but his care of them would extend to drying their tears personally.

Third, the Lord would remove the reproach of his people. God's people had suffered indignity and shame for various reasons during the course of history. The establishment of God's kingdom would once and for all demonstrate they had been right all along to follow their God, no matter the cost.

Isaiah repeated an assurance he had used in 24:3—"The Lord has spoken" (NASB). His people could count on him to judge sin wherever he found it, but they could also count on him to establish his kingdom and reign with them in triumph.

God's comfort brought great rejoicing among the people. They had trusted in him, waited on him, hoped in him, and now the king of the universe had delivered beyond their wildest dreams.

God Will Remove His People's Enemies (25:10–12)

The final aspect of God's restoration and blessing involved removal of his people's enemies. Interestingly, Moab is singled out for special attention. Perhaps at the time Isaiah prophesied, the Moabites posed a particular problem to God's people, a hypothesis that may explain Isaiah's lengthy prophecy against them earlier (15:1–16:14).

Another possibility is that Moab's pride lay at the root of the prophet's focus. Moab had spurned the offer of grace (16:3–6) and now would have no part in the new kingdom God was establishing. The disgusting nature of Moab's judgment highlighted the utter humiliation the nation would face.

Judah's Song of Deliverance (26:1–21)

The praise begun in 25:1–5 now resumed in Judah as the people joined together in song.

Judah's Praise (26:1–6)

Judah's praise included proclamation of God's deliverance and affirmation that God deserved their trust. The establishment of his kingdom had proven this once and for all.

The Lord Delivered Us!

Judah testified to God's deliverance (26:1–2). The Judeans had a strong city because God had built it. Further, he had built it with everlasting materials, including walls made of salvation. The imagery Isaiah used depicted walls especially capable of protecting the faithful and keeping out all enemies. The Lord had humbled those who thought themselves great; they had become so low the poor and oppressed could keep them at bay (26:6).

The Lord Deserves Our Trust!

Verses 3–4 form the heart of the song of praise. The Hebrew expression translated "perfect peace" is *shalom shalom*. The Hebrew language often emphasizes a concept through repetition (cf. 6:3, "holy, holy, holy"). *Shalom* embodies the concept of completeness. Every aspect of one's being is in perfect harmony with God's will. Double that completeness, and one has the blessing that comes to one who fully trusts the Lord. The masoretic marking between the two uses of the word suggests the reader of the Hebrew text pause slightly to highlight the effect.

The prophet described the Lord as an everlasting rock. The image portrayed is that of a huge, immovable rock cliff. Yahweh would provide his people rock-solid footing for life.

Judah's Prayer (26:7–21)

The text now shifts from praise to petition as the faithful speak their prayer to the Lord. Judah's prayer contains three elements: the contrast between the righteous and the wicked, a description of God's past dealings, and God's coming deliverance and wrath.

Two Attitudes: The Righteous and the Wicked (26:7–11)

The righteous spoke first. They described their life's path as "smooth" (26:7). Didn't their lives generally include as much or more hardship than the lives of unbelievers? Of course they did; however, knowing the Lord was with them every step of the way gave them a different perspective on life.

The Hebrew word translated "wait" (26:8) connotes an eager anticipation of what the Lord will do. The righteous

trust him completely, and they know he will come through for them. His glory was their sincere desire. Their thoughts of God consumed morning and evening times (26:9).

In contrast, the wicked wasted God's grace (26:10–11). They did not share a proper understanding of God, so they lived according to their own ways. God's day of judgment would consume them.

God's Past Dealings (26:12–18)

Isaiah continued to speak on behalf of the remnant. God's people had seen many rulers come and go and had come to understand through the process that only in the Lord God would they have real peace, real *shalom*. God was their source; they owed their very existence to him. He had blessed them with all they had. Earthly rulers had come and gone, but the Lord's hand remained.

God's people admitted their helplessness (26:17–18). Their condition was like that of a seemingly pregnant woman who went through the anguish of labor, only to have nothing to deliver. In contrast, God had brought salvation to the earth and raised up a people for himself.

God's Deliverance and Wrath (26:19–21)

Isaiah announced the deliverance God was planning for his people (26:19). Their dead would live again. But did Isaiah intend this figuratively or literally? In other words, did he mean the nation would live again, or that individual people from past ages would rise to new life?[3]

Most likely Isaiah described an actual resurrection from the dead. Four reasons support this understanding: (1) The hopelessness of 26:16–18 is not adequately countered by the promise of the nation's restoration. Many God-fearing ancestors had perished under evil rulers. (2) A literal resurrection appears to be the simplest, plainest reading of the text, especially in light of the references to those "who dwell in the dust" awaking and to the earth giving birth to its

Leviathan

dead. (3) Isaiah had already announced the swallowing up of death for all time (25:8), so the proclamation of resurrection makes the perfect corollary, as God's victory comprises all time. (4) The fact that the New Testament trumpets much more resoundingly the concept of the resurrection of the dead does not mean it was nonexistent or insignificant to an Old Testament audience.[4] The promise of resurrection thus gave God's people a future hope, not merely a present one.

God was about to shake the earth with his judgment, but he would protect his people as he did so (26:20–21). They would not be swept away with the wicked. God's invitation to enter their rooms and shut the doors may recall God shutting the door on Noah's family to protect them (Gn 7:1, 16).[5] Some also have seen in the imagery a reference to the exodus, when God's people shut their doors so that the death angel would pass by (Ex 12:22–23).[6] God would protect his own as he judged the earth.

Israel's Coming Salvation (27:1–13)

Isaiah had described the earth's destruction (24:1–23), victory over God's enemies (25:1–12), and Judah's song of deliverance (26:1–21). What more could he say?

In chapter 27, Isaiah further elaborated on Israel's coming salvation. God would destroy evil for all time, he would again care intimately for his people, and he would bring them home once and for all.

The Destruction of Evil (27:1)

Isaiah announced the destruction of **Leviathan**, the gliding, coiling serpent, the great sea monster. Whom did he intend by this designation?

Leviathan appears in four other Old Testament verses (Jb 3:8; 41:1; Pss 74:14; 104:26). The verses generally agree in associating Leviathan with the sea, as one of the creatures fitting the category

of "sea monster" (Heb. *tannin*, cf. Ps 74:13–14; see sidebar 8.1).

The discovery of the Ugaritic tablets has revealed stories of the god Baal and his battles with Yam, the god of the sea, and his associate Lotan, a name some scholars have linguistically linked with Leviathan.[7] No doubt such myths provided a general cultural background against which the Hebrews came to understand the concept of Leviathan, but it is doubtful Isaiah or the other biblical writers intended to allude specifically to the Canaanite deity.

More likely is the idea that Isaiah applied the concept of Leviathan to one of the great forces of evil God would subdue in the last days. The connection between Leviathan and both a serpent and a dragon suggests this when we look at the New Testament evidence. In the book of Revelation, the apostle John linked the concepts of serpent and dragon with Satan, the ultimate enemy (Rv 12:9; 20:2).

Israel's Position as God's Vineyard (27:2–6)

Isaiah employed the vineyard imagery he had used earlier (5:1–7), but with a new twist. In the first usage, the vineyard had proved unworthy and was exposed to God's judgment. Now Isaiah described God's careful protection and preservation of his vineyard, his people, emphasizing the intimate fellowship God wanted to have with them. He would make peace with all who sought him, and his people would grow as never before (see sidebar 8.2).

The Purpose behind God's Judgment (27:7–11)

Isaiah then returned to an issue facing his current audience. Why did his people continually face exile and warfare? Were they no different in the eyes of God than the other nations?

Isaiah's rhetorical questions (27:7) clarified the issue. The Lord had *never* struck his people with the same judgmental force as he had struck the nations who oppressed them. "Exile"

Sidebar 8.1
Biblical References to Leviathan

The term "Leviathan" occurs in the Old Testament five times. The following chart illustrates what we may learn about the term from its usages.

Reference	Meaning/Interpretive Data
Job 3:8	Job calls for the day of his birth to be cursed, but only those bold enough to "rouse Leviathan" should try it. Rousing Leviathan sounds like a formidable task, but no further description of him appears.
Job 41:1	God asks Job if Job is able to capture and domesticate Leviathan. The rest of Job 41 (41:2–34) describes Leviathan as possessing these characteristics: (1) so strong that men need spears and harpoons to defeat him (41:7); (2) unstoppable by one man (41:10); (3) possessing great teeth, scales, and armor (41:13–17); (4) having fiery eyes and a nose and mouth that exude fire (41:18–21); (5) invincible against human weapons (41:26–29).
Psalm 74:14	A list of God's mighty acts includes the defeat of Leviathan. Interestingly, the passage refers to God crushing Leviathan's *heads*, though the number of heads is not stated.
Psalm 104:26	A list of God's mighty acts includes the creation of Leviathan, whom God created to frolic in the sea.
Isaiah 27:1	Leviathan is described as a "gliding serpent" and "coiling serpent," a "monster of the sea." His judgment comes in the day of God's final judgment prior to the ultimate restoration of Israel.

In sum, Leviathan appears as a great monster of the sea, too big and strong for human beings to tame, but an animal God created for his purposes and whom God ultimately will destroy. Leviathan, living in the sea, stands for chaos and opposition to the created order, but as God brings his new order in the latter days, Leviathan will meet his end.

John the apostle may well have had Isaiah's reference to Leviathan as a serpent and dragon (27:1) in mind when he described Satan as "the dragon, that ancient serpent" (Rv 20:2). Leviathan's destruction affirms the Bible's assurance that God will one day destroy all evil for all time.

(27:8) may have included the Assyrian and perhaps later Babylonian exiles, but most likely refers to lesser occasions as well: all the times Israel's enemies had taken away captives.

God's judgment was intended to be redemptive in nature (27:9). The verse contains redemption concepts that also appeared in 6:7, where Isaiah experienced God's cleansing and atonement.[8] Thus, the exile to some extent served as a payment for the nation's sin. However, true repentance would be marked by destruction and/or removal of Jacob's idols, but meanwhile, such repentance had not come, so the conditions of judgment remained (27:10–11).

The Returning Remnant (27:12–13)

Threshing was the agricultural process by which grain was separated from the chaff. The Hebrew word translated "thresh" (27:12; Heb. *habat*) designated a more specific beating out process whereby the husks of grain were separated from the grain itself (Jgs 6:11; Ru 2:17). Isaiah probably used *habat* rather than the usual term for "thresh" (Heb. *dush*) to stress the Lord's extra tender care of his people, an interpretation supported by the fact that God would gather (Heb. *laqat*, "glean"; cf. 17:5; 24:13) his people "one by one."

Sidebar 8.2
Vineyard Images in Isaiah 5 and 27

Isaiah employs the vineyard image in two contexts: 5:1–7 and 27:2–6. In the first instance, the prophet stresses God's tender care, the vineyard's disappointing yield, and God's subsequent destruction of the vineyard. In the second, Isaiah describes God's tender care and love over the vineyard he has prepared just as he wants it. The following table highlights the similarities and contrasts:

	Isaiah 5	Isaiah 27
Prophetic genre	Song	Song
Vineyard owner	God	God
Location	Fertile hillside	Unnamed
Owner's care	Tilled soil Cleared out stones Planted choice vines Built a watchtower Cut out a winepress	Oversees it Waters it continually Guards it day and night Wards off briars and thorns
Vineyard's yield	Bad grapes	Exceedingly fruitful (fruit fills the world)
God's response	Calls for Judah to judge between God and vineyard. Decides to tear down vineyard, expose it to briars and thorns, withhold its rain.	God's pleasure toward his vineyard is evident. God calls all who will to make peace with him.

Isaiah 5 describes Israel and Judah's lack of response to God's tender care. Consequently, Isaiah warned, God would tear down the nation and expose it to the elements, probably a reference denoting the attack of other nations. God's people had answered his grace with sin and would now pay the price.

In contrast, Isaiah 27 heralds the great day of restoration. God appears as a proud vineyard owner, taking tender care of his vineyard and providing for its every need. In such fashion he will provide the ever-present care and love his people need, and as they respond to him, their lives will yield the abundant fruit they were designed to produce.

Isaiah's two vineyard prophecies set before his readers a choice. The vineyard song of chapter 5 emphasizes the sad consequences of refusing God's intervention in their lives. The vineyard song of chapter 27 describes the peace and harmony that come to lives surrendered to his care.

The outer designations of the Euphrates River and the Wadi of Egypt (the latter term refers not to the Nile but to a wadi at Egypt's northeastern border) are not intended to limit the extent of God's gathering but rather to denote the extent of his gracious work. He would leave no one behind.

The day of salvation would begin with a great trumpet sound that gathered God's people to Jerusalem (27:13). It is difficult to determine how much later-revealed eschatology—particularly concerning trumpets—one should read into Isaiah's words (Zec 9:14; Mt 24:31; 1 Cor 15:52; 1 Thes 4:16; Rv 11:15). At the same time, insofar as Isaiah 24–27, like these other passages, addressed similar concepts as the day of the Lord, the Lord's judgment of sinners, and ultimate salvation and the gathering of his people, it seems justifiable to link Isaiah's words with those of other biblical voices that spoke of God's coming everlasting kingdom.

Concluding Thoughts from Isaiah 24–27

As we come to the end of the "little apocalypse," four themes deserve special mention, and their consideration provides a good review of the section.

God Is in Control

First, God is in control. The theme of God's sovereignty runs throughout Scripture, but it is especially strong in Isaiah 24–27. From beginning to end, the Lord of Hosts is in charge of judgment and salvation, upheaval and order, scattering and gathering.

However, although God holds the universe in his hands, he also cares for his people one by one. Isaiah's message is that almighty God loves individuals and desires that they know and worship him.

God's Sovereignty Includes Judgment and Restoration

Second, God's sovereignty includes both judgment and restoration. God actively brings the judgment the earth's citizens deserve, but he also knows his own and makes a clear distinction in the process. He will judge sin, but he will also remove barriers to fellowship, swallow up death for all time, and comfort his own.

God Calls Us to Peace

Third, God calls us to peace, to *shalom*, to wholeness. Indeed, peace with God is what the life of faith is all about (Rom 5:1). Isaiah's testimony of nations coming to worship in Jerusalem again foreshadows the work of Jesus, who abolished the hostility between Jew and Gentile and reconciled them to each other and to God (Eph 2:14–16).

Great Days Are Coming!

Fourth, great days are coming. No matter what people have faced, no matter what they are facing, no matter what they will face, great days are coming. Life might bring experiences so difficult they wonder if they will be able to endure, but Isaiah announces that by God's grace, not only endurance is possible but also victory.

Isaiah's prophetic words remind those who would listen that one day God will more than make up for whatever happens in this life. He is keeping score, and he is preparing a kingdom for his own. Meanwhile, as his children yield to him and trust his work in their lives, they have intimate companionship with him as he makes them into what he wants them to be. In the great day ahead, death will be defeated once and for all, and sorrow and pain will be gone. And every day is one day closer to that time.

Study Questions

1. Identify Isaianic images from Isaiah 24–27 that John used in the book of Revelation. Consult a concordance if necessary.

2. Discuss the interplay of judgment and salvation motifs in Isaiah 24–27.

3. What New Testament concepts do you find anticipated in Isaiah 24–27?

Key Terms

apocalyptic

guilt

Leviathan

onomatopoeic

9 Oracles of Woe

Isaiah 28:1–33:24

Outline

- **Woe against Ephraim (28:1–8)**
- **Judgment and Restoration of Jerusalem (28:9–29:16)**

  Judgment against Jerusalem's Leaders (28:9–29)

  Woe against Jerusalem (29:1–16)
- **Restoration of Israel (29:17–24)**
- **Woe against Foreign Alliances (30:1–31:9)**

  The Futility of Appealing to Egypt (30:1–17)

  God's Restoration and Deliverance of Jerusalem (30:18–33)

  The Woe and Restoration Restated (31:1–9)
- **Hope Mixed with Woe: A Description of the Righteous Kingdom (32:1–20)**

  Characteristics of the Righteous Kingdom (32:1–8)

  Judgment, Mourning, and the Outpouring of God's Spirit (32:9–20)
- **Woe against Assyria (33:1–24)**

  Plea for Assyria's Destruction (33:1–9)

The Lord's Promise of Restoration (33:10–24)

Objectives

After reading this chapter, you should be able to

1. Describe the spiritual failures of Judah's leaders and general population (chaps. 28–29).
2. Explain the reasons behind Isaiah's warning against foreign alliances (chaps. 30–31).
3. Highlight further aspects of God's future kingdom (32:1–20).

Thus far in the book of Isaiah, the prophet has already used the word "woe" (Heb. *hoy*) twelve times. Each time he used the term, he introduced a judgment God would bring against one or more nations that had oppressed his people and/or ignored his sovereignty. Woe to the nations that opposed the Lord and his people!

In Isaiah 28–33, the word "woe" appears six times (28:1; 29:1, 15; 30:1; 31:1; 33:1). The last occurrence introduced a woe against Assyria, the nation whose empire dominated the ancient Near East at the time of Isaiah's prophetic ministry. This should not surprise us, since many of Isaiah's prophetic words (e.g., chaps. 13–23) focused on God's work among and against those nations that opposed him. Interestingly, however, the first four occurrences of the term "woe" in Isaiah 28–33 introduced woes against God's own people.

One of the people's most significant sins was turning away from the Lord to put their trust in earthly alliances with other nations, in particular Egypt. Isaiah warned that their plans would fail, and only those who trusted the Lord would find lasting security.

Woe against Ephraim (28:1–8)

When Tiglath-Pileser III of Assyria attacked Israel and Syria at the request of King Ahaz of Judah (2 Kgs 16:7–9), he annexed much of the northern kingdom of Israel, leaving Hoshea to rule a territory roughly the size of the tribal territory of Ephraim. Isaiah's reference to the northern kingdom as "Ephraim" rather than as "Israel" reflects this political reality.[1]

Isaiah pronounced woe to a kingdom that was fading fast. Its glory dimmed as its rulers and false prophets staggered from wine and strong drink (28:1, 3, 7–8), which they drank either to forget their troubles or to "stimulate their minds" to see visions.

The prophet did not specifically mention Assyria as his "powerful and strong" instrument whose force resembled "a hailstorm and a destructive wind" (28:2), but the allusion was clear. What Assyria would begin, it would finish—all by God's direction.

Again, the Lord would protect those who trusted in him (28:5–6). He would prove to be their source of strength, as well as the crown and wreath they would wear after coming through the time of testing triumphantly.

Judgment and Restoration of Jerusalem (28:9–29:16)

Isaiah now shifted his attention southward. Verses 9–13 could just as well apply to the northern kingdom, but verse 14 clearly links the application to Jerusalem.

Judgment against Jerusalem's Leaders (28:9–29)

Jerusalem's leaders had disregarded God, his word, and his prophets. Isaiah likened their spiritual understanding to that of infants and warned them the Lord would rebuild his people his way. A time of judgment would precede a time of restoration.

Immature People Don't Listen (28:9–13)

Isaiah asked rhetorical questions (28:9) that presented a ridiculous situation. Who was able to understand the meaning of God's teaching? Was it infants or those whose mothers had just weaned them? Of course not!

The spiritual level of understanding had declined drastically among God's people. Many interpreters believe verse 10 may be a children's nursery rhyme,[2] for when it is translated into Hebrew, it reads as follows:

tsav letsáv tsav letsáv,
qav leqáv qav leqáv
ze'er sham ze'er sham

The people's spiritual depth of understanding had become pitifully shallow and immature.

Isaiah declared that God's response to them would be at the level of their understanding (28:11, 13). He would speak to them with unintelligible speech that would sound to them like the nursery rhyme of verse 10. The unintelligible speech would fall from the lips of Assyrian conquerors. Imagine the fear of a conquered people trying to obey Assyrian orders when they didn't understand the language!

The Lord Rebuilds His Way (28:14–22)

The Lord challenged the prevailing thought of Jerusalem's rulers (28:14–15). The Hebrew word translated "scoffers" is related to the word translated "mockers" in Psalm 1:1 and underscores the contempt the leaders showed for God's truth.

Jerusalem's rulers thought they would escape judgment. It was as if they had made a covenant with death and the grave. They chose to trust in lies rather than in the Lord. The Hebrew word *sheqer*, translated "falsehood," occurs commonly in Jeremiah to describe Judah's false sense of security as the people trusted in the temple and their religious tradition (Jer 7:4, 8; 13:25; 28:15).

The Judeans thought themselves forever secure in their beloved Jerusalem—David's city—with God's temple in their midst. History would prove otherwise in the day of God's rebuilding (28:17–19).

The Lord would rebuild Jerusalem, but he would rebuild it his way, according to his plan (28:16–17a). He would use good building instruments such as justice and righteousness and provide a sure foundation through a "precious cornerstone." Those who would place their trust in him (lit. "believe") would find their trust well placed. Those who

persisted in unbelief would find sorrow at every turn (28:20, 22).

Isaiah's references to Mount Perazim and the Valley of Gibeon (28:21) recalled two great divine works. The first described God's work against the Philistines early in David's reign as Israel's king (2 Sm 5:17–20). The second recalled the sun standing still on the day of Joshua's victory over the southern coalition of kings when Israel conquered Canaan (Jos 10:12–14).

By pulling in these two events, the text emphasizes the work God will do in the day Isaiah described. Ironically, the same divine power that defended Jerusalem and God's people would now work *against* his people to bring judgment.

The apostles Paul and Peter (Rom 9:33; 1 Pt 2:6) applied Isaiah's words of 28:16 to Jesus Christ, the cornerstone of the church (Eph 2:19–20). God would one day rebuild his people on a whole new level, beyond anything Isaiah's hearers would have understood or even imagined.

The Parable of the Farmer (28:23–29)

Isaiah's parable of the farmer concludes this section. A farmer had to learn valuable lessons about diligence and patience. He could not plow and sow arbitrarily, and he needed to use his farming instruments properly in accordance with season and crop. God instructed the farmer, and in time, the farmer learned how to plant, grow, and harvest. Likewise, people also needed to learn from God regarding life's most important lessons. Following their own plans would never work.

Woe against Jerusalem (29:1–16)

Isaiah's woe against Jerusalem included three elements: God's siege of Jerusalem, God's spiritual judgment, and God's woe against the bold.

God's Siege of Jerusalem (29:1–8)

Commentators disagree over the meaning of the term "Ariel" (29:1).

Some have suggested "lion of God,"[3] while others have suggested the term perhaps means "altar hearth."[4] Though scholars have argued both sides based on linguistic evidence, "altar hearth" appears a better fit. Jerusalem, whose identity is hinted at in 29:1 and identified clearly in 29:8, both is and becomes a place of burning, a hearth for offering sacrifice. Moreover, a linguistically similar term in Ezekiel 43:15–16 clearly means "altar hearth." Finally, "lion of God" does not fit the meaning of 29:2 nearly as well.

Isaiah's words "add year to year and let your cycle of festivals go on" (29:1) were intended sarcastically (cf. Amos 4:4–5). Jerusalem's citizens may have thought their temple worship was proceeding appropriately, but actually they were just going through the motions—ritual for ritual's sake.

The prophet described God's coming judgment against the city (29:2–4), a judgment some scholars have identified with Sennacherib's invasion.[5] Isaiah made no specific identification, though the language of 29:7, when compared with 29:2–3, seems to link God's work of judgment with the use of human instruments such as other nations. Mourning and lamentation would ensue as the people found themselves ground into the dust.

However, Isaiah also described the defeat of Jerusalem's enemies (29:5–8). As suddenly as the Lord had brought judgment, he would bring deliverance to his people, summoning nature's forces against his people's attackers. The theme of the Lord's appearing to fight for his people just as all seems lost also occurs in Zechariah 14:1–5.

God's Spiritual Judgment (29:9–14)

The people's shallow practice of the sacrificial system (29:1) was symptomatic of a deeper spiritual issue. The people spoke words of praise to God, but their actions betrayed the true intentions of their hearts (29:13). Further, their worship focused merely on their traditions, not on God's revealed truth and not on their nurturing a relationship with him (see sidebar 9.1).

Consequently, the Lord had poured over his people a spiritual stupor (29:9–10). This judgment resulted in silence from those prophets and seers who might have alleviated the situation by proclaiming a divine message.

In fact, Isaiah likened his own message to a sealed scroll (29:11–12). Illiterate citizens couldn't read it anyway, and literate citizens couldn't read it because of its seal. Either way, the message wasn't read and applied to people's lives. The text also may provide another example of a prophet recording his message for use by his original audience (Jer 36:2; Heb 2:2–3).

Woe against the Bold (29:15–16)

Isaiah also warned the bold who made their own plans in defiance of God's intentions. These people thought they could hide their ways from him, but they could not. In fact, they totally misunderstood their place in the universe.

God had made them—he was the potter, they were the clay. They could never match God's wisdom; he had created them and knew them better than they knew themselves. They did not need to make their own plans or even to include God in their plans. Rather, they needed to align themselves with God's purpose for their lives.

Restoration of Israel (29:17–24)

Isaiah proclaimed a coming day that would turn people's hearts to the Lord. The deaf would hear, the blind would see, and the humble and needy would turn again to the Holy One of Israel (29:17–19). He would root out evildoers and oppressors.

In light of this, Isaiah had a special message for "the house of Jacob" (29:22–24). God's deliverance would also bring them spiritual renewal. They would respond to his work with lives

---

A Modern Application of Isaiah 29:13

Isaiah denounced his people for the shallowness of their religious faith. They worshiped according to traditions they had memorized, but they had no real grasp of God's written word. Consequently, while they honored God with their lips, their hearts were far from him.

Modern-day churchgoers can fall into the same pattern of life that Isaiah's people practiced. Many faithfully attend worship services and even Sunday school, but they rarely if ever open their Bibles during the week. The only biblical knowledge they have comes from what they hear on Sunday mornings. They ask questions in Sunday school class that begin something like, "Well, doesn't it say somewhere in the Bible that . . . ?" but they have no idea where to find the answer.

Today people have many Bible translations from which they may choose. Countless Bible study aids are available—concordances, dictionaries, commentaries, and other resources—to help people understand the text. Computer programs are available to enable Bible study at a depth earlier generations could often only dream of doing. Yet research indicates that Christians today know their Bibles no better than did other generations.

In many cases, the lack of interest in Bible study may indicate a deeper spiritual problem. If churchgoers have a shallow relationship with God, they naturally will not appreciate his word as much. Also, if they have not really embraced the concept that the Bible is God's word, they may not treat it with the respect it is due or be concerned about submitting to its teachings.

Ultimately, then, within the context of Christian faith, a love and desire to study God's word flows from a relationship with him. As believers draw close to him, they will naturally want to spend time in the Bible to get to know God better.

---

of holiness and would stand in awe of him.

Woe against Foreign Alliances (30:1–31:9)

During the years 1200–750 BC, many independent states sprang up in the ancient Near East because no major power existed. Assyria, Babylon, Hatti, and Egypt all were experiencing times of decline. Nations such as Syria, Philistia, Ammon, Edom, Moab, Phoenicia, Israel, and Judah vied for power and influence in their respective locations.

With the rise of Assyria around 750 BC, these smaller states faced the real possibility of subjugation or extermination. As they considered what to do, many sought rescue through alliances with other nations (cf. 7:1–9).

Isaiah 30–31 focuses on the sin of relying on alliances with other nations. First, the Lord wanted his people to look to him rather than to human strategies. Second, alliances with other nations typically involved treaties that called on the gods of both parties to judge whoever broke the treaty.[6] Thus, forming an alliance would have required Israel's and Judah's leaders to recognize, at least formally, the existence and power of another nation's gods.

The Futility of Appealing to Egypt (30:1–17)

Isaiah insisted that appealing to unreliable Egypt was futile. The people had committed two grave errors: they had made their own plans, and they had silenced God's plans.

People Make Their Own Plans (30:1–5)

Isaiah announced woe to Judah for its attitude, describing the Judeans as "obstinate children" (30:1). They carried out their own plans instead of consulting the Lord. The word translated "mine" (30:1) literally means "from me" and emphasizes that God was not the source of their strategies.

The words translated "form an alliance" can also mean "pour out a drink offering" and probably denote the offering made at the time of a political alliance. The people's sin had brought their situation on them, but they were "heaping sin upon sin" (30:1) by looking to Egypt for rescue.

Judah had already sent delegates to Egypt (30:4), but Isaiah pronounced the effort worthless and its outcome ruin. Egypt had a history of promising assistance that never came, a fact that would not escape Assyrian notice (36:6).

People Silence God's Plans (30:6–17)

Isaiah listed various animals that inhabited the Negev, Judah's southern desert region (30:6–7). The animals watched as Judah's envoys passed through, carrying the treasures with which they hoped to buy Egyptian support and protection. But Egypt, the object of their trust, would prove totally untrustworthy. The expression "Rahab the Do-Nothing" describes Egypt as at rest, at ease, rather than as providing aid.

The Lord instructed Isaiah to write down everything as a lasting witness (30:8). When it came true, people would know he had spoken God's truth. The people were unwilling to listen to the prophets and seers, instructing them instead to prophesy pleasant illusions that would help them feel better (30:10). They did not want to be confronted with the truth of their sin.

Consequently, sudden destruction was coming (30:12–14). The oppression and deceit the people had practiced would prove empty, and their wicked house would come crashing down on them, bringing total devastation. Isaiah told them that true strength lay in repentance and trust in the Holy One of Israel, but again, the people preferred their own ideas (30:15–16). In the end, however, they were doomed to fail, for God stood against them.

Temple of Ramses II. Egypt, for all its past glory, did not have the strength to hold off either Assyria or Babylon. (Courtesy of Todd Bolen/ BiblePlaces .com)

God's Restoration and Deliverance of Jerusalem (30:18–33)

Isaiah's words (30:15–17) sounded harsh, and they were. Nonetheless, the people should not think they lay beyond God's grace or that God no longer loved them. Indeed, the Lord was planning a great day of restoration. Jerusalem's restoration and deliverance would feature three aspects: the Lord teaching his people, bringing them great blessing, and displaying his warrior power to the nations.

The Lord Will Teach His People (30:18–22)

First, Isaiah described a God who longed to be gracious to his people if they only would cry to him for help (30:18–19). He intended the hardship they were experiencing to turn them back to him! Their teachers would teach them, but the Lord would teach them even more and guide their very steps (30:21). They would realize the worthlessness of their idols and images and cast them away (30:22).

The Lord Will Bring Great Blessing (30:23–26)

Second, Isaiah described a God who would bring great blessing. Nature flourished with abundant rain and streams, producing great crops and a rich land in which livestock would graze. What a contrast to the Judean wilderness, where shepherds had to search out water and vegetation. The reference to the "day of great slaughter, when the towers fall" (30:25) is probably a general designation for the judgment of his enemies. Isaiah's description of the intense brightness of the sun and the moon (30:26) appears to describe God's future kingdom.

The Lord Will Display "Warrior Power" (30:27–33)

Third, Isaiah described a God who would display his warrior power against the nations. He would shake the nations as if he held them in a sieve. He would sift out the bad for judgment as he displayed his burning fury (30:27–28).

Assyria would not escape God's wrath (30:31). As God displayed his fury, those who loved him would rejoice and celebrate his work on their behalf (30:29). He had prepared Topheth, the place of slaughter (cf. Jer 19:6), and its blaze would consume the wicked.

The Woe and Restoration Restated (31:1–9)

In chapter 31, Isaiah pronounced further woe to people who persisted in seeing Egypt rather than God as the answer to their problems. One day they would recognize the futility of placing their trust anywhere else. They trusted in Egypt when the fact of God's coming deliverance should have brought them to repentance.

People Trust in Egypt, Not in God (31:1–3)

Isaiah castigated the people. They had carefully assessed Egypt's strength—the number of its horses, the quality of its horsemen, and the strength of its chariots. But they would not look to the one who had created all nations. The Lord offered more than Egypt could ever provide, and in a moment, he could and would bring them low. Isaiah's words were unmistakable—*it is not God's will to deliver you through assistance from Egypt!*

The Lord's Deliverance Should Lead to Repentance (31:4–9)

Isaiah described a day when God would descend to do battle on behalf of his own (31:4–5). He would shield Jerusalem and his people as he fought for them.

The prophet called the people to repentance in light of the promise of God's deliverance (31:6–9). Israel had revolted against its God, but the day was coming when it would reject the idols it had fashioned from its gold and silver. No individual or nation would bring Assyria down; it would be the Lord's doing. Indeed, following the Lord's victory during the days of Hezekiah (chaps. 36–37), Assyria began a decline that ultimately would lead to its ruin.

Hope Mixed with Woe: A Description of the Righteous Kingdom (32:1–20)

Characteristics of the Righteous Kingdom (32:1–8)

Two characteristics of the righteous kingdom stand out in Isaiah's description. The first is upright leadership, and the second is societal rejuvenation.

Upright Leadership (32:1–2)

Upright leadership! Judean leaders had so often failed their subjects, but Isaiah promised a righteous king and just rulers alongside him. He used four similes to describe the blessing of this upright leadership (32:2). Though their positive intent is obvious, more detail on them appears in sidebar 9.2:

like a shelter from the wind
and a refuge from the storm,
like streams of water in the
desert
and the shadow of a great
rock in a thirsty land.

Societal Rejuvenation (32:3–8)

Societal rejuvenation was the second important feature of the kingdom God was bringing. Negative aspects of society became positive as people's eyes and ears were open to seeing and hearing truth. Rash decision makers received discernment, and stammerers spoke clearly.

In that day, people would see the fool and the wicked for what they really were (32:5–8). They had practiced ungodliness and spread falsehood and error. Societal rejuvenation included not only the addition of positive aspects but also the rooting out of the negative ones.

Judgment, Mourning, and the Outpouring of God's Spirit (32:9–20)

Isaiah 32:1–2 announced the establishment of righteous, upright leader-

---

Sidebar 9.2
Images of Upright Leadership in the Land of Judah

Isaiah used four similes to describe the blessing of upright leadership (32:2):

like a shelter from the wind
and [like] a refuge from the storm,
like streams of water in the desert
and [like] the shadow of a great rock in a
thirsty land.

The images Isaiah used become more vivid when one considers the Judean landscape. The wilderness and desert regions of Judah get as little as six inches of rainfall per year. Wind blows dust across the wasteland. Shepherds have to find shelter in caves or rock crevices. Streams of water are a welcome sight, and those who travel the area must know where they are, or they will die of dehydration. Even the presence of a great rock brings some relief from the heat through the shade it provides.

Plentiful water was rare in the Judean wilderness and desert; so was upright leadership in Judah. But Isaiah promised that one day, God would provide relief to a land thirsty for good leadership.

The wilderness of Judah's desert-like conditions normally provide little vegetation for its inhabitants. Isaiah compared good leadership to streams of water in such regions (32:2). (Courtesy of Todd Bolen/BiblePlaces.com)

ship. It was a great promise, but first would come days of judgment and mourning. God would deal with sin wherever he found it. Once he had done so, the outpouring of God's Spirit would usher in a grand new day.

Prelude to the Kingdom: Judgment and Mourning (32:9–14)

Isaiah called the complacent women of Judah to mourn. They felt secure, but within a year, hard times would come. Perhaps the prophecy dates just prior to Sennacherib's invasion during the reign of Hezekiah, when war brought difficult conditions.

Hard times were indeed coming, and the women would mourn the loss of crops and harvest (32:10–13), for the land's growth would either fail or be taken by an advancing enemy. Cities would disappear, and everything would seem lost.

The Outpouring of God's Spirit (32:15–20)

God's Spirit would bring the coming restoration at all levels. First, the land would become fertile (32:15). Even desert areas would become fertile fields. Second, animals would have plenty of places to graze in peace (32:20). Third, justice and righteousness would prevail in the land (32:16–17). Fourth, the people would enjoy lasting security (32:18).

The promise of lasting security must have sounded particularly significant to a people living in constant fear of attack from nations that bordered them. And of course, the threat of Assyria always loomed large. When God established his people in security with righteous leadership, then the real meaning of *shalom* would be evident. Isaiah promised it would come as the Spirit of God worked the divine will.

Woe against Assyria (33:1–24)

The word "woe" (Heb. *hoy*) introduces Isaiah 33, as it has other woe passages in this section (28:1; 29:1, 15; 30:1; 31:1). Although Isaiah does not specifically mention Assyria, it is clearly in view in light of the historical context.

Isaiah's hearers were beaten down and oppressed and also felt the weight of their own sin. The entire land mourned and suffered the affliction of Assyrian domination. Did his people really have any reason for hope? Would the Lord really arise on their behalf and rescue them? Isaiah's message brought strong reassurance to his audience; God had not forgotten them, and he would act soon.

Plea for Assyria's Destruction (33:1–9)

The word "woe" (33:1) heralded Assyria's doom. The Assyrians had destroyed others but had escaped destruction. They had dealt treacherously with others, but others had not had the power to reciprocate. When Assyria was finished with its destruction and treachery—a time determined by the Lord, not by Assyria—then Assyria would receive its measure of destruction and treachery. The Assyrians had not realized their role in the divine plan (10:5–7), but they would in that day.

Verses 2–4 comprise a prayer for deliverance. After the initial announcement of verse 1, God's people implored him for grace. He alone could be their strength, he alone could rescue them from their distress. His power alone could scatter the nations and put them in their place. Prayers such as this reflected an attitude God had wanted his people to have all along.

The Lord stood exalted (33:5–6). He would restore justice and righteousness to Zion and provide his people a sure foundation for life. He only asked that his people fear him.

Meanwhile, the land languished as the people waited for God's intervention (33:7–9). Brave men did not know what to do, peace delegations had failed, travel had ceased, and evil abounded. Even Sharon, Bashan, and Carmel—three northern regions known for their lush foliage and agriculture—withered away.

The Lord's Promise of Restoration (33:10–24)

The Lord quickly replied to the people's lament (33:10–14). He was ready to act; he would demonstrate his great works. He would consume "the peoples" (33:12), a reference to those who opposed him. He called on everyone near and far to consider his works and acknowledge him (33:13) and promised fear would grip them all (33:14). Who could stand before such power, before the consuming fire of God's judgment?

Isaiah then provided an answer to these questions (33:15–16). Those whose lives reflected their good inner character would receive God's blessing. They emptied their lives of evil practices and would not even contemplate evil. Rather, they filled their lives with God-honoring qualities.

Study Questions

1. What was Judah's sin in Isaiah 28:9–13? What steps should the people have taken to grow in their faith?

2. Describe what Judah could have done to overcome its spiritual stupor (29:9–14).

3. Why did Isaiah consistently condemn making alliances with other nations (chaps. 30–31)?

4. What are the main features of God's kingdom described in Isaiah 32?

Isaiah described features of God's great day of restoration (33:17–20). The people would behold the king's splendor and enjoy a spacious land. They would no longer face their arrogant enemies who had oppressed them and made their lives difficult. Rather, they would see Jerusalem as a beacon of peace, an immovable city of festivals and celebration.

Finally, God's great day of restoration would feature spiritual blessing (33:21–24). More important than anything else, the Lord would stand as their mighty one, their judge, their lawgiver, their king, their savior. They would experience the true meaning of salvation, and in that day, they would understand the true meaning of life. God in his love and grace had forgiven them and established them as his everlasting people.

10 Eschatological Summation

Isaiah 34:1–35:10

Outline

- **The Lord Will Avenge Himself against the Nations (34:1–17)**

  A Call to the Nations (34:1–4)

  Judgment against Edom (34:5–15)

  Summary Statement: You Can Count on It! (34:16–17)

- **The Redeemed See God's Salvation (35:1–10)**

  God Will Show His Salvation in Nature (35:1–2)

  God Will Encourage the Weary (35:3–6a)

  God Will Renovate the Land (35:6b–10)

- **Concluding Thoughts from Isaiah 28–35**

  God Desires His People to Follow His Plans

  God Hates Spiritual Complacency

  God Desires His People's Ultimate Allegiance

  God Has Exciting Days Ahead

Objectives

After reading this chapter, you should be able to

1. Describe features of God's final judgment.
2. Highlight features of God's coming salvation.
3. Summarize the main themes of Isaiah 28–35.

"Okay, let's wrap it up!" Maybe you've heard those words at the end of a lecture, a rehearsal, or a sports practice. Usually at that time, the leaders—be they professors, directors, or coaches—try to pull together what has been accomplished that day. They may restate the key points of a lecture or remind athletes of particular plays they've practiced.

Isaiah 13–23 presents the prophet's oracles against the nations. God was sovereign over these nations whether or not they realized it. Isaiah 24–27, the "little apocalypse," tied the oracles together by proclaiming God's sovereignty over the whole universe and the final judgment and victory he would accomplish on behalf of himself and his people.

Isaiah 28–33 contains several woes against those who made their own plans and ignored God's plans and direction. Many in Judah trusted in Egypt instead of in their God. Others, such as Assyria, trusted in themselves and their own might, as well as perhaps in their own worthless idols. The prophet assured his people that the Lord was their only real hope and even described the righteous kingdom God would reestablish under David's descendant.

Isaiah 34–35 function much like chapters 24–27 in that they tie off the previous section (chaps. 28–33). In fact, some scholars have also argued that the chapters (along with chaps. 36–39) form a literary bridge between 1–33 and 40–66.[1] Was the Lord really his people's only hope? Could they count on him to establish his kingdom and rescue them?

Isaiah assured his hearers the answer to both these questions was a resounding yes. The Lord would avenge himself against the nations, and the redeemed would see God's salvation.

The Lord Will Avenge Himself against the Nations (34:1–17)

Isaiah's description of God's vengeance against the nations included three sections. First, Isaiah called to the nations to prepare to experience God's wrath (34:1–4). Second, the prophet announced Edom especially would experience God's judgment (34:5–15). Third, Isaiah assured his hearers that God would accomplish all he said (34:16–17).

Bozrah, the capital of ancient Edom (Courtesy of Todd Bolen/ BiblePlaces .com)

Edom

vengeance

A Call to the Nations (34:1–4)

Isaiah began his oracle with a general call to all peoples and nations (34:1). Clearly his primary audience was Judah. Nonetheless, such words emphasize again the divine interest in people outside Judah's borders. Here the primary intention is to warn them of judgment, but other parts of Isaiah call them to salvation (45:22–23).

The Lord's wrath was about to descend on all nations (34:2). The words "will totally destroy them" might also be translated "has totally destroyed them." In the former reading, Isaiah's words function as a prediction of things to come. In the latter reading, the prophet's words represent a divine decree of judgment. The Hebrew verb used[2] typically referred to the giving over of things or persons to the Lord for destruction. Their armies would prove no match for his fury.

Isaiah described a scenario in which the Lord won absolute victory (34:3). The gruesome language emphasized total devastation. No one remained even to bury the dead.

The destruction had universal implications (34:4). Isaiah's apocalyptic language described the sky rolling up and the stars falling from heaven. Earth's judgment found its parallel among the heavenly elements.

Isaiah had used similar imagery earlier in his book (13:13), and he would do so again (51:6). Later biblical writers also used parallel images to describe the events preceding the coming of God's kingdom (Ez 32:7–8; Mt 24:29; Rv 6:12–14). The great day of God was on its way.

Judgment against Edom (34:5–15)

Edom's appearance in the midst of a prophetic statement of universal judgment appears somewhat odd. Most interpreters understand **Edom**, a historic "thorn in the side" for Israel and Judah, to represent the nations in general.[3] All who opposed the Lord would suffer the fate Isaiah now described for Edom.

Edom had received only minor treatment in Isaiah's oracles against the nations (chaps. 13–23; cf. 21:11–12). However, the great sword of God's wrath had "drunk its fill" in the heavenly realm—an expression indicating thorough judgment—and now descended on the land where Esau's descendants resided (34:5; Gn 36:1). The Hebrew word behind the expression "totally destroyed" is related to the word in 34:2; God had determined their utter destruction.

The "God as warrior" motif continues in 34:6–7. His judgment sword sliced through Edom's best as he prepared a sacrifice for himself from Edom's livestock. Bozrah, which appears again in 63:1, was Edom's capital city. Some scholars have suggested that the references to oxen and great bulls in 34:7 may refer to Edom's leaders.[4] Without them, society would be confounded (cf. Ob 8–9). The entire land would lie slaughtered.

Vengeance (34:8) suggests not merely the concept of revenge but also of making things right, of balancing the scales of justice. This is supported by the words "retribution" (Heb. *shillumim*, suggesting "making complete") and "cause" (Heb. *rib*). The latter word consistently carries a legal connotation, denoting a court case (1:23; 41:21; Jer 11:20; Hos 4:1). The Lord's judgment would provide the ultimate vindication for those who followed him.

Isaiah detailed Edom's complete destruction (34:9–15). It would become a fiery wasteland unsuitable for human habitation. The language of these verses closely parallels Isaiah's words against Babylon (13:19–22), further suggesting Edom's judgment represents the judgment on all nations.[5]

Edom's great desolation was accompanied by the growth of thorns and brambles and its inhabitation by unclean creatures (34:11, 13–15). The nesting and egg laying of these creatures suggested their continued established presence.

God would build his new city with justice as its measuring line and righteousness as its plumb line (28:17), but he would stretch over Edom "the measuring line of chaos and the plumb line of desolation" (34:11). The Hebrew words translated "chaos" and "desolation" are *tohu* and *bohu*, respectively, which occur together in Genesis 1:2 to describe the condition of the earth prior to God establishing its order. In effect, God was "un-creating" Edom.

Summary Statement: You Can Count on It! (34:16–17)

Verses 16–17 form a summary statement that gave the prophet's hearers a challenge: "Seek [or inquire] from the book of the LORD, and read" (NASB). What was this "book of the Lord"? The expression probably referred to the prophecies that Isaiah had already spoken. The prophet had earlier called his hearers back to God's written revelation (8:19–20). Here he probably intended to invite anyone who wished to verify the accuracy of his recorded words as the prophecy came to pass. God would fulfill his word to the letter.

Why could God's people count on Isaiah's words? Because God had given

the order. The perpetuity described in verse 17 echoed verse 10 and placed a final exclamation point on Isaiah's prophecy.

The Redeemed See God's Salvation (35:1–10)

The tone of Isaiah's words shifted abruptly in 35:1. Isaiah 34 described the bad news that awaited everyone who opposed the divine plan for the nations. But Isaiah 35 announced the joy the redeemed would see and experience as God brought his salvation to his people. This **redemption** featured three elements: God would show his salvation in nature, he would encourage the weary, and he would renovate the land.

God Will Show His Salvation in Nature (35:1–2)

Isaiah announced that the Lord would show his salvation in nature.

The Wadi Qilt east of Jerusalem toward Jericho. Isaiah 35 predicted the region would one day blossom like the fertile regions of Galilee. (Courtesy of Bryan E. Beyer)

The terms *midbar* (desert) and *arabah* (wilderness) do not necessarily connote a desert region. They do, however, often designate southern areas more suited to the pasturing of animals than to agriculture. But in the coming day of salvation, growth would spring up throughout such regions.

Isaiah compared the growth of the southern wilderness and desert to the best of Galilee and beyond. Galilee's northern position meant it received more rainfall and hence typically supported more of the land's agriculture. Today, the regions of Mount Carmel and the Sharon Plain remain quite green, even during the hot summer period when little if any rain falls and temperatures often reach 90 degrees Fahrenheit and higher.

If Judah's relatively barren areas became fertile and lush, many who struggled to maintain their livelihood might do quite well as the economy shifted from predominantly pastoral to predominantly agricultural. Most of Judah's citizens would have welcomed the fulfillment of Isaiah's promise. This agricultural rejuvenation displayed the glory of the Lord. Only he could do this work in a land whose climate stood against such a possibility.

God Will Encourage the Weary (35:3–6a)

A string of commands begins Isaiah's encouragement to the weary. The people were to strengthen their hands, knees, and hearts to prepare themselves for God's great work.

But why should feeble hands become strong? Why should shaky knees become steady? Why should people tell the fearful to be strong and lay aside their fear? After all, the people had seen so much oppression, so much domination, so much suffering.

Isaiah provided the answer to all these questions in 35:4—you should be strong and not fear because of God's promise to come, bring vengeance and retribution, and save his own. Living by the word of God would bring stability and strength; living by circumstances and feelings would only continue the weakness and fear. "Be strong," Isaiah encouraged his hearers. "God will save you!"

Isaiah also announced the miracles that would accompany God's salvation (35:5–6). Blind eyes would see; deaf ears would hear; lame legs would leap for joy; tongues that had never uttered a word would proclaim God's praise. God's work for his people would include a healing work in them.

Perhaps many in Jesus's day thought the fulfillment of Isaiah's words near as they witnessed Jesus's miracles (Mt 11:5). The final fulfillment of Isaiah's words, however, await the final coming of Christ's kingdom.

God Will Renovate the Land (35:6b–10)

After describing God's salvation of his people, Isaiah returned to the theme he had begun in 35:1–2. The Lord would renovate the land in an incredible way. The Hebrew terms *midbar* and *arabah* occur again in 35:6 in the same order as in 35:1, though the NIV reverses their translation. Water sustained life, and abundant water would bring life to formerly dry and desolate regions of Judah.

Even more significantly, Isaiah announced that God's renovation of the land would include spiritual renewal. God would prepare a highway for his people to travel, and its name would be "the Way of Holiness" (35:8). The term "holiness" described more those who traveled the road than the road itself.

Just as in English, the word "way" can have either a literal or a figurative meaning, so the Hebrew word for "way" (*derek*) can designate either literal or figurative concepts. Those who "walk in that way" are those whose lives display God's holiness, and only they may travel that road (35:8). Furthermore, security reigns on Holiness Highway; God will protect his redeemed from all wild animals and evildoers (35:9).

complacency

Such, Isaiah proclaimed, will be the future of God's people. The imagery of 35:10 is astounding. The Lord's ransomed will return to Zion amid celebration, singing, and joy. Even in modern Jerusalem, one often sees people carrying loads on their heads, but in that day, joy will adorn their heads like crowns. Gladness and joy will overwhelm God's people, driving away sorrow and despair.

Concluding Thoughts from Isaiah 28–35

At the beginning of the chapter, we noted that Isaiah 34–35 concludes Isaiah 28–33 in much the same way that Isaiah 24–27 concludes Isaiah 13–23. As we conclude our study of Isaiah 28–35, four themes deserve special mention. First, God desires his people to follow his plans. Second, God hates spiritual complacency. Third, God desires his people's ultimate allegiance. Fourth, God has exciting days ahead.

God Desires His People to Follow His Plans

God desires his people to follow his plans. Isaiah condemned the attempted alliances with Egypt because Judah was trying to make its own plans rather than consulting the Lord. The nation's future was at stake, and Judah was busy making its own plans instead of seeking the Lord through his word and through prayer.

God assured his people he would answer them if they called to him, but they did not call. Maybe they even intended to include the Lord in their plans, but the Lord wasn't seeking to be part of these plans. Rather, he wanted to include them in his plans. Even today, believers must align themselves with God's purpose for their lives.

God Hates Spiritual Complacency

Isaiah warned his people that God hated spiritual **complacency**. Their spiritual understanding remained at a nursery-rhyme level (28:10). They honored the Lord with their lips, but their hearts were far away; all they knew of him consisted of memorized traditions (29:13). Isaiah encouraged the people to grow in their relationship with the Lord.

God hates spiritual complacency no less today. Believers should seek to grow in their relationship with him. As they yield their lives to him and trust in the Holy Spirit's work in them, he will conform them to the image of Jesus (Rom 8:29; 2 Cor 3:18).

God Desires His People's Ultimate Allegiance

Isaiah exhorted his people—God desired their ultimate allegiance! He knew who opposed him, and their day was coming. Not a single promise he made concerning judgment would fail; all would happen just as he had said. Consequently, he desired their ultimate and absolute allegiance. Nothing less would do.

Many things in life clamor for people's attention today: money, power, status, even human relationships. None of these may necessarily be bad in and of itself, but the Lord desires his people's ultimate allegiance. Believers should

---

Study Questions

1. What were key aspects of Edom's judgment?

2. Why would agricultural blessing (particularly of Judah) have been so significant to Isaiah's audience?

3. What connection did Isaiah make between the kingdom's blessing and the expectations of the kingdom's citizens?

view everything else through the lens of their relationship with him.

God Has Exciting Days Ahead

Isaiah assured his people God had exciting days ahead. He would sweep away those who opposed him and his people. They could count on him to judge thoroughly and with absolute fairness. But he also knew his own and would not let them down or let them go.

Isaiah foretold a day when the earth would again yield abundant crops, when holiness would reign in the hearts of God's people, and when God's glory would display itself from one end of the universe to the other. Jesus will return and usher in an age beyond his people's wildest dreams. Isaiah announced this in the eighth century BC, but as the kingdom draws closer, the Bible calls believers to live in light of that coming reality (2 Pt 3:10–13).

Key Terms

complacency

Edom

redemption

vengeance

11 Highlights from Hezekiah's Reign

Isaiah 36:1–39:8

Outline

Objectives

After reading this chapter, you should be able to

1. Explain key chronological issues regarding the historical events of Isaiah 36–39.
2. Summarize the account of Sennacherib's invasion and defeat.
3. Discuss the key details regarding Hezekiah's illness, recovery, and visit from the Babylonian delegation.
4. Articulate the role of Isaiah 36–39 within the book of Isaiah.

Hezekiah

Sennacherib

After studying the first thirty-five chapters of the book of Isaiah, do you feel you're getting to know the prophet Isaiah well? Perhaps you do because you've read about Isaiah's call (chap. 6), his encounter with Ahaz (chap. 7), and, of course, his many prophecies. These chapters have provided much insight into Isaiah's personality and character.

Isaiah 36–39 provide insight into King Hezekiah's personality and character. The chapters describe three events: Sennacherib's threat and God's deliverance (36–37), Hezekiah's illness and recovery (38), and Hezekiah's visit with King Merodach-Baladan (39). If you read each of these stories carefully, you'll gain a better understanding of this great king of Judah.

Historical Questions concerning Isaiah 36–39

Except for the listing of his name in 1:1, Hezekiah appears by name in the book of Isaiah only in chapters 36–39 though he probably was the target of Isaiah's words in 22:8–11. However, in these four chapters, Hezekiah stands at the center of each account, and much of what he does has direct bearing on what the Lord is doing in Judah.

As we begin our study of Isaiah 36–39, historical questions emerge. What is the chronological order of the events of chapters 36–39? When exactly did King **Hezekiah** reign? When did **Sennacherib** invade Judah? When did the Babylonian delegation visit Hezekiah? And why did Isaiah arrange his material the way he did? Once we answer those questions, we may proceed with our interpretation of the events.

What Do We Know with Certainty from Isaiah 36–39?

To determine the correct chronological order of the events of Isaiah 36–39,

we must begin with the clues found in the biblical text and in extrabiblical material from that time. We must determine what we know with certainty and then move to various hypotheses as we deduce from the sources what is possible.

Bible scholars have long noted that chapters 36–37 follow chapters 38–39 chronologically.[1] Isaiah, then, clearly had a different purpose than to present a timeline of events as they happened. But how do we determine the correct order? Key factors in the determination include the following:

- Sennacherib ruled as king of Assyria from 704 to 681 BC. It seems certain that his siege of Judah and the surrounding area occurred in 701 BC, based on his own royal inscriptions.

- Merodach-Baladan ruled as king of Babylon from 721 to 710 BC and then briefly again in 703 BC prior to being killed.

- Hezekiah ruled as king of Judah either from 727 to 698 BC or from 715 to 686 BC. The former dates are suggested by a synchronism with Hoshea's reign (2 Kgs 18:1), while the latter dates are derived from a synchronism between 2 Kings 18:13, Isaiah 36:1, and Sennacherib's own inscriptions.[2]

- Isaiah 38:6 suggests that Hezekiah's sickness precedes Sennacherib's defeat, but also seems to suggest that the threat of Sennacherib's invasion is imminent.

- Isaiah 39:1 shows that the events of chapter 39 follow the events of chapter 38.

On the basis of this information, we may quickly settle the basic order of events. First, Hezekiah became sick but recovered (38). Second, a delegation from Merodach-Baladan visited Hezekiah (39). Third, Sennacherib invaded Judah, but God brought deliverance (36–37). But how do we harmonize these facts with the question of when Hezekiah reigned?

What Are the Most Likely Interpretations of the Evidence?

What are the most likely interpretations of the evidence? Three have been suggested.[3]

Interpretation 1: Part of Hezekiah's Reign Was a Co-regency

The first possible interpretation suggests that perhaps Hezekiah began ruling with his father Ahaz as part of a co-regency[4] in 727 BC and began ruling on his own in 715 BC. The expression "the fourteenth year of Hezekiah's reign" (2 Kgs 18:13) was calculated from 715 BC, when Hezekiah assumed sole control of the throne, and would thus be 701 BC.

The advantage of this interpretation is that we can harmonize all the data regarding the dates of Hezekiah's reign and Sennacherib's invasion of Judah.

The disadvantages are that (1) it requires an assumption of a co-regency without specific evidence, though we do know Judah's kings often utilized them, (2) it requires 2 Kings 18 to have two different reference points for Hezekiah's reign in the space of a few verses, and (3) it requires the Babylonian delegation's visit in 713–712 BC (Hezekiah was given fifteen years of additional life, 38:5), which many have argued fits better around 703 BC.

Interpretation 2: Hezekiah's "Fourteenth Year" Was Actually His Twenty-fourth

The second possible interpretation involves adding one letter (the letter *mem*) to the Hebrew text of 2 Kings 18:13 and Isaiah 36:1. Doing so would change "fourteenth" to "twenty-fourth." Thus, the biblical text would date Sennacherib's campaign against Judah as beginning around 703 BC, which would designate the time Hezekiah revolted and heard news of Assyrian reprisal,

not the actual time of Sennacherib's arrival.

The advantage of this view is that all the data again may be reconciled, and no co-regency needs to be assumed. The disadvantage is that while the textual emendation is small, no manuscript evidence suggests the twenty-fourth year of Hezekiah was intended in either 2 Kings 18:13 or Isaiah 36:1.

Interpretation 3: Hezekiah Ruled Later than Others Suggest

A third possible interpretation suggests dating Hezekiah's reign to 715–687 BC. This interpretation uses Sennacherib's fixed date of 701 BC as its reference point. As with the second interpretation, no co-regency is necessary.

The advantages of this view are that (1) it synchronizes 2 Kings 18:13, Isaiah 36:1, and Sennacherib's own inscription, and (2) it places the Babylonian delegation's visit around 703 BC, right after Hezekiah received his fifteen-year extension of life. The disadvantage is that it fails to account for the clear statement of 2 Kings 18:1, 9 that Hezekiah's reign overlapped Hoshea's reign.[5]

All three interpretations have their strengths and weaknesses, and the exact chronology of Hezekiah's reign remains difficult to determine. Interpretation 2 appears most likely, though perhaps the appearance of further historical evidence will one day settle the matter.

Why Are the Events Given in This Order?

Why, then, does Isaiah put the events in the order he does? The answer must be that it suited his greater purpose. The first part of the book (chaps. 1–33) focuses on Isaiah's day, when Assyria reigned as the dominant power in the ancient Near East. The second part of the book (chaps. 40–66) looks ahead to a time Babylon ruled the world, but when its reign was coming to an end.

Thus, Isaiah 36–37, with its emphasis on the Lord's defeat of Assyria, con-

Sidebar 11.1
Co-regencies in Israel and Judah

As sidebars 1.2 and 1.3 mentioned, Edwin R. Thiele's pioneering work in reconciling Israelite and Judean chronologies has proven invaluable in the field of Old Testament studies. One of the key aspects to Thiele's approach is recognizing the existence of co-regencies in Israel and Judah. In such cases, the given length of a king's reign may have overlapped with his father or son, and the years of the co-regency were credited to the reign of both kings. In other situations, rival kings may have contended for the throne.

Thiele argued for nine occurrences of co-regencies—three in Israel and six in Judah. Not all of these co-regencies are mentioned specifically in the biblical record, but Thiele believed the evidence warranted them. His approach has much to commend it, and later generations of scholarship have built on his foundation, though not everyone accepts all his conclusions.

Co-regencies and Rival Reigns in Israel and Judah

Israel	
Kings Involved	Reason for Co-regency
Omri and Tibni	Israel divided into two, Omri's side prevails (1 Kgs 16:21–22); Thiele argues that Kings understands Omri's twelve years as including the time of civil war.
Jehoash and Jeroboam II	Threat of imminent war requires Jehoash to establish his son as co-regent in case Jehoash dies in battle (2 Kgs 14:8–13; 2 Chr 25:18–23).
Menahem and Pekahiah	Israel again divided into two nations (Hos 5:5—Hosea's reference to Israel and Ephraim not only here, but elsewhere in the book); Thiele also suggests Pekah overlapped with both Menahem and Pekahiah, eventually becoming Israel's sole ruler.

Judah	
Kings Involved	Reason for Co-regency
Asa and Jehoshaphat	Asa becomes seriously ill, warranting the naming of Jehoshaphat as co-regent (1 Kgs 15:23; 2 Chr 16:12).
Jehoshaphat and Jehoram	Threat of imminent war requires Jehoshaphat to establish his son as co-regent in case Jehoshaphat dies in battle (1 Kgs 22:4, 32–33; 2 Kgs 8:16 specifically notes the co-regency).
Amaziah and Azariah/Uzziah	Amaziah taken prisoner in battle with Israel (2 Kgs 14:8–13, 21; 2 Chr 25:21–24).
Azariah/Uzziah and Jotham	Azariah/Uzziah struck with leprosy and thus needs to be isolated from the common people (2 Kgs 15:5 and 2 Chr 26:21 specifically mention the co-regency).
Jotham and Ahaz	Threat of war with Israel and Syria as Ahaz weighs his options and courts Assyria for protection (2 Kgs 16:7; see also Is 7 and this book's discussion of the Syro-Ephraimite War [735–732 BC]); a careful study of 2 Kings 15:32–16:9 shows that while Jotham was still king, Ahaz had the power due to his link with Assyria.
Hezekiah and Manasseh	Hezekiah becomes ill (2 Kgs 20:1–6; 2 Chr 32:24) and establishes his twelve-year-old son (2 Kgs 21:1) as co-regent; assuming he did so as early as feasible once Isaiah announced Hezekiah's fifteen-year extension of life, Manasseh would have been around twenty-seven when he began to reign by himself.

For more detail, see Edwin R. Thiele, *The Mysterious Numbers of the Hebrew Kings*, 3rd ed. (Grand Rapids: Zondervan, 1983), 61–65.

Lachish

cludes the "Assyrian section" of Isaiah, whereas the events of 38–39—particularly Isaiah's announcement about Hezekiah's descendants serving in Babylon—anticipate the Babylonian exile, as well as the news of release from Babylon that begins in Isaiah 40 and introduces the "Babylonian section" of the book of Isaiah.

Sennacherib's Threat and God's Deliverance (36:1–37:38)

The account of Sennacherib's threat and God's deliverance concludes the "Assyrian section" of the book of Isaiah (see preceding discussion). The text records an amazing and totally unan-

The Gihon Spring, Jerusalem's main source of water and beginning point of Hezekiah's Tunnel (Courtesy of Todd Bolen/ BiblePlaces .com)

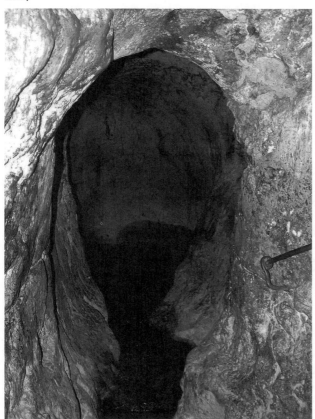

ticipated victory over Sennacherib's army as the Lord intervened on behalf of Judah in response to Hezekiah's prayer.

Sennacherib's Threat (36:1–22)

Sennacherib ascended Assyria's throne in 704 BC after the death of his father Sargon II (721–705 BC). The accession of a new king often provoked revolts of subject peoples, particularly in outlying areas where subduing the revolt would prove more time intensive and costly for a new monarch.

The book of 2 Kings records that Sennacherib's invasion of Judah came in response to Hezekiah's revolt (2 Kgs 18:7). Probably somewhat before this time Hezekiah began preparations for Assyrian reprisal by ordering the construction of a tunnel to divert water from the Gihon Spring, Jerusalem's water supply, to the Pool of Siloam on the city's west side (2 Chr 32:30; see sidebar 11.2). Perhaps Hezekiah was counting on Egyptian support that never came (2 Kgs 18:21). The account also notes Hezekiah's initial capitulation to the king of Assyria (2 Kgs 18:14–16).

Hezekiah sent a delegation to **Lachish**, a strategically located Judean city under Assyrian siege approximately thirty miles to Jerusalem's southwest. Sennacherib's siege of Lachish is well attested in Assyrian sources (see sidebar 11.2). Judah's king promised to bear whatever requirement Sennacherib might impose. Sennacherib required payment of three hundred talents of silver and thirty talents of gold—an amount perhaps exaggerated in Sennacherib's own inscription (see sidebar 11.3)—and Hezekiah immediately began complying.

Isaiah's account does not mention Hezekiah's revolt. The accounts of Kings and Isaiah may easily be reconciled, however, if we assume that as Hezekiah was in the process of gathering the silver and gold Sennacherib had demanded, the king of Assyria changed his mind and decided he wanted more.

145

Sidebar 11.2
The Siloam Inscription

In preparation for the Assyrian siege of Jerusalem, King Hezekiah ordered a tunnel dug from the Gihon Spring to bring its waters into the city of Jerusalem. By doing so, he hoped to secure the city's water supply. The tunnel meanders its way through approximately eight hundred meters of rock and ends at the Pool of Siloam.

Recent archaeological excavations in the region of the tunnel suggest that perhaps the Gihon Spring was already inside an outer wall of Jerusalem at the time Hezekiah ordered the tunnel dug. Perhaps the king feared the Assyrians would breach the outer wall and discover the water source. If this scenario is correct, then Hezekiah no doubt would have ordered the spring concealed, while at the same time being able to take advantage of its ever-flowing water.

Until recent years, the Pool of Siloam was marked by a structure from the Byzantine period. But in June 2004, a crew widening a nearby road inadvertently came across archaeological remains. These remains proved to be the original Pool of Siloam that existed in Jesus's day (Jn 9:7). Water from an aqueduct was actually still trickling into the pool area.

In 1880, an inscription (now known as the Siloam inscription) was discovered in the tunnel near the Pool of Siloam. It describes how the tunnel was dug.

This is the record of how the tunnel was breached.
While the excavators were wielding their pick-axes,
    each man towards his co-worker,
and while there were yet three cubits for the breach,
a voice was heard
    each man calling to his co-worker;
because there was a cavity in the rock extending from the south to the north.

So on the day of the breach,
the excavators struck,
    each man to meet his co-worker,
pick-axe against pick-axe.

Then the water flowed from the spring to the pool,
a distance of one thousand and two hundred cubits.
One hundred cubits was the height of the rock above the heads of the excavators.

Adapted from COS 2:145–46.

An Assyrian delegation came to Jerusalem demanding Hezekiah's surrender, and this is the point at which Isaiah's account begins.

The Setting (36:1–3)

In response to Hezekiah's revolt, Sennacherib invaded Judah and laid siege to Judah's leading cities (see sidebar 11.3). Sennacherib was focusing his personal attention on Lachish along Judah's coast when he sent a delegation to Jerusalem (2 Kgs 18:17). The chief spokesperson of this delegation was the field commander.[6]

The meeting occurred "at the aqueduct of the Upper Pool, on the road to the Washerman's Field" (36:2), the very spot where Isaiah had met Hezekiah's father Ahaz to discuss an earlier threatening military situation (7:3). Ahaz had rejected Isaiah's counsel and appealed to Assyria for assistance. Would Ahaz's

Sidebar 11.3
Sennacherib's Siege of Jerusalem

Among the many discoveries archaeologists have made, some of the most intriguing are the Assyrian and Babylonian royal annals. In them, the kings boast of their accomplishments in ways that often seem somewhat inflated. Among the records of Sennacherib, king of Assyria (704–681 BC), a reference to the king's battle with Hezekiah of Judah has been discovered, an excerpt of which appears below. Note Sennacherib's veiled admission that he did not conquer Jerusalem.

As for Hezekiah, the Judean, I besieged forty-six of his fortified walled cities and surrounding smaller towns, which were without number. Using packed-down ramps and applying battering rams, infantry attacks by mines, breeches, and siege machines, I conquered (them). . . . He himself, I locked up within Jerusalem, his royal city, like a bird in a cage. I surrounded him with earthworks, and made it unthinkable for him to exit by the city gate. His cities which I had despoiled I cut off from his land and gave them to Mitinti, king of Ashdod, Padi, king of Ekron and Ṣilli-bel, king of Gaza.

He, Hezekiah, was overwhelmed by the awesome splendor of my lordship, and he sent me after my departure to Nineveh, my royal city, his elite troops (and) his best soldiers, which he had brought in as reinforcements to strengthen Jerusalem, with 30 talents of gold, 800 talents of silver, choice antimony, large blocks of carnelian, beds (inlaid) with ivory, armchairs (inlaid) with ivory, . . . countless trappings and implements of war, together with his daughters, his palace women, his male and female singers. He (also) dispatched his messenger to deliver the tribute and to do obeisance.

COS 2:303.

son show more faith, or would history repeat itself?

Judah's delegation consisted of Eliakim, who was palace administrator (lit. "over the house"), Shebna the secretary (lit. "scribe"), and Joah the recorder. The Shebna and Eliakim mentioned here are probably the same as those mentioned earlier in the book of Isaiah, which shows Eliakim's assumption of Shebna's earlier duties had already occurred as Isaiah foretold (22:15, 19–21).

The Field Commander's Speech (36:4–22)

The field commander's speech was as much a propaganda campaign as anything else. If intimidation would bring Judah's surrender, all the better.

The field commander challenged the Judeans as he relayed his king's message. Wherein lay their confidence (36:4–7)? How did they hope to prevail against the Assyrian war machine? Would they trust in Egypt, whose reputation for providing false assurances

preceded it? Further, how could they trust in their God when Hezekiah had angered him by removing all his altars and high places? The Assyrians knew the Judeans well. The field commander was trusting that Hezekiah's religious reforms (2 Kgs 18:3–4) had not been received well by the general populace.

The field commander then encouraged surrender (36:8–10). After all, he boasted, the Judeans couldn't hope to win in a show of force, even if Assyria gave them two thousand horses. Finally, he appealed to divine direction—Yahweh himself had sent him.

Again, the Assyrians knew their enemy. They already had taken the northern kingdom, an event the biblical text would blame on Israel's persistent sin (2 Kgs 17:7–18). Perhaps the field commander could convince the Judeans they likewise were facing their own God's judgment.

The Judean delegation asked the field commander to speak in Aramaic instead of in Hebrew to keep their dis-

Entrance to the gate of ancient Lachish. Lachish battled both Sennacherib (701 BC) and Nebuchadnezzar (588/7 BC), eventually losing to both. (Courtesy Todd Bolen/Bible Places.com)

cussions private from common citizens listening from Jerusalem's wall (36:11). But a private conversation was the last thing the field commander desired; his purpose was intimidation. He responded that his message was for all Jerusalem, whose citizens would face horribly disgusting conditions if war ensued (36:12).

The field commander then proclaimed Sennacherib's ultimatum loudly in Hebrew so everyone could hear and understand (36:13–20). He urged the people not to trust in Hezekiah, who could not deliver them. He urged them not to trust in their God either, for no other gods of other nations had delivered them. Notice in particular his haunting question of verse 19: "Have they rescued Samaria from my hand?" Assyria had already conquered another kingdom that trusted in Yahweh (at least originally), and Judah would be next.

Eliakim, Shebna, and Joah returned inside the city and reported to Hezekiah the field commander's words (36:22). Their dejected state was evident by their torn garments; the situation seemed hopeless.

God's Deliverance (37:1–38)

Hezekiah's Initial Response (37:1–7)

Hezekiah's initial response to his delegation differed greatly from the response his father, Ahaz, had shown to Isaiah (7:1–9; 2 Kgs 16:7–10). Isaiah had assured Ahaz of God's deliverance, but Ahaz had refused to believe. At this point, Hezekiah had no assurance of God's deliverance but went to the temple to seek the Lord anyway.

Hezekiah also sought encouragement from Isaiah (37:2–4). The king likened the day to a day on which women in labor could not find the strength to deliver their babies! His graphic description emphasized the straits in which the Judeans found themselves. Hezekiah asked Isaiah to pray for God's intervention on behalf of those remaining in the land.

Isaiah sent a reply to Hezekiah (37:6–7). The king was not to fear, for God had the situation well in hand and knew Sennacherib's blasphemy. Sennacherib would return to his own land, where God would cut him down.

Now Hezekiah had two items to consider: the demonstrated power of Assyria as highlighted by the field commander's speech, and the promise of God's deliverance relayed by the prophet Isaiah. Which would he choose? Which would *you* choose?

Sennacherib's Second Message to Hezekiah (37:8–13)

Meanwhile, Sennacherib received a report that Tirhakah, Egypt's Ethiopian king, was marching against him (37:9). As he prepared to deal with Tirhakah, Sennacherib dispatched messengers to Hezekiah with more threats, lest Judah's king gain encouragement from news of support from Egypt.

The Assyrian messengers reiterated much of what the field commander had said and even took his threats to a new level (37:10–13). The field commander earlier had suggested the Lord God was on Assyria's side (36:7, 10); now the messengers urged the Judeans not to let their God deceive them. The messengers recited an even longer litany of defeated nations and gods. How could the Judeans possibly hope their God would save them?

Hezekiah's Prayer (37:14–20)

Hezekiah's response again revealed the depth of his faith and character. He spread the written ultimatum before the Lord in the temple and prayed fervently (37:14–15). He pleaded with God to give ear to all of Sennacherib's insults. Of course Sennacherib had defeated the gods of other nations—they were but wood and stone (37:18–19)! Hezekiah asked God to deliver Judah that all the earth might see the power of Judah's God. The king's prayer again indicates the sharp spiritual distinction between him and his father, Ahaz.

God's Prophecy through Isaiah (37:21–35)

The prophet Isaiah brought God's response to Judah's king. God had a message of his own for Sennacherib. In his arrogance, Assyria's king had not challenged Judah as much as he had challenged Judah's God, the Holy One of Israel (37:23). The battle had shifted to a whole new level; Yahweh's honor was now at stake, and he would intervene on behalf of his people.

Isaiah announced that God had made the Assyrian kingdom what it was (37:24–26). The prophet simulated the proud boasts Sennacherib and other Assyrian rulers before him had made, but each of them was only fulfilling God's plan for them. He knew their every move, and the time for their judgment had come. He would turn Sennacherib around and drive him back to Assyria (37:28–29).

How would Judah know this would happen? Isaiah promised his people a sign: by the third year, agriculture would return to normal (37:30–31). God's zeal would provide his remnant a display of his glory, and they would reap the benefit (37:32). Threats from Assyria would disappear.

God was determined to defend Jerusalem for David's sake (37:35). He had not forgotten his promise that if David's descendants were faithful, they would never lack a man on the throne (2 Sm 7:11–16; 1 Kgs 2:4). Hezekiah had placed his faith in the Lord when it really counted, and the Lord responded with a promise of deliverance.

God Fulfills His Word (37:36–38)

God fulfilled his promise of deliverance. The Lord's angel struck down the Assyrian camp, and Sennacherib and what was left of his army retreated to Assyria, receiving no more than what Hezekiah already had given him (2 Kgs 18:14–16). His royal inscription (see sidebar 11.3) boasted of shutting up Hezekiah "like a bird in a cage," conveniently omitting the fact that he was unable to capture the caged bird! About twenty years later, his sons murdered him, and his son Esarhaddon (680–668 BC) became Assyria's next king (37:38).

Manasseh

Hezekiah's Illness and Recovery (38:1–22)

Assuming our interpretation regarding the chronology of Hezekiah's reign is correct (see the discussion earlier in this chapter), Hezekiah probably became ill around 713–712 BC. Based on the fact that the king received a fifteen-year extension of life (38:5), one can count backward from 698 BC to arrive at the approximate time.

Isaiah Announces Hezekiah's Impending Death (38:1)

Hezekiah became seriously ill, and the message Isaiah brought him also was serious (38:1). Hezekiah was to set his estate in order so as to ensure a smooth transition of the monarchy, for his illness would end his life.

Hezekiah Prays to the Lord (38:2–3)

Hezekiah prayed fervently to his God. He asked him to remember his acts of faithfulness and loyalty and wept at the thought of his life ending. Hezekiah had no assurance God would even respond, since the prophet's announcement had not suggested his words were conditional.

Isaiah's Reply to Hezekiah (38:4–8)

Isaiah brought God's reply to Hezekiah. The Lord indeed had heard his prayer, seen his tears, and remembered his father David. He would add fifteen years to Hezekiah's life. The Lord also promised deliverance from Assyria, which had conquered the northern kingdom ten years earlier.

Isaiah even offered Hezekiah a sign that God would fulfill his word. He would cause the shadow on the stairway, which normally would lengthen as evening approached, to get shorter. Again, the contrast with Ahaz, Hezekiah's father, is clear. Ahaz refused to ask for a sign (7:12), but God gave his faithful king a sign before the king even asked.

Hezekiah's fifteen-year extension of life gave him the opportunity to exercise more faith when Sennacherib came against him a little more than ten years later. This great miracle would not have occurred if God had not spared Hezekiah's life. God had great plans for Judah's king.

Second Kings 21:1 records that **Manasseh**, Hezekiah's successor, was twelve years old when he began to reign. This means one of two things: (1) Manasseh was born during his father's fifteen-year extension of life. If this were the case, one of Judah's most evil kings would not have been born, and another of Hezekiah's descendants would have succeeded him instead. (2) Manasseh's reign began as a co-regency with his father from 696–686 BC.[7] In this case, Manasseh would have been in his early twenties when he assumed sole control of Judah's throne. Yet, in the providence and grace of God, Manasseh, despite his wickedness, would become part of the line of Jesus (Mt 1:10).

Hezekiah's "Psalm" (38:9–20)

Hezekiah wrote poetic verses after his recovery, and Isaiah included them in his account. The verses can be divided into two major sections. In the first section (38:9–15), Hezekiah described his anguish over the Lord's decree that he would die. In the second section (38:16–20), Hezekiah reflected on the grace God had extended to him and the lessons he had learned through his anguish.

Hezekiah Describes His Anguish (38:9–15)

Verses 10 and 11 both begin with the words "I said." In poetic verse, these words often introduce thoughts and feelings the writer had that turned out to be wrong (49:4a; Ps 30:6; Eccl 2:1; 7:23). Hezekiah recalled the painful thoughts his mind entertained prior to God's reprieve. He wrestled with the brevity of life but in the end resigned himself humbly to God's purpose (38:12–15).

Hezekiah Reflects on Lessons Learned (38:16–20)

Hezekiah then reflected on the lessons he had learned through his encounter with the Lord through Isaiah. The Lord had restored him (38:16), and somehow Hezekiah knew the initial judgment and reprieve would benefit him during his next fifteen years (38:17). He had new opportunity to testify to Yahweh's faithfulness (38:19) and pledged himself to a life filled with worship in God's temple (38:20).

Notes on Hezekiah's Recovery (38:21–22)

The details of verses 21–22 logically belong between verses 6 and 7 (cf. 2 Kgs 20:7–8), but for some unknown reason they appear here as final details of the account. Hezekiah's illness involved the swelling of a large boil, and when Isaiah told the king he would recover, the king asked for a sign, which Isaiah then assured him the Lord would provide.

Hezekiah's Visit with a Babylonian Delegation (39:1–8)

An old proverb says, "The enemy of my enemy is my friend." In Isaiah 39, this principle played itself out again as Babylon sought an alliance with Judah against Assyria.

Merodach-Baladan's Messengers Visit Hezekiah (39:1–2)

Merodach-Baladan's Initiative (39:1)

Sometime after Hezekiah recovered from his illness, a Babylonian delegation arrived in Jerusalem bearing letters and a gift for Judah's king. The delegation was sent by **Merodach-Baladan II**, king of Babylon.[8]

Merodach-Baladan ruled as king of Babylon from 721 to 710 BC and again in 703 BC. During the late eighth century BC, Babylon attempted to assert its independence when it perceived Assyrian weakness. Sargon II (721–705 BC) was able to subdue Babylon, and Merodach-Baladan fled into exile in Elam. When Sennacherib came to power, however, Merodach-Baladan returned and reestablished himself as Babylon's king in 703 BC. Assyrian forces finally scuttled Babylonian resistance, and Merodach-Baladan fled to Elam, where he subsequently died.

Merodach-Baladan's delegation clearly seems to have visited Hezekiah in hope of forming an alliance against Assyria. Of course, Judah's ultimate deliverance lay not in alliances but in trusting the Lord (30:1–2; 31:1).

Hezekiah's Foolish Response (39:2)

Hezekiah "received the envoys gladly" (lit. "rejoiced concerning them"). Perhaps his opinion of himself jumped a notch or two as he pondered that Babylon had actually contacted him for an audience. Hezekiah consequently set his heart on impressing his guests.

Hezekiah was pleased, and showed them everything that might impress them: silver, gold, spices, oil, weapons, and more. The last sentence of verse 2 suggests that perhaps Hezekiah's "tour" included even more than this—possibly showing the delegation everything it would ever wish to see. The delegation would leave with a thorough knowledge of Judah and its royal house.

Isaiah Speaks with Hezekiah (39:3–8)

Isaiah probably had already uttered some of his prophetic words against foreign alliances (30:1–2; 31:1). The prophet confronted the king, who admitted the delegation from Babylon had seen virtually everything he possessed (39:3–4).

Nebuchadnez-
zar II

Isaiah then shared with the king the Lord's message (39:5–7). Someday Babylon would become the dominant world power, and when it did, it would remember all the "goodies" back in Judah. The Babylonians would return, and some of Hezekiah's own descendants would pay the price of exile to Babylon.

Isaiah's response rang true with Hezekiah (39:8). In a moment of pride, he had shown a potential conqueror his assets and shared many of his secrets. His response could be construed as a somewhat selfish comment: "At least there will be peace in *my* day!" More likely, however, Hezekiah appreciated God's grace. The king's proud act of folly might have cost him his kingdom, but God would delay the Babylonian conquest for over a century.

Concluding Thoughts from Isaiah 36–39

Isaiah 36–39 ends with a look toward Babylon. Sennacherib's defeat in chapters 36–37 provided a foretaste of Assyria's coming doom. The Assyrians only exercised the power the Lord gave them, and when he determined they were finished, they were indeed finished. The great power of Isaiah's day was going down for good.

In that day, another power—Babylon—would rise to supremacy. Under their king **Nebuchadnezzar II** (605–562 BC), the Babylonians would expand their empire, and the Judeans would have to face the same questions they had faced during the heyday of Assyria's empire. Should they fight the Babylonians? Should they make peace with them? Should they form an alliance against Babylon with Egypt and/or other nations? Or should they trust in the Lord their God and serve him faithfully? The books of Kings and Jeremiah reveal that Judah made the wrong choices, which eventually led to ruin and exile.

Isaiah 39, with its account of the Babylonian delegation and Hezekiah's blunder, sets the stage for what comes next in the book of Isaiah. Judah's exile to Babylon would come, but it also would end, and God's people would come home again. Isaiah 40–66 announces a day when Judah would return and God would bless his people beyond their wildest expectations.

Study Questions

1. Put the events of Isaiah 36–39 in proper chronological order. What questions remain? What solution do you think best accounts for the evidence? Why?

2. Summarize the key issues surrounding Sennacherib's invasion and defeat.

3. Explain Hezekiah's failure with the Babylonian delegation (39:1–8).

4. What is the role Isaiah 36–39 plays within the book of Isaiah as a whole?

12 Introduction to Isaiah 40–66

Outline

- **Authorship and Date Issues**
  The Multiple Authorship View: Summary and Evidence
  The Single Authorship View: Summary and Evidence
  Authorship and Date Summary
- **Themes of Isaiah 40–66**
  God's People Are in Captivity because of Their Sins
  The Captivity Proves God Is God, because He Predicted It
  God Now Will Redeem His People—Through Cyrus and in Other Ways

Objectives

After reading this chapter, you should be able to

1. Summarize the arguments for the multiple authorship view of the book of Isaiah.
2. Summarize the arguments for the single authorship view of the book of Isaiah.
3. Articulate the three main themes of Isaiah 40–66.

Isaiah 40 begins abruptly, with its herald command, "Comfort, comfort my people," signaling the beginning of something new and exciting. Judah is coming home! God will redeem his people and establish his kingdom. Joy and celebration will replace despair and sadness.

Indeed, we have turned a significant literary corner as we begin Isaiah 40–66. Gone is the threat of Assyria; instead, the prophetic word ushers the people home from Babylon. Promises of judgment comprise a seemingly distant memory as promises of hope and renewal gush forth. The focus shifts largely to the future and the exciting things the prophet expects God to do after the Babylonian exile.

In the last two centuries, some scholars who have noted these and other differences between Isaiah 1–39 and 40–66 have suggested someone besides the prophet Isaiah wrote chapters 40–66. Other scholars have contended that despite the book's two major sections, Isaiah is nonetheless responsible for all sixty-six chapters.

This chapter will survey the basic arguments for multiple authorship and single authorship of the book of Isaiah. We will then conclude with a summary of the basic themes in Isaiah 40–66.

Authorship and Date Issues

The issues of authorship and date are linked in the discussion of Isaiah 40–66.[1] Simply stated, if Isaiah wrote chapters 40–66, then they originated in the late eighth or early seventh century BC. If he did not, then the door is open to suggesting a date sometime in the sixth century BC. In fact, some scholars have argued that parts of Isaiah 40–66 were written even later.[2]

Historically, the issue of authorship was a battle between those who held a high view of Scripture and those who did not. However, in recent years, some

evangelicals have also adopted the view that more than one author contributed to what we now know as the book of Isaiah.[3] Arguments for both positions appear below.

The Multiple Authorship View: Summary and Evidence

Those who argue for multiple authorship of Isaiah generally agree that Isaiah 40–66 comes from the later sixth century BC. The prophecies largely reflect the period immediately following the Judeans' release from captivity and return home to reestablish themselves in Judah. Some point to a future time.

Scholars have long used the name "Deutero-Isaiah" (i.e., "Second Isaiah") to denote the author of Isaiah 40–66. They believe he lived in the exciting days following Cyrus's decree that allowed the Jews to return to Judah. He saw the hand of God in the events of his day and proclaimed encouragement and salvation to God's people.

Some scholars have noted a further shift in prophetic tone and emphasis on the final establishment of God's universal kingdom toward the end of the book of Isaiah. For that reason, they have suggested Deutero-Isaiah wrote Isaiah 40–55, and a third author—"Trito-Isaiah"—was responsible for chapters 56–66.

Yet another variation of the multiple authorship view sees the names "Deutero-Isaiah" and "Trito-Isaiah" as designating not individuals but rather schools of disciples who continued in the spirit of their eighth-century-BC predecessor, Isaiah of Jerusalem (see sidebar 12.1). They did not merely record Isaiah's words but "continued" or "expanded" his prophetic ministry through their own words and writings. These writings consequently became attached to the prophecies of Isaiah.

Proponents of the multiple authorship view—whatever their particular convictions about the nature of Deutero-Isaiah and/or Trito-Isaiah—generally argue their position based on four factors. These factors include the

Sidebar 12.1
Authorship of Isaiah Issues

The following table summarizes the essence of the authorship of Isaiah 40–66 issue in terms of section divisions, authorship, and date. Naturally, views of individual scholars may vary slightly.

	One Isaiah	Deutero-Isaiah	Trito-Isaiah
Section Divisions	None (unity)	Chaps. 1–39 Chaps. 40–66	Chaps. 1–39 Chaps. 40–55 Chaps. 56–66
Author(s)	Isaiah of Jerusalem (i.e., the prophet Isaiah); may have been collected and/or edited by a disciple.	Chaps. 1–39: Isaiah of Jerusalem. Chaps. 40–66: Deutero-Isaiah, an anonymous prophet, perhaps a disciple of Isaiah's, or perhaps a modern name for a school of disciples.	Chaps. 1–39: Isaiah of Jerusalem. Chaps. 40–55: Deutero-Isaiah, an anonymous prophet, perhaps a disciple of Isaiah's. Chaps. 56–66: Trito-Isaiah, another anonymous prophet, perhaps a disciple of Isaiah's or of Deutero-Isaiah's, or perhaps a modern name for a school of disciples.
Date of Composition	Early seventh century BC	Late sixth century BC, at the time of Persia's rise to power.	Late sixth century BC, perhaps early fifth century BC.

For a thorough discussion of the evidence on all sides, including discussion of authorship, structure, and content, see John N. Oswalt, *The Book of Isaiah: Chapters 1–39*, New International Commentary on the Old Testament (Grand Rapids: Eerdmans, 1986), 3–60; and idem., *The Book of Isaiah: Chapters 40–66*, New International Commentary on the Old Testament (Grand Rapids: Eerdmans, 1998), 3–16.

time span of the book, different subject matter, different vocabulary and style, and the mention of Cyrus by name.

The Time Span of the Book

The historical setting of Isaiah 1–39 is primarily the eighth century BC, during the time of Isaiah's prophetic ministry (740–690 BC). Much of Isaiah 40–66, however—especially chapters 40–48—focuses on the period following King Cyrus of Persia's conquest of Babylon in 539 BC. Thus, the prophet begins his ministry around 740 BC, but the book also describes events and conditions that occurred two hundred years later. From a purely naturalistic perspective, a second author seems necessary.

The Different Subject Matter of 1–39 and 40–66

Proponents of the multiple authorship view also point out the presence of significant differences in chapters 1–39 and 40–66. Indeed, clear differences do exist. In chapters 1–39, the focus is on Assyria, the dominant power in the ancient Near East, and the judgment God will bring on his people and the world. Some messianic prophecies and other encouraging words are present, but all in all, the focus is Assyria and judgment.

In chapters 40–66, however, the focus is rescue and return from Babylon. The tone is uplifting and encouraging, and the primary issue is the redemption and salvation God is bringing his people, who are coming home. Stark differences such as these in subject matter suggest multiple authors.

The Different Vocabulary and Style of 1–39 and 40–66

Proponents of the multiple authorship view also note the significant differences in the vocabulary and style of chapters 1–39 and 40–66. Indeed, an analysis of the text confirms that the vocabulary is quite different. Common words of judgment (e.g., "woe," "judgment," "desolation") occur often in chapters 1–39, but infrequently in 40–66. On the other hand, uplifting words such as "cry aloud," "sing for joy," and "rejoice" occur often in chapters 40–66, but rarely in 1–39.

Scholars have also noted differences in writing style between chapters 1–39 and 40–66. The first part of the book features historical narrative: Isaiah's dialogue with Ahaz (7:4–17), Isaiah walking about naked and barefoot (20:1–6), Isaiah's dialogues with Hezekiah (37:1–7, 21–35; 38:1–8, 21–22; 39:3–8), and Sennacherib's invasion (chaps. 36–37). Isaiah 40–66, on the other hand, consists exclusively of poetic prophecy. Further, scholars of biblical Hebrew have suggested the poetry in 40–66 comprises some of the most beautiful in all the Old Testament and stands in contrast with the "lesser poetry" of the first thirty-nine chapters.

The Mention of King Cyrus by Name

Those who hold the multiple authorship view also point to the book's mention of King Cyrus of Persia by name. In 539 BC, Cyrus conquered Babylon. Isaiah 41:2–4, 25 alludes to a conqueror who serves as God's instrument, but Isaiah 44:28 and 45:1 mention Cyrus by name. In fact, Cyrus is designated God's shepherd and anointed one. The specific mention of the king's name suggests the prophet was prophesying at a time when the identity of Babylon's conqueror had become clear.

The Single Authorship View: Summary and Evidence

Despite this evidence, many evangelicals continue to maintain the single authorship view of the book. Some of their arguments are aimed at refuting those of the proponents of the multiple authorship view, while other arguments stand on their own to support the single authorship view.

Time Span of the Book Explained by Predictive Prophecy

Proponents of the single authorship view have argued that the time span the book covers (two hundred plus years) may be accounted for by the phenomenon of predictive prophecy. If God knows the future and can communicate it to his prophets, then Isaiah may well have spoken during his lifetime of events such as the return from Babylon that would not occur for some time. Only in a closed system—that is, one that does not allow for either God's existence or his ability to communicate with people—are multiple authors absolutely required.

Predictive prophecy also resolves questions such as the placing of Isaiah 13–14's judgment against Babylon first in the "Oracles against the Nation" section (chaps. 13–23; see earlier discussion). Isaiah placed Babylon first in the list because he knew on the basis of divine revelation that Babylon, not Assyria, would ultimately pose a larger threat to Judah.[4]

The Different Subject Matter of 1–39 and 40–66

Proponents of single authorship concede that the subject matter of chapters 1–39 and 40–66 is quite different. They argue, however, that one author is capable of writing on different subjects. For example, today's college students are capable of writing research papers on a biblical text, but also short essays on church history, European civilization, and more. They also may communicate with friends and family about other subjects. Those who maintain single authorship of the book of Isaiah merely want to allow Isaiah the same ability to write on different subjects.

The Different Vocabulary and Style of 1–39 and 40–66

Arguing for multiple authorship on the basis of different vocabulary and style falls victim to the same criticisms as arguing on the basis of different subject matter. Again, students' term papers and essay answers to test questions often use significantly different vocabulary and extraordinarily different style than emails to their friends on other college campuses. Professors write course materials, minutes of meetings, and personal correspondence, all of which use different vocabulary and style. Most of us typically use many different styles of writing depending on our purpose and audience, and our subject matter shapes our vocabulary. Different vocabulary and style can hardly rule out single authorship.

The Mention of King Cyrus by Name

Proponents of single authorship concede that the mention of a person by name is highly unusual in prophecy but offer two possible explanations. First, in 1 Kings 13:2, the same phenomenon occurs. An unnamed man of God prophesied King Josiah's coming and mentioned him by name, so such an event is not without precedent.

Second, some have suggested perhaps a scribe added Cyrus's name in 44:28 and 45:1 in the sixth century BC, when his identity became clear. Such action is known as a scribal gloss, and we know from textual evidence that sometimes glosses occurred during the process of textual transmission. However, there is no textual evidence to support such an argument for either 44:28 or 45:1. All Isaiah manuscripts have Cyrus's name in both verses.

Isaiah 36–39 and 2 Kings 18–20

The earlier discussion of Isaiah 36–39 presented evidence that chapters 38–39 chronologically precede chapters 36–37. However, chapters 36–37 conclude the Assyrian section of the book with the account of Sennacherib's defeat, whereas chapters 38–39 introduce the Babylonian section of the book with the account of Hezekiah entertaining the Babylonian delegation.

Such a literary rearrangement only makes sense, however, if the author knew that the Babylonian section of Isaiah (chaps. 40–66) was to be attached. Thus, it seems reasonable that whoever added chapters 40–66 must also be responsible for switching the order of chapters 36–37 and 38–39.

Interestingly, 2 Kings 18–20 presents the material in the same order as Isaiah 36–39, even though 2 Kings generally presents material in chronological order. This suggests that the writer of 2 Kings knew of Isaiah 36–39 and probably used it as one of his sources when compiling the books of Kings.

If scholars are right in dating the completion of the books of Kings to around 560 BC or shortly thereafter, then the book of Isaiah must have contained chapters 40–66 before then.[5] Such evidence does not require an eighth-century-BC date, but it does seem to negate the possibility of a later sixth-century-BC date.

Textual Evidence for Single Authorship

Proponents of single authorship also point out the lack of any evidence that the two sections of Isaiah ever existed separately. Granted, not as many Old Testament manuscripts exist as do New Testament manuscripts. Nonetheless, no Isaiah scroll has ever been discovered and no textual evidence has ever suggested a break occurs after chapter 39 and then chapter 40 starts anew. The famous Isaiah scroll, discovered at Qumran and now located in the Israel Museum, shows no such break between chapters 39–40.

New Testament Evidence

Proponents of single authorship also point to the New Testament use of the book of Isaiah. The New Testament writers cite or allude to different parts of Isaiah, attributing it all to the eighth-century-BC prophet.

Sometimes in quoting Isaiah, the New Testament writer prefaces his quotation with a phrase such as "as it says in Isaiah." Such instances might be understood as "in what we call 'the book of Isaiah.'" In such cases, the writer's

Qumran Cave 4, where many of the Dead Sea Scrolls were discovered. The Isaiah scroll contains the complete text of Isaiah, with no break between chapters 39 and 40. (Courtesy of Chris Miller)

purpose may not have been to ascribe authorship.

However, in other passages, the New Testament writers make the statement "Isaiah prophesied." In such instances, the link between author and book are stronger. Sidebar 12.2 highlights key usages of Isaiah's material by the New Testament writers, particularly as they bear on the question of Isaianic authorship.

The Mysterious Disappearance of Deutero-Isaiah

Proponents of single authorship grant the beauty of the Hebrew poetry of Isaiah 40–66. Indeed, it stands out among all the prophetic material. While some believe it odd to have two such different writing styles in the book of Isaiah, others argue it seems stranger still that such a gifted prophet-writer would vanish from the pages of history, his only legacy that of being known as "Deutero-Isaiah" and attached to a prophet of lesser writing skill.

Such superior writing would seem to demand a separate work if it came from a different author. But if all sixty-six chapters come from the eighth-century-BC prophet, no problem exists, and the joining of the material would be quite expected.

Authorship and Date Summary

To some extent, the question of single or multiple authorship hinges at least partly on whether one allows for the existence of a God who knows the future and who can communicate it to his servants the prophets. If the prophet is merely speaking his own mind, it is highly unlikely he will consistently prophesy factual material about the future. On the other hand, if prophets such as Isaiah did receive revelation from an all-knowing God, it was quite possible for them to speak with authority on future matters.

Those scholars who presume either (1) that there is no God, or (2) that if he exists, he does not communicate with people so specifically, naturally must presume a second or third author. For scholars who accept or allow the possibility of the existence of God and his direct work in human lives, the authorship question focuses primarily on the mention of Cyrus and whether God chooses to reveal his will that specifically to people.

A hard look at all the evidence suggests the single authorship view has much to commend it. God revealed aspects of the return from Babylon to his eighth-century-BC prophet, who recorded them for his generation and future generations. One author certainly can write in different styles and use different vocabulary, and textual evidence, the witness of the New Testament, and other factors appear to support this position.

Herbert Wolf,[6] while arguing for single authorship, suggests the terms "First Isaiah" and "Second Isaiah" might be used in much the same way as we refer to "First Timothy" and "Second Timothy." That is, the two are almost separate works (as 1 and 2 Tm are), and the terminology provides a useful distinction. Wolf's suggestion appears useful as long as those who hear the terms are clear on the speaker's intent.

Themes of Isaiah 40–66

Isaiah 40–66 focuses primarily on three themes. The first two appear more commonly in the earlier chapters, while the third appears throughout. The three themes are as follows: (1) God's people are in captivity because of their sins;

Sidebar 12.2
Isaiah and the New Testament: "What Was Spoken through the Prophet Isaiah"

The following chart shows a list of Isaianic quotations in the New Testament that appear to support a single authorship view by the New Testament writers. They do so in that they specifically mention Isaiah as speaking the words some scholars attribute to Deutero-Isaiah or Trito-Isaiah. Matthew, Luke, John, and Paul all cite material from Isaiah 40–66.

New Testament Reference	Isaiah Reference	Key Wording/Support
Matthew 3:3	40:3	(Describing John the Baptist) "This is he who was spoken of through the prophet Isaiah."
Matthew 8:17	53:4	(Describing Jesus's works of healing) "This was to fulfill what was spoken through the prophet Isaiah."
Matthew 12:17–21	42:1–4	(Describing Jesus's healing people and instructing them not to make him known) "This was to fulfill what was spoken through the prophet Isaiah" (Mt 12:17).
Luke 3:4–6	40:3–5	(Describing John the Baptist) "As is written in the book of the words of Isaiah the prophet" (Lk 3:3).
John 12:38	53:1	(Describing the unbelief of many in spite of witnessing Jesus's miracles) "This was to fulfill the word of Isaiah the prophet."
Romans 10:20–21	65:1–2	"And Isaiah boldly says" (regarding Israel's current state of unbelief as Paul writes).

See sidebar 21.1 for a more comprehensive list of Isaianic citations in the New Testament.

(2) the captivity proves God is God, because he predicted it; (3) God will now redeem his people—through Cyrus and in other ways.

God's People Are in Captivity because of Their Sins

Chapter 40 begins with the announcement that God is preparing a way for his coming glory and leading his people home. Why is this necessary? Because God's people are in captivity for their sins. They have received from the Lord punishment for their wickedness (40:2). The time has now come to judge other nations instead (43:3–4). Indeed, God was angry with his people and forsook them for a time (47:6; 54:7–8). The captivity was sin's sad consequence, and many prophets had predicted it.

The Captivity Proves God Is God, because He Predicted It

The captivity of God's people was not in any way the defeat of God. Rather, it *proved* he is God, because he predicted it. He had spoken over many generations, beginning with Moses (Lv 26:27–39; Dt 28:49–63) and later with the prophets (Am 2:4–5; Mi 3:12; Hb 1:5–11), of the awful judgments he would bring if his people refused to follow his covenant faithfully. The exile simply demonstrated God's power to make good on the terms of the covenant.

Key Terms

Deutero-Isaiah

Trito-Isaiah

Other gods, however, had no reason to boast. Isaiah challenged foreign gods to predict the future (or do anything) as a demonstration of their power, but there came only silence (41:21–29). Idols had no power to do what God could do, for they were the product of human hands (44:9–20). Even the gods of mighty Babylon would be proven powerless (46:1–2).

God Now Will Redeem His People—Through Cyrus and in Other Ways

Isaiah 40–66 announces that the time had come for God to redeem his people. He would lead them gently with his arms; he would carry them; he would sustain them (40:10–11). He would gather them from the nations and bring them back to Judah. God called King Cyrus as his instrument, his shepherd, his anointed one, to bring his people back to their land and establish them again (41:2–4; 44:28; 45:1).

The book of Ezra provides further details of those first days back in their land and the external and internal challenges God's people faced. Certainly those were exciting days for those who witnessed the reestablishment of Jerusalem and its temple.

However, Isaiah 40–66 takes the concept of redemption even further. The prophet had spoken earlier of a day of peace, a day of restoration that would bring blessing not only to the Jewish people but to all nations (2:1–4; 11:1–16).

In Isaiah 40–66, this concept moves to center stage. Isaiah's God calls the ends of the earth to turn to him for sal-

---

Study Questions

1. What are the main arguments that support the multiple authorship view of the book of Isaiah?

2. What are the main arguments that support the single authorship view of the book of Isaiah?

3. What are the three major themes of Isaiah 40–66?

---

vation (45:22–23). His servant will bring justice to the nations (42:3–4) but will also intercede for their sins (53:4–6). His messengers will proclaim his glory among all nations before the end comes, and God and his people will endure forever (66:19–23).

As you study Isaiah 40–66, keep these three themes in mind, for they appear again and again.

13 God's People Are Coming Home!

Isaiah 40:1–31

Outline

- **God Will Lead His People Home (40:1–11)**
  Comfort, Comfort My People (40:1–2)
  God Will Show His Glory (40:3–8)
  God's Coming Will Be Amazing (40:9–11)
- **Description of God's Wisdom and Power (40:12–31)**
  God Is a Wise Creator (40:12–17)
  God Is beyond Comparison (40:18–20)
  God Is the Sovereign (40:21–26)
  God Is Israel's Source of Strength (40:27–31)
- **Conclusion**

Objectives

After reading this chapter, you should be able to

1. Identify the two major sections of Isaiah 40.
2. Explain the relationship of Isaiah 40 to Isaiah 41–66.
3. Discuss how Isaiah affirms God as Israel's souce of strength.

Have you ever wished you could start over? Maybe you didn't apply yourself during the first part of a college course, and now you wish you had worked harder and received a higher grade. Perhaps a relationship began in the wrong way, and now you're having trouble smoothing things out. Maybe your team played poorly in the first part of the game, and catching up later was hopeless. Perhaps you wish you could take back angry words you spoke to someone.

In Isaiah 40, the prophet announced that God was giving his people a chance to start over. They had experienced the pain of exile and they had received the sad consequences of their sin, but God in his grace would give them another chance, just as he does with people today who seek his grace.

Isaiah 40 comprises an introduction to the rest of the book of Isaiah. The chapter can be divided into two major sections: verses 1–11 and verses 12–31. In the first section, Isaiah announces the great news: God will lead his people home. In the second section, Isaiah proclaims God's sovereignty and his power to bring his people home, to make good on what he promised in verses 1–11.

God Will Lead His People Home (40:1–11)

God's bringing his people home included three aspects. First, God would comfort his people. Second, he would show them his glory. Third, he would amaze them by his coming.

Comfort, Comfort My People (40:1–2)

The words "comfort, comfort" comprise a double imperative; the repetition emphasizes the urgency of the command (cf. "holy, holy, holy," 6:3; "perfect peace" [*shalom, shalom*], 26:3). The imperatives

are in the plural, which some scholars have suggested indicates God is calling to his heavenly court.[1] Probably, however, the prophet is merely announcing the command to everyone in a position to comfort God's people, perhaps prophets, priests, and other leaders.[2]

The expression translated "speak tenderly" (40:2) literally reads "speak to the heart" and occurs elsewhere to denote gentle, caring words (Ru 2:13; Hos 2:14). Jerusalem's hard service was over, its sin atoned for. "Double" may more have the sense of complete and total payment than of exactly double retribution.[3] The time for God's redemption had come.

God Will Show His Glory (40:3–8)

God would show his glory by preparing a way for his people. Some would struggle to believe, but God would encourage their hearts.

He Will Prepare a Way (40:3–5)

A voice called out the news; the language is reminiscent of Isaiah's temple vision (6:3–4). We should understand the commands to prepare the Lord's way "in the desert" and make a straight highway "in the wilderness" in light of the topography of the Judean wilderness.

Rugged hills and valleys extend from Jerusalem down to Jericho and the Jordan Valley. Jerusalem, at an elevation of approximately 2,500 feet, sits about 3,100 feet above the valley, which actually lies below sea level. Thus, the journey from Jericho to Jerusalem involved over fifteen miles of uphill walking.

Consequently, the leveling of the area's hills and valleys into a plain would be a truly incredible blessing. But even more than that, God would reveal his glory in such a way that all would see it. They could count on it, for he had spoken (40:5; cf. 24:3; 25:8).

Generations later, the ministry of **John the Baptist** fulfilled Isaiah's words (Mt 3:3; Mk 1:3; Lk 3:4–6; Jn 1:23). John

The Wadi Qilt's rugged terrain makes Isaiah's words of 40:3–5 all the more amazing. (Courtesy of Bryan E. Beyer)

preached a baptism of repentance in the Judean wilderness, the very area Isaiah described, and as John carried out his ministry, he prepared the way for the ultimate revelation of God's kingdom in Jesus of Nazareth.

He Will Encourage the Discouraged (40:6–8)

The scene now shifts from the heavenly realm to the earthly realm, from what God will do to how humanity responds. An unnamed listener receives God's command to "cry out" but responds dejectedly (40:6–7). How can mere people be expected to accomplish anything when they're like grass in comparison to God's majesty? Even the *thought* of leveling the Judean wilderness would be exhausting to many.

Perhaps the weight of exile also contributed to the feelings of dejection. Seventy years was a long time to wait, and it was ample time to become discouraged, even despairing. Indeed, during the exile, false prophets arose and stirred up false hope (Jer 28:1–4; 29:8–9). When the fulfillment of Isaiah's words came, how would the people know this really was the time to go home? And even so, their feeble human strength could never accomplish such an arduous task.

Isaiah again used images from the Judean wilderness. The hills display a lovely green richness in winter when the rains come, but when the eastern desert winds arrive in early spring, the vegetation dies and disappears within a matter of days. Such was the people's strength.

Nevertheless, the prophet assured the people all was well (40:8). They could count on God's word. He had said it, and everything would happen just as he said. He had kept his word of judgment, and he would keep his word of salvation.

God's Coming Will Be Amazing (40:9–11)

Isaiah then called on Zion to take the lead in announcing the exciting news to Judah's towns and villages (40:9). People formerly received news reports that began in Jerusalem, the capital, so it made sense for the same to happen now.

The words "Do not fear!" occur commonly over the next several chapters as the prophet used them to encourage his people. They could count on their God. They could count on his promises. Isaiah described the sovereign God as coming in power, ready to dispense reward and recompense as appropriate (40:10). Many struggled to believe it, but God *would* make it happen.

Isaiah also described the Lord as a shepherd (40:11). The images of carrying lambs and gently leading nursing ewes highlight the loving and tender care God extends to his own. A good shepherd knew his flock well and gave each animal the care it needed. So it would be with Judah's heavenly shepherd.

Thus, in verses 1–11, Isaiah announced comfort to God's people, described God's glory, and proclaimed both God's amazing power and his loving care as he tenderly nurtured them. But could God really do all of that? Some people struggled to believe because they needed a more comprehensive view of God. Isaiah would now provide that view.

Description of God's Wisdom and Power (40:12–31)

In verses 12–31, Isaiah provided his people a broader view of God by describing his wisdom and power. God was the wise creator, the incomparable one, the sovereign, and the source of Israel's strength. God was indeed powerful enough to bring his people home.

God Is a Wise Creator (40:12–17)

Ten Rhetorical Questions Make the Point (40:12–14)

Isaiah drove home his point with ten related rhetorical questions:

1. Who has measured the waters in the hollow of his hand?
2. Who marked off the heavens with the breadth of his hand?
3. Who has held the dust of the earth in a basket?
4. Who has weighed the mountains on the scales and the hills in a balance?
5. Who has understood the mind of the Lord?
6. Who instructed the Lord as his counselor?
7. Whom did the Lord consult to enlighten him?
8. Who taught the Lord the right way?
9. Who taught the Lord knowledge?
10. Who showed the Lord the path of understanding?

Isaiah's questions contrasted God's utter awesomeness with humanity's inability to contribute anything to creation. The answer to Isaiah's first four questions was "God." The answer to Isaiah's last six questions was "no one."

God's vastness also emerged in Isaiah's images. He held the earth's waters in his palms. He marked off the heavens with his hands. He knew how much dust the earth contained and the weight of the mountains and hills. And for all this creative activity, he needed absolutely no help. One need only to read Genesis 1–2 to see how God knew exactly what he was doing.

God's Power Dwarfs the Nations' Power (40:15–17)

By contrast, Isaiah proclaimed, the nations were powerless—as drops of water in a bucket, as dust on the divine scales (40:15). Lebanon's rich forests could not begin to provide a sufficient offering to honor him (40:16). Nations that thought themselves exalted he regarded as nothing (40:17). How could they compare to him?

God Is beyond Comparison (40:18–20)

Isaiah challenged the people to find an image that would compare with God (40:18). Would they resort to their idols? Idols were fashioned from things God had created by people God had created! How could such abominations compare to the incomparable one? Later, Isaiah would challenge the gods of the nations to demonstrate their power, but of course, they could not (41:21–29).

God Is the Sovereign (40:21–26)

Isaiah's four rhetorical questions (40:21) all demanded an affirmative answer. He was only stating the obvious—truth his hearers should have known.

God displayed his glory throughout the heavens (40:22). In contrast, earth's inhabitants seemed like mere grasshoppers. The Lord was not impressed with princes and rulers, who held leadership roles on earth (40:23). He determined the times of their rule and the territories over which they ruled (40:24). They could not stand before him.

The sovereign Lord again challenged the people to find one equal to him in any way (40:25). He guided their eyes heavenward to the stars some of them may have worshiped, which were actually objects of his creation (40:26). He had placed them there, and he had names for each one, whereas human beings could not even begin to count them.

Study Questions

1. How does Isaiah 40 prepare the reader for the rest of Isaiah's message?

2. Describe how the two main sections of Isaiah 40 fit together.

3. How does an understanding of Judah's geography reveal more clearly the impact of Isaiah's words to his hearers?

4. How can Isaiah's description of God's wisdom and power provide hope for believers today?

God Is Israel's Source of Strength (40:27–31)

Up to this point, Isaiah had painted an incredible picture of God. God had created everything that existed in heaven and on earth. He sustained everything by his strength, and no one in all the universe rivaled him.

Jacob Has Forgotten God's Strength (40:27)

The prophet now introduced an argument from the greater to the lesser. If God had done all of this, how could anyone think he could not do something as relatively simple as bringing his people back to Judah? How could people actually believe God didn't see their cause?

The All-Wise God Never Tires (40:28–29)

Isaiah then began the "grand finale" of his speech with two rhetorical questions: "Do you not know? Have you not heard?" (40:28). The obvious answer to both questions was "Of course!" Israel *certainly* should have understood the truths Isaiah was about to proclaim.

Isaiah declared that God's ways stood far beyond humanity's comprehension. He had created the universe; how would he grow tired watching over his people? Furthermore, he stood ready to strengthen his people, to renew the weary and the weak with strength and power.

Israel Must Hope in the Lord (40:30–31)

Isaiah contrasted society's normally strong and energetic people—youths and young men—with those who received their strength from the Lord. Even youths and young men would eventually grow weary, but those who placed their hope in the Lord would find strength for everything they needed (see sidebar 13.1). They would soar like eagles. They would run and walk and not grow weary.

Sidebar 13.1
Hope in the Bible

People today often use the word **"hope"** in a much different sense than the Bible does. Used as a verb, our modern word "hope" connotes wishful thinking, a desire that something will turn out the way we want, as the following sentences suggest:

"I hope the weather's nice so I can go fishing today."
"I hope he asks me out again."
"I hope I will get into the school I want."
"I hope there's a God, but I just don't know."

In contrast, hope in the Bible (both verb and noun forms) always denotes a confident, bold assurance in God to keep his word. Biblical hope is not wishful thinking because the fulfillment of God's promises is rooted in his righteous character. Two related ideas are the concepts of trusting and waiting. Isaiah 40:31 provides one such example of biblical hope, and other instances that suggest God's people can have hope in all circumstances are listed below:

Job 13:15	"Though he slay me, yet will I *hope* in him" (Job, expressing his hope in the face of extreme suffering).
Psalm 38:15	"I *wait* for you, O Lord; you will answer, O Lord my God" (David, confessing his sin, but trusting in God's forgiveness and restoration).
Psalm 130:5, 7	"I *wait* for the Lord, my soul *waits*, and in his word I put my *hope*. . . . O Israel, put your *hope* in the Lord, for with the Lord is unfailing love and with him is full redemption" (the psalmist, asking the Lord for mercy and recognizing none can stand on his own merit before God's holiness, but also affirming that hope is real in light of God's love, forgiveness, and salvation).
Isaiah 25:9	"In that day they will say, 'Surely this is our God; we *trusted* in him [NASB, "*waited for him*"], and he saved us'" (God's people praising him in the day of ultimate salvation).
Lamentations 3:21–24	"Yet this I call to mind and therefore I have *hope*: because of the Lord's great love we are not consumed, for his compassions never fail. They are new every morning; great is your faithfulness. I say to myself, 'The Lord is my portion; therefore I will *wait* for him'" (the writer of Lamentations, in Jerusalem's darkest hour following the destruction of the city by Nebuchadnezzar, appealing to God's compassion and faithfulness as a source of hope nonetheless).

The New Testament stresses that the foundation of believers' ultimate hope lies in the second coming of Jesus Christ (Ti 2:13; 1 Jn 3:3). Because of this, Jesus's followers also may stand strong in the face of current trials, which God uses to refine their character and to further strengthen hope in their hearts (Rom 5:2–5).

hope

Conclusion

Chapter 12 suggested three major themes for Isaiah 40–66: (1) God's people are in captivity for their sins; (2) This captivity proves God is God, for he predicted it; (3) God will now redeem his people—through Cyrus and in other ways.

Isaiah's words in chapter 40 form a foundation for chapters 41–66. God's people are coming home. God will prepare the way. He will shepherd his people. He has the power to do so too for he created and sustains the vast universe.

Isaiah's words provide encouragement to believers of all generations who face serious life challenges. Sometimes those challenges seem overwhelming, but Isaiah reminds us that the One to whom we pray is the One who spoke the universe into existence. He will give his people strength to accomplish whatever he sets before them.

Key Terms

hope

John the Baptist

14 Proclamation of Deliverance and Restoration

Isaiah 41:1–45:25

Objectives

After reading this chapter, you should be able to

1. Identify passages that point to Cyrus as God's instrument of redemption.
2. Discuss details of the first servant passage.
3. Support the concept of God's sovereignty in his people's restoration with key texts and themes from Isaiah 41–45.

Isaiah 40 heralded the good news—God's people were coming home! Isaiah announced the homecoming in grandiose terms. Prepare a way in the wilderness! Level the hills and valleys! God would lead and shepherd his people as he brought them to their land again.

Further, Isaiah described God's amazing power to bring his people home. He had created the universe and sustained all of it by his power. Consequently, he could accomplish something as relatively small but as incredibly significant as bringing his people back to their land.

God's people were in captivity for their sins. The captivity had proved he was God, for he had predicted it. Now, however, he planned to redeem them through Cyrus and in other ways. As chapters 41–45 unfold, we'll see these themes emphasized repeatedly.

The Coming Deliverance (41:1–29)

The deliverance Isaiah described in chapter 41 contained three major aspects. First, the prophet introduced Cyrus, God's instrument to rescue his people. Second, Isaiah described Israel, the Lord's servant, introducing a concept he would develop further later in the book. Third, Isaiah prosecuted the Lord's case against false gods. Only the Lord had predicted the captivity, and only he had the power to guide history as he wished.

Introduction of Cyrus (41:1–7)

Isaiah did not introduce Cyrus by name until 44:28. The allusions in the following verses, however, clearly describe Persia's leader who conquered Babylon in 539 BC.

Coastlands Called as Witnesses (41:1–4)

Isaiah called the coastlands and the peoples to stand in silence before God (41:1). Probably "coastlands" and "peoples" are better translations than "islands" and "nations" for the Hebrew words that appear here. "Coastlands" occurs again in 41:5, where it parallels the phrase "ends of the earth." The prophet also invited the peoples to "renew their strength," a direct parallel to the language of 40:31 that described the blessing of those who hope in the Lord. Other peoples as well could find such blessing if they sought him.

Isaiah called the coastlands and the peoples to testify to God's work. The NIV's translation "let us meet together at the place of judgment" also could be translated "let us come together for judgment" (NASB). The latter rendering probably fits the context better. Isaiah was inviting people who had seen God's work to testify to that work.

Verse 2a asked a question: "Who has stirred up one from the east, calling him in righteousness to his service?" Verse 4b answered the question: "I, the LORD—with the first of them and with the last—I am he" (see sidebar 14.1). Between the question and the answer came a description of God's strong instrument. He subdued nations and kings as he conquered new territory. Cyrus clearly fit Isaiah's description.

The text's point is clear. What god had the power to raise up such a world leader and bless him in such a way? Only the Lord God, the deity of seemingly insignificant Judah! God had used Assyria and Babylon as his instruments of judgment, and now he would use Cyrus as his instrument of blessing.

Coastlands Tremble in Fear (41:5–7)

As stated earlier, the parallel references to renewing strength in 40:31 and 41:1 subtly extended the invitation of salvation to the ends of the earth. As many people witnessed God's work, however, fear gripped them, and they

I Am He, the First and the Last

The expressions "I am he" and "I am the first and the last" occur several times in Isaiah 40–48. They complement well the threefold emphasis of Isaiah 40–66: (1) God's people are in captivity for their sins; (2) the captivity proves God is God, because he predicted it; (3) now God will redeem his people through Cyrus and in other ways! The Lord is "he," the only one with the power to make good on his promises. He is also "the first and the last," the beginning and the end of everything. He holds history in his hands; he is its source and its ultimate destination. The expressions also appear in the book of Revelation, where they describe the Lord God and his risen one, Jesus Christ.

The usages of the expressions are closely parallel, as the following table illustrates:

"I Am He" (Related Expressions Noted)

Verse	Emphasis
Isaiah 41:4*	God has raised up Cyrus to deliver his people.
Isaiah 43:10	God wants his people to understand that he alone is God.
Isaiah 43:11	God proclaims he is the only savior ("I, even I, am the Lord").
Isaiah 43:12	God has revealed all, saved all, announced it to all ("I am God").
Isaiah 43:13	God has always been "he"—"from ancient days" he is God.
Isaiah 46:4	God is Israel's creator, sustainer, and rescuer.
Isaiah 48:12*	God has called Israel; he emphasizes his uniqueness by describing how he created heaven and earth and foretold his purpose regarding Babylon.

"I Am the First and the Last" (Related Expressions Noted)

Verse	Emphasis
Isaiah 41:4*	God raised up Cyrus to deliver his people ("I, the LORD—with the first of them and with the last"; literally "I, the Lord, am the first and with the last").
Isaiah 43:10	God says, "Before me no god was formed, nor will there be one after me," and calls on his people to bear witness to this fact.
Isaiah 44:6	God is unique as Israel's King and Redeemer, the almighty One; he challenges other gods to recall their works of the past or to predict their future works.
Isaiah 48:12*	God emphasizes his uniqueness as the one who called his people; he created heaven and earth and foretold his purpose regarding Babylon.
Revelation 1:8	"I am the Alpha and the Omega . . . who is, and who was, and who is to come"; use of alpha, the first Greek letter, and omega, the last Greek letter, parallels "first and last" concept, as does the second part of the description; context describes Christ freeing believers from their sins to serve God the Father.
Revelation 1:17	The risen Christ uses the expression to reassure the fearful John, who has just seen his glorious appearance; verse 18 describes how Christ holds the keys of death and Hades (future oriented).
Revelation 2:8	The expression is used in the introduction to the letter to the church of Smyrna and is linked with the death and resurrection of Jesus, suggesting that the impact of Jesus's death and resurrection spans all history.
Revelation 22:13	Three parallel expressions, "the Alpha and Omega," "the First and the Last," and "the Beginning and the End," summarize John's description of history's dramatic conclusion with the second coming of Jesus, the final judgment, and the ushering in of God's eternal kingdom.

*These verses contain both the expression "I am he" and "I am the first and the last."

Both Isaiah and John proclaim the Lord's sovereignty. God holds past, present, and future in his hands, and all of history points to him.

responded by seeking their own deliverance through the idols they had worshiped for generations. Craftsman teamed with goldsmith to prepare an idol that would stand firm without tottering. Isaiah consistently contrasted the worthlessness of idols with God's all-embracing power (40:19–20; 41:21–29; 44:9–20; 46:5–7).

The people's response made no sense in light of Isaiah's proclamation of God's power. The exile proved God was God because he had predicted it. Now he was bringing his people home, using Cyrus as his instrument. What an awesome work! And what was the response of many? They built idols. Ironically, human beings created the idols they worshiped, making them from materials the Lord had created.

Israel, the Lord's Servant (41:8–20)

Beginning in 41:8, Isaiah introduced a concept to which he often would return in chapters 40–66. That concept was servanthood. (See sidebar 14.2.)

The word "servant" appears forty times in the book of Isaiah. Only nine occur in chapters 1–39, whereas thirty-one occur in 40–66. Frequently the term designates the nation of Israel. In other instances it denotes an individual. The servant concept will be discussed further in chapter 17 of this book.

In 41:8, the servant's identity is clear. Note the parallelism for emphasis:

> But you, O **Israel**, *my servant*,
> **Jacob**, *whom I have chosen*,
> **you descendants of Abraham**, *my friend*,

The words in bold designate Israel as the servant and also remind Isaiah's hearers of the nation's rich heritage. Jacob's name was changed to Israel as a result of his striving for God's blessing (Gn 32:24–28), and Abraham trusted faithfully in God's promise to make him a father of many nations (Gn 12:1–3). The words in italics are relationship words, emphasizing Israel's special relationship to God.

God had called Israel from the ends of the earth (41:9). Exile had spread many of his people far apart geographically, but the time of their restoration was at hand. Consequently, they were not to fear (41:10, 13). The Lord would strengthen them and uphold them. Their enemies would feel shame as God's intervention ended their opposition (41:11–12).

The label of "worm" (41:14) for Jacob has seemed odd to some. It probably was intended to designate the relatively weak and powerless state in which the nation found itself apart from God's restorative work. The Holy One of Israel—a term common in Isaiah—now appears as the one who will redeem them from their captivity and exile. In fact, Isaiah said, God would even use Israel as his threshing sledge of judgment (41:15–16). Israel would rejoice in him.

The imagery of 41:17–20 would have spoken powerfully to those who had spent time in the Judean desert. (See also the discussion of 40:3–5 in the preceding chapter.) Rivers and springs do not flow on the barren heights nor in the valleys, and pools of water and springs, let alone various types of trees, are definitely not a common sight. Such a rejuvenation of this land could only find its explanation in God's creative work.

The Lord's Case against False Gods (41:21–29)

One of the major themes in Isaiah 40–66 is "this captivity proves God is God, because he predicted it." Isaiah 41:21–29 strongly trumpets that theme.

The Lord's Challenge to False Gods (41:21–24)

The Hebrew word translated "case" (*rib*, 41:21) often appears in legal contexts. In effect, the Lord—Jacob's king—was calling the false gods into court.

Sidebar 14.2
The Term "Servant" in Isaiah

Verse(s)	Referent
14:2	Nations (servants of Israel in day of restoration)
20:3	Isaiah
22:20	Eliakim, officer of Hezekiah's court
24:2	Servant in general (swept away in God's judgment)
36:9	Officials of Sennacherib, king of Assyria
36:11	Judean officials (responding to Sennacherib's representative)
37:5	Officials of Hezekiah
37:24	Officials of Sennacherib
37:35	David
41:8	Israel
41:9	Israel
42:1	Jesus (Mt 12:18–21)
42:19 (2)	Israel
43:10	Israel
44:1	Israel
44:2	Israel
44:21 (2)	Israel
44:26	Prophets
45:4	Israel
48:20	Israel
49:3	Israel

Verse(s)	Referent
49:5	Israel (but servant has a mission to Israel)
49:6	Israel (Acts 13:47, remnant of Israel)
49:7	Israel (or perhaps messianic)
50:10	Isaiah? Jesus? (context unclear; no NT references)
52:13	Jesus (NT evidence)
53:11	Jesus (NT evidence)
54:17	Israel/God's people in general (plural)
56:6	Foreigners (NIV says "worship him," but the Hebrew says literally "to be his servants")
63:17	Israel or God's people in general (plural)
65:8	Israel or God's people in general (plural)
65:9	Israel or God's people in general (plural)
65:13 (3)	Israel or God's people in general (plural)
65:14	Israel or God's people in general (plural)
65:15	Israel or God's people in general (plural)
66:14	Israel or God's people in general (plural)

As we try to determine the intended referent of each use of the term "servant," we should apply the following criteria:

1. Context: What are the clues in the verse and verses immediately surrounding the term? (In some cases, of course, the verse may clearly identify the referent.)
2. New Testament citation: Does the New Testament cite the passage and confirm a referent?
3. Direct or secondary fulfillment: If the New Testament cites the passage and confirms a referent, does that limit Isaiah's meaning to the New Testament identification, or could Isaiah's historical context provide a different referent?

The Lord challenged the idols to prove their power (41:22–23). Could they predict future events and then bring them to pass, so that all could know their might? Could they testify to past things they had done—present a "résumé" of their sovereign works? A sarcastic tone is clear in verse 23: "Do something, whether good or bad, so that we will be dismayed and filled with fear." The NASB's rendering, "Indeed, do good or evil, that we may anxiously look about us and fear together," also conveys this sarcasm.

The initial verdict came down (41:24). Idols were nothing (or perhaps literally "from nothing") and could testify to no significant work in the universe. Isaiah pronounced a curse on everyone who would choose idols over the Lord.

The Lord's Presentation of His Own Works (41:25–27)

The Lord now presented evidence for *his* sovereignty. First, he described one he had raised up to bring down other rulers (41:25). Indeed, Cyrus (here unnamed) would do God's bidding and even call on God's name (2 Chr 36:22–23; Ez 1:1–4).

One might wonder how Cyrus comes both "from the north" and "from the rising sun" (41:25). The solution lies in recognizing both Cyrus's location and his route of travel. The Persian kingdom lay due east of Judah. However, any Mesopotamian ruler traveling to Judah would follow the Euphrates River northwest and then descend southward into the region.

The Lord had announced this plan from long ago; no one else had joined him in doing so (41:26). He had planned Judah's judgment and had announced Judah's restoration (41:27).

The Lord's Conclusion (41:28–29)

As the Lord performed his work with his people, no other deity in the universe had provided him counsel, let alone an answer to any of his questions (41:28). Consequently, the final verdict came down (41:29) in language similar to 41:24. All idols were false, nothing![1] Their deeds amounted to nothing at all. In fact, Isaiah even compared their idols to "confusion" (Heb. *tohu*), a term that described the state of the universe prior to creation (Gn 1:2).[2]

The Role of the Lord's Servant (42:1–25)

Isaiah's earlier mention of the Lord's servant (41:8) was a reference to Israel. The servant he now described was a person.

Description of the Servant (42:1–9)

Isaiah's description of the servant included two primary aspects. First, he described the servant's ministry as the servant faithfully carried it out. Second, he described the servant's Lord, who would empower him for that ministry.

The Servant's Ministry (42:1–4)

Isaiah first described the servant's ministry as marked by God's presence (42:1). The Lord upheld him and delighted in him (42:1). Further, God would put his Spirit on his servant, as he had with past prophets and kings (1 Sm 11:6; 16:13; 2 Chr 20:14). Indeed, God's leading continues to mark God's servants throughout the book of Isaiah.

Second, the servant's ministry was marked by startling contrast (42:3). The contrast lay between the servant's mild demeanor and his significant accomplishments. He did not announce his coming with loud pomp and was so gentle that he would not even crush a bruised reed or extinguish the smoldering wick of an oil lamp. Nonetheless, he would bring forth justice with perfect faithfulness. "Justice" here almost certainly denotes more than merely redressing crime. Rather, it designates a society that functions according to God's design.[3]

Third, the servant's ministry was marked by relentless determination (42:4). He would stay the course until he had established justice on the earth. Even the coastlands (see also 41:1) would place their hope in his instruc-

Septuagint

tion—a reference to the extent of his leadership.

The Servant's Lord (42:5–9)

The Lord continued to speak; the statement "This is what God the LORD says" (42:5) further stressed his endorsement of his servant. The Lord had created the universe and given life to all people; he was certainly able to lead his servant.

Righteousness would shape the servant's ministry, as would the Lord's personal guidance (42:6). The expressions "covenant for the people" and "light for the Gentiles (or nations)" are parallel. The first suggests that the servant would mediate God's special covenant relationship with his own. The second indicates the servant would shine the light of God's truth on peoples who had not yet experienced it. This latter concept occurred earlier in Isaiah (2:3; 11:10; 19:18–25), and the prophet would continue to develop this theme later in his book.

The covenant of people and the light to the Gentiles that the servant brought included special blessings (42:7). Blind eyes would see, and captives would be released from prison.

Who had planned his servant's special ministry? It was the Lord himself (42:8–9). His very name—Yahweh—emphasized his presence with his people.[4] He would not share his glory with another. He and only he had earlier proclaimed events that now had happened, and he also continued to announce new things he would do.

The Servant's Identity

In contrast to the use of the term "servant" in 41:8, where the referent was clearly identified as Israel, the Hebrew text does not mention the identity of the servant in 42:1–9. Interestingly, the **Septuagint** (an early Greek translation of the Old Testament) renders 42:1 as follows:

Behold, Jacob my servant, whom I will uphold;

Israel, my chosen one, in whom my soul delights.

As interesting as this variant is, we should reject it for two reasons. First, when comparing different textual readings, preference is normally given to the more difficult reading, since it is more likely a scribe would attempt to simplify a passage than to make it more obscure. Second, preference is normally given to the shorter reading, since it is more likely a scribe would add a clarifying note than delete anything. Indeed, the names "Jacob" and "Israel" may have been added to the later Greek text to emphasize the nationalistic interpretation over and against an individual (and possibly messianic) interpretation.

The New Testament asserts that Jesus fulfilled Isaiah's words during his earthly ministry. The Gospel of Matthew records how Jesus performed great works of healing yet warned those who received such blessings not to make their healing widely known (Mt 12:15–16). Matthew 12:17–21 states that by acting in this way, Jesus fulfilled Isaiah's words of 42:1–4.[5] Jesus quietly, but with relentless determination, pursued the will of God and accomplished it to the fullest (Jn 17:4). Jesus's death on a cross satisfied God's demand for ultimate justice, but Jesus's final establishment of justice in God's kingdom will occur when he returns.

Triumph, Judgment, and Indictment (42:10–25)

The remainder of Isaiah 42 voices themes of triumph, judgment, and indictment. God had triumphed and deserved his people's praise (42:10–13). Yet God had much judgment left to administer to those who persist in idolatry (42:14–17). Finally, God chastised his wayward servant, describing the sin that had led to the exile (42:18–25).

A Hymn of Triumph (42:10–13)

The good news of 42:1–9 led to Isaiah's command to "sing to the LORD a new song" (42:10). The inclusion of the "ends of the earth" as well as "islands" (or "coastlands") again emphasizes the intended extent of God's kingdom and suggests that more than Judah's return is intended here.[6]

Isaiah's summons alternated between the distant lands and the nearer ones. Those who sailed the sea and lived in the coastlands should praise God, as should the nomads of Kedar in the Arabian desert and those who lived in Sela, later Petra (42:11). God would go forth as a warrior, and his triumph over his enemies was certain, so all should give him glory (42:12–13).

An Announcement of God's Judgment (42:14–17)

Isaiah compared God's sudden judgment of the world to the onset of labor for a pregnant woman (42:14). Just as the soon-to-be mother has a job to do when labor comes, so the Lord would act after a period of waiting.

God would lead those who trusted in him and would never forsake them (42:16). But those who persisted in idolatry would experience nothing but shame and devastation (42:15, 17). He who brought streams in the desert (41:18) could just as quickly dry up the land.

An Indictment of God's Servant (42:18–25)

Isaiah's words against God's servant (42:18–20) appear startling in light of the servant's glowing description earlier (42:1–4). How could the servant in whom God delighted (42:1) now be described as "blind" and "deaf" to the things of God (42:19)? How could the servant see but pay no attention, have open ears but hear nothing (42:20)? Note the close parallel with the language of 6:9.

The answer lies in recognizing the fluid nature of the term "servant." Isaiah 41:8 designated Israel as God's servant, whereas 42:1–9 portrayed God's servant as an individual. The current passage no doubt intends the national interpretation as in 41:8.

Assuming Isaiah intended us to understand the servant of 42:18–20 as Israel, the flow of the three servant passages in Isaiah 41–42 becomes clear. It is as if God were saying, "Israel, you're my chosen servant. Don't fear, because I'm with you. I know you feel like a worm, but my power will give you all the strength you need to accomplish my will (41:8–14). Consider my ideal servant who will come one day (42:1–9). My Spirit will guide him, and he will bring justice to all the earth. Learn from him. By contrast, you're still spiritually blind and deaf (42:18–20). You're not fully seeing, hearing, or embracing the plan I have for you."

Isaiah upheld the Lord's instruction (Heb. *torah*, 42:21), the teaching to which the prophet had earlier encouraged God's people to turn rather than to idols and spirits (8:19–20). But God's people had in effect given themselves over to plunderers by persisting in their sin (42:22).

Isaiah stated the critical issue as clearly as he could (42:23–25). Had Israel become plunder of its own accord or by a fluke of history? Absolutely not! Rather, the Lord had brought judgment on his people for their sin, but they had not realized it. No one had stopped to consider that the Lord had brought their suffering in order to turn them back to him.

Israel's Redemption from Babylon (43:1–45:25)

Isaiah 43–45 announces Israel's redemption from Babylon. Israel's restoration would come through God's power, and he would bestow on his people lasting blessing. His superiority to idols was obvious, and he would put them and those who worshiped them to shame. Finally, he would restore Israel through Cyrus, his anointed shepherd. But in the final analysis, he would call the world—not merely Israel—to reconciliation with him.

Israel's Restoration through God's Power (43:1–13)

A message of restoration seems quite unexpected in light of the strong language of the preceding section (42:18–25). Nonetheless, the introductory words "But now" link the text that follows with the preceding passages and suggest that the prophet is building on his previous statement, getting to the crux of his prophecy. Isaiah proclaimed the Lord's determination to restore and rebuild his people.

Israel's Restoration (43:1–7)

Isaiah could confidently proclaim God's ability to restore his people, because God had created them and made them a nation (43:1). Again, he encouraged them not to fear, for they were God's own possession, and he had redeemed them.

God's presence meant his people could count on deliverance in the midst of trials (43:2). By using fires and floods as extreme examples of conditions against which God's preservation would prevail, Isaiah could assure the people that the Lord would also preserve them through lesser challenges. And for the first time in the book of Isaiah, the Lord referred to himself as his people's Savior (43:3), a title that would appear again (43:11; 45:15, 21; 49:26; 60:16; 63:8). God's salvation included Judah's physical deliverance from Babylon but also a personal faith relationship with him.

The Lord's judgment on his people was over, and now he would judge others in their place (43:3–4). He would gather his sons and daughters from every direction, and their homecoming would bring him glory (43:5–7).

God's Power (43:8–13)

Isaiah's reference to "those who have eyes but are blind" and those "who have ears but are deaf" (43:8) parallel his words of 42:18–19. God summoned his people to testify to the nations and peoples who also assembled at his command (43:9); and he reiterated his earlier questions (cf. 41:22–23, 26). The god who could demonstrate his ability to guide history was alone the true God!

The Lord now turned to his spiritually blind and deaf people, who nonetheless could serve as his witnesses (43:10). Note the close proximity of the word "servant," which may suggest the servant's role included serving as a witness. Centuries later, Jesus would tell his disciples, "You will be my witnesses" (Acts 1:8), for they had seen his saving work firsthand.

Isaiah proclaimed the Lord's absolute sovereignty (43:11–13). No other savior existed, and he expected his people to testify to that fact. They had seen him work with their nation, for blessing and for judgment. Further, no other deity could rescue and save his own as he had done. Such verses may also lie behind similar statements that we find in the early church regarding Jesus (Acts 4:12). A key theme of Isaiah 40–66 was sounded again: the captivity and rescue proved he was God, because he had predicted it.

God's Blessing on Israel (43:14–44:8)

Isaiah's announcement of God's coming blessing on Israel highlighted four key concepts. First, God was his people's redeemer, who had ransomed them from slavery in Babylon (43:14–21). Second, Israel had been the transgressor, who had received its just reward (43:22–24). Third, Israel's sin had led God to take action as judge (43:25–28). Fourth, God remained ever gracious, extending forgiveness to Israel, his servant (44:1–8).

God the Holy Redeemer (43:14–21)

God's redemption of his people also implied judgment on Babylon (43:14). The Babylonians would flee along the Tigris and the Euphrates rivers in a futile attempt to escape. Could God exodus

Spirit

really fulfill his promise? Of course! He was Yahweh, the holy one, king of his people whom he had created (43:15).

Isaiah reminded his people of God's amazing work during the **exodus** from Egypt (43:16–17). But they were not to dwell on the past, for their Lord was about to perform a new work among them (43:18–21). His "making a way in the desert" (43:19) recalled his faithful provision for his people during the wilderness wanderings. He had tenderly cared for them, and he would again.

Israel the Transgressor (43:22–24)

Tragically, Israel had not come to the point where it sought God's forgiveness. No earnest cry of repentance was forthcoming; no sacrifices appeared to implore God's favor. The people had wearied the Lord with their sins and offenses. God was much more ready to bless them than they were ready to receive that blessing.

God the Judge (43:25–28)

Isaiah again introduced legal language to outline God's case against his people. The Lord had blotted out their sins and transgressions *for his own sake*. Did God's people *really* think they stood innocent before him? Absolutely not! Rather, Israel had been sinful from the beginning.

Isaiah consequently promised God's judgment of all sin (43:28). Some interpreters have read the Hebrew verbs in this verse as past tense, which is possible,[7] though it may be Isaiah is stressing the general principle of God's ongoing judgment of sin wherever he finds it.[8]

God the Ever Gracious (44:1–8)

Isaiah 44:1–8, like 43:1, begins with the words "But now," indicating a link with the preceding section as the prophet issued a new proclamation. Everything Isaiah asserted about God's people and their rebellion in 43:22–28 was true, but God nonetheless had great plans for his own.

Again, Isaiah described Israel as God's chosen servant, who should not

fear (44:1–2). The Lord would bring agricultural blessing through the provision of abundant water (cf. 41:18; 43:19), but more important, he would pour out his **Spirit** on his people, causing their spiritual flourishing to parallel nature's blessing (44:3–4). God's Spirit would instill in them a deeper understanding of God's ownership of their lives (44:5). The apostle Paul would later write that God's Spirit marked believers as God's possession as they awaited their final redemption (Eph 1:13–14).

Isaiah's stringing together of God's names ("the LORD, Israel's King and Redeemer, the LORD Almighty," 44:6) further emphasized the power of God alone to bring about these great promises. He was the "first and the last," the beginning of all and the end of all (see sidebar 14.1). The Lord boldly challenged any would-be rival to speak up regarding either the past or the future (44:7). However, God's people were not to fear—he, their rock, had predicted all events long ago, and they were his eyewitnesses (44:8).

God's Superiority to Idols (44:9–23)

Despite the case Isaiah had built for God's utter sovereignty and ownership of his people, some persisted in idolatry, as the next prophetic statement demonstrates. Isaiah used vivid imagery to illustrate the futility of idolatry (44:9–20) and reminded the people the Lord should be the sole focus of their worship (44:21–23).

The Futility of Idolatry (44:9–20)

Isaiah began with a general denunciation of idolatry (44:9–11). Those who made and worshiped idols revealed their own ignorance and acted to their own shame. Their work and worship were worthless.

Isaiah then illustrated the futility of idolatry with a detailed description that included the idol's creation and ended with the worshiper falling before the idol (44:12–20). The almost comical portrayal brought home

Baal idol from Tyre. Idols were produced in various sizes besides the larger ones Isaiah described. (Courtesy of Biblical Illustrator © copyright 2007, LifeWay Christian Resources of the Southern Baptist Convention. All rights reserved. Used by permission.)

the depth of the people's spiritual blindness.

Blacksmith and carpenter worked together in the idol-making process (44:12–14). The carpenter secured the wood from the forest, while the blacksmith overlaid the object with metal. The work was hard, and he grew tired—making a "god" was not easy! The idol maker cooked his food using part of the wood as fuel, while bowing to the part he had made into an idol (44:15–17).

Isaiah decried the incredible spiritual blindness present in idol manufacturing (44:18–20). The idol manufacturers completely missed the obvious truth—a tree that served as fuel to cook their meal could have no spiritual power over them—and worshiped a lie they themselves had created (44:20).

A Reminder to Israel (44:21–23)

Isaiah reminded Israel of its special relationship to the Lord. He had made Israel, and Israel was his servant. He had cleansed them of their sins and called them to repent, to turn back to him. Nature, whose elements the idol makers had tried to turn into gods, now joined in praise to the true God.

Israel's Restoration through Cyrus (44:24–45:25)

The last few verses of Isaiah 44 provide another argument from the greater to the lesser (cf. 40:12–26, 27–31). Isaiah began with a description of God's creation of the universe and moved from

there to a description of God's redemption of his people through a particular king at a particular time in history.

Isaiah 45 announces the Lord's special use of Cyrus, king of Persia, as his instrument to bring God's people home. But as the chapter continues, Isaiah announces God's invitation to everyone to turn to him and be saved. The third theme of Isaiah 40–66—"Now God will redeem you, through Cyrus and still other means"—comes through clearly as God proclaims his call to the ends of the earth.

God's Sovereign Control over Cyrus (44:24–45:8)

Isaiah began with the big picture (44:24). God had created all things in heaven and on earth, and he had done so alone.

The prophet then moved into the earthly realm (44:25). God's wisdom far exceeded that of diviners and false prophets. He fulfilled the words of his servants the prophets, who brought his message to his people (44:26). He promised to rebuild Jerusalem and Judah, and now he would do so. Indeed, fulfilling this promise was a small thing compared to parting the waters during the exodus (44:27). The sovereign Lord would make a shepherd of Cyrus, a Persian monarch, and accomplish his will through him, even the rebuilding of Jerusalem (44:28).

Isaiah announced the Lord's personal word to Cyrus (45:1–7). He called Cyrus "his anointed," using the Hebrew word *mashiach*, from which the word "messiah" comes. Typically in the Old Testament, the term designated either priests or kings, though prophets were also anointed (see sidebar 14.3). The anointing designated the Lord's choosing someone for a special purpose. The description of Cyrus as "messiah" is the only time in the Bible that a Gentile is so designated. But the Lord would use him—as he had used Assyria and Babylon—to achieve his purposes, because he was Lord not only of his people but of the entire world.

Sidebar 14.3
Uses of the Term *Mashiach* in the Old Testament

The following chart gives the references and referents for uses of the term *mashiach*, "anointed one," in the Old Testament. Most occurrences clearly denote kings, though a few refer to priests or others. The New Testament points to Jesus as the ultimate *mashiach* (or Messiah).

Uses of *Mashiach*, "Anointed One"		
Priests	**Kings**	**Other**
Leviticus 4:3, 5, 16	1 Samuel 2:35 (unnamed, proves to be Saul)	2 Samuel 1:21 (Saul's shield)
Leviticus 6:22	1 Samuel 12:3, 5 (Saul)	1 Chronicles 16:22 (Israel's leaders in the wilderness)
	1 Samuel 16:6 (unnamed, proves to be David)	Psalm 105:15 (Israel's leaders in the wilderness)
	1 Samuel 24:6 (2), 10 (Saul)	
	1 Samuel 26:9, 11, 16, 23 (Saul)	
	2 Samuel 1:14, 16 (Saul)	
	2 Samuel 19:21 (David)	
	2 Samuel 22:51 (David)	
	2 Samuel 23:1 (David)	
	Psalm 2:2 (Israel's king)	
	Psalm 18:50 (David)	
	Psalm 20:6 (David)	
	Psalm 28:8 (David, or Israel's king in general)	
	Psalm 84:9 (Israel's king)	
	Psalm 89:38, 51 (Israel's king)	
	Psalm 132:10, 17 (David, Israel's king in general)	
	Isaiah 45:1 (Cyrus)	
	Lamentations 4:20 (Judah's king)	
	Daniel 9:25, 26 (possibly the Messiah, Cyrus, or a priest)	

God acted through Cyrus for three reasons. First, he wanted Cyrus to know his power (45:2–3). The Lord had summoned him by name and would work through him, though Cyrus had not acknowledged him (45:5).[9]

Second, God acted through Cyrus for the sake of Israel his servant (45:4). He was acting in history to redeem his people once again, and Cyrus was his chosen instrument.

Third, God acted through Cyrus so that all people everywhere might know the Lord as the one true God, unmatched in all the universe (45:6). God created light and darkness and brought peace and calamity as he willed (45:7). He called to the heavens to rain down righteousness that salvation might spring up, for the time of deliverance had come (45:8).

God's Control over All (45:9–25)

Isaiah emphasized three things in this final section. First, he pronounced woe against the defiant (45:9–13). The clay did not question the work of the potter, and newborns did not talk back to their parents. How dare people question the sovereign Lord's work when the evidence was so clear? He had created the earth and controlled it and would use Cyrus to free his people.

Second, Isaiah announced God's people's deliverance from foreigners and idols (45:14–17). As he had said before (43:3), Egypt, Cush, and the Sabeans would fall before them in defeat.

Study Questions

1. Locate the passages that speak of Cyrus as God's instrument.

2. List key details of Isaiah 42:1–4 and compare it with Matthew 12. How did Matthew understand Jesus as fulfilling Isaiah's words?

3. Identify texts that assert or demonstrate God's superiority to idols.

4. How do you think most of Isaiah's Judean hearers responded to the prophet's universal call to salvation (45:22–23)? To what extent does ethnic prejudice hinder the spread of the gospel today?

Key Terms

exodus

gospel

Septuagint

Spirit

gospel

Idol manufacturers would experience shame, and Israel would be saved forever.

Third, Isaiah proclaimed God's uniqueness (45:18–25). The Lord, the Creator, had spoken openly, never in secret, and had accomplished everything that he said he would (45:18–19). He reminded idolaters that their gods could not save them. Only he, the righteous Savior, held past, present, and future in his hands (45:20–21).

Using language that Isaiah's nationalistic Jewish audience must have found quite surprising, the prophet called the whole earth to turn to Yahweh and be saved (45:22). Every knee would bow to him, every tongue would swear allegiance, and only in him would they find righteousness and strength (45:23–24). "All the descendants of Israel" (45:25) may even designate all people who cast their lot with the Lord (Gal 3:29),[10] but it also may simply highlight Israel's special blessing among the redeemed.

Isaiah's universal offer of salvation anticipates Jesus's instructions to his disciples to reach all nations with the **gospel** (Mt 28:18–20; Acts 1:8). Just as Isaiah was the Lord's human instrument to announce his salvation, so the Lord uses believers today to advance his kingdom by calling others to join it.

15 The Fall of Babylon

Isaiah 46:1–47:15

Outline

- **God versus Babylon's Idols (46:1–13)**
  Babylon's Idols Are Humiliated (46:1–2)
  God's Assurance to Israel (46:3–4)
  The Futility of All Idols Anywhere (46:5–7)
  God's Uniqueness (46:8–13)
- **Taunt against Babylon (47:1–15)**
  Babylon's Shame Exposed (47:1–4)
  Babylon's Royalty Deposed (47:5–7)
  Babylon's Bereavement and Judgment
  Disclosed (47:8–15)

Objectives

After reading this chapter, you should be able to

1. Summarize Isaiah's condemnation of Babylon's idols and all other idols (46:1–13).
2. Discuss the main aspects of Isaiah's taunt against Babylon (47:1–15).

Akitu festival

Bel

Marduk

Nabu

Every time I teach Old Testament Survey, I know students will ask certain questions. They always want to discuss Genesis 1–2 and views of creation. They always ask about the Lord hardening Pharaoh's heart in the book of Exodus. They always have questions about messianic prophecies. I've adjusted the amount of class time I spend on these and other topics to give time for such questions, because I anticipate students will always raise these issues.

Perhaps Isaiah 46–47 anticipates a question Isaiah's audience may have had. Isaiah 40–45 contains exciting proclamations of God's power and his rescue and salvation of his people. He would bring them home through King Cyrus, and God's plans for redemption included even more than that. But Isaiah's hearers may have wanted to ask: "Isaiah, if Persia will rescue us one day, what about Babylon?"

Isaiah 46–47 addresses this important question. Ultimately, Isaiah assures his audience, Babylon will fall. It will fall to Cyrus, yes, but more significantly, it will fall because God has decreed that Babylon's days are over.

God versus Babylon's Idols (46:1–13)

Remember the second theme of Isaiah 40–66? "The captivity proves God is God, because he predicted it." Earlier God had challenged idols and false gods to prove their power and had shown them powerless. Chapter 46 announces the logical implications of these truths for the false deities worshiped in the Babylonian empire.

Babylon's Idols Are Humiliated (46:1–2)

Isaiah's discourse began abruptly with an allusion to the Babylonian New Year (*Akitu*) festival.[1] This lavish festival normally lasted eleven days, and idols of all major deities of the Babylonian pantheon were brought to Babylon to participate in a grand parade (see sidebar 15.1).

However, the event Isaiah described sounded far from grand. His mocking language described the idols as stooping, as bowing low, as utterly humiliated (46:1). Even the animals that pulled the wagons on which the idols stood seemed to feel the burden of their worthless load (46:2). The gods looked not like rulers, but like defeated spoils of war.

Isaiah highlighted only two of Babylon's major deities. **Bel**, or **Marduk**, was head of the pantheon. **Nabu** (Nebo) was Bel's son, god of writing and wisdom as well as patron deity of the scribes. But these supposedly powerful and wise gods could not stop Cyrus, let alone the Lord's sovereign purpose.

God's Assurance to Israel (46:3–4)

Isaiah now addressed the remnant of God's people. They needed to hear his words, believe them, and live by them. The prophet declared God had brought the nation into existence and sustained it to maturity. He promised his presence with his children even into their old age. He would rescue them and bring them home. If he could bring down Babylon, he could rescue his people.

The Futility of All Idols Anywhere (46:5–7)

Isaiah's two rhetorical questions (46:5) challenged the people to ponder God's greatness. *In no way* was the Lord comparable to the idols hunched over on Babylonian wagons.

Isaiah reminded the people of an idol's source—it had to be made by humans, so how could it have power over humans? The prophet mockingly described the pitiful spiritual state of those who spent their time and money crafting images that could not move, answer them, or save them from calamity (46:6–7).

Sidebar 15.1
The Babylonian *Akitu* (New Year) Festival

The Babylonian new year festival occurred just before the spring equinox, during the first eleven days of the month of Nisannu. Its basic features included the following:

- Time was set aside for ritual purification and prayers.
- The entire Epic of Creation (**Enuma Elish**), which highlighted Marduk's place as head of the Babylonian pantheon (some believe the epic was portrayed dramatically), was recited.
- The king appeared and entered the inner sanctuary after the high priest removed all the king's royal insignia. The priest then slapped the king and pulled his ears, signifying the king's humiliation before Marduk. At this time the king would confess his loyalty to Marduk during the past year and swear it for the coming year. After the king received his royal insignia again, the high priest would slap the king's face again. Tears that appeared on the king's face showed his true repentance and the pleasure of Marduk at his humility.
- Later that evening, the king formally "took Marduk's hand" in a procession through Babylon, further signifying his loyalty, submission, and partnership with Marduk.

Joan Oates, Babylon
(London: Thames and Hudson, 1979), 175–76.

Depiction of the Babylonian god Bel (in earlier times Marduk) as a dragon. Isaiah highlighted Bel's coming humility in the face of Babylon's destruction. (Courtesy of Biblical Illustrator © copyright 2007, LifeWay Christian Resources of the Southern Baptist Convention. All rights reserved. Used by permission.)

God's Uniqueness (46:8–13)

Enuma Elish

Isaiah highlighted the Lord's impatience with his rebellious people with the three imperatives of 46:8. How long would it take for his people to understand that the Lord stood supreme in the universe? No one else came close to matching him.

Isaiah announced three demonstrations of God's supremacy over all other gods (46:10–11). First, he had announced the end from the beginning and had foretold the future. Second, he established his sure purposes and

did what he said he would do. Third, he had called Cyrus, a "bird of prey," to accomplish his will.

Many Judeans stubbornly refused to believe God would bring them home (46:12). Their evil lives contrasted sharply with the righteousness to which their God called them. But the Lord encouraged them to cease their stubbornness. He would bring his righteousness to the very people who had wandered away from it (46:13). They would not have to wait long to see his salvation.

Taunt against Babylon (47:1–15)

After describing the humiliation of Babylon's deities and thereby alluding to Babylon's downfall (46:1–2), Isaiah focused his prophetic attention on Babylon again. He had announced Babylon's judgment in general fashion earlier in his book (chaps. 13–14). Now, having shared more details of the return from exile in chapters 40–46, he targeted Babylon with yet more words of judgment. Indeed, a comparison with chapters 13–14 reveals how much more personal the judgment seems in the current text, with the Lord speaking directly to the soon-to-be-conquered enemy.[2]

Babylon's Shame Exposed (47:1–4)

Isaiah began the taunt against Babylon with two commands: sit in the dust and sit on the ground without a throne (47:1). The first points to Babylon's humiliation and mourning; in fact, a similar expression describes (1) Nineveh's king during the days of Jonah (Jon 3:6), and (2) Job during the days of his affliction (Jb 2:8).

Isaiah used feminine imagery to describe the city. The expression "Virgin Daughter of Babylon" (47:1) may seem surprising in view of Babylon's spiritual impurity (47:12–13). The reference probably denotes the city as yet untouched by an invader.

The expression "Daughter of the Babylonians" literally reads "daughter of the Chaldeans." The **Chaldeans** were the tribal group that achieved domination over Babylon and hence became known as the Babylonians. The two terms are basically interchangeable when speaking of this period of history, though "Chaldeans" preserves the people's ethnic designation.

Isaiah used captivity language to describe Babylon's coming lot (47:2–3). The Lord would subject the Babylonians to the shameful treatment they had inflicted on others. Grinding flour on a millstone was tedious work usually reserved for slaves, and slaves did not need to veil themselves or otherwise cover their beauty. "Nakedness" and "shame" may parallel the refer-

ences from 47:2, or perhaps may designate the horrors sometimes inflicted on captive women (Jer 13:26–27; Ez 23:10; Na 3:5).[3]

Isaiah proclaimed the identity of the one who would bring Babylon's shame (47:4). The Lord Almighty, the Holy One of Israel, would accomplish this. Babylon's judgment was the necessary prerequisite to the Lord's redemption of his people. Similar doxologies occur elsewhere in Isaiah and especially in Jeremiah.[4]

Babylon's Royalty Deposed (47:5–7)

Silent darkness (47:5) was not the usual habitation of a "queen of kingdoms." However, it would fit Babylon on the day that God deposed it.

Isaiah revealed the real reason behind Judah's exile (47:6). The exile came not because of Babylon's overpowering might, but because of Judah's sin. God had given Judah into Babylon's hands, but Babylon had shown no mercy. Babylon was an instrument of God's judgment but had overstepped its prerogatives by its arrogance and pride (47:7).

Babylon's foolish confidence, expressed in the thought "I will continue forever—the eternal queen!" (47:7) was accompanied by other foolish thoughts (47:8, 10). The Lord would prove them all wrong.

Babylon's Bereavement and Judgment Disclosed (47:8–15)

Years of Babylonian supremacy had established a sense of false security in Babylon (cf. Dn 4:29–30). In fact, in 539 BC on the night the Persians took Babylon, Babylon's officials may have been taken totally by surprise (Dn 5). The NIV's "lounging in your security" (Is 47:8) conveys the nuance of complacency and false confidence apparent within the kingdom's capital.

Babylon's arrogance culminated in its boast, "I am, and there is none besides me"—almost exactly what the Lord had asserted of himself earlier (45:22). Bab-

Study Questions

1. How do the prophet's words in 46:1–2 show his familiarity with the Babylonian *Akitu* festival?

2. Summarize the taunt against Babylon in Isaiah 47; of what sins was the nation guilty?

Key Terms

Akitu festival

Bel

Chaldeans

Enuma Elish

Marduk

Nabu

ylon seemed confident it would not suffer widowhood or bereavement; that is, nothing disastrous would ever befall the city. But Isaiah assured Babylon: "Both of these will overtake you in a moment, on a single day" (47:9). He likened Babylon's devastation to that of a woman whose husband and children all died the same day.

Babylon trusted in many things for its security (47:9–10). Its religious leaders led the people astray with acts of sorcery and divination.[5] Its wise men thought their wisdom and knowledge would carry the day. But they would not be able to reason or conjure their way out of the judgment soon to come (47:11).

Isaiah warned Babylon to brace itself for the inevitable (47:12–15). He mockingly invited the people to persist with their spells and sorceries—as if these would save them. Those who consulted the stars would find nothing in the heavens that halted God's judgment. They would find nothing even to save themselves, let alone the people and the kingdom (47:14). All they could do was wait for destruction.

Isaiah's message to Babylon brought home what every nation on earth needed to understand. Nations ruled only by God's grace, and when they had served his purpose, he would bring them down. He would judge their sin and those who mistakenly thought their own wisdom or strength had attained their lofty positions would receive the due penalty of their arrogance.

The universe would have *only one* who would remain to say, "I am, and there is no one besides me." The Lord of Hosts was his name.

16 Israel's Release and Exaltation

Isaiah 48:1–52:12

Outline

- **Israel's Stubbornness versus God's Stubborn Grace (48:1–22)**
  Israel's Stubbornness (48:1–5)
  God's Even More Stubborn Grace (48:6–22)
- **The Lord's Servant and Israel's Return (49:1–26)**
  The Lord's Servant (49:1–7)
  Israel's Return (49:8–26)
- **God and His Servant (50:1–11)**
  God's Rebuke to Israel (50:1–3)
  The Servant's Testimony (50:4–11)
  The Servant's Identity
- **Encouragement to the Righteous (51:1–16)**
  Look to the Past (51:1–3)
  Look to the Future (51:4–6)
  Look to the Present (51:7–8)
  Isaiah's Prayer (51:9–10)
  God's Response (51:11–16)
- **Good News for Jerusalem (51:17–52:12)**
  Jerusalem the Drunkard (51:17–23)
  Jerusalem the Free (52:1–6)
  Jerusalem the Rejoicing (52:7–12)

Objectives

After reading this chapter, you should be able to

1. Describe God's persistent measures to lead and restore his people (48:1–20).
2. Compare and contrast the key aspects of the two servant passages (49:1–7; 50:4–11).
3. Highlight the main points of Isaiah's encouragement to the righteous and good news to Jerusalem (51:1–52:12).

grace

Isaiah 48–52 highlights further details of Israel's release and exaltation. Judah's prophet continued to announce the exciting plans God had for his people.

Some struggled to believe the words Isaiah proclaimed. But Isaiah encouraged his people—God had not forgotten them. His grace would surpass their stubbornness. His servant would minister among them, and God would bring them home. Isaiah proclaimed good news for Jerusalem, a city whose judgment was now coming to an end and whose day of freedom would bring great rejoicing.

Israel's Stubbornness versus God's Stubborn Grace (48:1–22)

Isaiah 48 features a tension between two opposing forces—Israel's stubbornness and God's even more stubborn **grace**. One could almost say the Lord was determined to bless his people whether or not they wanted that blessing.

Israel's Stubbornness (48:1–5)

Isaiah focused on three aspects of Israel's stubbornness. He reminded the people of their election, detailed their sin, and proclaimed their inexcusability.

Israel's Election (48:1a)

Isaiah used the expressions "house of Jacob," "called by the name of Israel," and "line of Judah" to stress how God had chosen his people centuries earlier. God had established his covenant with Jacob and changed his name to Israel (Gn 32, 35). Jacob's son Judah became the progenitor of what would become the heart of the southern kingdom. In light of these ancient blessings, why would Judah remain so stubborn?

Israel's Sin (48:1b–2)

Isaiah accused Israel of merely going through spiritual motions that lacked any real substance. The people took oaths in God's name, and Jerusalem's inhabitants prided themselves on their exalted citizenry. But God was a God of truth and righteousness—two virtues seriously lacking among his people.

God's children may have sworn public allegiance to him, but their attitudes and actions betrayed their sinful hearts. Their lives should have reflected the qualities of their heavenly Father, just as they should today (1 Pt 1:15–16).

Israel's Inexcusability (48:3–5)

Isaiah declared that Israel stood without excuse. The Lord had warned the people of impending judgment time and time again through his prophets, and then he had acted. He knew their stubborn hearts and announced his judgment beforehand so they could not blame their misfortune on their idols. In fact, their idolatry brought them nothing but trouble.

God also declared these things ahead of time so the people would have a record of them, because he knew their stubborn hearts. He had acted according to his faithful character, even in judgment.

God's Even More Stubborn Grace (48:6–22)

Despite Israel's stubbornness, Isaiah nonetheless announced God's determination to bless his people. In doing so, the prophet stressed four aspects of God's grace: his patience, his openness, his instruction, and his redemption.

God's Patience (48:6–11)

God called the people together; would they not admit the truth of what he had said (48:6)? But then God assured them that he would reveal to them hidden things they had not known (48:7). He would reveal a new work he was about to perform.

The Lord then put the situation in proper perspective (48:8–9). Israel had proven a rebel from the beginning of its existence. Nevertheless, God had withheld his wrath for his own glory and to display grace toward his people. Of course, judgment finally did come.

The exile had become the time of Israel's refinement (48:10–11). God had used his people's affliction to test them and strengthen them in their walks of faith. The apostles Paul and James also recognized the potentially good side of afflictions and trials in believers' lives (Rom 5:2–4; Jas 1:2–4). Ultimately, all happened for God's glory. He would not share his glory with another.

God's Openness (48:12–16)

The Lord's statement, "I am he; I am the first and I am the last" (48:12), provided a strong basis for what followed. God was the beginning, the source of everything that existed, and he also was the goal to which all history pointed. He had created the universe, and it responded to his direction (48:13). Generations came and went, but God remained through them all (see sidebar 14.1).

The Lord reiterated his earlier challenge (48:14). Who among all the world's idols had foretold everything he had done? Who else could claim credit for all of this? No one! Cyrus, the Lord's "chosen ally," would bring Babylon's defeat.

Isaiah explained that no one should have been surprised by anything God was doing (48:16). God had not spoken in secret. Now God's Spirit again spoke through Isaiah, confirming everything he had done and would do.

God's Instruction (48:17–19)

Isaiah further stressed the Lord's authority (48:17). The Lord was Israel's redeemer, the Holy One, Israel's covenant God. This redeeming, holy God was also Israel's teacher. He had laid the path he desired before them through his word.

The Lord lamented the fact that his people had not listened to him (48:18).

What peace and righteousness they would have enjoyed had they listened and obeyed! Their descendants would have been innumerable. God's people needed to understand that they could not selectively obey God's commands, but rather they were to follow them completely.

God's Redemption (48:20–22)

Notice how in this chapter the prophet has gone back and forth, alternately discussing what God has done and what Israel has not done. God has predicted; God has forewarned; God has acted. Israel has turned a deaf ear; Israel has refused to listen; Israel has been rebellious since day one.

Isaiah's joyful announcement of God's redemption (48:20–21) recalled the days of Israel's exodus from Egypt, when the people were driven out because the Egyptians feared God's plagues (Ex 12:31–33, 39). The prophet reminded God's people of the blessing their ancestors had experienced during their wilderness days (48:21). God provided them water in the desert and provided for their other needs as well. He would do so again as he brought them home from Babylon.

The chapter's final warning that the wicked will receive no peace (48:22) stands in stark contrast to the positive tone of the text immediately preceding it. Some scholars have consequently suggested it is a later gloss, though no textual evidence supports this assertion.

However, the verse fits well if one understands it as continuing the wilderness imagery Isaiah began in the preceding verse. During the days of the wilderness wanderings, God displayed his power and care for his people in many ways, but many nonetheless refused to place their faith in him. Those who persisted in their rebellion ultimately perished. Isaiah's warning to the wicked reminded his hearers that God's blessing was linked to his people's faithfulness.

The Lord's Servant and Israel's Return (49:1–26)

The theme of the Lord's servant begins Isaiah 49. Following this, Isaiah announced further details of Israel's return to the land. God would guide them, overcome their doubts, and vindicate his own cause.

The Lord's Servant (49:1–7)

The term "servant" appears in the book of Isaiah twenty-two times, thirteen of which occur in Isaiah 40–66. Of these latter usages, most have linked the servant with Israel, though a few usages designate others (44:26). However, one occurrence thus far had a messianic fulfillment (42:1–4; Mt 12:18–21). Isaiah 49:1–7 focuses on this servant's call, cry of complaint, and confirmation in a new task.

The Servant's Call (49:1–3)

The servant called the islands and distant nations to witness his proclamation (49:1; cf. 41:1). Clearly his announcement had implications extending far beyond Israel's borders.

First, the servant described God's call as resting on him since birth (lit. "from the womb").[1] God had set him apart from the beginning of life. The servant thus joined others in Scripture specifically mentioned as set apart for God's purpose even before they were born (Jer 1:4–5; Lk 1:13–17, 31–33; Gal 1:15). Of course, all believers have this special status (Eph 1:4–5).

Second, the servant received special authority from the Lord (49:2). His statement "He made my mouth like a sharpened sword" designates the authority of the servant's word. The apostle John used similar imagery to describe the authority of Jesus Christ at his second coming (Rv 19:15).

Third, the servant had a special purpose. A "polished arrow" would fly straight and true, free from imperfections that might cause it to turn in flight. The expression "concealed me in his quiver" symbolizes the warrior's saving the arrow for just the right shot.

Verse 3 appears to settle the servant's identity with the words, "You are my servant, Israel." However, other issues contribute to the final identification, as we will see later.

The Servant's Cry (49:4)

The Lord's servant described his frustrating ministry. He felt as if his work was for no purpose, perhaps because he had seen few results. The expression "in vain and for nothing" translates the Hebrew words *tohu* and *hebel*. *Tohu* appears in Genesis 1:2 to describe the earth's formlessness prior to God's bringing a created order. It also occurs many times in Isaiah.[2] *Hebel* is the word that appears regularly through Ecclesiastes, translated "meaningless" or "vanity" (Eccl 1:2).[3]

In spite of his feelings of hopelessness, the servant expressed hope that the Lord would grant him justice. He was certain God took note of his faithfulness and ultimately would reward him.

The Servant's Confirmation (49:5–7)

The Lord answered his servant in a way that probably surprised him. He had originally called the servant to "bring Jacob back" and "gather Israel" (49:5). However, he would now expand the servant's ministry worldwide. God's servant would become "a light for the Gentiles" and would thereby bring God's salvation "to the ends of the earth" (49:6). The servant may have been "despised and abhorred" (49:7) by many, but now rulers would bow to his message as they recognized God's blessing on him.

One can only imagine the servant's thoughts as he pondered an even greater task. Yet, he had confessed a knowledge of the Lord's hand on him, so he knew he could count on the Lord for even bigger responsibilities, as large as they may have loomed.

The Servant's Identity

As stated above, the words of 49:3, "You are my servant, Israel," do not settle the issue of the servant's identity. How can Israel have a mission to itself (49:5–6)? For this reason, many interpreters have looked beyond the simplest understanding of the term "Israel."

One option is to understand the servant as the Messiah.[4] Certainly much of the language of the passage fits the New Testament description of Jesus. First, the clear parallel between the sword imagery of 49:2 and Revelation 19:15 has been noted above. Second, the servant's discouragement may parallel Jesus's marveling at the people's unbelief (Mk 6:6), as well as his painful psychological struggles in the Garden of Gethsemane and on the cross (Mt 27:46; Lk 22:39–46; Heb 5:7–10). Third, the servant's description as "despised and abhorred" (49:7) parallels 53:3, as well as the Gospel narratives that highlight Jesus's rejection by many. Fourth, the concept of the servant taking God's message of salvation to the ends of the earth fits the concept of Jesus's sacrifice, which covers the sins of all who place their faith in him, as well as his commission to his disciples (Mt 28:18–20; Acts 1:8).

Biblical evidence also supports understanding the servant as the faithful remnant of Israel. During the apostle Paul's first missionary journey, he and Barnabas testified of Jesus to their audience at Antioch of Pisidia (Acts 13:14–50). They cited themselves as the fulfillment of Isaiah 49:6; God had commissioned them as a light to the Gentiles (Acts 13:47). Thus, this view suggests the faithful within Israel were given the responsibility to spiritually awaken their own nation, but God also sent them to the ends of the earth.

A blending of these views may be best. Perhaps we should understand Isaiah's words as finding fulfillment in the work of both Jesus and his church, inasmuch as the book of Acts suggests the early church continued the ministry of Jesus.

Israel's Return (49:8–26)

As Isaiah continued describing Israel's return home, he stressed three items: God's guidance of his servant, Zion's doubts, and God's vindication.

God's Guidance of His Servant (49:8–13)

The servant's role included mediating God's covenant with his people (49:8; cf. 42:6). He also would play a role in restoring and reassigning the land, as well as proclaiming deliverance to the oppressed (49:9).

Isaiah then used shepherd imagery to describe the blessing that the day of salvation would bring (49:9–12). The Lord's "sheep" (his people) would find ample pastureland and would not suffer from hunger, thirst, or heat. He would lead them and guide their steps. In fact, he would bring them in from everywhere.

Isaiah called heaven and earth to rejoice (49:13). The Lord would comfort his people and demonstrate great compassion toward them.

Zion's Doubts (49:14–21)

Isaiah anticipated Zion's doubts (49:14). Seventy years of exile had taken their toll. Consequently, many people struggled to believe God cared about them anymore. They felt as abandoned and forgotten as they had the day Jerusalem fell (Lam 5:22).

Isaiah brought God's reply (49:15). Could a nursing mother forget her baby? Could she fail to have compassion on her little one? Of course not! First of all, her breasts would become engorged with milk, and she would feel the need to nurse her baby for her own relief. But second and most important, the maternal bond she had with her child made the thought of abandoning the child unthinkable (see sidebar 16.1).

Isaiah then applied this life illustration to God's care for his people, taking it to a new level. All the nursing mothers of Judah would abandon their little ones before the Lord would ever forget his people. In other words, it wasn't going to happen.

Sidebar 16.1
Feminine Imagery in Isaiah 40–66

The book of Isaiah is full of feminine imagery. The prophet uses these images to enhance his people's understanding of God and his relationship with his people. Consider the following chart; you may wish to look up the verses for further study on the topic.[5]

Feminine Relationships	Feminine Activities and Attributes	Feminine Persons, Real and Abstract
Mother/Child: 49:1–7, 14–15, 19–23; 54:1, 4; 60:4; 66:13	*Pregnancy*: 44:2, 24; 46:3–4; 49:1, 5, 15	*Humanized Nations*: 47:1–3, 6–9; 51:17–18; 66:10–11
Daughter/Parent: 43:6; 49:22; 50:1; 52:2; 60:4, 14; 62:11–12	*Birthing*: 7:14–15; 37:3; 42:14; 66:7	*Perverse People/ Leaders*: 3:16–4:1; 57:3
Bride/Groom: 49:18; 61:10; 62:4–5	*Nursing*: 40:11; 49:15, 22–23; 60:16; 66:11–12	*Sarah*: 51:1–2

Of course, the announcement of Immanuel's birth (7:14–15) provides one of Isaiah's most powerful images.

Isaiah's uses of these images prove complementary to his greater purpose, particularly in chapters 40–66. The great spiritual compassion God pours out on his people stresses God's intimate nurture of them, as well as their vital dependence on him.

Isaiah's words also speak to us today. Through the prophet's use of feminine images, believers recognize that God's fatherhood does not preclude all motherly qualities. The father-daughter imagery, as well as the husband-wife imagery, speaks to the different aspects of the family relationship that God has with them. Finally, Isaiah's reference to Sarah reminds us that our heritage is rooted in both genders. The prophet's words encourage today's readers to pursue a more complete and balanced understanding of both God and self.

Further, Isaiah asserted, the Lord had inscribed his people on his palms and constantly viewed their city walls (49:16). How could he forget them? What assurance! God's people found life in God's "waiting room" difficult, but he would act soon.

Isaiah addressed the nation in 49:17–21, challenging it to look around and see the day of salvation dawning. Its children would return from everywhere and become its ornaments. Its enemies would be far away, and the nation would be astounded at the number of children (i.e., citizens) it had in spite of its days of exile and affliction.

God's Vindication (49:22–26)

The Lord himself would orchestrate Israel's day of salvation (49:22). He would raise the standard to signal the procession home. Isaiah continued to address the nation as he announced a day when foreign royalty would bow to Israel. The imagery is reminiscent of 2:1–4, where the prophet described nations streaming to Jerusalem to learn God's ways in the last days.

God would defeat Israel's oppressors even as he saved his own (49:25–26). In that day, all the world would know who reigned as God—the Savior, the Redeemer, the Mighty One of Jacob!

God and His Servant (50:1–11)

In Isaiah 42, the prophet had contrasted God's ideal servant (42:1–9) with his currently wayward servant (42:18–20). Now, Isaiah began with a rebuke of God's people for their sins. He then introduced God's servant, who described his ministry in his own words.

God's Rebuke to Israel (50:1–3)

Isaiah functioned as God's mouthpiece as he placed the blame for the captivity squarely on Israel (50:1). He likened the exile to God's writing Israel a certificate of divorce for the indecency he had found in them (Dt 24:1–4). The sins of the people of Israel had created a spiritual separation between them and their God.

The Lord further clarified the situation (50:2–3). He was more than able to save his people, but when he had called to them, no one answered or listened. The exile did not come because the Babylonians or other foreign powers became too strong for God. Rather, the terrible price the people of Israel paid came solely because of their sin.

The Servant's Testimony (50:4–11)

Isaiah presented the servant's testimony in the first person, in effect allowing the servant to speak for himself. The servant's speech emphasized three areas: the servant's strength, the servant's suffering, and the servant's challenge.

First, the servant described his strength (50:4–5). He had the tongue and the ear of a disciple. He listened to the Lord, his master, who instructed him on what to say in each situation. He followed the Lord obediently.

Second, the servant described his suffering (50:6–7). He was humiliated for God's cause—beaten, mocked, spit upon. Yet, he remained steadfast to that cause (set his face like flint) because he knew the Lord would sustain him and ultimately vindicate him (see sidebar 16.2).

Third, the servant described his challenge (50:8–9). As he reflected on God's protection and vindication, he found himself able to stand strong. Who could accuse him, who could bring charges against him, who could condemn him? No one who mattered! *The Lord God* was on his side. Centuries later, the apostle Paul would draw on the servant's challenge as he described the firm standing of those who place their faith in Jesus (Rom 8:31–39, esp. 33–34).

Isaiah then concluded the chapter with an exhortation (50:10–11). Who among his audience feared the Lord and demonstrated that fear by following the word of God's servant? Only in trusting the Lord would people find deliverance and help for every need. They were to walk in the spiritual light God provided, not in their own light. Following their own ways would only lead to ruin.

The Servant's Identity

The text does not identify the servant of Isaiah 50. Some interpreters have suggested the prophet intended himself.[6] Certainly this is possible. Though we have no specific evidence from the text of Isaiah that he suffered in this way, we do know that prophets sometimes faced abuse for their messages (Jer 20:1–2; 38:4–6).

Similarities between the servant's words and the life of Jesus suggest a messianic connection. Interestingly, the New Testament does not cite 50:4–9 as fulfilled in Jesus, but neither does it cite the announcement in Isaiah 9:6–7. A text may still refer to Jesus even though the New Testament doesn't mention it. The suffering Jesus experienced at his trial, coupled with his firm resolve to stand strong in doing his Father's will, make him a likely candidate for the servant.

Isaiah 50:10–11 also provides a challenge to a life of servanthood. Isaiah challenged his hearers to follow the Lord as faithfully as the Lord's servant did. The servant found his fulfillment in pursuing God's fulfillment, God's glory. Nothing else really mattered.

Sidebar 16.2
Following God When It Hurts

Second Corinthians 5:15 says, "And he [Jesus] died for all, that those who live should no longer live for themselves but for him who died for them and was raised again." Followers of Jesus thus have new marching orders. They live to serve him, to fit into his plan. He does not exist to fit into theirs.

Sometimes following Jesus means facing difficult circumstances. A woman loses her job for sharing her faith, missionaries' financial support dries up and they must return home, or a couple's neighbors shun them for "being too righteous." In such circumstances, believers must come back to the fundamental question: "What has God called me to do?"

Sometimes the world today views followers of Jesus as out of touch or even insane because of the choices they make in following what they perceive as God's will for their lives. A doctor may be asked, "Why, when you worked so hard to put yourself through medical school, do you work in a culture where your pay for surgery is a few bunches of bananas rather than several thousand dollars?" Others may question why a couple would sell a lucrative business and use the money to pay tuition for training to do church-related ministry. It just doesn't make sense to those without spiritual awareness.

For the servant in Isaiah 50, God's calling was the key issue. God called him, and God gave him the strength to respond to that call. He remembered God's faithfulness in the past and consequently trusted him in the present.

God will probably give his followers more significant ministry opportunities as they show themselves faithful, but sometimes he calls his children to tasks that even they do not understand. In such times, they must remember the servant's example and choose to trust God, which will lead to results that will honor him.

Encouragement to the Righteous (51:1–16)

Isaiah 51 begins with a threefold challenge: look to the past, look to the future, and look to the present. The Lord has done great things in the past and will do great things for his people in the future, so they can trust him for the present. Isaiah's prayer then follows, along with God's response to that prayer.

Look to the Past (51:1–3)

Isaiah now addressed those in his audience who wanted to pursue the Lord and his righteousness. They could receive encouragement by looking to the past.

Isaiah took them back to their roots. He reminded them how the Lord had created their nation through an elderly couple—Abraham and Sarah—who were unable to have children. Yet God blessed them and gave them Isaac, from whom came Jacob and his sons. God's hand on the nation was evident from the beginning; he would not leave them now.

Look to the Future (51:4–6)

Isaiah also challenged his hearers to look to the future. First, he described the justice that would come for all nations (51:4–5). God's law would become a standard for all peoples, and they would look to him for justice. And the Gentiles would actually become part of God's people. Prophetic words such as these emphasize again that God's desire to reach the nations is not exclusively a New Testament concept.

Second, Isaiah called everyone to reflect on God's power (51:6). The Lord had created heaven and earth, but both of these would pass away one day. His salvation and righteousness, however, would last forever, as would those who had placed their trust in him.

Look to the Present (51:7–8)

Isaiah then brought his audience back to the present. He challenged those who held God's law in their hearts not to fear the reproach and/or persecution others brought against them. Their enemies' plans would come to nothing, but God's salvation and righteousness would last. The vindication of God's own would certainly come.

The Bible calls God's people to live in the present in light of the past and the future. God's work in the past enables his children to trust him for the present. His faithfulness in the past enables us to trust his promises for the future. We gain encouragement to live for him in light of the amazing future God is planning. And yet the Bible always calls us to live faithfully in the present, challenging us to consider the difference God's work in the past and the future will make in our lives today (2 Pt 3:10–11; Rv 22:17).

Isaiah's Prayer (51:9–10)

Isaiah called on the Lord to confirm the promises of action that appeared earlier in the chapter. The prophet asked him to demonstrate the same power he had displayed in his past victories.

The imagery of "Rahab" and "that monster" (51:10) recalls Egypt and Pharaoh (cf. 30:7; Ps 87:4; Ez 29:3). In defeating Egypt, the Lord also demonstrated his power over Egypt's gods (Ex 12:12).

Isaiah also recounted the Lord's parting the waters so his people could cross (51:10). Isaiah 51:11 closely parallels 35:10, with its uplifting announcement of the redeemed returning to Zion with joy. God was, in effect, preparing a "second exodus."

God's Response (51:11–16)

Isaiah proclaimed God's response. The Lord brought comfort to his people. Why did they continue to fear humans who persecuted them, when their comforter had made the universe (51:12–13)?

Isaiah proclaimed that the time of deliverance was at hand (51:14–16). Prisoners would be set free; God had his hand on his own, and he who had created the universe would not forget his own.

Good News for Jerusalem (51:17–52:12)

Isaiah 51:17–52:12 focuses on proclaiming good news for Jerusalem. This good news describes Jerusalem in three ways: Jerusalem the drunkard, Jerusalem the free, and Jerusalem the rejoicing.

Jerusalem the Drunkard (51:17–23)

Isaiah called to Jerusalem to wake up, to rouse itself from its drunken stupor (51:17). Its judgment was complete—it had completely drained the cup of God's wrath and was staggering from the effects.

The concept of the cup of God's wrath is common in prophetic oracles (Jer 25:15, 17, 28; Ez 23:31, 32, 33; Hb 2:16) and appears again in 51:22. To drink the cup of God's wrath is to take in the full measure of God's judgment. Nations who opposed God's people also drank it according to God's timing (Ob 16). This image of the cup of God's wrath was probably foremost in Jesus's mind when he prayed in the Garden of Gethsemane (Mt 26:39, 42; see sidebar 16.3).

Jerusalem's helplessness was obvious (51:18). No one could assist her, for all her children had drunk of the cup (51:19–20). All felt the effects of God's judgment.

Sidebar 16.3
Jesus and the Cup of God's Wrath

The image of the cup that appears in the prophetic writings also appears in the life of Jesus in the New Testament. During his earthly ministry, Jesus referred to the cup he must drink (Mt 20:22). In the Garden of Gethsemane, he also asked that the cup he was about to drink might be taken from him (Mt 26:39, 42). Ultimately, of course, he accepted his Father's will and went to the cross.

The cup of which Jesus spoke was also probably the cup of God's wrath. More than Jesus feared the physical pain of death by crucifixion, he likely dreaded the spiritual separation from God the Father that would occur as Jesus hung on the cross and took on the world's sin (2 Cor 5:21).

The New Testament affirms that Jesus's death satisfied God's righteous wrath against sin. Consequently, God stays true to his character with respect to his infinite sense of justice while also allowing sinners to come into his presence through Jesus's sacrifice. Indeed, the concept of the cup of God's wrath, when applied to Jesus's death, further testifies to God's amazing love on behalf of sinners.

his prerogative to take his people and redeem them for his purpose.

Many nations had oppressed, mocked, and belittled the people of God (52:4–5). Egypt, Assyria, and Babylon had all done so in turn. But in the day of deliverance, God's people would know and call his name again (52:6). God had predicted it, and he would make good on his prediction.

Jerusalem the Rejoicing (52:7–12)

Jerusalem's day of freedom became a day of rejoicing. The feet of the messengers were beautiful in that those feet brought the news of God's deliverance (52:7). The announcement of peace and salvation rang from the mountaintops.

Jerusalem's watchmen were the first to see the runner approaching with the news, and they shouted joyfully together (52:8). The text does not tell us who the watchmen were. Some interpreters have connected them with prophets, who are elsewhere called watchmen (Ez 3:17; 33:2, 7), though nothing here requires them to be. The watchmen may simply add to the imagery of a runner bringing the message of God's deliverance to a city that desperately needed to hear it. They led the people in rejoicing as the Lord's glory returned to Zion.

The Lord had indeed restored Zion (52:9–10). When the time of salvation came, the Lord "rolled up his sleeves" (lit. "bared his arm") before the nations and manifested the salvation of his people before them. The text does not reveal why the Lord wanted all the nations to see him save his people, but probably he displayed his glory so that

At the same time, Isaiah assured his hearers that Jerusalem's rescue was certain (51:21–23). God would "sober Jerusalem up" by removing from it the cup of his judgment. Instead, he would give the cup to the nations that had opposed Jerusalem, and they would face his judgment.

Jerusalem the Free (52:1–6)

Isaiah announced the glad day when Jerusalem would again know freedom (52:1–2). Jerusalem's deliverance involved two aspects: removing the evidence of its slavery, such as dust and chains, and adorning itself with splendid garments as befit its royalty.

The Lord had a right to step in and redeem Jerusalem (52:3). He had chosen to give his people into captivity for their sin, not because he owed another kingdom anything. Therefore, it was

Key Term

grace

Study Questions

1. What steps did Isaiah say the Lord took to overcome Israel's stubbornness?

2. What common themes appear in the two servant passages (49:1–7 and 50:4–11)? What differences?

3. Explain Isaiah's encouragement to God's followers through appeals to the past and future.

4. Summarize Isaiah's description of Jerusalem (51:17–52:12). Why do you think Jerusalem receives so much attention in Isaiah?

they too might one day come to share in it (cf. 45:22–23).

God called his people to depart Babylon as a pure people (52:11). As they had purified themselves in earlier days prior to God's great works (Ex 19:10–15; Jos 3:5), the people were now to leave behind all of Babylon's impurities. Isaiah's commands reminded the people they could not fully pursue God's holiness and at the same time cling to their evil ways.[7]

Finally, God's people would not leave Babylon in a panic or frenzy (52:12). The Lord would lead them out in an orderly fashion, protecting them front and rear.

Indeed, Isaiah's words came true to the letter. Cyrus's decree (Ezr 1:1–4) in 539/538 BC led to Sheshbazzar, Zerubbabel, and other Jewish leaders reclaiming the temple vessels and proceeding to Judah in an orderly procession (Ezr 1:5–11).

Isaiah's words of deliverance heralded a glad day when Judah would return from exile. He then went beyond these images to describe God's servant, whose work would bring a salvation with ramifications far beyond deliverance from Babylon (52:13–53:12).

17 The Suffering Servant

Isaiah 52:13–53:12

Outline

- **The Servant's Introduction (52:13–15)**
  The Servant's Wisdom (52:13)
  The Servant's Exalted Status (52:13)
  The Servant's Appearance (52:14)
  The Servant and the Nations (52:15)
- **The Servant's Rejection (53:1–3)**
  The Struggle to Believe in the Servant (53:1)
  The Servant's Ordinary Beginnings (53:2a)
  The Servant Has No Special Appearance (53:2b)
  The Servant Faces Derision and Rejection (53:3)
- **The Servant's Suffering (53:4–6)**
  The Servant's Suffering Is Substitutionary
  The Servant's Suffering Is from God
- **The Servant's Death (53:7–9)**
  The Servant Goes Quietly to Slaughter (53:7)
  The Servant Dies for God's People (53:8)
  The Servant Dies Innocent (53:9)
- **The Servant's Triumph (53:10–12)**
  God Made the Servant a Guilt Offering (53:10)

The Servant Will See His Descendants (53:10–11)
The Servant Will Justify Many (53:11)
The Servant Receives God's Reward (53:12)
- **The Servant's Identity**
  Isaiah
  Israel
  The Remnant of Israel
  Jesus the Messiah
- **Jesus and Servant Leadership**

Objectives

After reading this chapter, you should be able to

1. Name the five main points of the servant passage.
2. Summarize the issues surrounding the servant's identity.
3. Explain the New Testament evidence that points to Jesus as the servant.

Probably no chapter in all of Old Testament prophecy has generated as much discussion as Isaiah 53. Over the centuries, scholars have studied it in depth to glean from it the richness of its message. And beyond that, the question remains: What, if any, is the application of the prophetic message to the twenty-first century?

As we study this important text, we will first attempt to discern its pertinent details—details on which scholars have expressed fairly consistent agreement. We then will survey three possible interpretations and give a rationale for each.

The prophetic unit we commonly call "Isaiah 53" actually begins in 52:13. The passage contains fifteen verses and divides symmetrically into five three-verse sections. These five sections describe the servant's introduction, the servant's rejection, the servant's suffering, the servant's death, and the servant's triumph.

A first-century tomb with flat stone to block the tomb entrance, the kind of tomb into which Jesus's body was placed (Courtesy of Bryan E. Beyer)

The Servant's Introduction (52:13–15)

The passage begins somewhat abruptly following the scene of Jerusalem rejoicing (52:7–12). The Hebrew word *hinneh*, translated "see" or "behold," indicates the beginning of a new section.

In this introductory section, Isaiah described the servant's wisdom, exalted status, appearance, and relationship to the nations.

The Servant's Wisdom (52:13)

Isaiah said the Lord's servant would act wisely. Some translations read "My servant will prosper," which can be misleading if we understand prosperity as financial gain. However, the Hebrew word *sakal* typically describes someone with advanced insight, wisdom, knowledge, or understanding (41:20, "understand"; Jer 23:5, "reign wisely"; Dn 1:17, "understanding").

The Servant's Exalted Status (52:13)

Isaiah described the Lord's servant as "raised and lifted up." The Hebrew words behind this expression (*rum* and *nasa'*, respectively) are the same two words Isaiah used to describe the Lord's majesty in the temple vision (6:1). Many interpreters see this parallel in the text as intentional, thereby suggesting the servant is more than an ordinary human being.[1]

The Servant's Appearance (52:14)

Our discussion of 52:14 involves two issues. First, we must determine who is the object of the verb "appalled." Second, the verse describes the servant's disfiguration, presumably at the hands of others.

"Appalled at *You*" or "Appalled at *Him*"?

English translations of 52:14 differ slightly in one important way. The question lies in whether to read the verse "there were many who were appalled at *him*" or "there were many who were appalled at *you*." The difference in translations is due to a variation in the manuscripts involving two Hebrew letters that look quite similar (see sidebar 17.1).

Sidebar 17.1
Illustration of "At You" and "At Him" in Isaiah 52:14

The early manuscripts render the Hebrew expression in Isaiah 52:14 either "many were appalled *at you*" or "many were appalled *at him*." Students should remember that Hebrew reads from right to left, so the question concerns the last (leftmost) letter of each word. The first three are identical.

עָלֶיךָ "at you" (Masoretic Text [MT], Septuagint [LXX])
עָלָיו "at him" (Syriac, Targum)

The two letters in question are ו (*vav*) and ך (final *kaph*). One can see how in the later Hebrew script, though distinctions exist, the letters might be confused if handwritten. In earlier periods of the Hebrew script (shortly after Isaiah), the distinction between the two letters was even less pronounced. A scribe may have thought "at him" was correct because all the other references in the passage referred to "him." However, the more difficult reading has the support of the two best manuscripts (Masoretic Text and Septuagint) and may well be correct. If so, the Hebrew text clearly distinguishes the servant from Israel.

The Masoretic Text (the most reliable Hebrew manuscript) and the Septuagint (the Greek translation of the Old Testament) agree on the reading "you." The agreement of these two witnesses is strong evidence in favor of understanding "you" as the correct reading. Later manuscripts have the reading "him."[2]

The NASB adopts the reading "you" and adds the words "my people" in italics, thereby indicating the words are not present in the original text, in order to clarify what it believes is the correct meaning. Indeed, understanding "you" as the proper reading does lead one to surmise that Isaiah is distinguishing the servant from Israel.

Isaiah's point would be that just as many were appalled at Israel's disfigured appearance in the exile, so the servant's appearance was marred as well. On the other hand, reading "him" in 52:14 does not rule out distinguishing the servant from Israel.

The Servant's Disfiguration

Regardless of how we understand the Hebrew textual variant at the begin-ning of the verse, it is clear many were appalled at the servant's disfigured appearance. The text does not indicate how the servant came to be disfigured and marred, only that it was so.

The Servant and the Nations (52:15)

Already in the first few verses of this servant passage, the text makes it clear that the servant's ministry affects not only Israel but also the nations.

The Servant Sprinkles Nations

Isaiah said the servant would sprin-kle many nations. Some scholars have debated the use of the Hebrew word *nazah*, here translated "sprinkle," and suggested—based on the Septuagint reading—that the word should be translated "startle" or "surprise." This theory, however, has difficulty reconcil-ing the Hebrew to this meaning.[3]

If in fact the idea of "sprinkle" is correct, the connotation is probably priestly, since the word is typically used in a cultic sense.[4] The servant somehow intercedes on behalf of the nations as a priest might do. Exactly how he does this is not revealed until later.

The Servant Shuts Kings' Mouths

Isaiah said the earth's kings would shut their mouths because of the servant. Through the servant's ministry, these rulers would come to understand truths they had never formally encountered. As they observed his life, their unexpected understanding would lead them to silence. Indeed, the servant had quite a ministry if he could silence the world's leaders.

The Servant's Rejection (53:1–3)

After the amazing statement of 52:15 that the servant would silence the earth's rulers, one would expect an announcement of the servant's universal acceptance. Instead, Isaiah now described the servant's rejection.

The Struggle to Believe in the Servant (53:1)

Isaiah asked two rhetorical questions: "Who has believed our message?" and "To whom has the arm of the Lord been revealed?"

The questions anticipate a less-than-ideal reception for God's servant. Were someone to answer the questions in light of what follows, the answers would be something like this: (1) "Very few people" and (2) "The Lord's arm (i.e., his work) was revealed widely through the servant, but few believed the Lord would work in that way."

The Servant's Ordinary Beginnings (53:2a)

Many may have rejected the servant because of his ordinary beginnings. They didn't expect him to grow up in their midst just like everyone else. A young plant doesn't suddenly burst on the scene; rather, it pushes itself gently through the dirt into the light. Likewise, the servant's arrival was unassuming.

Interestingly, the Hebrew word translated "root" (*shoresh*) may subtly link the servant to other Isaianic texts that use this imagery to describe a special divine work (11:1, 10; 37:31). The servant's humble beginnings would not limit his amazing accomplishments.

The Servant Has No Special Appearance (53:2b)

Isaiah described another reason the servant may have faced rejection: nothing was particularly special about his appearance. Nothing about his stature naturally attracted attention. The Hebrew word translated "beauty" or "form" (*to'ar*) designated a person's physical features. The Hebrew word translated "majesty" or "greatness" (*hadar*) designated more a quality of being.

The servant stood out in neither way. Consequently, few initially thought him of any importance.

The Servant Faces Derision and Rejection (53:3)

Isaiah said people struggled to believe in the servant because of his ordinary beginnings and lack of special appearance or demeanor. He also described the servant as despised and rejected.

The servant did not follow what most people think of as the path to leadership. Rather, 53:3 indicates more a sweeping rejection by the general populace. The servant's life was marked by sorrow and emotional pain, and he knew suffering and grief well.

Isaiah's likening the servant to "one from whom men hide their faces" stresses the servant's ostracism by those among whom he ministered. Again, he stressed that many people did not esteem him as anyone special.

The Servant's Suffering (53:4–6)

Isaiah had already described the servant's rejection with its accompanying emotional pain and sorrow. In this next section, physical pain was added to the servant's suffering. And yet something was different about that suffering. First, the servant's suffering was substitutionary; that is, he suffered for others, not for himself. Second, the servant's suffering actually came from God's hand.

The Servant's Suffering Is Substitutionary

Isaiah described the servant's suffering as substitutionary. The servant did not suffer for his own sin and wrongdoing; rather, he took on himself the sin of others. In doing so, he brought peace and well-being to their lives. Notice the contrasts presented in sidebar 17.2.

Isaiah described God's people as straying sheep (53:6). They followed their own needs and ways. But the servant remained focused on his task, willingly taking on what the Lord gave him.

The Servant's Suffering Is from God

Isaiah added an interesting twist to his description of the servant. The servant's suffering actually came from God. Many prophets experienced suffering and persecution because they boldly proclaimed God's truth to a rebellious audience (1 Kgs 19:1–2; 22:26–27; Jer 20:1–2). But this servant was different. The same divine hand that enabled him to serve also brought suffering on him.

Twice in this section Isaiah stressed this concept. First, the people themselves somehow recognized God's hand in the servant's suffering, even as he took upon himself the people's infirmities and sorrows (53:4). Second, the Lord laid the iniquity of all the people on his servant, even as they spiritually wandered astray (53:6).

This concept of substitutionary suffering at God's hand for the sins of others is unique to Isaiah in the Old Testament prophetic corpus. Servants of God sometimes suffered as they ministered, and God's hand sometimes used suffering as his instrument to mold people into his image. But no other servant or prophet actually suffered *for* the sins of the people, taking their punishment and allowing them to go free.

The Servant's Death (53:7–9)

The servant's suffering led to his death. He went quietly to slaughter, dying for God's people, though he himself remained innocent of wrong.

The Servant Goes Quietly to Slaughter (53:7)

Isaiah described the servant as silent amid oppression and affliction. Usually, people who are in the right at least have something to say to defend themselves. Even orphans and widows, who often were not in a position to defend them-

guilt offering

selves because they didn't have the necessary societal clout, would at least try to do so (1:17, 23). But the servant suffered in silence.

Isaiah described the servant as going "like a lamb to the slaughter" and silent "as a sheep before her shearers." He endured it all without protest.

The Servant Dies for God's People (53:8)

As the servant was taken away to judgment, all appeared lost. The question "Who can speak of his descendants?" is again rhetorical, anticipating a reply of "no one." The servant had no descendants to continue his name or his ministry.

The expression "land of the living" is a common poetic expression designating life.[5] Consequently, to be cut off from the land of the living was to die. Hezekiah had despaired during the days of his own illness that he would no longer see the Lord in the land of the living (38:11).

Isaiah added an almost parenthetical note reminding his audience that the people actually deserved the servant's lot. Nevertheless, he had died for their transgressions.

The Servant Dies Innocent (53:9)

The servant's death highlighted two stark contrasts. First, his death and burial were linked with both wicked men and a rich man. Some commentators have suggested the parallelism between wicked and rich signifies a negative connotation for the latter, though nothing in the text suggests this. Mysteriously, the servant was associated with both the wicked and the wealthy as he died.

Second, the servant died for a sinful people, but he died innocent. The Hebrew word translated "violence" is *hamas*, a word that carries with it the notion of unjust violence (Ob 10; Hb 1:2, 3).[6] The servant committed no violence or deceit, yet he died in shame.

The Servant's Triumph (53:10–12)

After three sections describing the servant's rejection, suffering, and death, one does not expect a section denoting the servant's triumph. Indeed, this servant took a very different path to victory.

Isaiah announced four aspects related to the servant's triumph. First, God made the servant a **guilt offering**. Second, the servant would see his descendants. Third, the servant would justify many. Fourth, the servant would receive God's reward.

God Made the Servant a Guilt Offering (53:10)

Isaiah explained the ultimate reason behind the servant's death: "It was the LORD's will to crush him." A slightly more literal translation (NASB) reads, "The LORD was pleased to crush Him." Either way, the prophet places ultimate responsibility on the Lord for the servant's death. Why would the Lord delight in such an act?

Isaiah also described the servant's life as a guilt offering.[7] The Bible uses the term "guilt" in a legal sense. The term denotes a condition in which sinners find themselves regardless of how they feel about their sin. The concept of guilt here is identical to its use in our modern legal system. To find a defendant guilty means the defendant committed the crime and therefore owes restitution. The amazing fact regarding the servant in 53:10 is that the giving of his life provided restitution for others, not for himself.

The Servant Will See His Descendants (53:10–11)

Isaiah's words in 53:8 suggested the servant's generation would end with the servant. No descendants would be forthcoming. But now Isaiah announced, "He will see his offspring and prolong his days" (v. 10). Somehow,

justify

the servant who died would yet see his descendants.

Further, the Lord's good pleasure or will would "prosper in his hand" (53:10). The same Lord who willed that the servant be crushed now willed that he prosper.

The Servant Will Justify Many (53:11)

The legal language continued as Isaiah described the servant's triumph. The servant had been despised, rejected, condemned, and put to death. But he would know satisfaction following his anguish.

The servant was earlier described as raised, lifted up, and highly exalted (52:13). Now Isaiah described him as the Lord's righteous one. The servant had demonstrated his own righteousness through his willingness to follow his Lord's will completely. Now he saw the fruit of his labor.

The Hebrew word translated "**justify**" and the Hebrew word translated "righteous" are from the same Hebrew root (*tsadaq*). Again, the sense is legal, for one who was justified was declared not guilty. However, the servant did not justify himself, for he was innocent (53:9). Rather, he justified the many, whose sins he bore (53:12). Because he bore their sins, they were counted not guilty. Had they been guilty? Yes. But not anymore.

Isaiah thus described a servant despised, rejected, and put to death. But in the end, the servant gained God's approval, which ultimately was all that mattered. Through his faithful ministry, the servant demonstrated himself righteous. The divine verdict was "not guilty."

The Servant Receives God's Reward (53:12)

Isaiah used the language of battle to describe the victorious servant. He would receive a portion with great ones and divide the spoils with the strong. We should probably understand the initial "I" of 53:12 as God speaking,

thereby registering divine approval. And the servant gained his victory by pouring himself out unto death.

Notice the careful distinction in Isaiah's description. The servant "was numbered with the transgressors." Although he was not a transgressor, he cast his lot with them. Further, he bore their sin and interceded for them. Such was his path to victory.

The Servant's Identity

As stated in the introduction to this chapter, Isaiah 52:13–53:12 stands as one of the most analyzed and debated passages in the Bible. But after all the analysis and debate conclude, typically four theories remain regarding the identity of the servant. The consensus is that the servant is either Isaiah, Israel, a remnant of Israel, or Jesus the Messiah.

Isaiah

Some scholars have suggested the servant could be Isaiah.[8] According to this view, Isaiah was presenting a veiled autobiographical account of his prophetic ministry. He had no special appearance that anyone should think anything of him, and eventually the people rejected him. He suffered for the people's sins and eventually died, but ended victorious because God blessed his ministry and gave him his eternal reward.

This interpretation, however, fails on many accounts. The Scriptures give no suggestion elsewhere that any prophet ever suffered for the sins of the people. True, prophets suffered, because their uncompromising stance toward God and his message ran counter to their hearers' prevailing thoughts and practices. But Scripture gives no hint of a substitutionary suffering by which Isaiah or any other prophet paid a price on behalf of the nation.

Jewish tradition also is strangely silent on such a view. It suggests Isaiah was martyred during Manasseh's reign by being placed between two boards and sawn in half but does not allude to Isaiah 53 in its description. Isaiah's death does not seem to have fulfilled prophecy in any way.

Israel

A second view suggests Israel fulfilled Isaiah's description of the suffering servant.[9] According to this interpretation, the kings of the earth (52:15) became amazed when they realized the impact the nation of Israel had upon the world. Isaiah 53:1–12 then largely reflects the thoughts of the nations, who saw Israel as a suffering servant of its God.

The nations were astounded; who would have believed Israel was anything special? Here was a nation well acquainted with grief and sorrow. Yet, it carried the sin of the world on itself. Israel's suffering led to the nations' healing and redemption. The nations had all gone spiritually astray, and the Lord laid their iniquity on Israel. Israel's quiet suffering through all it endured from nations such as Egypt, Assyria, and Babylon brought hope and reconciliation to the world.

This interpretation also fails on several points. First, 52:14 distinguishes Israel from the servant unless we adopt the textual variant with lesser support (see sidebar 17.1).

Second, there is no suggestion in the Bible that Israel or Judah ever suffered for the sins of other nations. They suffered at the hands of other nations, but not on their behalf. Such a suggestion totally contradicts 2 Kings 17 and the book of Lamentations, which clearly place the blame for the Assyrian and Babylonian conquests on the sin and faithlessness of Israel and Judah. It would be inconsistent for Isaiah, who lived during the time of Israel's fall to Assyria, to suggest that Judah's northern neighbor was guiltless, let alone that Israel's suffering was really for the sins of others.

Third, the idea of Israel's interceding for the nations (53:12) around them is inconsistent with Isaiah's oracles against the nations, as well as the general indictment the prophets place on them. Unless Isaiah 53:12 alone mentions it, the Old Testament is silent on such a concept.

The Remnant of Israel

Some interpreters have suggested that the servant is not Israel but rather the faithful remnant of Israel.[10] This has many parallels with the previous view and also has many of the same drawbacks.

According to this view, during the time of Israel's growth as a nation, the remnant was following the Lord faithfully. As the nation began to stray spiritually, the remnant remained quietly steadfast. As Israel began to suffer for its sins, the remnant suffered most of all, for it had remained faithful to the Lord yet had to endure God's judgments. Only later did Israel reflect on this fact and realize what the remnant had done.

This view may see 53:1–12 as the rest of Israel speaking rather than as the nations speaking, as in the earlier view. Who would have believed such things would befall the faithful remnant?

As stated, the remnant view struggles with the same difficulty as the Israel view. Especially noteworthy is the problem of the remnant allegedly suffering for the sins of the nation. Again, the faithful suffered because of the sins of others and may have even faced persecution from their own, but they did not pay the price of others' sins. More people than merely the remnant went into exile following the Assyrian conquest. Isaiah does indeed speak of a future remnant, but he never suggests the remnant suffered in the place of its fellow citizens.

Jesus the Messiah

The Christian church since its beginning has believed Jesus of Nazareth fulfilled Isaiah's words regarding the servant. Evidence for this view comes largely from the New Testament itself

Sidebar 17.3
Citations of Isaiah 52:13–53:12 in the New Testament

Isaiah Verse(s)	New Testament Citation(s)
52:15	Romans 15:21
53:1	John 12:38; Romans 10:16
53:4	Matthew 8:17
53:7–8	Acts 8:32–33 (Septuagint)
53:9	1 Peter 2:22
53:12	Luke 22:37

The significant usage of this passage by many New Testament writers provides early testimony to the link the early church made between Isaiah's words and the life and ministry of Jesus.

Targum

Rashi

and is supported by early Christian and Jewish writings.

Evidence from the New Testament

The New Testament cites the book of Isaiah over sixty times. Seven of these come from Isaiah 52:13–53:12 (see sidebar 17.3).

All seven usages link the servant of Isaiah with Jesus. Paul applied 52:15 to the concept of nations coming to faith in Christ (Rom 15:21) and also applied 53:1 to unbelieving Jews, as did John (Jn 12:38; Rom 10:16). Matthew associated Jesus's healing works with 53:4 (Mt 8:17). Luke recorded the Ethiopian official's reading of 53:7–8 and described Philip's explanation of its link with Jesus (Acts 8:32–35). Peter used 53:9 to testify to Jesus's sinlessness (1 Pt 2:22). Finally, Jesus cited 53:12 in testifying of himself (Lk 22:37).

Further details from Jesus's life also fit point by point with Isaiah's description of the servant (see sidebar 17.4). Isaiah's words describe events from the beginning of Jesus's ministry to its culmination in the resurrection. Certainly this is more than coincidence.

Isaiah 52:13–53:12 is the fourth and final servant passage of Isaiah 40–66 (42:1–9; 49:1–7; 50:4–11; 52:13–53:12). We have already noted the link between Jesus and 42:1–9, as well as possible messianic links with 49:1–7 and 50:4–11. It thus seems justifiable to entertain the notion of another messianic fulfillment in 52:13–53:12, despite other clear Isaianic references to Israel as the servant (41:8; 43:10; 44:2).

The New Testament, the most historical and well-documented record of Jesus's life and ministry,[11] must be taken seriously in its claims regarding Jesus's fulfillment of Isaiah's words. People who observed Jesus's ministry firsthand saw in him an undeniable connection with the suffering servant. People may choose to accept or reject their testimony, but they cannot deny the unanimity of the New Testament witness.

Evidence from Early Jewish and Christian Writings

A survey of the literature from the period of the early church reveals surprising evidence. As one might expect, the church fathers see Jesus as the fulfillment of Isaiah 52:13–53:12. However, early evidence from Judaism also suggests Isaiah's words describe the Messiah.

The **Targum** to Isaiah, an early Aramaic witness to the Hebrew Old Testament, interestingly adds the words "The Messiah" after the words "my servant" in 52:13. And the Targum does not stand as a lone witness. Jewish authorities who debated early church leaders did not believe the Messiah was Jesus, but they agreed Isaiah's words described the Messiah.[12]

The first known Jewish commentator to suggest that Israel might be the suffering servant was **Rashi**, who lived in the eleventh century AD. Rashi found his supporters, but Jewish commentators after Rashi sometimes disagreed with him, arguing the messianic view but distinguishing the Messiah from Jesus as earlier Jewish interpreters had done.

Sidebar 17.4
Jesus and Isaiah 53

Isaiah 52:13–53:12 (often simply called "Isaiah 53") forms one of the Old Testament's most remarkable prophecies concerning Jesus Christ. The following chart summarizes Isaiah's words and how Jesus fulfilled them:

Verse	The Servant's Description	Fulfillment in Jesus
52:13	Raised, lifted up, exalted	God exalted him and will exalt him fully at the second coming (Phil 2:9–11)
52:14	Appearance disfigured	Received beating at his trial (Mt 26:67)
52:15	Sprinkled many nations	Sprinkling of his blood brings forgiveness (1 Pt 1:2)
53:3	Despised and rejected	Many rejected him, especially the leaders (Jn 11:47–50)
53:4–6	Suffered for our sin; stricken by God	Died for our sin according to God's plan (1 Cor 15:3)
53:7	Silent before oppressors	Silent before accusers at his trial (Mk 14:60–61)
53:8	Killed for his people's sin	Died for our sin (2 Cor 5:14–15)
53:9	Assigned a grave with the wicked and rich, but did no wrong	Crucified between two robbers, buried in a rich council member's tomb (Mk 15:27–28, 43–46)
53:10	Lord's will to crush him; he will see his offspring	God prepared him as an offering for sin (Rom 5:9; 2 Cor 5:21)
53:12	Receives great reward because he poured out his life	Receives great reward because he poured out his life (Phil 2:9–11; Heb 1:3–4)

This evidence is important because sometimes one gets the impression Judaism has always maintained the servant is Israel, whereas the church has believed the servant is Jesus. Actually, both Judaism and Christianity appear to have been united for a millennium in believing 52:13–53:12 described the Messiah. The difference of opinion lay only with the issue of the Messiah's specific identity.

Jesus and Servant Leadership

The New Testament and evidence from the early church period argue strongly that the servant of Isaiah 52:13–53:12 is Jesus of Nazareth. By his life and ministry, Jesus fulfilled Isaiah's words to the letter.

Jesus's life teaches much about servant leadership. Jesus told his disciples that he came to serve others (Mk 10:45).

Key Terms

guilt offering

justify

Rashi

Targum

Study Questions

1. List the five main sections of Isaiah 52:13–53:12.

2. Summarize the details of the servant's life and ministry.

3. Discuss the various arguments related to identifying the servant.

4. Why do the New Testament writers see Jesus as the servant? Cite key verses in your answers.

He also contrasted the leadership of his day with the servant leadership he expected of his disciples (Mt 18:25–28). At his last meal with his disciples before his death, he served them by washing their feet, thereby giving them an example of humility (Jn 13:1–17).

Jesus modeled servant leadership in that he showed the disciples he led a life totally yielded to God, his Father. Through his total surrender, he won ultimate victory.

The servant is first and foremost a slave. Slaves have no rights; they find their fulfillment in doing the will of their master. The New Testament asserts that believers have become slaves to God through Jesus Christ (Rom 6:22). These believer-slaves find their fulfillment in his fulfillment, their ultimate joy in knowing his will is done through them. Indeed, for the New Testament writers, becoming a slave of Christ brings the greatest freedom one can attain.[13]

18 Celebrating the Return

Isaiah 54:1–59:21

Outline

- **Jerusalem's Rebirth (54:1–17)**
  The Command to Celebrate the Rebirth (54:1–3)
  The Lord's Plan concerning the Rebirth (54:4–10)
  The Establishment of the Rebirth (54:11–17)
- **Call to Trust in God (55:1–13)**
  Buy True Riches (55:1–2)
  Remember David (55:3–5)
  Yield Yourselves to God! (55:6–13)
- **Foreigners Join God's Family (56:1–8)**
  Call to Righteous Living (56:1–2)
  Call to Eunuchs and Foreigners (56:3–8)
- **Israel's Sins Answered with God's Healing and Restoration (56:9–57:21)**
  Israel's Sins (56:9–57:13)
  God Brings Healing and Restoration (57:14–21)
- **Call to True Righteousness (58:1–14)**
  True Discipleship (58:1–2)
  True Fasting (58:3–12)
  True Sabbath Observance (58:13–14)

- **Israel's Sin and God's Deliverance (59:1–21)**
  Israel's Sin (59:1–15a)
  God's Deliverance (59:15b–21)

Objectives

After reading this chapter, you should be able to

1. Summarize Isaiah's description of Jerusalem's rebirth (54:1–17).
2. Discuss Isaiah's challenge to trust in God and his promises (55:1–13).
3. Explain key issues related to life in God's covenant community (56:1–8; 58:1–14).

I recently attended a conference dealing with change in the local church. One of the speakers asserted that most church people need to hear a new idea fifteen to twenty times before they grasp it fully, let alone decide to adopt it. Change often comes slowly, because people are either comfortable with the way things are or have decided to settle for the way things are.

Isaiah has already proclaimed the good news of God's people returning to their land in a number of ways. God was redeeming his people—through Cyrus and in other ways. In Isaiah 54–59, he continued to emphasize this important theme as he reassured his people of God's amazing coming work.

Jerusalem's Rebirth (54:1–17)

The idea that Jerusalem could be reborn after seventy years sounded strange to many. Nevertheless, Isaiah insisted it would happen. He commanded the people to celebrate Jerusalem's rebirth, declared the Lord's plan for it, and announced its establishment.

The Command to Celebrate the Rebirth (54:1–3)

Isaiah's command to celebrate Jerusalem's rebirth contains two important aspects. The barren people and land would become fertile, and the people would multiply.

The Barren Become Fertile (54:1)

Isaiah's command for the barren woman to celebrate introduced immediate tension into his prophecy. Barrenness was *not* something women celebrated. But Isaiah quickly went on to explain that the "desolate" (i.e., barren) woman would now have many children.

The comparison of the desolate woman with "her who has a husband" may provide clarification as to Isaiah's usage of the term "barren." He might have been comparing a married barren woman with a married woman who had already borne children. But more likely he was using "desolate" to describe a divorced woman. This interpretation agrees with his imagery in 54:6. God was taking Israel, the bride he had forsaken into exile, back again.

The apostle Paul cited Isaiah 54:1 when he compared those who sought to make themselves right with God by keeping the law of Moses with those who placed their faith in Jesus Christ (Gal 4:27). And just as in Paul's day God was working in a way people didn't expect, so Isaiah announced a new work God would perform among his people. They didn't expect to return from exile, but they would, and when they did, God would bless them beyond their dreams.

The People Multiply (54:2–3)

Isaiah instructed the people to spread their tents out, to expand their territory. They needed to make room for all the people God would bring home and raise up.

Today some countries talk about limiting the growth of their population. China has taken intentional steps to do so. But this was not Isaiah's perspective. The more people Israel had, the better.

The words "You will spread out to the right and to the left" would probably have reminded Isaiah's hearers of God's blessing to Jacob at Bethel (Gn 28:14). The Lord had promised Jacob that his descendants would spread out (*parats*, the same Hebrew word) to the west, the east, the north, and the south. Now the return of God's people to the land would lead to dispossessing other nations and resettling desolate cities. The Hebrew root *shamam*, "desolate," is used of both the woman (54:1) and the cities (54:3), a fact that strengthens the identity of the barren woman of 54:1.

hesed

The Lord's Plan concerning the Rebirth (54:4–10)

Isaiah presented three aspects of the Lord's plan concerning Jerusalem's rebirth. First, the Lord had redeemed his people. Second, the Lord had disciplined his people, but now that disciplinary action was complete. Third, the Lord promised to keep his people forever.

The Lord Has Redeemed His People (54:4–6)

Isaiah encouraged his hearers not to fear shame and disgrace (54:4). He introduced two themes that he would then comment on a few verses later: the shame of Israel's youth and the reproach of Israel's widowhood.

The Lord Almighty, the Holy One of Israel, was Israel's husband. The concept of redemption here (Heb. verb *ga'al*) denotes buying back or taking back. In this case, the Lord was calling back to himself the wayward bride he had disciplined for a time during the exile. He had married her during her youth, and she had known the feeling of widowhood during the time of the exile, but now God's redemption had come.

The Lord's Discipline Is Now Complete (54:7–8)

Why did the exile happen? Isaiah asserted that the Lord had dealt with his people through a "disciplinary abandonment," an abandonment they knew only briefly in comparison with the long time he had known them (54:7). He would now restore them with deep compassion.

In a "surge of anger" (54:8), the Lord had turned his face from his people. Again, Isaiah adds, "for a moment," in contrast to the long time he had endured their sin. But now, he would gather them with "everlasting kindness."

The rich Hebrew term *hesed* is rendered "kindness" here. It occurs over one hundred times in the Old Testament with a wide range of meanings. Here, it parallels compassion, so "kindness" or "tenderness" fits well. Elsewhere *hesed*

denotes God's covenant love—all that comes to his children because they are his people.

The Lord Will Keep His People Forever (54:9–10)

Isaiah reached back to the book of Genesis for an illustration that would drive home the magnitude of God's redemptive promise (54:9). God made a covenant with Noah after the flood destroyed all humanity except Noah and his family (Gn 9:8–17). He promised to put his rainbow in the clouds as a reminder that he would not destroy the earth again. The Lord was equally serious now about his commitment to his people. He would not exile them again.

Isaiah also added a promise related to nature. The mountains and hills would dissolve before God's "unfailing love"—again, he used the term *hesed*—would ever depart from his people. The expression "covenant of peace" denotes a covenant whose chief feature would be lasting *shalom*. The compassionate Lord of Israel would bring it about.

The Establishment of the Rebirth (54:11–17)

The establishment of Jerusalem's rebirth naturally involved the rebirth of the city itself, which would be rebuilt. But it would not really be a city without a people to inhabit it. In 54:11–17, Isaiah focused on these two aspects of the rebirth.

The City (54:11–12)

Isaiah described the city as "afflicted" and tossed about as a ship beset by storms (54:11). Indeed, Jerusalem had seen its share of affliction. But now the Lord would rebuild his beloved city's foundations and walls with precious stones (54:12).

Such a description is similar to the apostle John's description of the new Jerusalem (Rv 21:18–21). Perhaps Isaiah saw the same images John saw in Revelation, though John added more detail. No doubt Isaiah was again describing the coming golden age of peace and righteousness he himself had described on many occasions (2:1–4; 11:1–10; 35:1–10).

Israel never added precious stones to Jerusalem's foundations and walls; doing so would have prompted enemy attack. If, however, Isaiah was describing the day of God's coming kingdom, when enemies would no longer threaten his people, Jerusalem could display whatever kind of ornamentation it pleased.

The People (54:13–17)

Isaiah described the people who would accompany the Lord's reestablishment of Jerusalem. First, their children would be the Lord's disciples (54:13). A disciple is one who learns from his master. These disciples would carefully follow the instruction of their God, a commitment that would bring them lasting peace.

Second, the Lord promised his people would be far from oppression (54:14–17). No weapons would overtake them, and any opposition would meet quick defeat. Promises of security meant much to people with many hostile neighbors.

Isaiah closed this chapter with a final word of encouragement—"This is the heritage of the servants of the LORD" (54:17). As discussed in the previous chapter of this book, a servant is a slave—someone who finds his own fulfillment in doing his master's will. Israel served a loving master who had its best interests at heart, knew his people better than they knew themselves, and treated them as his own children.

Call to Trust in God (55:1–13)

In light of the amazing promises Isaiah had announced in the previous chapter, he now called on his people to place their absolute trust in God. How could they do anything else? He com-

manded them to buy true riches, to remember David, their greatest king, and to yield themselves totally to God.

Buy True Riches (55:1–2)

As he had done in 54:1, Isaiah now introduced tension in his opening statement (55:1). He invited his hungry and thirsty hearers to purchase all they needed—without cost! He even appealed especially to those with no money. All were welcome to buy goods. But how could people purchase goods if they had no money?

Isaiah then drove home his point (55:2): "Why spend money on what is not bread, and your labor on what does not satisfy?" The people's priorities were completely backward. They spent their money on things that could never bring them ultimate satisfaction.

On the other hand, God's offer of a saving relationship with them was free, yet it would provide them lasting satisfaction. Why would they take their hard-earned money and try to buy happiness, when in the end they would discover that what really mattered in life was free?

The New Testament alludes to Isaiah's words twice. Jesus called the spiritually thirsty to come to him and drink (Jn 7:37–39). The living waters that would flow from them symbolized the coming Holy Spirit. The apostle John alluded to Isaiah's words when he invited all his readers to come to Jesus, thereby receiving "the free gift of the water of life" (Rv 22:17).

Remember David (55:3–5)

Isaiah challenged his hearers to remember David, their great king of old. They needed to listen to the Lord and receive his instruction and thereby receive the blessings of God's covenant with David.

Listen and Live (55:3a)

Isaiah further challenged his hearers to listen and to live (55:3). They were to come to God, incline their ears to him, and listen.

covenant

Often a big difference exists between hearing and listening. Hearing may mean simply the detection of sounds. However, listening usually implies a receptive attitude, a taking to heart of what has been heard. Isaiah called his audience to hear and to listen, to listen and to obey.

Receive the Blessings of David's Covenant (55:3b–5)

The Lord promised an everlasting covenant to those who listened and responded to his offer (55:3). This was not a new covenant but the blessings of the **covenant** he had already made with David (2 Sm 7:8–16). The Hebrew word *hesed* again appears here as in 54:8, 10. Here it denotes the faithful love that God promised David. All the faithful would receive that love.

The passage certainly has messianic overtones. David's legacy of leadership was well known during Isaiah's time, and when the new David (cf. 11:1) appeared, nations would again take notice.

The commands in verse 5 are in the singular form, whereas the commands of verses 1–3 are in the plural.[1] This may suggest that the words of verse 5 are intended for the new David, the Messiah.[2] Nations will hasten to him not to make military peace, as they might have with David, but rather to make their spiritual peace. They will see the splendor with which the Lord will endow his chosen people.

Yield Yourselves to God! (55:6–13)

Isaiah called his people to yield themselves completely to God. They needed to seek him, to marvel at his word, and to claim his promises.

Seek Him (55:6–7)

First, Isaiah called God's people to seek the Lord and call on him "while he is near" (55:6). The sentiment is much like Paul's admonition to the Corinthian church: "In the time of my favor I heard you, and in the day of salvation I helped you" (2 Cor 6:2).[3] Some people in Isaiah's audience may have had their own timetable for deciding to follow God, but for Isaiah, the time was now.

Second, Isaiah called God's people to full-scale repentance (55:7). They needed to turn from sin to God. Not only did people's ways need to change, but their thoughts did too. The prophet called his people to change both externally and internally, for if the heart did not change, righteous deeds would not last.

The Hebrew word translated "turn" (55:7) literally means "repent" or "return."[4] For the Hebrews, repentance meant turning back to the God of their ancestors, returning to the covenant.

Third, Isaiah assured God's people that the repentant could count on God's forgiveness. Those who turned to him would find him ready to grant mercy and pardon.

Marvel at His Word (55:8–11)

Isaiah now voiced the Lord's own words. God's thoughts and ways were far beyond those of his people (55:8–9). He had already commanded them to forsake their own ways and thoughts (55:7). Now, he challenged them to consider the infinite difference between his ways and theirs.

Isaiah called his audience to put their trust in a God whose ways and thoughts infinitely surpassed theirs. Certainly they could fear such a God, but how could they trust him?

The answer lay in the fact that God was loving and trustworthy. He did not act arbitrarily, as the false gods of neighboring peoples typically did. They could count on the consistency of his character, and therefore, it didn't matter if they couldn't grasp the significance of everything he was doing.

Isaiah likened God's word to rain and snow (55:10–11). The rain and the snow watered the earth and produced many favorable results, accomplishing everything for which God sent them. Likewise, God's word, which he sent to his people through his prophets, would accomplish its purpose.

Claim His Promises (55:12–13)

Isaiah concluded his portrayal of the day of salvation with vivid imagery. Peace and joy would accompany God's people, and as they went out, God would lead them (55:12).

All nature would rejoice as well. The day would be as if the mountains and hills shouted along with the people, and the trees added their applause. Clearly Isaiah was using figurative language to describe nature's renewal.

God's work will be so evident that it will provide testimony to God's name (NIV "renown" captures the sense well). The additional usage of the word "sign" (Heb. 'ot) further emphasizes the miraculous extent of the nation's renewal.

Isaiah's words were not intended to depict the return from exile. Rather, they looked ahead to a day when God would usher in his everlasting kingdom. Only in that day would his work be so evident, so dazzling, so complete. Nature would rejoice and so would God's people.

Foreigners Join God's Family (56:1–8)

Isaiah's announcement that foreigners would join God's family must have surprised and perhaps even angered many in ethnocentric Israel. It was one thing to suggest the nations would one day obtain blessing from their relationship with God's people, but it was quite another to assert that they would stand before God on equal spiritual footing. But this was not the first time Isaiah had proclaimed such an idea, and it would not be the last.

Isaiah first called his people to righteous living in light of their relationship with God. He then reassured foreigners and eunuchs that God had not forgotten them and in fact would bless them beyond their hopes.

Call to Righteous Living (56:1–2)

Isaiah challenged his people to practice justice and righteousness (56:1). They needed to live in the light of God's coming salvation. The prophet's words parallel the challenges of John the Baptizer and of Jesus to prepare for the imminent arrival of God's kingdom (Mt 3:2, 17).

Isaiah pronounced blessing on those who kept from evil, but he also singled out **Sabbath** observance for special mention (56:2). He would do so again later (56:4, 6; 58:13–14). Why would Isaiah single out Sabbath observance?

Probably Isaiah mentioned Sabbath observance because it so clearly typified a covenant lifestyle. One refrained from evil but was also careful to observe God's other commands. Ceasing to work one day in seven provided an obvious testimony to everyone around.

Call to Eunuchs and Foreigners (56:3–8)

Isaiah now singled out two groups—eunuchs and foreigners. Though they had different reasons, both these groups believed they would not enjoy God's lasting blessing to the same extent others would.

Word to the Eunuchs (56:3–5)

Isaiah told the eunuchs not to be discouraged. God would reward their faithfulness. Isaiah described what God was looking for: observing the Sabbath, choosing what God delighted in, holding firm to details of the covenant (56:4). Such faithful followers would receive an everlasting name that would not disappear. Eunuchs would produce no earthly families, but they would enjoy all the blessings of God's heavenly family (see sidebar 18.1).

Word to the Foreigners (56:6–8)

Isaiah described the faithful foreigners (56:6). They served the Lord and loved his name. They avoided

Sidebar 18.1
Singleness and the Christian

Isaiah's words of encouragement to eunuchs (56:3–5) underscore an important spiritual principle: God's blessing and approval surpass anything else in life. In Isaiah's day, there were men who because of physical deformity could not have sexual relations. Others (e.g., superintendents of the royal harem) were made eunuchs specifically to prevent them from having sexual relations.

In a society where descendants preserved the family name and provided for one's future, eunuchs may well have felt they had nothing significant to anticipate as they contemplated their future. However, Isaiah assured them God would provide them a name and an honored place in his future kingdom.

Jesus discussed the issue of celibacy in Matthew 19:10–12. He had just proclaimed a high standard for marriage and marital fidelity (Mt 19:3–9), and his disciples' astonishment was reflected in their comment: "If this is the situation between a husband and wife, it is better not to marry" (Mt 19:10). Jesus replied as follows:

> Not everyone can accept this word, but only those to whom it has been given. For some are eunuchs because they were born that way; others were made that way by men; and others have renounced marriage because of the kingdom of heaven. The one who can accept this should accept it. (Mt 19:11–12)

Jesus was not saying everyone should choose singleness. He did say that some may choose to remain single so their attention and energy may be more completely devoted to pursuing God and his kingdom. In fact, Jesus's words in verse 12 appear to commend such a choice.

The apostle Paul also addressed the issue of marriage and singleness in 1 Corinthians 7. He affirmed that most people marry, and that if they choose to do so, they do not sin (1 Cor 7:36), for each has his own gift from the Lord (1 Cor 7:7). However, Paul warned married people or those intending to marry that marriage brought special challenges and also divided one's attentions between the Lord and one's spouse (1 Cor 7:28, 32–34). He also suggested singleness provided a freedom to serve the Lord unreservedly.

In the end, while Paul found great joy in singleness (1 Cor 7:7, 40), he urged all believers to live contentedly in whatever state God called them (1 Cor 7:17, 24). Though we live in a world where most people marry, the Bible portrays singleness as a state with great kingdom potential.

profaning the Sabbath and held to his covenant.

Faithfulness was more important than bloodline (see sidebar 18.2). The Lord would bring them to his holy mountain and bless them with a presence in the temple courts (56:7). The Lord would be well pleased with the sacrifices they offered. God desired that his house be called a house of prayer by *all* nations. He would gather others besides those he already had gathered (56:8).

Jesus made use of both Isaiah's and Jeremiah's words as he drove the money changers from the temple area (Mt 21:13; Mk 11:17; Jer 7:11). The Lord desired his temple to be a place of prayer, but they had made it a den of robbers.

Israel's Sins Answered with God's Healing and Restoration (56:9–57:21)

Isaiah denounced Israel's sins. Nonetheless, God would bring healing and restoration. Those who sought him would see the day of blessing.

Israel's Sins (56:9–57:13)

Isaiah said his people stood guilty of spiritual blindness, injustice, and idolatry. These three categories of sin often go together. Spiritual blindness leads to injustice because people don't realize humanity's moral law is rooted in God's righteous nature. Idolatry comes when people try to make God in their own image, rather than realizing that they are made in God's image.

Spiritual Blindness (56:9–12)

Isaiah denounced Israel's spiritual blindness. God had elsewhere warned he would bring wild animals against his people. Isaiah now called the beasts of the field and forests to come devour the people (56:9).

The term "watchmen" (56:10) probably designated prophets but may have referred to leaders in general. Those who kept guard were like mute dogs, unable to sound the alarm and warn others of an enemy's approach. Dogs who loved to sleep did *not* make good watchdogs.

The dogs and the shepherds had one thing in common: they sought their own gain, not the welfare of their flock (56:11). The latter entertained themselves with strong drink and assured themselves that life's circumstances would never change for them (56:12). Such an attitude led to their self-serving agenda. They would soon discover that God was, in fact, doing something new among his people.

Injustice (57:1–2)

Isaiah denounced the injustice that was rampant in society. Not only did righteous people suffer and even die unjustly, but no one seemed to notice (57:1). Widespread apathy allowed the oppressors to gain total control.

Nonetheless, Isaiah hinted at the hope that awaited those who died unjustly (57:2). They would know God's peace and find rest. This can hardly be simply a reference to the grave but is rather a reminder of a life to come in which God will right all wrongs.

Idolatry (57:3–13)

Isaiah also denounced the people's idolatry. He described them as children of sorcery, adultery, and prostitution, as

Sidebar 18.2
Faithfulness over Bloodline

Much of the Old Testament story focuses on the nation of Israel. God called Abraham out of Ur and led him to a land Abraham did not know. God then gave him a son after testing Abraham's faith for almost twenty-five years. From Abraham and Sarah came Isaac, and to Isaac and Rebekah were born Esau and Jacob. God changed Jacob's name to Israel, and in doing so, God defined his chosen nation.

Nonetheless, the Bible gives many examples of non-Israelites who found favor with God. Jethro, Moses's father-in-law, served the Lord as a priest of Midian prior to God's call of Moses (Ex 3:1). Rahab, the prostitute from Jericho, cast her lot with God's people and put her faith in God, and God spared her life (Jos 2:8–11; 6:22–25; Heb 11:31). She later would become an ancestor of Jesus (Mt 1:5). Likewise Ruth, the Moabite woman, affirmed her faith in God and became part of Bethlehem's community and another ancestor of Jesus (Mt 1:5). Through the witness of his Hebrew slave girl, Naaman the Syrian was led to Elisha, who cured him of his leprosy (2 Kgs 5:1–14). And Isaiah's closing chapter confirms God's proclamation of his glory to all nations and his choosing of priests from all nations (Is 66:19–21).

The New Testament also affirms the importance of faithfulness over bloodline. Jesus affirmed the faith of non-Israelites during his public ministry (Mt 15:28; Lk 7:9; 17:17–19). Paul wrote that true Jewishness was a matter of the heart (Rom 2:28–29; 9:6). And the book of Ephesians heralds as its central point the fact that Jesus, by his death, broke down the wall of hostility that existed between Jews and Gentiles so that he might redeem them into one body, the church (Eph 2:14–16). The redeemed of all ages, who come from all the world's ethnic groups, share a common salvation in Christ (Rv 7:9–10).

The sexual imagery of 57:8 probably suggests fertility rites were part of the people's idolatry. The people had abandoned their true love—the Lord Yahweh—to worship idols (a dominant theme of the prophet Hosea). Isaiah said the people had actually worn themselves out with all their idolatry (57:10), yet they would not repent.

The Lord questioned why the people did not fear him (57:11). He promised judgment on them, and when it came, he would leave them to cry to their idols for deliverance—a deliverance that would not come (57:12). Again, the Lord held out hope for those who cast their lot with him (57:13).

God Brings Healing and Restoration (57:14–21)

Isaiah's description of God's bringing healing and restoration had four phases. First, the Lord would build a highway to bring his people home. Second, he would clarify the nature and intent of his judgment. Third, he would proclaim the restoration itself. Fourth, he would warn the wicked they would have no peace apart from him.

God's Highway Built (57:14)

Isaiah functioned as a construction foreman, giving orders to build God's highway. Every obstacle needed to be cleared so that his people might have a smooth place on which to return. The language is reminiscent of other Isaianic highway imagery (35:8; 40:3–4). One can better appreciate the magnitude of this accomplishment when one understands the rugged nature of Israel's topography.

God's Judgment Is Temporary (57:15–17)

Isaiah described the stark contrast between God's nature and God's expectation for humanity (57:15). The Lord was high and exalted, awesome and holy, but dwelt with the contrite and lowly in spirit. He looked specifically for those who humbled themselves and recognized their need for God. He

rebels and liars (57:3–4). They continued the sins of past generations.

The prophet described the idolaters' wickedness (57:5–10). Their lust burned everywhere, and they sacrificed their children to false gods. They built worship sites on hills all over the land and even brought idols and other pagan symbols into their homes (57:7–8).

discipleship

fasting

would provide them strength to live as he expected.

God's judgment was a response to the people's persistent sin. Nevertheless, he assured his people his anger would not remain (57:16–17).

God's Restoration Is Coming (57:18–19)

Isaiah described the restoration God was bringing. He would heal, guide, and comfort them (57:18). Those who mourned would praise him and receive his peace and healing (57:19).

Warning for the Wicked (57:20–21)

Isaiah closed the chapter with a solemn warning for the wicked. Those who persisted in their evil had no hope of participating in the great day of restoration.

Isaiah described the wicked as the unresting sea, whose waves continued to churn and toss mud (57:20). They had no spiritual foundation on which to stand. Further, they would not receive the peace God promised to those who followed him (57:21).

Isaiah 40–66 contains twenty-seven chapters. At the end of each unit of nine chapters (48, 57, 66), the prophet announces a warning to evildoers,[5] though he does elsewhere as well. The prophet proclaimed a great day of restoration for God's people, but he also reminded them that God requires his people to respond to his grace with repentance and faith. Great blessing lay ahead for God's people, but not for those who persisted in evil.

Call to True Righteousness (58:1–14)

Isaiah called his people to display true righteousness. He wanted their lives to reflect the image of their God.

In chapter 58, Isaiah took up three aspects of true righteousness: true dis-

cipleship, true fasting, and true Sabbath observance.

True Discipleship (58:1–2)

True **discipleship** always involves learning and following. A disciple learns from the master and follows the master. One who only learns but does not apply learning for life change is not truly a disciple.

Isaiah announced Jacob's sinful state. The key words were "seem eager" (58:2; NASB "delight"), which occur twice. The people inquired of their God and wanted to know him and be near him. But the following verses make clear that they were not as ready to follow him from their hearts.

True Fasting (58:3–12)

The people complained because God was not honoring their **fasting** (58:3). They abstained from food and humbled themselves (at least they thought so), yet God seemed unimpressed.

Isaiah explained the reason for God's failure to honor the people's fasting (58:3–4). No heart change occurred. The people continued exploiting their workers and quarreling, their edginess no doubt intensified by their hunger and their frustration at God's lack of response. Such a situation would never receive God's blessing.

Isaiah contrasted the people's current situation with the scenario God desired (58:5–7). Sincerity and humility needed to accompany their fasting. But sincerity and humility were best evidenced by *action*, not by words. The Lord wanted to see them cease injustice and oppression, share food with the hungry, and take care of others' needs (see sidebar 2.2).

Fasting that produced a change of heart in God's people would bring God's approval (58:8–12). The Lord's presence would surround them, and he would quickly answer their prayers. Their spiritual darkness would give way to the light of God's ways, and the Lord would refresh their souls. They would rebuild ancient cities that had long lain in ruins. God's presence would bring them the ability and resolve to accomplish everything he set before them.

True Sabbath Observance (58:13–14)

Isaiah described two vital characteristics of true Sabbath observance. First, true Sabbath observance meant turning aside from one's own routine and pleasure. People must not focus on their own cares and concerns as they might the other six days of the week.

Second, true Sabbath observance meant delighting in the day and honoring the Holy One of Israel with it. It was a day when God's people could take their minds off their everyday cares and focus their attention on him. He had blessed them with the command to rest one day in seven. Doing so recognized God as Lord of all time.[6] The Lord promised to exalt those who took delight in his Sabbath because they took delight in him.

Israel's Sin and God's Deliverance (59:1–21)

As Isaiah continued his prophetic pronouncements, he returned again to the issue of Israel's sin. God's people had seriously strayed from his ways; few if any stood for truth, justice, and righteousness.

Nevertheless, Isaiah also heralded a coming day when God's deliverance would be realized. The Lord would fight for his people, defeating their enemies and bringing his Redeemer to Zion.

Israel's Sin (59:1–15a)

Isaiah first described Israel's problem of sin in the most basic of terms. He then focused on specific sin problems. Finally, he painted a tragic picture of

sin's result in the nation both corporately and individually.

The Basic Problem (59:1–2)

Isaiah declared that the people's basic problem was that their sin had separated them from God. Over the years, Israel had drifted farther and farther away. God was still there, seeking a relationship, but Israel kept drifting. God had the strength to save and the will to listen, but Israel wasn't interested.

The Specific Problem (59:3–8)

Isaiah described his people's sin as involving the entire body (59:3, 4, 6, 7). Their hands and fingers were stained with the guilt of innocent blood. Their lips and tongues spoke lies and other wicked things, never justice or integrity. They conceived trouble and gave birth to evil. Their hands held acts of violence, while their feet rushed to sin. They stained their minds with evil thoughts.

The people placed their trust in *tohu* (59:4; NIV "empty arguments"). This term described the universe prior to God's creating it (Gn 1:2) and also often designated idols and/or the futility of idol worship. Their lives thus had no spiritual substance.

The Result of Sin (59:9–15a)

The people had filled their lives with sin. Consequently, justice and righteousness stood far from them (59:9). They were so far from spiritual light that they groped along in spiritual darkness, stumbling and moaning for justice that never would come (59:10–11).

Isaiah confessed that the people's sins were many (59:12–15a). His words bear a general resemblance to the prophet Daniel's confession (Dn 9:1–19). Daniel confessed the nation's sin, including himself among the transgressors, and Isaiah did the same here. The society was so full of sin that no place remained for justice, righteousness, truth, and honesty (59:14–15a).

Sidebar 18.3
The Isaianic Background of Ephesians 6

In Ephesians 6:11–18, the apostle Paul describes the armor believers are to put on to stand against Satan and his evil forces. He describes the following items:

- The belt of truth
- The breastplate of righteousness
- The readiness of the gospel of peace covering one's feet
- The shield of faith
- The helmet of salvation
- The sword of the Spirit (= God's word)

Paul also mentions prayer under the guidance of the Holy Spirit for every circumstance.
   As he wrote, Paul applied much Isaianic imagery:

Image	Ephesians Verse	Isaiah Verse
Belt of truth	6:14	11:5
Breastplate of righteousness	6:14	59:17
Gospel of peace	6:15	52:7
Helmet of salvation	6:17	59:17
Sword of Spirit/word of God	6:17	49:2

Each of the Isaianic passages concerns God's work of salvation. Chapters 11 and 49 focus specifically on the Lord's Servant/Messiah, whereas chapters 52 and 59 focus on God's coming kingdom in general.
   Paul made a powerful point as he adapted Isaiah's words to believers. The armor God used to bring salvation may now be used *by believers* to withstand the forces of evil on a daily basis.

God's Deliverance (59:15b–21)

Isaiah announced God's coming deliverance. He finished his description of Israel's sad situation and emphasized God's preparation to deliver his people. Finally, he described deliverance accomplished in all its glory.

The Sad Situation (59:15b–16a)

The Lord saw the lack of justice in the land. Amazingly, no one rose to intervene on behalf of God's people. In similar fashion, the Lord would later tell the prophet Ezekiel's audience that he had looked for a man to stand in the gap on behalf of God's people but had found none in Ezekiel's generation either (Ez 22:30).

Preparation for Deliverance (59:16b–17)

Isaiah now described the Lord's dramatic intervention. He put on his armor to do battle, but his battle armor looked quite different from ordinary armor. Righteousness—so lacking in society—was the Lord's breastplate, a helmet of salvation sat on his head, and a cloak of zeal enfolded him. Isaiah's imagery forms the foundation of Paul's thinking when he encouraged believers to put on the full armor of God (Eph 6:10–18; see sidebar 18.3).

Study Questions

1. What are the key details in Isaiah's description of Jerusalem's rebirth (54:1–17)?

2. Discuss Isaiah's use of paradox in 55:1–2.

3. In what ways do Isaiah's words support the idea that faithfulness to God is more important than bloodline?

4. How can Christians today honor the Sabbath/Lord's day principle?

Key Terms

covenant

discipleship

fasting

hesed

Sabbath

Interestingly, Isaiah did not mention the Lord needing any offensive weapons. Apparently his strong arm was all he needed.[7]

Deliverance Accomplished (59:18–21)

Isaiah assured his hearers deliverance would be accomplished. First, God's wrath would be poured out on his enemies (59:18). His wrath would extend to the islands (or coastlands), a term Isaiah had used before to indicate distant regions (41:1, 5).

Second, the nations would fear God's name (59:19). From the east to the west, they would revere him and know his glory.

Third, a redeemer would come to Zion and save the repentant ones of Jacob (59:20). The New Testament sheds light on the identity of this redeemer. The apostle Paul used this verse in his letter to the Romans when he described the great day when all the redeemed would see their salvation as Jesus Christ returned to establish his kingdom (Rom 11:26–27).

Fourth, the Lord would establish an everlasting covenant with his people (59:21). His Spirit would rest on his children forever, and they would see his Spirit rest on their children and grandchildren as well. Throughout all generations, the Lord would be there.

Isaiah's words of the everlasting covenant dovetail with Jeremiah's description of the new covenant God would establish (Jer 31:31–34). These words find their ultimate fulfillment in Jesus Christ, who will one day fulfill the prophet's words. Indeed, the New Testament provides us a more complete context in which we can understand Isaiah's already amazing words.

19 The Grand Finale of God's Restoration

Isaiah 60:1–66:24

Outline

- **Zion Glorified (60:1–22)**
  The Nations See God's Glory (60:1–3)
  Jerusalem's Population, Wealth, and
  Relationship with Other Nations Grow
  (60:4–16)
  God's Special Blessing Rests on His
  People (60:17–22)
- **God's Further Restoration (61:1–11)**
  God's Spirit-Led Anointed One (61:1–3)
  Israel's Rebuilt Cities (61:4–9)
  Israel's Exultation (61:10–11)
- **Zion's Marriage to God (62:1–12)**
  The Marriage Itself (62:1–5)
  The Watchmen's Reward (62:6–9)
  God's Redeemed (62:10–12)
- **Judgment of the Nations (63:1–6)**
  The Judge Identified: God the Warrior
  (63:1–3)
  The Reason for Judgment Declared
  (63:4–6)
- **Prayer for God's Intervention (63:7–64:12)**
  God's Tenderness and Compassion
  (63:7–14)

Isaiah's Plea for Help (63:15–64:12)
- **Blessing for God's Servants (65:1–25)**
  Destiny of Believing and Unbelieving
  Israel (65:1–16)
  New Heavens and a New Earth
  (65:17–25)
- **The Ultimate Conclusion (66:1–24)**
  Judgment and Restoration of Jerusalem
  (66:1–14a)
  Final Wrath and Glory of God
  (66:14b–24)

Objectives

After reading this chapter, you should be able to

1. Summarize Isaiah's description of God's final restoration of his people.
2. Provide details about God's Spirit-led anointed one (61:1–3).

As I write this chapter, the Christmas season is approaching. I especially love the looks of wonder and excitement on children's faces this time of year. Children often can hardly wait to open their packages, and when they receive just what they wanted, the expressions on their faces are priceless.

As we have studied Isaiah's book, we have seen images that would have filled Isaiah and his hearers with wonder and excitement. God would judge their enemies and rescue his people. He would establish his kingdom forever. Jerusalem would become a focal point of God's redemptive purpose. God's servant the Messiah would triumphantly complete his ministry and receive his eternal reward. Many may have wondered if the good news Isaiah proclaimed could really be that good.

As the prophet concluded his book, he proclaimed many themes, some of which he had already announced. Zion's exaltation and marriage to God, God's anointed one, Jerusalem's rebuilding, God's final judgment of sin, God's glory among the nations, and God's creation of new heavens and a new earth all appeared as Isaiah directed his prophetic drama to a grand finale.

Zion Glorified (60:1–22)

Isaiah described Zion's glorification as including three aspects. First, the nations would see God's glory. Second, Jerusalem's population and wealth would grow as its relationship with the nations changed. Third, God's special blessing would rest on his people.

The Nations See God's Glory (60:1–3)

Isaiah called God's people to rise and shine with the light that had come upon them (60:1). And what was that light? It was the Lord's glory. Isaiah foretold a day when as spiritual darkness covered the earth, nations would be drawn to Israel's light (60:2). Kings also would join the procession (60:3).

The imagery is different from that of 2:1–4 but probably refers to the same event. In chapter 2, the nations stream to Jerusalem to learn of God's ways. Here kings and nations are attracted to the light of God's glory.

Jerusalem's Population, Wealth, and Relationship with Other Nations Grow (60:4–16)

Jerusalem's Population (60:4)

Isaiah called his people to look around them; they would see their sons and daughters coming home! Here the terms "sons" and "daughters" probably designate Israelites, though Isaiah has already described the nations also sharing in God's glory.

Jerusalem's Wealth (60:5–9)

Nations would bring their wealth to Israel from land and sea (60:5–7). The resultant blessing to the nation would be obvious, but more importantly, these foreign nations also would bring praise to the Lord, and their offerings would burn on Jerusalem's altar.

The Lord had glorified his people (60:8–9). Treasure came in from everywhere to the honor of the Holy One of Israel. In light of the context, "sons" (60:9) may actually include foreigners who placed their faith in the Lord. God desired to expand his kingdom to reach the entire world.

Jerusalem's Relationship with Other Nations (60:10–16)

Isaiah's description of the nations' future relationship with Jerusalem and God's people was one that included both submission and partnership. The nations would worship with the Israelites, but foreigners would rebuild Jerusalem's walls and kings would bring their bounty (60:10–12). The city gates would be open continually—a reference to lasting security, but also to circumstances that provided opportunity for a continual flow of trea-

anointed one

sure to Zion. Judgment awaited those who did not serve God's people (cf. Zec 14:16–19).

The nations would not only worship with the Israelites but would also recognize God's special blessing on the nation (60:14–15). The people would enjoy the best that the nations had to bring and would delight in God their Savior and Redeemer (60:16). The nursing mother imagery hints at the nurturing, nourishing care the nations would offer Israel.

God's Special Blessing Rests on His People (60:17–22)

The special blessing God would place on his people was threefold. It would include good administration, everlasting light, and blessed people.

Good Administration (60:17–18)

Isaiah described a wonderful improvement in building materials: bronze to gold, iron to silver, wood to bronze, and stone to iron (60:17). Moreover, righteousness and peace would govern Israel, eliminating violence and ruin.

Everlasting Light (60:19–20)

Isaiah's imagery ascended to the apocalyptic level, describing a new sphere of existence. Sun and moon would no longer be needed, for God's glory would light his people forever. Probably Isaiah saw the same future time the apostle John did when he spoke of the new Jerusalem (Rv 21:23). Life as God's people experienced it would cease as God took them to a whole new level.

Blessed People (60:21–22)

Isaiah promised God's people would be righteous and would "possess the land forever" (60:21). The prophet had already announced this pledge many times, but such a promise bore repeating, because it was hard to imagine after so many years of fear and insecurity.

Isaiah had described the Messiah as God's branch who would rule the nations (11:1). He now used the same Hebrew word (*netser*, "shoot") to describe his choice people, whom he had prepared for this glorious purpose. When the perfect time came, the Lord would fulfill his word swiftly.

God's Further Restoration (61:1–11)

Isaiah added other dimensions to his description of Israel's coming golden days. God's Spirit-led anointed one would arise and work God's purpose. Israel's cities would be rebuilt. Isaiah rejoiced as he saw Israel's exultation bring glory to Israel's God.

God's Spirit-Led Anointed One (61:1–3)

The text uses the first person, giving the impression that God's **anointed one** is speaking. Isaiah described this individual's source of strength and his task and ultimate purpose.

The Anointed One's Source of Strength (61:1a)

The anointed one's source of strength was the Lord's Spirit. God had anointed him, as he had anointed prophets, priests, and kings before him. God's Spirit empowered him to do God's will (cf. 42:1).

The Anointed One's Task and Ultimate Purpose (61:1b–3)

The anointed one's task had several dimensions. First, he was to "preach good news to the poor." (The Hebrew word translated "poor" also can mean "afflicted.") The poor faced many challenges, and because of their economic disadvantage, their lives rarely changed for the better. However, this messenger was specifically sent to the poor and afflicted.

Second, the anointed one was to "bind up the brokenhearted." That is, he was to bring a ministry of comfort

Sidebar 19.1
Why Are the Poor Especially on God's Heart?

Isaiah spoke often of God's care for society's underprivileged. He warned those who oppressed the poor that God saw and would bring vengeance (1:23; 3:14–15; 5:23; 10:1–2). He also spoke of the coming one who would proclaim good news to the poor (61:1–3).

Jesus also reached out to the underprivileged. He had compassion on the discouraged multitudes (Mt 9:36) and encouraged the weary to come to him for rest (Mt 11:28–30). He also promised the poor in spirit that heaven would be theirs (Mt 5:3).

Why are the poor the special focus of God's concern? And what is it that renders them ready to respond to God's offer of salvation? Philip Yancey, in his book *The Jesus I Never Knew*, discusses insights he acquired from Monika Hellwig's *Jesus, the Compassion of God*, and shares the following "advantages" the poor have over others:

1. The poor know they are in urgent need of redemption.
2. The poor know not only their dependence on God and on powerful people but also their interdependence with one another.
3. The poor rest their security not on things but on people.
4. The poor have no exaggerated sense of their own importance and no exaggerated need of privacy.
5. The poor expect little from competition and much from cooperation.
6. The poor can distinguish between necessities and luxuries.
7. The poor can wait, because they have acquired a kind of dogged patience born of acknowledged dependence.
8. The fears of the poor are more realistic and less exaggerated because they already know that one can survive great suffering and want.
9. When the poor have the gospel preached to them, it sounds like good news and not like a threat or a scolding.
10. The poor can respond to the call of the gospel with a certain abandonment and uncomplicated totality because they have so little to lose and are ready for anything.

People with many material things may place more confidence in them than they should and in the end find that they don't provide lasting satisfaction or meaning in life. The poor, on the other hand, know they are needy, and as they turn to God, they find life's ultimate meaning.

Adapted from Philip Yancey, The Jesus I Never Knew *(Grand Rapids: Zondervan, 1995), 115.*

and encouragement to the discouraged and downcast.

Third, the anointed one was to proclaim freedom and release to captives and prisoners. Those who had lost their rights and status would regain them.

Fourth, the anointed one was to proclaim "the year of the LORD's favor and the day of vengeance of our God" (61:2). The Lord's favor would especially rest on those Isaiah had already mentioned: society's underprivileged (see sidebar 19.1). "Vengeance" here need not denote revenge; it may in fact refer to God simply restoring a proper balance in society by righting inequities.[1]

The anointed one's ministry would produce wonderful results (61:3). Zion's ashes would turn to beauty, her mourning to gladness, and her despair to praise. God's planting of his shoot (60:21) would find its ultimate fulfillment in the people God would grow through the ministry of his anointed one (61:3). Indeed, bringing God glory was the anointed one's ultimate purpose.

The Anointed One's Identity

New Testament evidence again points to Jesus as the fulfillment of Isaiah's words. Luke 4:16–30 describes Jesus's visit to his hometown of Nazareth, a visit that provoked a heated reaction to the Galilean prophet.

Jesus entered the synagogue on the Sabbath and stood up to read. When handed the scroll of Isaiah, he opened it and read what we now know as Isaiah 61:1–2. He then told those present that the Scripture he had just read was fulfilled that day in their presence.

The people appreciated Jesus's eloquent and gracious teaching, but they also wanted to see him perform miracles similar to those he had done in Capernaum. Jesus affirmed the difficulty of a hometown accepting one of its own as a prophet. When he cited Old Testament accounts of God visiting foreign people who were more ready to receive God's message than the Israelites were, many became enraged. They wanted to throw Jesus over the cliff at the edge of town, but he passed through the crowd and returned to Capernaum.

Isaiah's depiction of the anointed one's ministry well describes Jesus of Nazareth. Jesus regularly ministered to the poor and reached out to the underprivileged of society (Lk 15:1–2, 7; 19:2–10). In fact, he sometimes exalted them over the self-righteous people of his day, who often had a hard time recognizing their own sin (Lk 18:9–14).

Finally, Jesus's ministry brings to dramatic conclusion God's redemptive purpose. Through Jesus's death and resurrection, the year of God's favor is established and proclaimed.

Israel's Rebuilt Cities (61:4–9)

Isaiah had earlier described Israel's glorious return as its sons and daughters came from everywhere. He now described the gloriously rebuilt cities they would occupy as they returned home. The ruins would be rebuilt with foreign assistance, and in that day, the people would be sanctified as God's covenant was realized.

Ruins Rebuilt (61:4)

Isaiah proclaimed the rebuilding of ruined cities. The Hebrew terms[2] emphasize the total and lingering devastation and desolation that had consumed the region for such a long time.

The seeming hopelessness of rebuilding the desolate cities paralleled Ezekiel's later words of seeming hopelessness as he described God's people in his famous dry bones passage (Ez 37:11). In both instances, all seemed lost, but God would bring hope out of hopelessness and life out of desolation.

Foreigners Employed (61:5)

Working the fields—whether pastoral or agricultural—was difficult, unglamourous work. Usually tending the sheep was something reserved for the younger members of the family (1 Sm 16:11). Isaiah assigned these tasks to foreigners in the coming day. Foreigners would serve the people of Israel, not oppress them.

People Sanctified (61:6–7)

Isaiah now incorporated Levitical imagery. God's people would be sanctified—set apart for his priestly service. They would intercede on behalf of the nations. The nations would serve the Israelites physically and provide for them materially, and the Israelites would serve their spiritual needs.

Isaiah's twofold reference to a double portion (61:7) emphasizes Israel's special place of prominence among the nations. Like the firstborn, who normally received a double portion of the family inheritance (Dt 21:17), so Israel would enjoy God's special blessing.

Covenant Realized (61:8–9)

The covenant God had made with Abraham and confirmed again and again throughout Israel's history now would reach its ultimate fulfillment. The God who loved justice and faithfulness would bring these qualities to fruition in his people's lives. Generation after generation of Israelites would receive the recognition of nations that they were truly blessed.

Israel's Exultation (61:10–11)

Isaiah now expressed his own excitement as he anticipated the day he announced. Perhaps he spoke for the nation as he proclaimed his joy.

Isaiah compared the celebration to the pomp and circumstance that accompanied a wedding. He also likened the day to a day of agricultural abundance—only with righteousness and praise springing up instead of produce.

Zion's Marriage to God (62:1–12)

Isaiah now carried through the imagery of bride and bridegroom he had just introduced (61:10). The Lord would join himself to Israel, his bride, forever. The watchmen who had longed for the day would at last see it, and God's redeemed would see their final salvation.

The Marriage Itself (62:1–5)

Isaiah's description of Zion's marriage to God included three aspects: God's determination to bring about the marriage, Zion's beautiful ornamentation, and the wedding celebration itself.

God's Determination (62:1)

Isaiah earlier had described God's determination to judge sin and lead his people home. Like a woman in labor with a job to do, he would accomplish his work (42:14–17). Now Isaiah again affirmed God's resolve to complete his redemptive work. For the sake of his beloved Jerusalem, he would not be silent until he saw her righteousness and salvation shine forth.

Zion's Ornamentation (62:2–3)

Nations and kings would see the beauty of God's bride. Her beauty was not external but lay in her righteousness and glory. Isaiah would develop the concept of Zion's new name (62:2) a

few verses later. Her Lord had made her into a bride of beauty, like a crown jewel in his hand (62:3).

The Wedding Celebration (62:4–5)

Zion's judgment had been so thorough that neighboring nations knew her as one deserted and desolate. But she would now receive new names, signifying her new relationship to the Lord her husband. "Hephzibah" means "my delight is in her" and "Beulah" means "married."

Verse 5 may read either "your sons will marry you" or "your maker (or builder) will marry you," depending on how one understands the Hebrew.[3] The parallelism of the second half of the verse suggests the Lord is in view, so "maker" may be preferred.

As special as Zion's wedding day would be for Zion, Isaiah affirmed that the day would be even more special for God. The prophet used the illustration of a bridegroom rejoicing as he saw his bride in the wedding ceremony. So the Lord would rejoice over his people.

The Watchmen's Reward (62:6–9)

The term "watchmen" probably designates Israel's prophets and "prayer warriors," who at last can celebrate the salvation they have prayed for and announced.

The Watchmen's Faithfulness (62:6–7)

The Lord had posted watchmen around Jerusalem's walls. In contrast to watchmen who sounded the alarm only if potential danger threatened, these watchmen called aloud to the Lord day and night. They asked him to honor his promises concerning Zion and kept pleading until he did so. Jesus similarly told his disciples that the Lord honored the persistent prayers of his children (Lk 18:1–8).

The Lord's Oath (62:8–9)

The Lord announced an oath. Once the day of redemption and salvation came, hostile foreigners would never again steal the fruit of Zion's labor. Those who grew it and harvested it would eat it and glorify God amid lasting security.

God's Redeemed (62:10–12)

In language reminiscent of 40:3, Isaiah called the people to prepare the way for God's coming salvation. The expression "banner for the nations" parallels an earlier phrase regarding the root of Jesse (11:10).

The Lord's announcement of salvation would spread worldwide (62:11). Everyone would see his care for his own as he brought them home. They would also see him as their Redeemer and Savior, and their lives would reflect his holiness (62:12). Isaiah then proclaimed two more names that Jerusalem would own in that day—"sought out" (NASB) and "city no longer deserted."

Judgment of the Nations (63:1–6)

Isaiah complemented his repeated assurance to his people that God would save them with repeated assurances that God would judge their enemies among the nations. The Lord would put on his warrior apparel and crush the opposition.

The Judge Identified: God the Warrior (63:1–3)

Isaiah described God as a warrior coming from Bozrah, Edom's capital, with crimson stains on his garments (63:1). The Edomites, descendants of Esau, often displayed hostility against God's people.[4] Perhaps Isaiah uttered this prophecy during a time of Edomite hostility and hence portrayed the Lord as coming most directly from there. The stains on the Lord's garments came from the nations' blood as he trampled them in his fury (63:2–3).

The Reason for Judgment Declared (63:4–6)

The Lord declared the reason he had judged the nations. His appointed time—"the day of vengeance"[5] (63:4)—had arrived, but no one came to join him in fighting the nations. Consequently, the Lord again bared his arm (cf. 62:8) and defeated the nations himself.

Prayer for God's Intervention (63:7–64:12)

Isaiah prayed for God's intervention. He described God's tenderness and compassion toward his people in former times despite Israel's stubbornness and pleaded for God's help again. Only in absolute dependence on him would they find salvation.

God's Tenderness and Compassion (63:7–14)

In his description of God's tenderness and compassion, Isaiah contrasted God's lovingkindness with Israel's stubbornness. The people of Israel often answered God's grace with sin, yet he persisted in his desire to win them to him.

God's Lovingkindness (63:7–9)

The Hebrew word translated "kindnesses" is *hesed* (see discussion of 54:8, 10, and 55:3). Here it denotes acts of covenant love that God extended to his people. Isaiah noted some of God's most significant acts of *hesed* to remind the people of his faithfulness and praiseworthiness.

The Lord acted in history to deliver his people from Egypt (63:8). The "angel of his presence" denotes the angel who led the Israelites during their days in the wilderness after the Lord delivered them from the Egyptians (Ex 23:20–23; 33:2). God led them every step of their journey (63:9).

Israel's Stubbornness (63:10–14)

However, Israel's stubbornness displayed itself as God's people turned their backs on him (63:10). God's discipline, which came swiftly, turned the people's attention to the former days when God performed great works among them (63:11–13). God gave them rest (63:14), though Israel's history was one of frequent regression into sin, as the book of Judges clearly testifies.

Isaiah's Plea for Help (63:15–64:12)

Isaiah pleaded with the Lord for help. The prophet longed for God's coming kingdom, not for a regression into sin, which so often had marred Israel's history. He asked God to restore the nation, pleaded once again for earth-shaking judgment to show the world God's greatness, and confessed the nation's absolute dependence on God.

Plea for National Restoration (63:15–19)

Isaiah asked God to look down from heaven and see his people. They were a sad lot whose own ancestors would not even have recognized them (63:16). Why did God withhold his compassion and tenderness? No doubt Isaiah longed for God's intervention all the more because he had seen a vision of God's coming kingdom.

Isaiah wondered aloud why the Lord allowed his people to wander from the truth and begged for God's intervention (63:17). He projected onto himself the pain Judah would experience one day as the sanctuary lay in ruins at the hands of Babylonian invaders (63:18). What was the purpose of this extended Babylonian domination?

Plea for Earth-Shaking Judgment (64:1–4)

Isaiah pleaded with God to bring earth-shaking judgment. If the Lord would come with all his power, the whole earth would tremble (64:1–2). Certainly, Isaiah thought, the nations would tremble in fear were God to so show himself. History had never witnessed such awesome works as God had brought in past days (64:4).

Confession of Dependence on God (64:5–12)

Isaiah confessed the people's deep need for the Lord. Given the fundamentally sinful condition of human hearts, how could they possibly hope to sustain a relationship with an utterly holy and righteous God (64:5)?

The people were spiritually defiled, and their feebly small righteous acts counted for nothing in God's sight (64:6). The term "filthy rags" probably denotes stained menstrual cloths, a sign of ritual impurity, and provided a powerful contrast with God's righteousness.

Isaiah declared that God was the potter, and his people the clay (64:8). Their only source of worth and purpose lay in him; therefore, they were absolutely dependent on him to rescue them from their spiritual dilemma (64:9). Jerusalem was devastated, and the temple burned; the people couldn't endure anymore (64:11).

Isaiah again pondered aloud how long the Lord would allow such tragedy to continue. Having received a glimpse of the judgment that would occur before the final restoration, the prophet raised the hard questions he knew God's people of the Babylonian exile would be asking. The book of Lamentations likewise raised such questions as the nation struggled under the weight of God's judgment.

Blessing for God's Servants (65:1–25)

Isaiah's further description of the blessing that would come to God's servants included even more dramatic elements as the prophet moved toward the conclusion of his book.

First, Isaiah described the ultimate destiny of believing and unbelieving

Israel (65:1–16). God was not going to bless his people regardless of the circumstances. He was looking for those willing to serve him wholeheartedly.

Second, Isaiah described the creation of a new heaven and a new earth (65:17–25). Jerusalem would become a place of special blessing, and the people would be especially blessed. Isaiah also reintroduced earlier kingdom imagery as he looked ahead to God's coming kingdom.

Destiny of Believing and Unbelieving Israel (65:1–16)

Isaiah's description of the destiny of believing and unbelieving Israel divided into two fairly even sections. In the first (65:1–7), the prophet depicted the judgment of the rebellious. In the second (65:8–16), he contrasted the rebellious with the Lord's servants, who would enter his kingdom.

The Judgment of the Rebellious (65:1–7)

The Lord now spoke, using Isaiah as his mouthpiece. He had called openly to his people when they were not seeking him, and they had found him (65:1). However, the Israelites' spiritual track record was one of stubbornness and obstinacy (65:2).

The Lord further described the rebels (65:3–5). They sacrificed using inappropriate sacrifices and worship sites, sat among the graves expecting a word from the dead, ate pork, and yet considered themselves holier than others.

The Lord's anger fumed as he described his people's sin (65:6–7). He warned them he would repay them in full for all their sin.

The Contrast between God's Servants and the Rebellious (65:8–16)

Isaiah contrasted the lot of God's servants with the lot of the rebellious people he had just described. God knew his own, and he would spare them from judgment (65:8). He would act on their behalf and make them heirs to the land (65:9).

The Sharon plain (65:10) was a historically fertile area that began near Joppa and extended northward to Mount Carmel. God said he would bless the Sharon plain with lush pastureland, meaning he would make the area even more desirable than it already was. The Valley of Achor, located on the Jordan plain near Jericho, was a barren area historically associated with the stoning of Achan (Jos 7:26). The Lord would take it and make it useful for his people.

However, the rebellious would not fare so well. They had not heeded the Lord's persistent instruction and now they would pay the price (65:12). Isaiah contrasted the incredible blessing of the Lord's servants with the absolute rejection and desolation of the rebellious (65:13–15).

Fittingly, the section ends with two references to "the God of truth" (65:16). The Hebrew word translated "truth" is related to our word "Amen." The Hebrew root 'aman means "to be confirmed or established." God's people could count on him to confirm and establish all he said he would do. The apostle Paul expressed a similar concept when he affirmed, "For no matter how many promises God has made, they are 'Yes' in Christ" (2 Cor 1:20).

New Heavens and a New Earth (65:17–25)

Isaiah 65:17 begins with the announcement that the Lord will create new heavens and a new earth. The expression immediately calls to mind Revelation 21:1 and John's vision of the new Jerusalem descending from heaven.

Evangelical interpretations of details of this passage differ, though all agree it announces God's coming kingdom through Jesus Christ. Isaiah moved freely between details of the eternal kingdom and details that seem to describe an earthly existence in which heaven is not yet realized (65:20). For him, such details are part of the grand time to come.

premillennial

For many evangelicals, a comparison of this text with Revelation 20–22 suggests that a **premillennial** understanding best fits the passage's details. According to this view, Christ reigns on earth a thousand years with his saints prior to the final judgment of evil and entry into the eternal state embodied by the new Jerusalem.

Jerusalem a Special Blessing (65:17–19)

Jerusalem would become a place of special blessing in the age to come. Former things would be forgotten (65:17; cf. 43:18) in the face of the new work God was doing. The city would become a place of so much rejoicing that weeping and sorrow would no longer be heard (65:18–19). The sad aspects of the past would be swept away by the abundance of God's blessing.

The People Especially Blessed (65:20–24)

Isaiah described three special features of the people's blessing. First, long life would be the rule in the coming age (65:20). Someone who died at the age of one hundred would be counted as one who died as a youth. People would assume serious sin had occurred in the life of anyone who did not reach such an age (see sidebar 19.2).

Second, God's people will enjoy the fruit of their labor (65:21–23). They will build houses and live in them and will maintain ownership of their fields and vineyards. Each generation will see God's continued blessing. Such promises would mean much to people accustomed to raids on their land.

Third, God's blessing would come even before the people would ask. The

---

Sidebar 19.2
Sin and Missing the Mark

The Bible teaches that all people everywhere are sinners. This teaching is not always popular in today's world, where many believe people are basically good and that our own intellect and initiative will ultimately bring the solution to the world's most significant problems. At the heart of humanity's problem is the problem of sin, which has corrupted every aspect of our nature (Eph 2:1–3).

The Hebrew verb *hata'* literally means "to miss the mark." That is, people fall short of the holy, righteous standard God has set. We miss the bull's-eye; in fact, even the best people don't come anywhere close to it. This concept of sin involving missing the mark is illustrated in two biblical passages where the word *hata'* is translated in its literal sense.

First, Judges 20 describes intertribal warfare between Benjamin and the other tribes of Israel. Benjamin's army included seven hundred stone slingers. The slingers were extremely accurate with their weapons, so much so that they "could sling a stone at a hair and not miss" (20:16). The Hebrew word translated "miss" is *hata'*.

Second, Isaiah 65 describes the great new kingdom that God would usher in. Old age would be the norm; in fact, Isaiah said, "he who fails to reach a hundred will be thought accursed" (65:20 NASB). The Hebrew word translated "fails to reach" is once again *hata'*.

These two passages illustrate the basic meaning behind the concept of sin. All people have sinned and missed the mark of God's expectation (Rom 3:23). The Bible asserts that only through faith in Jesus and his finished work can anyone attain the righteous standard God requires.

shalom

linear view of
history

Lord promised, "Before they call I will answer; while they are still speaking I will hear" (65:24). Such a response from the Lord would come only from a deep and abiding relationship, a relationship in which his people were totally aligned with his will and purpose.

Flashback to 11:6 (65:25)

Isaiah 65:25 provides a literary "flashback" to 11:6. Isaiah linked his description of the new heavens and the new earth with his earlier description of God's kingdom. God's *shalom* would be so complete that it would prevail even among natural enemies in the animal kingdom.

The Ultimate Conclusion (66:1–24)

Isaiah 66 presents the prophet's ultimate conclusion, his eschatological finish. Fundamental to Isaiah's thinking is a **linear view of history**—that is, *history is going somewhere*. God created the world and his people. He raises up nations and guides them to their predetermined ends. And in the fullness of time, he will bring all history to a grand conclusion as he ushers in a world and a kingdom without end.

Isaiah first described Jerusalem's judgment and restoration (66:1–14a), topics he had dealt with before but to which he now would return one last time. Second, he described God's final wrath and glory. Isaiah's story was a story about God's people, but first and foremost, it was a story about God.

Judgment and Restoration of Jerusalem (66:1–14a)

Three themes appear in Isaiah's final announcement of Jerusalem's judgment and restoration. First, the sovereign Lord delights in the humble (66:1–2). Second, the Lord will encourage the faithful (66:3–6). Third, the Lord

will bring about Jerusalem's rebirth (66:7–14a).

The Sovereign Lord Delights in the Humble (66:1–2)

Isaiah described the Lord as an almighty sovereign, who sat in heaven with earth as a footstool (66:1). What could people possibly offer him that he did not have? What character qualities would win his attention and admiration?

The Lord then declared whom he esteemed, and his answer may have surprised many. The Lord esteemed those who were humble and contrite in spirit (66:2). Those who truly followed him knew their place in the universe; God was God and they were not. They trembled at his word, receiving it as their instruction for life, for they realized he knew them better than they knew themselves.

The Lord Encourages the Faithful (66:3–6)

The Lord encouraged the faithful who maintained their faithfulness through difficult circumstances. Many had chosen their own ways, but to the Lord their deeds and rituals were an abomination (66:3–4).

In contrast, those who trembled at the Lord's word would see their vindication (66:5). They had suffered mocking and derision from their kinsmen but had stood firm, just as Jesus encouraged his followers to do (Mt 5:11–12). The world would soon come crashing down on God's enemies (66:6).

The Lord Brings about Jerusalem's Rebirth (66:7–14a)

The Lord used the image of childbirth to illustrate the great work he was about to perform (66:7–9). He described a woman who gave birth quickly and practically without labor or pain. Could it really be so? Further, could a country actually be born in one day? God's rhetorical questions (66:9) assured his people that he was ready to act and to act quickly. The nation's recovery would occur so dramatically that the

Jerusalem as it appears today from the Mount of Olives. Isaiah described Jerusalem's exaltation in the days of God's kingdom. (Courtesy of Heather Stancik)

eschatological

only explanation possible would be the touch of almighty God.

Isaiah described Jerusalem as a nursing mother ready to take her children to her breasts (66:10–11). The people would receive her comfort, nourishment, and nurture. A great sense of peace would flood them as their mother carried them along (66:12–13). Isaiah also described the Lord as comforting his people with motherly compassion. Everyone would rejoice as they realized the time God had promised had finally come.

Final Wrath and Glory of God (66:14b–24)

Isaiah concluded his book with one final cycle of familiar themes. First, he announced God's judgment against all sin. Second, he proclaimed the sending of messengers through the world to declare his glory. Third, he portrayed the blessing that would come to all nations. Fourth, he closed his book with a final warning to the wicked.

Judgment against All Sin (66:14b–17)

Isaiah's image of God the warrior (cf. 63:1–6) reappeared and took on new dimensions. The Lord mounted

his chariot in preparation for the final battle with those who opposed him (66:15). The text's **eschatological** perspective is clear. The Lord would judge sin wherever he found it.

The Sending of Messengers (66:18–19)

Isaiah had already spoken many times of God's glory among the nations (e.g., 2:1–4; 11:1–10; 45:22–23; 52:15). The prophet again announced God's intention to gather nations and tongues to see his glory (66:18).

But then Isaiah added a new, previously unmentioned aspect. The Lord would send messengers to the nations who would declare his glory (66:19). Such a statement anticipates Jesus's words as he sent his disciples into the world to reach the nations (Mt 28:18–20).

Scholars differ somewhat as to the identification of the places to which the messengers go.[6] The identification is rendered more difficult because of the various ways the Hebrew may be translated.[7] Most agree Tarshish is probably Spain, and Javan probably denotes Greece. Libya (Heb. *Put*) was located in northern Africa, and the Lydians lived in Asia Minor, as the people of

Tubal probably did (Ez 39:1). The term translated "islands" has occurred many times already in Isaiah·to denote the ends of the earth.[8] Thus the proclamation of God's messengers will know no limits.

The Blessing of Nations (66:20–23)

Isaiah declared that the resultant blessing to the nations would be staggering. All Israel's brothers would be brought to Jerusalem as an offering to the Lord. The context of the word "brothers" suggests the term refers to more than the Israelites. Isaiah may be describing no less than the true and complete Israel, comprised of the faithful of all ages.[9]

The Lord promised he would also choose from among the nations' gathered brothers for his priests and Levites (66:21). If indeed the interpretation suggested in the previous paragraph is correct, Isaiah's words anticipate Peter's instruction regarding the priesthood of all believers (1 Pt 2:9–10).

The Lord also promised that in the age to come, God's people and their descendants would endure forever (66:22). Everyone from everywhere would come to bow before the Lord (66:23), just as he earlier announced they would do (45:23).

Key Terms

anointed one

eschatological

linear view of history

premillennial

shalom

Final Warning to the Wicked (66:24)

Isaiah's opening words to Judah set before the people the choice to believe or not to believe, to obey or not to obey, to follow or not to follow (1:16–20, 27–31). The prophet now described the glorious lot of those who chose to believe, to obey, to follow. He closed his book with one final warning to the wicked. Perhaps he did so because he thought the people of his day might be moved more by threats than by promises.

Isaiah described a fire that would not go out on the wicked (66:24). Jesus picked up the wording when he said, "Their worm will not die, nor will their fire be quenched" as he described the torment of hell (Mk 9:48). Again, the eschatological dimensions of Isaiah's words appear obvious. The prophet is depicting not a small judgment framed in history, but God's final judgment of those who oppose him.

Isaiah's picture of victorious believers viewing the destruction of those who opposed God does not form a pleasant ending to the book of Isaiah. And yet the Scriptures assure believers that such a perspective helps one to appreciate the salvation that comes through a faith relationship with the Lord. The good news of God's salvation is good news precisely because the bad news is so bad.

And so as we come to the end of Isaiah, we discover that the prophet begins and ends with Yahweh, the sovereign Lord of history. The vision Isaiah

---

Study Questions

1. Compare Isaiah 61:1–3 and Luke 4:16–30. How did Jesus fulfill Isaiah's words? Why did Nazareth's population get upset with him?

2. Compare and contrast Isaiah 65–66 with Revelation 20–22.

3. How does Zion's marriage to God (62:1–12) parallel Christ and the church in the New Testament?

received (1:1) came from God, and at the end of Isaiah's prophecy, all nations recognize God's supremacy either willingly or unwillingly (66:23–24). Not only is history going somewhere, but fundamentally, history is not about humanity but about the God of humanity, the God of the universe. The apostle Paul's words provide an excellent summary of Isaiah's message:

"For from him and through him and to him are all things.

To him be the glory forever! Amen." (Rom 11:36)

20 Isaiah and the Old Testament

Outline

- **Isaiah's Use of Earlier Old Testament Material**
  Isaiah's References to Historical People, Places, and Events
  References to the Torah
- **Isaiah's Use in Later Old Testament Material**
  Cases of Dependence or Interdependence
  Further Uses of Isaianic Motifs

Objectives

After reading this chapter, you should be able to

1. Identify key people, places, and events that Isaiah cites from earlier Old Testament material.
2. Discuss the book of Isaiah's use of the Torah.
3. Explain how the book and/or its common motifs were used in later Old Testament material.

The book of Isaiah has had profound impact on the rest of the Bible. Indeed, the Bible would have quite a different look if it lacked Isaiah.

Isaiah highlights many key themes of Scripture. His use of the expression "Holy One of Israel" sets the Lord apart as the sovereign God of the universe. Isaiah's emphasis on his people's covenant obligations direct them back to their spiritual heritage. His focus on the nations reveals God's intent both to judge them and to bring them his salvation. Finally, the prophet's proclamation regarding the Messiah and the messianic kingdom lays a strong foundation for the New Testament's proclamation of Jesus and his kingdom.

The book of Isaiah also forms a "bridge" between the Old and the New Testament. The prophet drew upon the rich heritage provided by the biblical writers who preceded him. In turn, the New Testament writers made frequent use of Isaiah's material.

This chapter will explore the book of Isaiah's contribution to the Old Testament by focusing on two main areas: Isaiah's use of earlier Old Testament material and Isaiah's use in later Old Testament material.

Isaiah's Use of Earlier Old Testament Material

Isaiah's message built on the foundation of prior Old Testament material, even though all of what we now know as the Old Testament was not yet complete. The prophet called the people's attention to God's earlier revelation, urging them to heed its demands for their own good. To some extent, then, his message was a call to embrace the old, not merely to look to something new.

Isaiah's use of prior material took two forms: references to historical people, places, and events and references to the

law of Moses. His references to the law of Moses included important concepts such as festivals, offerings, and sacrifices, as well as leaders, social justice, and holiness and righteousness.

Isaiah's References to Historical People, Places, and Events

Isaiah referred to many historical people, places, and events to drive home his points. Mainly, he described God's former great works among his people to encourage them to put their faith in him for the present and future. Some of the more prominent examples are highlighted below.

God as Creator

Genesis 1:1 affirmed God's creation of all that existed over and against the pagan polytheistic understanding of the world's beginning. Isaiah's emphasis of this concept reminded his people of God's continued sovereign guidance over their lives. The Lord had created heaven and earth (42:5; 44:24) and knew the stars by name (40:26). He and he alone had accomplished it (45:18), and consequently, God's people could count on him to rescue them from exile and establish them in the land again (40:27–31).

The Days of Noah

Isaiah drew a comparison with "the days of Noah" (54:9) to reassure his people of God's blessing. After the great flood, God had promised never to flood the earth again (Gn 8:21–22). Likewise, Isaiah promised that when the day of Israel's final restoration came, the Lord would never remove his covenant love and blessing from them again (54:9–10).

The Patriarchs

Isaiah directed his hearers' attention to Abraham four times (29:22; 41:8; 51:2; 63:16). In doing so, he reminded his people of their precious heritage as well as their covenant responsibilities. His common use of the name Jacob as a designation for Israel also reinforced these concepts (e.g., 2:5–6; 10:20–21;

40:27; 44:1–2; 60:16). God's relationship with Israel had begun long ago and would continue through Jacob's descendants.

Sodom and Gomorrah

The Bible records God's destruction of Sodom and Gomorrah because of the cities' extreme wickedness (Gn 18:20; 19:24–25). Isaiah shocked his hearers by describing Jerusalem's sin as rivaling that of these cities (1:9–10; 3:9). In doing so, he implied the punishment these cities received might also come to Jerusalem.

Isaiah also indicated the depth of Babylon's impending doom by likening its destruction to the destruction of Sodom and Gomorrah (13:19). No one would ever inhabit the city again.

The Exodus and Wilderness Wanderings

The books of Exodus and Numbers record how God led his people out of Egypt and through the wilderness to Canaan. Isaiah recalled God's defeat of Egypt and his parting the waters for his people as a demonstration of God's power and presence for his future work (10:24, 26; 51:10; 63:11–13). The prophet also utilized the imagery of a pillar of fire and a pillar of cloud (Ex 40:36–38) to describe the Lord's care for Zion in the messianic kingdom (4:5).

The Valley of Gibeon

The city of Gibeon overlooked the Aijalon Valley, where the Lord made the sun stand still during Joshua's battle against the southern coalition of Canaanite kings (Jos 10:12–14). Isaiah's allusion to this miracle (28:21) helped his people understand the magnitude of God's future work on their behalf.

The Battle of Midian

The book of Judges records how Gideon of the tribe of Manasseh defeated the Midianites and brought peace to Israel (Jgs 6–7). Isaiah's allusion to "the day of Midian's defeat" (9:4) and his mention of how the Lord "struck down Midian" (10:26) reminded his people that the Lord had the power to defeat every oppressor if they trusted in him.

David

Isaiah highlighted God's covenant with King David (2 Sm 7) and its benefits to God's people in several prophetic oracles. The designation "house of David" for Judah's royal line occurs three times (7:2, 13; 22:22), and Hezekiah is noted as being of Davidic ancestry (38:5). The linkage between David and Jerusalem also appears (22:9; 29:1), with God's interest in the city linked with his covenant with David (37:35).

David's name also occurs in connection with future promises, including those of the messianic kingdom (9:7; 16:5; 55:3). David thus stands as a channel for God's blessing to his people—past, present, and future.

References to the Torah

Isaiah also held the law of Moses in high regard and used its teachings as a foundation for much of his message. Only God's word provided the people the spiritual light they needed to live as God expected, as the following verses emphasize:

> When men tell you to consult mediums and spiritists, who whisper and mutter, should not a people inquire of their God? Why consult the dead on behalf of the living? To the law and to the testimony! If they do not speak according to this word, they have no light of dawn. (8:19–20)

Festivals, Offerings, and Sacrifices

The festival of the new moon occurs only in the first and last chapters (1:13–14; 66:23), and the Sabbath appears in close proximity to the new moon references (1:13; 66:23). In Isaiah 1, the prophet describes these festivals as worthless before God because those who celebrate them are living evil lives. In Isaiah 66, the Sabbath and the new moon festivals mark the blessing and order of God's kingdom. Isaiah also spoke of proper Sabbath observance as something that brought God's blessing and favor (56:2, 4, 6; 58:13).

References to offerings and sacrifices occur commonly in Isaiah. People sometimes provoked God by offering sacrifices to other deities (40:20; 57:5–6; 65:3, 7) and by bringing offerings when their hearts were not right (1:11, 13; 66:3). However, God declared he would again accept them in the day of his blessing (56:7; 60:7)—even the sacrifices other nations offered (19:21)! He stood ready to receive the offerings of those who brought them with genuine repentance and humility.

However, the most significant offering was one the Lord himself offered—his servant, whose life became a guilt offering for God's people (53:10). The servant quietly resigned himself to God's purpose, even though that purpose included dying a wrongful death. In the end, however, the Lord highly exalted his servant, who gave himself as a ransom for many (53:12; Mk 10:45).

Leaders

Leaders set the tone for the people they led. Good leaders who followed the teachings of Torah would seek to maintain the people's focus on the Lord and godly principles. Bad leaders who sought only their own gain would produce a "whatever is best for me" attitude among the general population. Of course, those who worshiped idols would quickly drag the common people down with them.

Isaiah addressed the problem of bad leadership early in his book (1:10). Evil rulers sought their own profit rather than serving those they led (1:23). The Lord would put an end to bad leadership in Judah (3:14), and when he did, confusion would reign for a time (3:6–7). Those who only looked after their own interests would flee in the face of danger rather than trying to stand against it (22:3).

Isaiah assured his people the Lord could handle the world's rulers too. He would bring down Babylon's king (14:5, 9) and Egypt's leaders (19:13). He

raised up nations and reduced them to nothing in accordance with his grand purpose (40:23–24). Isaiah's "Oracles against the Nations" (chaps. 13–23) assume the concept of God's sovereignty over all nations and peoples.

Isaiah promised, however, that just as the Lord could and would judge bad leadership, he also would one day raise up good leadership. Compassionate and honest leaders such as Eliakim would find their place in God's plan (22:20–23).

God's coming kingdom would also feature righteous leadership under the Messiah's rule. Justice and righteousness would prevail (32:1–2). Those in authority would bow to the Lord's servant (49:7). Harmony would return to nature under the root of Jesse's leadership as he led by the power of God's Spirit (11:1–10).

Social Justice

When a religious leader asked Jesus to articulate the greatest commandment of all, Jesus replied:

> "Love the Lord your God with all your heart and with all your soul and with all your mind." This is the first and greatest commandment. And the second is like it: "Love your neighbor as yourself." All the Law and the Prophets hang on these two commandments. (Mt 22:37–40)

In other words, a proper relationship with the Lord is primary. People's ability to love and serve others flows from their relationship with the Lord. In similar fashion, the first four of the Ten Commandments focus on our relationship with God, while the last six focus on our relationship with others.

Isaiah mentioned his people's iniquity in his opening comments (1:2, 4). Once the people turned their backs on the Lord, the Holy One of Israel, their relationships with their fellow citizens likewise degenerated.

For Isaiah, as for other prophets, social justice was the logical product of a

holiness

righteousness

good relationship with the Lord. Those who loved and followed him would align their attitudes and behavior with his teachings. Those who did not follow him would make their own rules for living.

Isaiah denounced the people's lack of concern for orphans and widows—generally society's powerless (1:17, 23). A mark of society's integrity was how it treated such groups. Issues of right and wrong were not to depend on one's economic or social status. Those who robbed the poor and powerless of their rights and dignity would answer to Yahweh (3:13–15).

Taking a stand for social justice meant living by God's definitions of good and evil, not by another's (5:20), and standing for right regardless of its profitability (5:23). Enacting evil statutes deprived the needy of justice and robbed righteous people of their due (10:1–2). Isaiah called his people to demonstrate their faith by fair and compassionate treatment of everyone (58:6–7). In the messianic age to come, social justice would pervade society—another indication that such issues are important to God's heart (11:4; 25:4; 60:18).

Feeding the poor, providing shelter for the homeless, working for civil rights, and fighting abortion are technically not part of the Christian gospel, but they should be a natural product of a relationship with God. Care for people's physical and social needs results from believers learning to share God's concerns for people created in his image (see sidebar 2.2).

Holiness and Righteousness

The basic meaning of the word "holy" is "set apart." God was wholly set apart from his creation, and God's people were to live lives set apart from the nations around them. Leviticus 19:2b summed up the issue well: "Be holy because I, the LORD your God, am holy."

God's **holiness** comprised a central theme in Isaiah's temple vision as the prophet heard one seraph call to another: "Holy, holy, holy is the LORD Almighty" (6:3). The designation of God as "the Holy One of Israel" occurs thirty-one times in the Old Testament, and twenty-five of those are in Isaiah.[1]

Isaiah affirmed God's holiness with this name but also used the term "holy" in reference to God elsewhere (5:16; 8:13; 40:25; 43:15; 52:10; 57:15; 63:10–11). God's holiness was to reflect itself in his people (4:3; 6:13; 29:23; 30:29) and in Jerusalem, his holy city (11:9; 27:13; 48:2; 52:1; 57:13). Holiness would especially be a mark of God's people and Jerusalem in the messianic age (4:3; 11:9; 35:8). As people reverently celebrated the Sabbath, they set it apart as holy in contrast to other days (58:13). Angels, God's holy ones, also marched to do his bidding (13:3).

Righteousness, a positive quality of goodness that led to good and right action, also figured prominently in Isaiah's message. Above all, righteousness was a divine attribute.

Of the approximately sixty occurrences of the words "righteous," "righteousness," and "righteously," over one-third refer to God. Some describe the righteous character that drives him to judge his people and the nations (5:16; 10:22; 28:17). Other uses denote God's desire to bring righteousness to his people (33:5; 42:6; 45:24; 51:5, 8; 56:1; 61:10).

Most references to righteousness designate God's people, either as some were then (3:10; 57:1), as God's desire for them now (5:7; 26:7; 33:15; 46:12; 48:1, 18), or as the ultimate goal for them in the messianic age (26:2; 45:8, 25; 60:21; 61:3, 10). They had fallen from their righteous state, but he would restore them (1:21, 26–27).

Isaiah clearly possessed a strong knowledge of the law of Moses and the Old Testament historical material that preceded him. He built his prophetic message on that foundation. As we shall now see, later Old Testament writers also built on Isaiah's message.

literary
dependence

literary inter-
dependence

Isaiah's Use in Later Old Testament Material

Some parts of later Old Testament material appear related to Isaianic material. In some cases, literary dependence or interdependence may be seen. In other cases, writers simply appear to have built on an Isaianic motif.

Cases of Dependence or Interdependence

Literary dependence means a writer borrowed or adapted material from an earlier source to a significant extent. In such cases, a relationship between the two texts is clearly observable, and one text is clearly primary.

Literary interdependence means two texts are connected in some clear way. However, in such cases, even though a relationship between the two texts is clearly observable, the direction of influence is unclear.

Dependence: Isaiah 36–39 and 2 Kings 18–20

Scholars have long noted that the events of Isaiah 36–37 historically follow the events of Isaiah 38–39. Usually this is explained in light of Isaiah's literary purpose. Isaiah concluded the "Assyrian section" of his book (chaps. 1–35) with an account of Assyrian defeat (chaps. 36–37), pointing to Assyria's ultimate demise. He then concluded with an account that suggested Hezekiah's descendants would one day serve in Babylon. Thus, Isaiah 39 introduces the "Babylonian section" that begins with Isaiah 40.[2]

Interestingly, the book of 2 Kings, which generally assumes a chronological approach in presenting its material, presents the events in the same order. Though the text is not copied verbatim, the dependence on Isaiah is obvious. This dependence raises an interesting issue.

The switching of the order of these events in Isaiah only makes sense if Isaiah 40 follows Isaiah 39. Therefore, the section some designate as Deutero-Isaiah and assume was written sometime after Cyrus's decree in 539 BC must have been attached to Isaiah 1–39 prior to the adaptation of chapters 36–39 by the writer of Kings.

However, most scholars assign a date of around 560–550 BC for the completion of the material in Kings. This would push the writing of Isaiah 40–66 earlier than multiple authorship advocates can allow. While not proving the single author view of Isaiah, this evidence does create problems for the multiple authorship view of Isaiah.[3]

Interdependence: Isaiah 2:1–4 and Micah 4:1–4

Isaiah 2:1–4 and Micah 4:1–4 bear a striking resemblance to each other. The two texts are virtually identical, though very minor wording differences exist.

Since Isaiah's and Micah's ministries overlapped to a significant degree, one cannot conclusively argue for Isaianic or Mican priority. Nonetheless, the texts seem clearly related. Some scholars have suggested—though no solid evidence exists—that both Isaiah and Micah adapted the words from a known eighth-century-BC hymn.[4]

Further Uses of Isaianic Motifs

The following motifs bear some resemblance to later Old Testament material, and no strong dependence on Isaiah is here suggested. The purpose of this section is merely to note that several important Isaianic themes find further treatment in later Old Testament books.

Holy One of Israel

The expression "Holy One of Israel" occurs twenty-five times in Isaiah, always as a designation for God. It occurs only six times outside Isaiah: 2 Kings 19:22 (parallel to Is 37:23); Psalms 71:22; 78:41; 89:18; Jeremiah 50:29; 51:5. The following is a brief analysis:

2 Kings 19:22: The verse is parallel to Isaiah 37:23 (part of a larger portion of material borrowed from Isaiah by the writer of Kings, discussed above); Sennacherib of Assyria, by his haughty arrogance, has challenged the Holy One of Israel.

Psalm 71:22: The occurrence here is the expression's only use in book 2 of the psalter; it appears in an ascription of praise to God (71:22–24). The psalm is anonymous.

Psalm 78:41: The usage appears in a section in which Asaph (see psalm heading) describes Israel's rebellion in the wilderness despite witnessing God's many miracles. If the psalm heading identifies the author and if the Asaph mentioned was David's lead musician (1 Chr 25:1), the psalm dates prior to Isaiah's time.

Psalm 89:18: The usage appears in a hymn extolling God's majesty. The author, Ethan the Ezrahite (see psalm heading), affirms his and Israel's allegiance to the Holy One of Israel. If Ethan the Ezrahite is the same man mentioned in 1 Kings 4:31, this psalm may date to the same general period as Psalm 78.

Jeremiah 50:29: Jeremiah uses the expression in the context of a siege against Babylon. Babylon's arrogance generally parallels that of Sennacherib in Isaiah 37:22–23.

Jeremiah 51:5: Jeremiah affirms that despite the guilt Israel and Judah bear, neither has been forsaken by the Holy One of Israel. The Lord's judgment now comes to bear on Babylon instead.

Other than the direct parallel of Isaiah 37:23 and 2 Kings 19:22, nothing in the other references suggests a direct parallel or dependence on Isaiah. Psalm 78 and 89 may well precede Isaiah, and although Jeremiah's two uses of the expression find similar contexts in Isaiah, no clear literary connection may be drawn.

Oracles against the Nations

Isaiah's "Oracles against the Nations" section (chaps. 13–23) finds its strongest parallels in Jeremiah 46–51 and Ezekiel 25–32. Amos and Zephaniah also speak against other nations, but in a much more limited sense (Am 1:3–2:3; Zep 2:4–15).

The prophets' oracles against other nations proclaim the powerful truth that the Lord God is sovereign over *all* nations, not merely Israel and Judah. Such a concept stood in stark contrast to the polytheistic views of surrounding nations, who generally believed divine sovereignty was more localized. Isaiah, Jeremiah, and Ezekiel all share this conviction, as do Amos, Zephaniah, and other prophets such as Obadiah and Nahum who announced God's judgment over a particular foreign nation.

However, besides sharing this common conviction, the prophets do not seem to have depended on one another for their oracles against the nations. The prophets denounce the nations in different order and use their own unique approaches. A few motifs appear common to all of them, though these motifs are likely part of a general approach prophets took in pronouncing judgment on nations.

One particular emphasis in Isaiah, however, is God's desire to reach all nations with the news of his salvation. Isaiah saw a day when all nations would stream to Jerusalem (2:1–4), a day when God would gather his people again (11:11–16). But he also proclaimed a God whose heart desired the ends of the earth to turn to him for salvation (45:22–23). He would reconcile Egypt and Assyria to serve him alongside Israel (19:18–25). He even planned to send his messengers to proclaim his glory among the nations (66:19).

Although elements of this concept appear elsewhere in the prophets (Jer 47:7; Jl 2:28–32; Zep 3:9–10) and in the book of Psalms (9:11; 18:49; 45:17; 96:3, 7, 10), no one developed it as thoroughly as Isaiah did. This topic will be the focus of our concluding chapter.

The Davidic Branch

The concept of the branch appears in Isaiah only twice. In the first occurrence (4:2), the branch appears as a glorious part of God's coming kingdom. The Lord purges evil from his people and establishes his close, intimate presence among them as in the days of the wilderness wanderings (4:4–6).

In the second Isaianic occurrence (11:1), the branch is the root of Jesse—a clear Davidic connection. God's Spirit empowers the branch with wisdom and understanding, and he will rule with justice (11:2–4). Harmony results in nature, and the Lord will gather the remnant of his people from everywhere (11:6–16).

Jeremiah built on Isaiah's foundation with two references to the Davidic branch that are closely parallel. In the first reference (23:5–6), Jeremiah described the Lord's raising up a righteous branch of David who would prosper as a king as his people lived in security. This branch had a name—"The Lord Our Righteousness."

In the second reference (33:15–16), Jeremiah expressed the same sentiments but added a word about the continuity of Levitical service and sacrifice as well. This linkage between kingship and priesthood finds fullest expression in Zechariah.

Zechariah's two usages of the term "branch" focus on Joshua, the high priest. In the first (3:8), the Lord's messenger had just given Joshua new clothes, symbolizing God's cleansing of the priesthood. Zechariah then announced the coming of a branch to bring in a wonderful new age. In Zechariah's second reference (6:12), Joshua received a crown, and the prophet proclaimed the branch would build God's temple and bring peace between the offices of king and priest (6:13).

The New Testament does not develop the branch motif directly. However, it does apply the concepts linked to the branch to one person. The New Testament writers proclaim Jesus as the son of David (Mt 1:1; 21:9), our great high priest (Heb 7:22–25), and the source of our righteousness (Rom 3:21–22; 2 Cor 5:21). These three concepts find their convergence in him.

The prophet Isaiah built on the foundation of Moses and other early biblical writers. He drew from the Torah for both teaching and illustrative material. He directed his hearers back to their spiritual heritage and to the God who had given it to them. Isaiah challenged his people to remember God's great works for them and to live righteously as his covenant people should.

Those who followed Isaiah also built on this stream of religious faith. One of Isaiah's grandest contributions was his exalted view of God. First, the Lord was the Holy One of Israel. His holiness set him apart, and he called people everywhere to submit to his righteous standards. As they followed him, they would become more like him.

Second, Isaiah also proclaimed God as Lord of all nations whether or not those nations knew it. He had made them what they were, and he would judge them in his perfect timing. His sovereignty did not end at Israel's borders.

Third, Isaiah described God as a God intimately involved in human history. He had carved out a people for his name, and he was guiding history toward the establishment of his kingdom, when all nations everywhere would recognize his majesty and rule. He would restore David's throne and

Study Questions

1. How does the book of Isaiah make use of earlier Old Testament material? Cite key people, places, and events.

2. Provide examples of the prophet's allusion to the Torah.

3. How were later Old Testament writers influenced by the book of Isaiah?

establish Jerusalem as his centerpiece of worship again.

As we have seen in this chapter, other Old Testament writers expanded on Isaiah's teachings. But the ultimate fulfillment of Isaiah's words awaited the coming of the particular son of David of whom Isaiah and others spoke. The New Testament proclaims that son of David as Jesus, and it is to the New Testament's use of Isaiah we now turn.

Key Terms

holiness

literary dependence

literary interdependence

righteousness

21 Isaiah and the New Testament

Outline

- **Direct Fulfillment of Isaiah's Words**
  Jesus's Person and Work
  Jesus's Eschatological Kingdom
  John the Baptizer
- **Secondary Fulfillment/Application of Isaiah's Words**
  Jesus's Person and Work
  People's Unbelief
  God's Salvation
  Church Life
- **Allusions to Isaiah's Words**
  Isaiah 8:12–13
  Isaiah 22:13
  Isaiah 40:6–8
  Isaiah 61:6
- **Conclusion**

Objectives

After reading this chapter, you should be able to
1. Cite key New Testament passages that proclaim a direct or secondary fulfillment of Isaiah's words.
2. Discuss how Isaiah's words point to Jesus's person and works.

The previous chapter examined how the book of Isaiah profoundly affected the Old Testament. Isaiah sometimes echoed themes from earlier writers as he called people to faithful living under the Lord's covenant. Isaiah also presented new themes and emphases. Later Old Testament writers also took Isaiah's message and drew on it as it suited their own purposes.

Isaiah's contribution to the New Testament also becomes evident when we examine the data. Approximately one out of every seventeen verses contains material that comes directly from Isaiah.[1] The New Testament writers clearly knew the book of Isaiah well.

The New Testament writers' use of Isaianic material falls into three categories. First, New Testament writers point to events in Jesus's life and in the life of the church as directly fulfilling Isaiah's words. Second, New Testament writers make secondary application of Isaiah's words to situations in Jesus's life or the life of the early church. Third, New Testament writers use Isaiah's words because his words, while not directly related to the point they are making, nonetheless fit the sense of what they want to say. A thorough study of every verse is not possible within the scope of this book, but I have tried to highlight the most significant aspects.

In some cases, interpreters will disagree over whether a fulfillment is direct or secondary, or whether the New Testament usage represents a secondary fulfillment or merely uses the words because they fit the New Testament context. Consider some or all of them for yourself and draw your own hermeneutical conclusions.

Direct Fulfillment of Isaiah's Words

The New Testament passages that declare a direct fulfillment of Isaiah's words fall into two main categories: those regarding Jesus's person and work and those regarding his eschatological kingdom. A few passages blend these two concepts, while one deals with John the Baptizer.

Jesus's Person and Work

Isaiah's prophecies about Jesus's person and work sometimes find their fulfillment in Jesus himself. At other times, they find their fulfillment in his body, the church.

Jesus Himself

The Gospel writer Matthew saw a fulfillment of Isaiah's words in Jesus's public ministry (Is 9:1–2; Mt 4:15–16). The light to which Isaiah referred was the glory and the spiritual light of Jesus, whose ministry was concentrated in Galilee of the Gentiles, especially the region on the northern shore of the Sea of Galilee.

Matthew also saw in Jesus the fulfillment of Isaiah's first servant song (Is 42:1–4; Mt 12:18–21). As Jesus performed works of healing among the crowds, he often insisted that those he healed tell no one. The passage contrasts Jesus's seemingly gentle approach with his effectiveness at accomplishing God's purpose.

Of course, many New Testament witnesses linked the fourth servant song (Is 52:13–53:12) with Jesus. John considered Isaiah's words as he marveled at the unbelief of many to whom Jesus spoke (Is 53:1; Jn 12:38). Matthew saw Isaiah's words fulfilled in Jesus's healings (Is 53:4; Mt 8:17). When the Ethiopian official puzzled over the identity of the servant, Philip began proclaiming Jesus to him, beginning at that very place in Isaiah (Is 53:7–8; Acts 8:32–33).[2] Peter reminded his readers of Christ's suffering for our healing, despite his innocence (Is 53:5, 9; 1 Pt 2:22, 24). They had been wandering sheep who had returned to Jesus, their shepherd (Is 53:6; 1 Pt 2:25). Finally, Jesus himself affirmed his link with Isaiah's words when he described himself as "numbered with the transgressors" (Is 53:12; Lk 22:37).

New Testament Citations of the Book of Isaiah

The chart below demonstrates the remarkable impact Isaiah's message had on the New Testament writers. As you peruse the information, note both the number of citations and the large number of New Testament books in which they occur.

Isaiah	New Testament Reference	Isaiah	New Testament Reference
1:9	Romans 9:29	43:20	1 Peter 2:9
6:9	Luke 8:10	43:21	1 Peter 2:9
6:9–10	Matthew 13:14–15	44:28	Acts 13:22
	Mark 4:12	45:21	Mark 12:32
	Acts 28:26–27	45:23	Romans 14:11
6:10	John 12:40	49:6	Acts 13:47
7:14	Matthew 1:23	49:8	2 Corinthians 6:2
8:8, 10 (LXX)*	Matthew 1:23	52:5	Romans 2:24
8:12–13	1 Peter 3:14–15	52:7	Romans 10:15
8:14	Romans 9:33	52:11	2 Corinthians 6:17
	1 Peter 2:8	52:15	Romans 15:21
8:17 (LXX)*	Hebrews 2:13	53:1	John 12:38
8:18	Hebrews 2:13		Romans 10:16
9:1–2	Matthew 4:15–16	53:4	Matthew 8:17
11:10	Romans 15:12	53:7–8 (LXX)*	Acts 8:32–33
22:13	1 Corinthians 15:32	53:9	1 Peter 2:22
25:8	1 Corinthians 15:54	53:12	Luke 22:37
26:20	Hebrews 10:37	54:1	Galatians 4:27
28:11–12	1 Corinthians 14:21	54:13	John 6:45
28:16	Romans 9:33; 10:11	55:3 (LXX)*	Acts 13:34
	1 Peter 2:6	56:7	Matthew 21:13
29:10	Romans 11:8		Mark 11:17
29:13 (LXX)*	Matthew 15:8–9		Luke 19:46
	Mark 7:6–7	59:7–8	Romans 3:15–17
29:14	1 Corinthians 1:19	59:20–21	Romans 11:26–27
40:3	Matthew 3:3	61:1–2	Luke 4:18–19
	Mark 1:3	61:6	1 Peter 2:9
	John 1:23	62:11	Matthew 21:5
40:6–8	1 Peter 1:24–25	64:4	1 Corinthians 2:9
40:13	Romans 11:34	65:1	Romans 10:20
	1 Corinthians 2:16	65:2	Romans 10:21
42:1–4	Matthew 12:18–21	66:1–2	Acts 7:49–50

*LXX = the Septuagint

Adapted from The Greek New Testament, *ed. Kurt Aland et al.,*
3rd ed. (London: United Bible Society, 1975), 899.

Luke saw in Jesus's Nazareth ministry the fulfillment of Isaiah's Spirit-led minister prophecy (Is 61:1–2; Lk 4:18–19). Jesus read the passage in Nazareth's synagogue and proclaimed the arrival of the Lord's favor that day, to the surprise and confusion of those who heard.

God was building a people for his name. Isaiah announced the Lord was laying a foundation for that work in Zion, with a precious cornerstone (Is 8:14; 28:16). Both Peter and Paul affirmed that Jesus was the cornerstone for the great house of people that God was building (Rom 9:33; 10:11; Eph 2:20; 1 Pt 2:6, 8).

Jesus also alluded to Isaiah's words as he preached to the crowds (Is 54:13; Jn 6:45). The time for the Lord to teach his children directly had come—in Jesus.

Finally, Matthew joined the concepts of Isaiah 62:11 and Zechariah 9:9 as he saw Jesus riding into Jerusalem on Palm Sunday (Mt 21:5). Israel's salvation had come.

Jesus's Work through His People

Isaiah's words about Jesus's work sometimes found their fulfillment in the church. Paul proclaimed to the crowd at Antioch of Pisidia that the church fulfilled its mission when it followed the Lord's command to be a light to the nations as Isaiah had prophesied (Is 49:6; Acts 13:47).

Jesus gave his disciples the Great Commission task of proclaiming the gospel to the ends of the earth (Mt 28:18–20). As they did, Paul argued, many Israelites remained in unbelief, but Gentiles who were not seeking God suddenly found themselves receiving his offer of salvation (Is 65:1–2; Rom 10:20–21).

The clear parallel between Isaiah 66:19–20 and Matthew 28:18–20 makes it likely that Paul viewed Isaiah 65:1–2 as beginning its direct fulfillment in his day. However, Isaiah's words may also be viewed as an indictment against Israel's general unwillingness to seek the Lord over the generations. In this case, the verses find a secondary fulfillment in Paul's letter to the Romans.

Jesus's Eschatological Kingdom

The New Testament writers also affirm that Isaiah's announcement of God's eschatological kingdom is fulfilled in Jesus. The root of Jesse, led by God's Spirit, will execute justice for the nations (Is 11:1–5). Peace will come to the earth, and as it does, the Gentiles will come to faith in fulfillment of God's promise (Is 11:10). Indeed, the apostle Paul's desire to see the Gentiles reconciled to God drove him to proclaim Christ in new places (Rom 15:12, 20–21).

The New Testament confirms that this age of peace and righteousness will begin with the second coming of Christ. Isaiah described God's great work in bringing a redeemer to Zion (Is 59:20). This redeemer would affirm God's covenant through God's Spirit, and his kingdom would last forever (Is 59:21). Paul cited these verses as descriptive of the great day when Jesus returns and Israel at last will recognize its Messiah (Rom 11:26–27).

Isaiah mentioned two other exciting aspects of Jesus's coming kingdom. First, every knee would bow to the Lord (Is 45:23). Interestingly, Paul applied to Christ words that originally applied to God (Phil 2:10–11). The world at last would recognize its true Savior and Sovereign.

Second, the Lord would bring an end to death and suffering. Isaiah described a day when the Lord would prepare a lavish banquet for all peoples. He would remove the spiritual barrier between himself and them, and he would swallow up death for all time (Is 25:6–8).

The **resurrection** was the last major topic in Paul's letter we know as First Corinthians (1 Cor 15:12–58). Paul described the certainty of Christ's resurrection and its impact on all believers—when he returns, they will rise as he did (1 Cor 15:20–22). Paul assured his readers that in that day, Isaiah's

repentance

words would come true (1 Cor 15:54). Death, the last enemy, would be destroyed forever (1 Cor 15:26).

John the Baptizer

Isaiah 40:3 forms part of the prologue (40:1–11) in Isaiah's initial oracle of encouragement to a people struggling to believe the Babylonian exile could actually end. The verse reads as follows:

> A voice of one calling:
> "In the desert prepare
> the way for the LORD;
> make straight in the wilderness
> a highway for our God."

The Synoptic Gospel writers Matthew, Mark, and Luke all cite this passage as fulfilled in John the Baptizer's ministry (Mt 3:3; Mk 1:3; Lk 3:4–6). Luke's citation is the most complete. John preached a baptism of **repentance** to prepare people for God's coming kingdom. Further, the Gospel of John reveals that John the Baptizer saw himself as the fulfillment of Isaiah's words (Jn 1:23). However, John also clearly recognized his role as a forerunner, announcing the ultimate fulfillment of God's kingdom in Jesus (Jn 1:26–27, 29–31).

Secondary Fulfillment/ Application of Isaiah's Words

The New Testament passages that present a secondary fulfillment or application of Isaiah's words fall into four categories: Jesus's person and work, people's unbelief, God's salvation, and church life.

Jesus's Person and Work

Three Isaianic passages find secondary fulfillment in Jesus's person and work in the New Testament. Two foreshadow Jesus's birth, while one is applied to his resurrection.

Jesus's Birth (Is 7:14; 8:8, 10; Mt 1:23)

As Israel and Syria tried to convince Judah to join its coalition against Assyria in 735–734 BC, Isaiah desperately tried to convince Ahaz, Judah's king, to trust in the Lord rather than in Assyrian might (Is 7:3–15; 8:1–4). When Ahaz refused to ask the Lord for a sign, Isaiah offered one instead, linked to the birth of a son. This son would be named Immanuel (God is with us), even though circumstances suggested God was far from Judah.

Matthew saw an even greater fulfillment of Isaiah's words in the birth of Jesus (Mt 1:23).[3] In Jesus, God's Son, God is truly now with us to a degree that he never was before. Matthew proclaimed that God in the flesh now walked among us, a fact the apostle John would also later record (Jn 1:14). Jesus's virgin birth also sets him apart from the rest of humanity, stressing his heavenly origin and preserving his sinless nature.

Jesus's Resurrection (Is 55:3; Acts 13:34)

In Isaiah 55, the prophet called his people to reconcile themselves to God. They were spending their money on things that did not bring lasting fulfillment, when the lasting fulfillment they could find in their God was free.

On his first missionary journey, Paul revealed the full intent of Isaiah's words to a crowd at Antioch of Pisidia (Acts 13:34). The ultimate fulfillment of God's granting people "my faithful love promised to David" (Is 55:3) came through Jesus's resurrection from the dead. Indeed, the New Testament proclaims that Jesus's resurrection is the source of the full blessings of our eternal life (Rom 5:9–10; 1 Cor 15:20–22).

People's Unbelief

The New Testament applies Isaiah's words about people's unbelief to two

257

categories of people. Sometimes it refers to Israel's unbelief, while at other times, it denotes the unbelief of people in general.

Israel's Unbelief

Israel's unbelief had a long history (Dt 9:6–24) and typifies the human struggle to believe God's promises. Isaiah described how God's grace alone preserved a remnant for Israel (Is 1:9), a fact Paul later affirmed (Rom 9:29). A spirit of stupor prevailed on the nation from Isaiah's day to Paul's day (Is 29:10; Rom 11:8). Isaiah and Jesus affirmed that the people of Israel honored God with their lips, while their hearts remained far from him (Is 29:13; Mt 15:8–9; Mk 7:6–7).

All four Gospel writers quoted all or part of Isaiah 6:9–10, which forms part of the foundational aspect of Isaiah's call (Mt 13:14–15; Mk 4:12; Lk 8:10; Jn 12:40; Acts 28:26–27). Israel continued to see and hear without real perception and understanding even to the time of Jesus's and the apostles' ministry.

God's name was blasphemed during Isaiah's day (Is 52:5). Paul, in building his case for all humanity lying in sin's grip, applied Isaiah's words to hypocritical Jews of his day (Rom 2:24). Their sinful lives made a mockery of God's name among the Gentiles.

Jesus applied another passage from Isaiah (56:7) in similar fashion. The money changers and merchants of the temple area had made God's temple, which should have been a house of prayer, a den of robbers (Mt 21:13; Mk 11:17; Lk 19:46). The way people treated the temple grounds spoke volumes about the real attitudes of their hearts.

Israel's unbelief stands as a testimony to the human condition. The biblical record asserts that everyone lies in sin's grip and has a deep spiritual need only God can meet (Rom 3:9).

People in General

The New Testament applies a few verses from Isaiah to the unbelief of people in general. Paul found Isaiah's description of God destroying the wisdom of the wise useful as he addressed the people of the Corinthian church, who lived in a society that prided itself on its knowledge and wisdom (Is 29:14; 1 Cor 1:19). And as he described the human condition, Paul found Isaiah's list of sinful practices a good commentary (Is 59:7–8; Rom 3:15–17).

God's Salvation

Isaiah announced God's coming salvation throughout his book. He called people to embrace the Lord's offer to be saved (45:22) and indicated that his salvation was sure (62:1–3). The New Testament writers applied various salvation themes to the contexts in which they found themselves.

The Lord was a God worthy of the people's trust (Is 8:17–18; Heb 2:13). Paul used Isaiah's declaration of God bringing salvation at the proper time, applying it to the Corinthians when he wrote, "I tell you, now is the time of God's favor, now is the day of salvation" (2 Cor 6:2). The time had come for people everywhere to embrace the salvation God had prepared for them. No one could even imagine all the blessings God had in store for his children (Is 64:4; 1 Cor 2:9).

Paul and Peter also applied Isaiah's words about Israel's status as a chosen people to God's chosen people the church. The church, like Israel, was a holy nation, a people for God's own possession (Is 43:20–21; 1 Pt 2:9).[4]

Paul also combined Isaiah's command for the barren woman to rejoice and cry aloud (Is 54:1) with Israel's early history of the births of Ishmael and Isaac (Gn 16:1–16; 21:1–7). Isaac was the child of promise, the son of a free woman. Likewise, the church's children are children of God's promise, born by the Spirit, not by the flesh (Gal 4:21–31).

Isaiah's words of salvation also find their fulfillment in the proclamation of the gospel message. Isaiah announced, "How beautiful on the mountains are the feet of those who bring good news" (Is 52:7). Paul applied these words to

world evangelization

the church as he stressed the urgency of **world evangelization** (Rom 10:9–15). God's plan to reach the world involved believers sharing their faith with unbelievers; he had no other plan.

Isaiah's last servant passage (52:13–53:12) described how the servant's ministry would bring an understanding to kings of the world (52:15). Paul applied Isaiah's words to himself as he spoke of his personal desire to proclaim the gospel to unreached peoples (Rom 15:21). He saw his calling primarily as taking the gospel where no one had heard it before. Many missionaries today claim a calling similar to Paul's.

Church Life

Many of Isaiah's teachings naturally apply to the church because they contain moral instruction based on God's earlier revelation. It is impossible to know the full extent of Isaiah's contribution in this regard, since other Old Testament writers echoed the same themes. However, two passages were specifically cited and applied to church life: Isaiah 28:11–12 and 52:11.

Isaiah 28:11–12

Isaiah 28:11–12 indicted the people for their childish understanding of God's truth. God assured them that he would speak to them in judgment through the unintelligible speech of a foreign, conquering people.

As Paul wrote the Corinthian church regarding spiritual gifts, he put the gift of tongues in perspective by applying Isaiah's words. Just as God had spoken to his people through foreign tongues in judgment, he could also speak in foreign tongues as a sign of his presence to unbelievers in Paul's day (1 Cor 14:21–25). Nonetheless, he instructed the church not to make more of this gift than God had intended (1 Cor 14:18–19).

Isaiah 52:11

Isaiah called the exile generation to flee Babylon. The time of deliverance had come. As they left, they were to touch nothing unclean and were to purify themselves.

As Paul challenged the people of the Corinthian church to separate themselves from the world to serve God, he cited Isaiah's words (2 Cor 6:17). The God of history called his people to a very different lifestyle than that of the world. Christians were more than merely forgiven. The Holy Spirit lived in them to help them live like Jesus, and thus their whole manner of life was to give testimony to their relationship with God.

Allusions to Isaiah's Words

In a few instances, the New Testament writers adapted Isaiah's words for their own purposes. The connection in these occurrences appears more remote; probably the writers used Isaiah's words because they conveyed the sense of what they wanted to say. Citing Scripture was deemed valuable, even if it was used only in an illustrative sense.

Isaiah 8:12–13

Isaiah 8:12–13 challenged the Judeans to see the Lord of Hosts as their only true refuge. They did not need to fear earthly powers, but rather, they needed to trust the Lord alone. Quoting Isaiah, Peter instructed his readers not to fear or be disturbed as they faced the world's persecution, but to set apart Jesus as Lord in their hearts (1 Pt 3:14–15).

Isaiah 22:13

The context of Isaiah 22:13 indicates God's impending judgment of those who ignored him and his ways as they went about their daily lives. They lived life by the motto, "Let us eat and drink, for tomorrow we die!"

In 1 Corinthians 15, Paul expounded the doctrine of the bodily resurrection. He insisted on the absolute necessity of Christ's resurrection. If Christ had never risen from the dead, Christians were without hope. In fact, Paul suggested if that were the case, the words of Isaiah's opponents were true: "Let us eat and drink, for tomorrow we die" (1 Cor 15:32). Of course, Paul went on to validate Christ's resurrection and all its consequent blessings on those who place their faith in him (1 Cor 15:20–28, 35–58).

Isaiah 40:6–8

Isaiah 40:6–8 represents the prophet's hypothetical answer to a discouraged people. Seventy years of exile was a long time; could God really bring them home? Isaiah insisted on both the validity of God's promise and his power to make it happen. God's word would stand forever.

Peter encouraged his readers that their hope was imperishable. It would never fade away, because it was founded on God's promise. They had been born again through the word of God, and drawing on Isaiah's words, Peter assured them God's word would stand forever (1 Pt 1:24–25).

Isaiah 61:6

The last example of New Testament allusions to Isaiah's words is based on Isaiah 61:6. There the prophet looked forward to a day when God's people would serve as his priests and ministers. Their service on his behalf would reach a level it had never reached in all their history.

For Peter, the dawning of Christ's church had brought that day. He affirmed that the Christians to whom he wrote were a royal priesthood and a holy nation. They belonged to God, and he had called them for a purpose: to "declare the praises of him who called you out of darkness into his wonderful light" (1 Pt 2:9). For Isaiah and for Peter, God's call came to people not merely so that they might glory in their own relationship with him. Rather, God's call meant aligning themselves with God's purpose to reach the world with his salvation.

Conclusion

Isaiah's impact on the New Testament is obvious. Many writers recorded the direct fulfillment of Isaiah's words through events in their days. Usually these events centered around the person and work of Jesus Christ and his coming kingdom.

The New Testament also identifies many secondary fulfillments and applications of Isaiah's words. These focus on Jesus's person and work, people's unbelief, God's salvation, and life in Christ's church. Isaiah's grand messages regarding covenant living, rebuking sin, and announcing God's salvation naturally rang out all the louder to Jesus's followers, who saw these themes gain even more meaning when applied to the life of their Lord.

Finally, many New Testament writers alluded to Isaiah's words merely because the expressions he used fit their purposes for particular points they wished to make. In general, Isaiah's context roughly paralleled their situations, and they felt free to link their writings with this ancient prophetic voice. In doing so, they affirmed again

---

Study Questions

1. What are the most significant links between the book of Isaiah and the New Testament? Give several examples.

2. How did New Testament writers understand Jesus's person and work in relation to Isaianic prophecy? Discuss key passages the New Testament applied either directly or secondarily to Jesus.

3. Given all the prophetic material about Jesus in the book of Isaiah, how clearly do you think Isaiah understood Jesus's coming ministry? Defend your answer.

the timeless impact of God's word across the generations.

As stated earlier in the chapter, Isaiah's impact on the New Testament extends far beyond the sum of the citations given in this book. The New Testament writers saw themselves as those on whom the fulfillment of the ages had come. Consequently, they felt a kinship with the prophetic voices that in past generations had kindled the hope of God's coming kingdom and salvation.

What the prophets "saw and welcomed . . . from a distance" (Heb 11:13), the New Testament writers proclaimed

Key Terms

repentance

resurrection

world evangelization

in all its fullness: God's salvation has come to the world through Jesus Christ, his Son. And how will news of this salvation reach the world? We will examine that issue in the final chapter.

22 Isaiah and the Great Commission

Outline

- **Foundational Questions**
  How Do the Creation Mandate and the Great Commission Mandate Differ?
  What Is Israel's Relationship to the Great Commission?
- **God and the Nations in Isaiah**
  God Will Judge the Nations
  God Will Show Himself Unique as He Judges False Gods
  God Will Bring the Nations to Himself
- **The Great Commission Implications of the Book of Isaiah**
  God Is Unique among All Gods
  God Is Sovereign over All Nations and Peoples
  God's Heart for the Nations Is Apparent
  God Will Reach the Nations through His People
- **Conclusion**

Objectives

After reading this chapter, you should be able to

1. Define and distinguish the creation mandate and the Great Commission mandate.
2. Discuss Israel's centripetal and centrifugal witness to the nations.
3. Explain God's plan for the nations as revealed in Isaiah.
4. Summarize the Great Commission implications of the book of Isaiah.

creation mandate

World evangelization is a primary emphasis of the New Testament. It proclaims that God has acted in history to redeem people through his Son, Jesus, whose death and resurrection secured the salvation of all who put their faith in him. The New Testament places a high priority on reaching people with the news of God's salvation through Jesus Christ.

Reaching the nations with God's message of salvation was clearly a high priority for Jesus. The Gospels and Acts record four different postresurrection occasions when Jesus commissioned his disciples with the task of world evangelization (Mt 28:18–20; Lk 24:46–49; Jn 20:21–23; Acts 1:7–8). The early church clearly understood that Jesus gave the task not only to the twelve apostles but to all believers of all time. Everyone is to have a part in this great cause.

The God of the Bible is a sending God. The Hebrew word for "send" (*shalah*) occurs over eight hundred times in the Old Testament, and in over two hundred of those occurrences, God appears as the subject. Many of those describe God sending people to do his work.[1] Interestingly, the Greek verb *apostello*, from which we get our word "apostle," translates the vast majority of these uses of *shalah* in the Septuagint.[2]

After addressing three foundational questions, this chapter will survey the concept of nations and peoples in the book of Isaiah. It will then provide an overview of the topic of God and the nations, followed by some concluding thoughts on the Great Commission implications of the book of Isaiah.

Foundational Questions

Two foundational questions merit exploring. First, how do the creation mandate and the Great Commission mandate differ? Second, what is Israel's relationship to the Great Commission?

How Do the Creation Mandate and the Great Commission Mandate Differ?

The Bible records both a creation mandate, that is, a mandate to humanity regarding its duties within the created order (Gn 1:26–28; 9:1–7), and a Great Commission mandate, which Jesus gave his disciples after his resurrection (Mt 28:18–20; Lk 24:46–49; Jn 20:21–23; Acts 1:7–8). We will consider the characteristics of each to clarify important differences.

The Creation Mandate

The **creation mandate** appears as the culmination of God's creative process in the book of Genesis. The text records how God created humanity in his own image and then pronounced the following mandate in the form of a blessing:

> God blessed them and said to them, "Be fruitful and increase in number; fill the earth and subdue it. Rule over the fish of the sea and the birds of the air and over every living creature that moves on the ground." (Gn 1:28)

After the great flood, the text records God's restatement of the creation mandate to Noah and his family:

> Then God blessed Noah and his sons, saying to them, "Be fruitful and increase in number and fill the earth. The fear and dread of you will fall upon all the beasts of the earth and all the birds of the air, upon every creature that moves along the ground, and upon all the fish of the sea; they are given into your hands. Everything that lives and moves will be food for you. Just as I gave you the green plants, I now give you everything. But you must not eat meat that has its lifeblood still in it. And for your lifeblood I will surely demand an accounting. I will demand an accounting from every animal. And from each man, too, I will demand an accounting for the life of his fel-

stewardship

low man. Whoever sheds the blood of man, by man shall his blood be shed; for in the image of God has God made man. As for you, be fruitful and increase in number; multiply on the earth and increase upon it." (Gn 9:1–7)

The creation mandate has three basic characteristics. First, it commands good **stewardship** of the earth's resources. God commanded humanity to populate the earth. As people did so, they were to subdue the earth and have dominion over all creation. Adam had begun this dominion by working the land in the garden of Eden (Gn 2:15) and by naming the animals, thus demonstrating a certain authority over them (Gn 2:19).

At the same time, this great authority also came with great responsibility. When people chose to stay in one place rather than obey God's command to fill the earth, he confused their languages, thus "forcing" them to fulfill his command (Gn 11:1–9).

Today God expects people to show good stewardship over the earth's resources. Recognizing that everything in life comes to us as a gift should encourage good and careful use and discourage careless, wasteful use.

Second, the creation mandate applies God's principles to human relationships. Since people are created in God's image, we have a responsibility to treat one another with dignity and respect. As originally given, the mandate spoke specifically against the taking of another individual's life. However, God's judgment of the world for its sin (Gn 6–8) reveals his concern for justice and righteousness to prevail in society. As people live according to the moral principles that flow from God's own character, they experience life as it was meant to be.

Third, the creation mandate focuses on the present age. God has put humanity on this earth to live life as he intended it. As they live according to his laws, the earth remains the peaceful and blessed place he created it to

be. However, when people abandon God's principles and substitute their own, society suffers.

Thus, the creation mandate commands good stewardship of the earth's resources, applies God's principles to human relationships, and focuses on the present age.

The Great Commission Mandate

The New Testament records four[3] occasions when Jesus gave his disciples the Great Commission:

1. And Jesus came up and spoke to them, saying, "All authority has been given to Me in heaven and on earth. Go therefore and make disciples of all the nations, baptizing them in the name of the Father and the Son and the Holy Spirit, teaching them to observe all that I commanded you; and lo, I am with you always, even to the end of the age." (Mt 28:18–20 NASB)
2. Then He [Jesus] opened their minds to understand the Scriptures, and He said to them, "Thus it is written, that the Christ would suffer and rise again from the dead the third day; and that repentance for forgiveness of sins would be proclaimed in His name to all the nations, beginning from Jerusalem. You are witnesses of these things. And behold, I am sending forth the promise of My Father upon you; but you are to stay in the city until you are clothed with power from on high." (Lk 24:45–49 NASB)
3. So Jesus said to them again, "Peace be with you; as the Father has sent Me, I also send you." And when He had said this, He breathed on them, and said to them, "Receive the Holy Spirit. If you forgive the sins of any, their sins have been forgiven them; if you retain the sins of any, they have been retained." (Jn 20:21–23 NASB)
4. He [Jesus] said to them, "It is not for you to know times or epochs which the Father has fixed by His

own authority; but you will receive power when the Holy Spirit has come upon you; and you shall be My witnesses both in Jerusalem, and in all Judea and Samaria, and even to the remotest part of the earth." (Acts 1:7–8 NASB)

The **Great Commission mandate** also has three basic characteristics, but they differ markedly from the creation mandate.

First, the Great Commission mandate involves a sacred stewardship in matters pertaining to the spiritual realm. Whereas the creation mandate encourages good stewardship over earthly resources, the Great Commission mandate encourages good stewardship over heavenly resources. Far from managing earth's treasures, which only last for this lifetime, the Great Commission mandate encourages people to store up heavenly treasure (Mt 6:19–21). Jesus likewise encouraged his followers to invest their earthly resources for eternal causes (Lk 16:9–11).

Second, the Great Commission mandate involves establishing eternal relationships through reaching people with God's eternal truth. Earthly relationships do not lie at the core of the Great Commission mandate, but heavenly relationships do. In particular, the Great Commission mandate calls people to a personal relationship with God through faith in his Son, Jesus Christ (Rom 3:21–31; Eph 2:8–9).

Third, the Great Commission mandate includes an emphasis on eternity. This earthly life becomes merely a tool to invest in what is truly lasting. Whereas the creation mandate involves teaching people to live as God intended for them to live on earth, the Great Commission mandate focuses on preparing them for eternal life—an abundant life that begins when they place their faith in Jesus (Jn 10:10; 17:3).

Thus, the Great Commission mandate focuses on the spiritual realm, stresses establishing eternal relationships, and directs people toward eternity. Both the creation mandate and the Great Commission mandate come from God and form important parts of his plan for his creation. And though the creation mandate is temporary—lasting only as long as the created order lasts—it provides the context in which the Great Commission mandate is carried out.

What Is Israel's Relationship to the Great Commission?

Most interpreters agree that the Bible teaches the nation of Israel had a role to play in the accomplishment of the Great Commission.[4] Most also agree that Israel's role differs at least somewhat from that of the church.[5] Israel's witness to the nations contained both *centripetal* and *centrifugal* aspects.

A Centripetal Witness

Israel's witness to the nations contained a centripetal aspect; that is, it was to draw people to God's light. People who witnessed Israelite society and interacted with Israelites were to see a

(Courtesy of the International Mission Board)

centripetal witness

centrifugal witness

quality of life so unique and blessed, they would want it for themselves. Moses anticipated such a **centripetal witness** for Israel when he instructed them about their future days living in the land of Canaan:

> See, I have taught you decrees and laws as the LORD my God commanded me, so that you may follow them in the land you are entering to take possession of it. Observe them carefully, for this will show your wisdom and understanding to the nations, who will hear about all these decrees and say, "Surely this is a wise and understanding people." What other nation is so great as to have their gods near them the way the LORD our God is near us whenever we pray to him? And what other nation is so great as to have such righteous decrees and laws as this body of laws I am setting before you today? (Dt 4:5–8)

The laws God had given his people were intended as a blessing, not as a curse or a burden. His statutes revealed his character, and as his people lived by them, they would reveal his character to one another and to the nations around them.

Israel's position as a land bridge between Asia, Europe, and Africa meant that peoples from all over the ancient Near East passed through its territory on a regular basis.[6] The nation was the site of much commerce and was also exposed to many foreign cultural influences. The biblical writers called the people to live in such a way that people of other nations would observe the difference in their lives and want to know more about their God.

A Centrifugal Witness

Israel's witness to the nations also contained a centrifugal aspect; that is, Israel was to share its spiritual light with others.

God's initial call to Abram (later Abraham) made it clear that the divine purpose was to bless both Abram's line and the peoples of the world through him:

> The LORD had said to Abram, "Leave your country, your people and your father's household and go to the land I will show you.
> "I will make you into a great nation
> and I will bless you;
> I will make your name great,
> and you will be a blessing.
> I will bless those who bless you,
> and whoever curses you I will curse;
> and all peoples on earth
> will be blessed through you."
> (Gn 12:1–3)

Notice especially the last part of the last sentence: *all peoples on earth will be blessed through you.* That is, Abram would somehow become a channel of blessing to the world.

The apostle Paul saw in Genesis 12:3 the Spirit of God actually proclaiming the gospel message to Abram (Gal 3:8). Did God expect the same kind of **centrifugal witness** from Israel as he did from the church?

The earlier portions of the Old Testament demonstrate God's desire to reach people outside the bounds of Israel with his grace. For example, Melchizedek, king of Salem, served as a priest of the Lord, calling him "God Most High" (Gn 14:18–20). Likewise, Jethro, Moses's father-in-law, served as a priest of Midian (Ex 3:1) and praised the Lord for his rescue of Israel from Egypt (Ex 18:10–11).

God also demonstrated his glory to the nations through his miracles in Egypt during Israel's slavery there. Many outside Israel heard of these amazing works and trembled in fear at the reports (Jos 2:8–11; 1 Sm 4:8).

Unfortunately, few appear to have responded to God's witness of himself. Scripture records Rahab's faith among the people of Jericho (Jos 2:8–11). She had heard the same reports others had heard but chose to respond in faith.

Likewise, Ruth, a Moabite woman, chose to cast her lot with God's people rather than return to Moabite culture after her Israelite husband died (Ru 1:16–17).

Both Rahab and Ruth experienced God's abundant blessing; in fact, both became part of the ancestry of Jesus Christ (Mt 1:5)! When we read their stories, we wonder how God might have blessed others if they had chosen to respond as well.

Many psalms also call other nations to join in praising God (Pss 66:1, 8; 67:1–7; 96:1–13; 98:1–3). He had done great works and commanded that the nations hear. Of course, some of Israel's witness may have occurred as foreign peoples traveled through Israel's territory and encountered testimony to Israel's God. However, the boldness of these psalms in urging the nations to hear suggests more than a centripetal witness within Israel.

The prophetic books also proclaim many examples of a call to centrifugal witness. The Lord sent Jonah to Nineveh with a message that ended up being one of grace (Jn 3:1–10). Jeremiah ministered primarily in Judah, but the Lord appointed him a "prophet to the nations" (Jer 1:5). Joel predicted a day when all flesh would receive God's Spirit (Jl 2:28–32). Zephaniah proclaimed a time when all the nations would serve the Lord together (Zep 3:9).

Among all the prophetic books, however, Isaiah has the most to say regarding God reaching out to peoples and nations. In fact, the book of Isaiah contains over two hundred usages of the most common Hebrew terms for "nations" and "peoples." As in other biblical books, these words emphasize groups of people and/or ethnic groups rather than land or territory.

As we study the concept of the nations in Isaiah, we will investigate Isaiah's contribution to the Great Commission mandate. What, in fact, is God's relationship to the nations in Isaiah? Is Israel's witness in Isaiah centripetal or centrifugal? And what are the Great Commission implications of the book of Isaiah?

God and the Nations in Isaiah

An examination of God and the nations in Isaiah reveals three basic principles to which the prophet returns again and again. First, God will judge the nations. Second, God will show himself unique as he judges false gods. Third, God will bring the nations to himself.

God Will Judge the Nations

Central to Isaiah's theology is the fact that God is sovereign over all nations. Isaiah's prophetic oracles against the nations (chaps. 13–23) declare this again and again. God rules even nations as large and powerful as Babylon (13:1–14:23), Assyria (14:24–27), and Egypt (19:1–17), decreeing their ruin according to his timetable.

At the same time, Isaiah assures us, God also pays attention to smaller peoples such as Moab (15:1–16:14), Damascus (17:1–3), and Tyre (23:1–18).

Isaiah stresses that the Lord is sovereign over these peoples whether or not they recognize it. Assyria, for example, was unaware of the role it played as God's instrument of judgment (10:5–11; 37:22–26). Babylon also needed Isaiah's perspective on its own victories (47:6–7). The Lord would lay low Babylon's arrogance and pride (13:19; 14:11–15). He would also reduce Egypt's wisdom to folly (19:11–15).

God's judgment would come upon the entire earth. The earth would fall in the day of the Lord's wrath (24:1–13). All the universe would quake in the face of his power, and the casualties would be enormous as the Lord himself defeated the nations in battle (34:1–4; 63:1–6).

Isaiah boldly announced that God was sovereign over all nations and had the right to judge them for their sin. He

divination

would do so when he saw fit. However, Isaiah also announced that the sovereign God had more than judgment to accomplish in his dealings with the nations.

God Will Show Himself Unique as He Judges False Gods

Isaiah announced God's judgment not only against the nations but also against the gods of the nations. As he judged them, he would show them powerless and demonstrate his own uniqueness.

God Will Judge False Gods

Isaiah said God would judge false gods in every society. The prophet also declared that God's judgment would begin with the idols his own people worshiped.

God's people were influenced by spiritual customs from all over the ancient Near East, adopting practices of superstition and **divination** (2:6–8). God would shame those who trusted in them (42:17), and they would fling their idols away (2:18, 20). As he displayed his own glory, his people would feel great shame at the feeble idols they had trusted (1:29).

Isaiah described the intense spiritual warfare going on among his people (44:9–20). Individuals planted trees, grew them to maturity, then cut them down to use for idols. The deep spiritual stupor that had overcome them hindered them from seeing their folly. Isaiah warned idolaters that in the day of God's judgment, their idols would not save them (57:13). God was tired of seeing his people provoke him to his face (65:3; 66:3).

Isaiah also announced the Lord's judgment on the gods of other nations. Egypt's idols would tremble at God's majestic arrival (19:1). In that day, the Egyptians would cling desperately to the very idols that stood powerless to intervene on their behalf (19:3).

Isaiah described with mocking derision Babylon's parade of deities in the day of God's judgment (46:1–2). They would be ashamed to show their faces. Babylon's many sorcerers, magicians, and astrologers would not be able to save the nation (47:8–15). The Lord would shut down the spiritual forces to which the Babylonians appealed.

In sum, Isaiah asserted God's right and power to judge false gods whether he found them among his own people or among other peoples. Spiritual pretenders or would-be rivals to his glory would come to an end.

God Will Show Himself Unique

Related to the concept of God judging false gods is the concept of God showing himself unique. Indeed, the two concepts overlap in that God's judgment of others reveals his own supremacy. The book of Isaiah portrays a God who is like no other, who has absolutely no rival in the universe.

Isaiah proclaimed a God who was unique in that he had revealed his word to his people. The prophet called them to live by its instruction:

> When men tell you to consult mediums and spiritists, who whisper and mutter, should not a people inquire of their God? Why consult the dead on behalf of the living? To the law and to the testimony! If they do not speak according to this word, they have no light of dawn. (8:19–20)

Isaiah also proclaimed a God who was uniquely proactive in human history. The Lord called idols into his courtroom, challenging them to declare their past accomplishments, to predict the future, to do anything that might reveal their power (41:21–23). But no response was forthcoming from images that in reality were less than nothing and could not even give the Lord an answer (41:24, 28–29). The Lord, on the other hand, had raised up Cyrus and was bringing his people home, all in fulfillment of his promises (41:25–27).

In several places in Isaiah 40–66, Isaiah reiterated the Lord's challenge to his rivals. God had demonstrated his absolute uniqueness, and no rival came close to his power:

> This is what the LORD says—
> Israel's King and Redeemer,
> the LORD Almighty:
> I am the first and I am the last;
> apart from me there is no
> God. . . .
> You are my witnesses. Is there
> any God besides me?
> No, there is no other Rock; I
> know not one. (44:6–8)

> And there is no God apart
> from me,
> a righteous God and a Savior;
> there is none but me. (45:21)

> To whom will you compare me
> or count me equal?
> To whom will you liken me
> that we may be compared?
> (46:5)

Why did Isaiah go to such lengths to highlight the sharp contrast between God's power and the idols' powerlessness? Because God's people were stubborn and refused to embrace the truth. Therefore, he said, God announced his works in advance, so that his people could not credit idols with having done them (48:5). They had seen all his work

(43:10–13), and he would not yield his glory to another (48:11).

God Will Bring the Nations to Himself

This third theme appears somewhat surprising in light of the first two. God will judge the nations. He will show himself unique as he judges false gods. But Isaiah also proclaimed God's grace in all its fullness. God would bring salvation to the nations as he brought them to himself.

Isaiah described two features of God's salvation among the nations. First, the nations would come to him. People would stream to Israel to learn of him and come to know him. But second, and even more amazing, *God would reach out to them.*

The Nations Will Come to Him

Isaiah uttered many prophetic speeches in which he described the nations coming to the Lord. As peoples from everywhere streamed to Jerusalem to learn more of his ways, true peace would come and war would end forever (2:1–4).

Jerusalem's restoration would climax God's great work, and many nations would contribute to that event (66:10–13). Gifts would come from everywhere (18:7), and foreigners would help rebuild Jerusalem's walls and would contribute to the land's economy (60:10; 61:4–6). Blessings would then come to the nations in the form of righteousness and praise to God (61:11).

Isaiah affirmed that God had plenty of room for non-Israelites in his kingdom. Faithfulness to the Lord was much more important than bloodline (56:3). The Lord would make his temple a house of prayer for all nations, not merely for Israel (56:7). In fact, one day, God would reconcile Egypt and Assyria—two bitter enemies—to each other and to Israel, and the three nations would worship the Lord together (19:18–25).

Isaiah also spoke of the significant role the nations would play in God's

(Courtesy of the International Mission Board)

plan in the messianic kingdom. They would be God's instruments to bring his children home (49:22–23). Nations would stream to the spiritual light God provided, bringing Israel's sons and daughters with them (60:1–9).

In the great day to come, the Lord would remove the barrier to intimate fellowship that lay like a sheet across the nations (25:7). The root of Jesse would stand as a banner for all peoples (11:10) when he brought peace to the world (11:1–9). God's servant would bring justice and hope to the nations (42:1–4). The nations would see Israel's righteousness, and Jerusalem would become an object of praise throughout the earth (62:2, 6–7).

God Will Reach Out to the Nations

Isaiah clearly foresaw a day when nations would come to Jerusalem and to God. But even more amazing, he foresaw a day when God would reach out to the nations. They would come to him, to be sure, but he also would go to them.

The two aspects of the nations coming to God and God reaching out to them occur in two passages that describe the messianic kingdom. Isaiah 2:3 contains both aspects:

> Many peoples will come and say,
> "Come, let us go up to the mountain of the LORD,
> to the house of the God of Jacob.
> He will teach us his ways,
> so that we may walk in his paths."
> The law will go out from Zion,
> the word of the LORD from Jerusalem.

The first part of the verse suggests that the nations are drawn to Jerusalem. The second part describes Jerusalem as a "spiritual hub" from which the word of God goes forth. Jesus seems to have alluded to this concept as he commissioned his disciples for their mission following his resurrection (Lk 24:46–47).

Isaiah's root of Jesse prophecy (11:1–16) also contains elements about God reaching the nations. His righteousness and justice extend to the ends of the earth (11:4), as does the knowledge of the Lord (11:9). The raising of a banner indicates the Messiah's signaling the people to rally to him (11:10, 12), and the building of a highway from Assyria (11:16) seems God's doing to bring people to him.

Isaiah also described the witness the Lord provided through the suffering servant Messiah. Isaiah 52:15 describes what the earth's kings somehow perceived through the servant's mission:

> Kings will shut their mouths
> because of him.
> For what they were not told,
> they will see,
> and what they have not
> heard, they will understand.

Spiritual light and insight came to the earth's leaders, who do not seem to have been seeking this truth when it suddenly came upon them in a powerful way.

God's invitation to the nations reaches its highest point in 45:22–23:

> Turn to me and be saved,
> all you ends of the earth;
> for I am God, and there is no other.
> By myself I have sworn,
> my mouth has uttered in all integrity
> a word that will not be revoked:
> Before me every knee will bow;
> by me every tongue will swear.

One could not find a clearer invitation to the nations. Isaiah's God called the world to turn to him and saw the day when every knee would bow to him.

And how would God reach the nations? He would reach them through his people. Isaiah 49:6 describes the work of the servant:

> It is too small a thing for you to
> be my servant
> to restore the tribes of Jacob
> and bring back those of Israel
> I have kept.
> I will also make you a light for
> the Gentiles,
> that you may bring my salvation to the ends of the earth.

As we saw in our discussion of this passage earlier (chap. 16), there are reasons to support both a messianic interpretation and a "remnant" interpretation. But in either case, the Messiah's role in reaching the Gentiles would be accomplished largely through his servants, his disciples (Acts 13:47).

Finally, in his concluding prophetic announcement, Isaiah proclaimed God's sending of messengers to distant lands with news of God's glory:

> "I will set a sign among them, and I will send some of those who survive to the nations—to Tarshish, to the Libyans and Lydians (famous as archers), to Tubal and Greece, and to the distant islands that have not heard of my fame or seen my glory. They will proclaim my glory among the nations. And they will bring all your brothers, from all the nations, to my holy mountain in Jerusalem as an offering to the LORD—on horses, in chariots and wagons, and on mules and camels," says the LORD. "They will bring them, as the Israelites bring their grain offerings, to the temple of the LORD in ceremonially clean vessels. And I will select some of them also to be priests and Levites," says the Lord. (66:19–21)

These verses contain three elements. First, Isaiah described a day when God would send his messengers to the distant nations to declare his glory. Second,

these messengers would bring God's children home. Third, God would select priests and Levites from their number.

God's desire to reach the nations with his glory is clear. Further, the context suggests "brothers" (66:20) and denotes more than Israelites.[7] God's plan includes a new priesthood created from all nations, not only from Levi's line through Aaron (1 Pt 2:9).

Thus, Isaiah describes a God who will both announce his glory and actively pursue people to embrace it. Nations will be drawn to his light, but he will also reach out to them through his chosen messengers.

The Great Commission Implications of the Book of Isaiah

In the preceding two chapters, we have discussed Isaiah's contribution to the Old Testament and have also examined his contribution to the New Testament. But what are the Great Commission implications of Isaiah's book? How does Isaiah's message lay a foundation for the greatest message of all?

Four themes especially stand out. First, God is unique among all gods. Second, God is sovereign over all nations and peoples. Third, God's heart for the nations is apparent. Fourth, God will reach the nations through his people.

God Is Unique among All Gods

Isaiah describes a God who is unique among all gods. His God has created everything that is. His God has done great wonders among his people, though many refused to believe in him despite those wonders. Nonetheless, God demonstrated his uniqueness even in predicting his people's exile.

Sidebar 22.1
Great Commission Resources: Learning More

The following list is by no means exhaustive but provides good resources about the world's people groups and the extent to which the gospel has reached them.

International Mission Board (www.imb.org): An agency of the Southern Baptist Convention. Its Web site provides links to a wide range of information for students, missionaries, churches, and researchers.

Joshua Project (www.joshuaproject.net): A Web site designed to bring definition to the unfinished task of reaching the world.

Operation World (www.gmi.org/ow): The OW Web site exists primarily to provide information for people who want to pray for specific parts of the world. A book version is also available: Patrick Johnstone, Jason Mandryk, and Robyn Johnstone, *Operation World: When We Pray God Works*, 21st ed. (Gabriel Resources, 2001).

People Groups (www.peoplegroups.info): People Groups focuses on the people groups within North America and provides current census information for cities, states, and provinces.

US Center for World Mission (www.uscwm.org): USCWM aims to mobilize workers and resources for the unreached peoples. Their Web site contains links to publications, resources and training materials for missionaries, pastors, and church members.

No other god had been able to do such wonders.

Isaiah's God would not share his glory with another. In fact, other gods were really not gods at all.

God Is Sovereign over All Nations and Peoples

Isaiah's God reigned as sovereign over all nations and peoples. He sustained all the earth by his power. He raised up nations and brought them down as he pleased. Many did not even realize they were his instruments, but they were.

Isaiah testified that God had guided his people through days of blessing and judgment. But God also knew the thoughts and hearts of other peoples. He would act in history on their behalf, just as he had earlier among the people of Israel. One day, they all would bow before his majesty.

God's Heart for the Nations Is Apparent

Isaiah proclaimed a sovereign God whose heart for the nations was apparent. True, God would judge those who opposed him, and the day of the Lord would find him judging sin wherever he found it. But Isaiah's God also desired to see the nations turn to him and be saved.

Isaiah saw a day when foreigners would rebuild Jerusalem. They would become part of God's people, for God valued faithfulness to him more than bloodline. People of all nations would serve him as he removed all barriers to fellowship. He would do more than accept their worship; he would actually welcome them into the family.

God's passion to see the nations turn to him thunders through Isaiah's message. It was a concept many Israelites may have struggled to understand, while others probably rejected it due to their ethnocentric thinking. But Isaiah's message was clear: God desired to see the nations turn to him.

God Will Reach the Nations through His People

Isaiah declared that God would reach the nations through his people. He would do so by two means, for which we earlier in this chapter used the terms *centripetal* and *centrifugal*. First, God's people would live the truth. Second, his people would take God's message to other people.

273

(Courtesy of the International Mission Board)

lives reflected the glory of the God they served. As God's people lived in this way, other people would want what they had and turn to Israel's God.

His People Will Take God's Message to Other People

Isaiah also proclaimed a God who was so eager for other nations to see his glory that he would send his messengers to the distant nations. They would declare his glory among the peoples and bring light to the spiritually needy world. These nations would then join the procession home—home to God and his ways.

Isaiah saw a new age in which the Lord would have at his banquet table people from all nations. In fact, the Lord was determined to bring them to that table. He had used the kings of the earth as his instruments of judgment, but now he would use ordinary people as his instruments of salvation, to reconcile the world to himself.

Conclusion

The prophet Isaiah thus continued the great themes of Scripture. He built on the lives and messages of earlier men and women of God, who lived faithfully as they saw in life a purpose much greater than themselves (Heb 11:13–16). As he did so, he anticipated the complete and final witness the New Testament would bring.

Indeed, the New Testament echoes Isaiah's words. God is unique among all gods, and his sovereignty extends throughout the universe. His heart for the nations is evident, and he has sent his only Son, Jesus Christ, to secure the salvation of all who place their faith in him. He calls people everywhere to turn to him and desires to send his message of salvation to all peoples and nations through those who already know him.

As we have seen, the concept of a Great Commission was no mystery to Isaiah. It likewise should be no mystery

His People Will Live the Truth

Isaiah called God's people to live the truth of God's word as they went about their daily lives. The Lord had positioned them on the land bridge between three continents, and peoples from all over the ancient Near East regularly traveled through their territory. As they did so, what would they see? God desired that they would see a people different from the rest, a people whose

Study Questions

1. How do the creation mandate and Great Commission mandate differ?

2. Compare and contrast the concepts "centripetal witness" and "centrifugal witness."

3. List key terms from Isaiah that point to God extending his salvation to people of other nations.

4. To what extent do you think Jesus's Great Commission (Mt 28:18–20) represented a new strategy to reach the world with the message of God's salvation? In formulating your answer, consider all you have read in the book of Isaiah.

to Christians today. A cause so urgent to God's heart must be on the hearts of his people. Our task is to consider how we might invest our lives in the most strategic manner possible to accomplish the Great Commission, that all nations everywhere might give glory to the Holy One of Israel.

Key Terms

centrifugal witness

centripetal witness

creation mandate

divination

Great Commission mandate

stewardship

Notes

Chapter 1 Who Was Isaiah, and What Do We Know about Him and His Book?

1. Is 2:1; 13:1; 20:2; 37:2, 21; 38:1; 2 Kgs 19:2, 20; 20:1; 2 Chr 26:22; 32:20, 32.

2. *Megillah*, 10:2; that Isaiah was the nephew of King Amaziah, see *b. Sota* 10b.

3. The dates in this book, unless otherwise noted, follow the chronology of Edwin R. Thiele's *Mysterious Numbers of the Hebrew Kings*, new rev. ed. (Grand Rapids: Zondervan, 1983).

4. The pseudepigraphal *Ascension of Isaiah* 5:1–16 attests to this; see also *b. Yebamot* 4:13; cf. *Sanhedrin* f. 103b.

5. Thiele, *Mysterious Numbers of the Hebrew Kings*, 64.

6. The other occurrences are 2 Kgs 19:22; Pss 71:22; 78:41; 89:18; Jer 50:29; 51:5.

Chapter 2 Isaiah's Opening Words to God's People

1. Hans Wildberger, *Isaiah 1–12: A Commentary* (Minneapolis: Fortress, 1991), 3–4; H. C. Leupold, *Exposition of Isaiah* (Grand Rapids: Baker Academic, 1976), 1:53; Otto Kaiser, *Isaiah 1–12: A Commentary*, trans. John Bowden, 2nd ed. (Philadelphia: Westminster, 1983), 1–5; John D. W. Watts, *Isaiah 1–33*, Word Biblical Commentary 24 (Waco: Word Books, 1985), 3–8.

2. "Sennacherib's Siege of Jerusalem," trans. Mordechai Cogan, in *COS* 2:302–3; Arthur Ferrill, *The Origins of War: From the Stone Age to Alexander the Great* (London: Thames and Hudson, 1986), 71–77.

3. Edward J. Young, *Book of Isaiah* (Grand Rapids: Eerdmans, 1972), 1:68–70; Joseph A. Alexander, *Commentary on the Prophecies of Isaiah* (Grand Rapids: Zondervan, 1953), 88.

Chapter 3 God's Call to Live in Light of the Future

1. Carl Friedrich Keil and Friedrich Delitzsch, *Commentary on the Old Testament*, trans. James Martin (Grand Rapids: Eerdmans, 1969), 7.110–12.

2. Millard Erickson, *A Basic Guide to Eschatology* (Grand Rapids: Baker Academic, 1998); Darrell L. Bock, ed., *Three Views on the Millennium and Beyond* (Grand Rapids: Zondervan, 1999); Richard J. Mouw, *When the Kings Come Marching In: Isaiah and the New Jerusalem*, rev. ed. (Grand Rapids: Eerdmans, 2002).

3. Alexander, *Commentary on the Prophecies of Isaiah*, 122–23; Leupold, *Exposition of Isaiah*, 1:102–4; Ardis Parlin, "What Is the Meaning of 'the Branch of Jehovah'? Isaiah 4:2" (PhD diss., Grace Theological Seminary, 1968).

4. John H. Walton, Victor H. Matthews, and Mark W. Chavalas, *The IVP Bible Background Commentary: Old Testament* (Downers Grove, IL: InterVarsity, 2000), 589–90; I. Howard Marshall et al., eds., *New Bible Dictionary*, 3rd ed. (Downers Grove, IL: InterVarsity, 1996), 1224–25.

5. Walter Brueggemann, *Isaiah 1–39* (Louisville: Westminster/John Knox, 1998), 48–49; Elbert Russell, "Paronomasia and Kindred Phenomena in the New Testament" (PhD diss., University of Chicago, 1919).

Chapter 4 Isaiah's Call to Prophetic Ministry

1. See the discussion in Brevard S. Childs, *Isaiah: A Commentary* (Louisville: Westminster/John Knox, 2001), 51–54.

2. Keil and Delitzsch, *Commentary on the Old Testament*, 7.1:189–92; Brueggemann, *Isaiah 1–39*, 58–59.

3. Keil and Delitzsch, *Commentary on the Old Testament*, 7.1:189–90; Watts, *Isaiah 1–33*, 74.

Chapter 5 The Signs of Immanuel and Maher-Shalal-Hash-Baz

1. For background on the Syrians/Aramaeans and their role in the ancient world, see Wayne T. Pitard, "Aramaeans," in *Peoples of the Old Testament World*, ed. Alfred J. Hoerth, Gerald L. Mattingly, and Edwin M. Yamauchi (Grand Rapids: Baker Academic, 1994), 207–30.

2. See the annals of Tiglath-Pileser III in "Tiglath Pileser III," trans. K. Lawson Younger Jr., in *COS*, 2.117A–F:284–92.

3. Sargon II boasts of conquering Samaria, capital of the northern kingdom of Israel, apparently finishing the job his father Shalmaneser V began; see 2 Kgs 17:1–6 and the annals of Sargon II in "Sargon II, The Annals," trans. K. Lawson Younger Jr., in *COS* 2.118A:293.

4. See the comments of Young, *Book of Isaiah*, 1:271; and Wildberger, *Isaiah 1–12*, 295.

5. KJV, NKJV, NIV, NASB, TLB, NLT, YLT.

6. RSV, NRSV, TAB.

7. TEV and see also John H. Walton, "Isa 7:14: What's in a Name?" *Journal of the Evangelical Theological Society* 30 (1987): 289–306.

8. J. Alec Motyer, *The Prophecy of Isaiah: An Introduction and Commentary* (Downers Grove, IL: InterVarsity, 1993), 84–86; Young, *Book of Isaiah*, 1:283–91; Keil and Delitzsch, *Commentary on the Old Testament*, 7.1:216–20.

9. Gleason L. Archer, "A Reassessment of the Value of the Septuagint Version of Isaiah for the Purpose of Textual Criticism," (paper presented at the national meetings of the Evangelical Theological Society, Dallas, 1983).

10. See George Adam Smith, *Isaiah*, ed. W. Robertson Nicoll (New York: Armstrong and Son, 1903), 114–15.

11. Herbert M. Wolf, *Interpreting Isaiah: The Suffering and Glory of the Messiah* (Grand Rapids: Zondervan, 1985), 91; Ronald Youngblood, *The Book of Isaiah: An Introductory Commentary*, 2nd ed. (Grand Rapids: Baker Academic, 1993), 48.

12. Walton, "Isa 7:14," 295–97; George E. Wright, *Book of Isaiah* (Richmond: John Knox, 1961), 40.

13. Motyer, *Prophecy of Isaiah*, 85.

14. 2 Chr 32:30 (NASB) refers to the "upper outlet of the waters of Gihon," thus implying the existence of at least one other.

15. Young, *Book of Isaiah*, 1:305; Wolf, *Interpreting Isaiah*, 94; John N. Oswalt, *The Book of Isaiah: Chapters 1–39*, New International Commentary on the Old Testament (Grand Rapids: Eerdmans, 1986), 225.

Chapter 6 God's Kingdom Will Surpass All Earthly Kingdoms

1. Bill T. Arnold and Bryan E. Beyer, *Encountering the Old Testament* (Grand Rapids: Baker Academic, 1999), 42–43.

2. E. M. Blaiklock, "Decapolis," in *The Zondervan Pictoral Encyclopedia of the Bible*, ed. Merrill C. Tenney (Grand Rapids: Zondervan, 1975), 2:81–84.

3. The Masoretic Text actually has *pel'i*, a form of *pele'*.

4. Such uses of *gibbor* to describe God's power argue against distinguishing between the concepts of "mighty" and "almighty" as Jehovah's Witnesses try to do when explaining Is 9:6.

5. For a comprehensive article on the Assyrians, see William C. Gwaltney Jr., "Assyrians," in *Peoples of the Old Testament World*, 77–106.

6. Is 9:4 (9:3 in the Masoretic Text); 10:5, 15, 24; 14:5; 28:27; 30:31–32.

7. The biblical text specifically notes Hoshea as paying tribute to Shalmaneser (727–722 BC). This shows that Hoshea remained loyal to Assyria after the death of Tiglath-Pileser III.

8. Edgar W. Conrad, *Reading Isaiah* (Minneapolis: Fortress, 1991), 43; John F. A. Sawyer, *Isaiah* (Philadelphia: Westminster, 1984), 1:112; Watts, *Isaiah 1–33*, 150.

9. J. Ridderbos, *Isaiah*, trans. John Vriend, Bible Student's Commentary (Grand Rapids: Zondervan, 1985), 113–15; Youngblood, *Book of Isaiah*, 53; Oswalt, *Book of Isaiah: Chapters 1–39*, 264.

10. Motyer, *Prophecy of Isaiah*, 121.

11. Ridderbos, *Isaiah*, 127; Harry Bultema, *Commentary on Isaiah*, trans. Cornelius Lambregtse (Grand Rapids: Kregel, 1981), 145–49.

12. Motyer, *Prophecy of Isaiah*, 125–26; Young, *Book of Isaiah*, 1:394–95.

Chapter 7 Oracles against the Nations

1. See, for example, the boasts of Tiglath-Pileser I (1114–1076 BC) in Bill T. Arnold and Bryan E. Beyer, eds., *Readings from the Ancient Near East: Primary Sources for Textual Study* (Grand Rapids: Baker Academic, 2002), 137–44.

2. For a comprehensive article on the Babylonians, see Bill T. Arnold, "Babylonians," in *Peoples of the Old Testament World*, 43–75.

3. Recent scholarly consensus places Joel around 500 BC. See Leslie C. Allen, *The Books of Joel, Obadiah, Jonah and Micah*, New International Commentary on the Old Testament (Grand Rapids: Eerdmans, 1976), 19–25.

4. On this force of the Hebrew pausal form, see Wilhelm Gesenius, *Hebrew Grammar*, ed. E. Kautzsch (Oxford: Clarendon, 1910), 96.

5. For more on the Medes, see Edwin M. Yamauchi, "Persians," in *Peoples of the Old Testament World*, 107–10.

6. "Shalmaneser III (858–824): The Fight against the Aramean Coalition," trans. F. Delitzsch and D. D. Luckenbill, in *ANET*, 278a; "Nebuchadnezzar II (605–562): The Expedition to Syria," trans. Zehnpfund-Langdon, in *ANET*, 307; "A Hymn Celebrating Assurnasirpal II's Campaigns to the West," trans. Victor Hurowitz, in *COS* 1:471; "The Sippar Cylinder of Nabonidus," trans. Paul-Alain Beaulieu, in *COS* 2:311–12.

7. Ridderbos, *Isaiah*, 142; Sawyer, *Isaiah*, 1:144–45; David L. McKenna, *The Communicator's Commentary: Isaiah* (Dallas: Word, 1994), 1:178–81.

8. See the boasts of Tiglath-Pileser I in Arnold and Beyer, *Readings from the Ancient Near East*, 137b; and of Esarhaddon in "Esarhaddon (680–669): The Fight for the Throne," trans. R. Campbell Thompson, in *ANET*, 289a.

9. For a comprehensive article on the Assyrians, see Gwaltney, "Assyrians," in *Peoples of the Old Testament World*, 77–106.

10. For a comprehensive article on the Philistines, see David M. Howard, "Philistines," in *Peoples of the Old Testament World*, 231–50.

11. For a discussion of the issues surrounding the chronology of Hezekiah's reign, see Thiele, *Mysterious Numbers of the Hebrew Kings*, 134–38.

12. Motyer, *Prophecy of Isaiah*, 147; "Tiglath-Pileser III (744–727): Campaigns Against Syria and Palestine," trans. D. D. Luckenbill, in *ANET*, 282–84; "Sargon II (721–705): The Fall of Samaria," trans. D. D. Luckenbill, in *ANET*, 284–87; "Sennacherib (704–681): The Siege of Jerusalem," trans. D. D. Luckenbill, in *ANET*, 287–88; "Tiglath-Pileser III," trans. K. Lawson Younger Jr., in *COS* 2.117A–F:284–92; "Sargon II," trans. K. Lawson Younger Jr., in *COS* 2.118A–J:293–300; "Sennacherib," trans. Mordechai Cogan, in *COS* 2.119A–E:300–305.

13. For a comprehensive article on the Moabites, see Gerald L. Mattingly, "Moabites," in *Peoples of the Old Testament World*, 317–33.

14. Adapted from Arnold and Beyer, *Encountering the Old Testament*, 232.

15. "Tiglath-Pileser III (744–727): Campaigns against Syria and Palestine," trans. D. D. Luckenbill, in *ANET*, 282; "Sargon II (721–705): The Fall of Samaria," trans. D. D. Luckenbill, in *ANET*, 287; "Sennacherib (704–681): The Siege of Jerusalem," trans. D. D. Luckenbill, in *ANET*, 287; "Esarhaddon (680–669): The Fight for the Throne," trans.

R. Campbell Thompson, in *ANET*, 291; "Tiglath-Pileser III," trans. K. Lawson Younger Jr., in *COS* 2.117D:289; "Sennacherib's Siege of Jerusalem," trans. Mordechai Cogan, in *COS* 2.119B:303.

16. For a comprehensive article on the Syrians/Aramaeans, see Pitard, "Aramaeans," in *Peoples of the Old Testament World*, 207–30.

17. Arnold and Beyer, *Readings from the Ancient Near East*, 145; "Tiglath-Pileser III (744–727): Campaigns against Syria and Palestine," trans. D. D. Luckenbill, in *ANET*, 282–83; "Tiglath-Pileser III," trans. K. Lawson Younger Jr., in *COS* 2.117A:285–86.

18. "Tiglath-Pileser III (744–727): Campaigns against Syria and Palestine," trans. D. D. Luckenbill, in *ANET*, 284; "Tiglath-Pileser III," trans. K. Lawson Younger Jr., in *COS* 2.117B:288.

19. For more on Cush, see H. C. Leupold, "Cush," in *Zondervan Pictorial Encyclopedia of the Bible* 1:1047–48.

20. The use of the Hebrew participle *medabberot* suggests this.

21. J. Alec Motyer, *Isaiah: An Introduction and Commentary* (Downers Grove, IL: InterVarsity, 1999), 174, argues for the former, while Childs, *Isaiah*, 151–52, argues for the latter.

22. Motyer, *Isaiah*, 177; "Tiglath-Pileser III," trans. K. Lawson Younger Jr., in *COS* 2.117A–B:286–87; "Sargon II," trans. K. Lawson Younger Jr., in *COS* 2.118A, D:293, 296; "Sennacherib," trans. Mordechai Cogan, in *COS* 2.119:301; "Ashurbanipal (668–633)," trans. D. D. Luckenbill, in *ANET*, 297–301.

23. See William A. Ward, "Phoenicians," in *Peoples of the Old Testament World*, 183–206.

24. Motyer, *Isaiah*, 193.

25. Keil and Delitzsch, *Commentary on the Old Testament*, 7:411–14. Childs, *Isaiah*, 169, sides with the Babylonian interpretation of 23:13, though he concludes this in part because he believes Is 13–23 was heavily edited during the sixth century BC.

Chapter 8 The "Little Apocalypse"

1. Childs, *Isaiah*, 179.

2. Four Hebrew verbs are preceded by their infinitive absolute form, a structure that strengthens the verbal idea.

3. Scholars who argue for a literal resurrection of the dead include Leupold, *Exposition of Isaiah*, 412–14; Otto Kaiser, *Isaiah 13–39: A Commentary*, trans. R. A. Wilson (Philadelphia: Westminster, 1974), 215–20; Oswalt, *Book of Isaiah: Chapters 1–39*, 485. Scholars who argue for a figurative interpretation include Hans Wildberger, *Isaiah 13–27: A Continental Commentary* (Minneapolis: Fortress, 1997), 570; Alexander, *Commentary on the Prophecies of Isaiah*, 430–32; Youngblood, *Book of Isaiah*, 79.

4. Motyer, *Isaiah*, 218–20.

5. Childs, *Isaiah*, 192.

6. Motyer, *Isaiah*, 220.

7. "Ugaritic Myths: The Balu Myth," trans. Dennis Pardee, in *COS* 1.86:241–74.

8. Note the presence in both 6:7 and 27:9 of the Hebrew words *'avon* (guilt), *hatta't* (sin), *sur* (taken away) in 6:7, (removal) in 27:9, and *kipper* (atone).

Chapter 9 Oracles of Woe

1. See Oswalt, *Book of Isaiah: Chapters 1–39*, 506.

2. See Watts, *Isaiah 1–33*, 363; Oswalt, *Book of Isaiah: Chapters 1–39*, 512; Kaiser, *Isaiah 13–39*, 245.

3. Sawyer, *Isaiah*, 1:238; Watts, *Isaiah 1–33*, 381.

4. Keil and Delitzsch, *Commentary on the Old Testament*, 7.2:17; Alexander, *Commentary on the Prophecies of Isaiah*, 461.

5. Motyer, *Isaiah*, 237.

6. Arnold and Beyer, *Readings from the Ancient Near East*, 98, 100.

Chapter 10 Eschatological Summation

1. Childs, *Isaiah*, 255, argues this interpretation, though Childs unnecessarily posits multiple sources.

2. Heb. *haram*. The noun form, *herem*, also occurs with similar meaning; cf. "devoted (to the Lord)" and "devoted things" (Jos 6:17–18).

3. Motyer, *Isaiah*, 270; Childs, *Isaiah*, 256; Youngblood, *Book of Isaiah*, 98; Christopher R. Seitz, *Isaiah 1–39* (Louisville: Westminster/John Knox, 1993), 237.

4. Motyer, *Isaiah*, 271; Keil and Delitzsch, *Commentary on the Old Testament*, 7.2:71–72.

5. Childs, *Isaiah*, 257.

Chapter 11 Highlights from Hezekiah's Reign

1. Motyer, *Isaiah*, 220–21; Keil and Delitzsch, *Commentary on the Old Testament*, 7.2:82; Kaiser, *Isaiah 13–39*, 367.

2. Thiele, *Mysterious Numbers of the Hebrew Kings*, 174–76, argues that the synchronisms between Hezekiah and Hoshea are "late and artificial" because the final editor of Kings did not understand the principle of dual dating.

3. A thorough discussion of the issues appears in Oswalt, *The Book of Isaiah: Chapters 1–39*, 674–75.

4. Edwin R. Thiele discusses the phenomenon of co-regency in *Mysterious Numbers of the Hebrew Kings*, 61–65.

5. Thiele, *Mysterious Numbers of the Hebrew Kings*, 174–75; see also 61–65 on the phenomenon of co-regency.

6. The expression translated "field commander" (*rab shakeh*) literally means "cup bearer" but by this time had come to mean a leading administrative official.

7. Thiele, *Mysterious Numbers of the Hebrew Kings*, 176–77.

8. J. A. Brinkman, "Merodach Baladan II," in *Studies Presented to A. L. Oppenheim*, ed. Robert D. Biggs and John A. Brinkman (Chicago: Oriental Institute, 1964), 6–53.

Chapter 12 Introduction to Isaiah 40–66

1. For a comprehensive discussion of authorship and date issues, see John Oswalt, *The Book of Isaiah: Chapters 40–66* (Grand Rapids: Eerdmans, 1998), 3–6.

2. For those supporting a later, third Isaiah, see P. A. Smith, *Rhetoric and Redaction in Trito-Isaiah: The Structure, Growth, and Authorship of Isaiah 56–66* (New York: Brill, 1995); John D. W. Watts, *Isaiah 34–66*, Word Biblical Commentary 25 (Waco: Word Books, 1987), 368.

3. Watts, *Isaiah*, 1–33, xix, xxiv, xxxii–xxxiv; John Goldingay, *God's Prophet, God's Servant; A Study in Jeremiah and Isaiah 40–55* (Exeter: Paternoster, 1984), 11–12.

4. Some scholars see Is 13–14 as written later; see Wright, *Book of Isaiah*, 52–53; Sawyer, *Isaiah*, 1:134.

5. John H. Walton, "New Observations on the Date of Isaiah," *Journal of the Evangelical Theological Society* 28 (1985): 129–32.

6. Wolf, *Interpreting Isaiah*, 36–37.

Chapter 13 God's People Are Coming Home!

1. Motyer, *Prophecy of Isaiah*, 299.

2. Oswalt, *Book of Isaiah: Chapters 40–66*, 50.

3. Ibid., 43n5.

Chapter 14 Proclamation of Deliverance and Restoration

1. The Hebrew term may mean "wickedness" or "nothing" depending on one's reading of the text.

2. The expression in Gn 1:2 "formless and empty" translates the Hebrew *tohu ve-bohu*.

3. Oswalt, *Book of Isaiah: Chapters 40–66*, 110.

4. The name Yahweh (Heb. *YHWH*) comes from the verb "to be" and emphasizes God's presence with his people. See, e.g., Ex 3:14, where God says "I AM WHO I AM" and where this verb occurs.

5. Note Matthew's words (12:17): "This was to fulfill what was spoken through the prophet Isaiah." He then follows with a quote from Isaiah 42:1–4; see sidebar 12.2.

6. Oswalt, *Book of Isaiah: Chapters 40–66*, 123–24.

7. The LXX supports the emendation of the Hebrew text, and the change is possible without altering any of the original consonantal text. Nonetheless, the principle of preserving the more difficult reading suggests the future (Heb. imperfect) tense should be maintained.

8. Oswalt, *Book of Isaiah: Chapters 40–66*, 162n68.

9. Cyrus's decree (Ezra 1:2–4) does not imply Cyrus was a true believer. The Persians were known for accommodating all subject peoples as far as possible.

10. Motyer, *Prophecy of Isaiah*, 367.

Chapter 15 The Fall of Babylon

1. Joan Oates, *Babylon* (London: Thames and Hudson, 1979), 175–76.

2. In Is 14:12–20, Isaiah speaks directly to Babylon's king, whereas in 47:1–15, the Lord speaks through Isaiah to the nation.

3. Oswalt, *Book of Isaiah: Chapters 40–66*, 242.

4. Is 48:2; 51:15; 54:5; Jer 10:16; 31:35; 32:18; 33:2; 46:18; 48:15; 50:34; 51:19, 57.

5. See the Babylonian temple program for the *Akitu* festival in Arnold and Beyer, *Readings from the Ancient Near East*, 128–33.

Chapter 16 Israel's Release and Exaltation

1. A more literal rendering of the Hebrew text reads: "The Lord called me from the womb; from (the time I was in) my mother's inward parts he mentioned my name."

2. Is 24:10; 34:11; 40:17, 23; 41:29; 44:9; 45:18, 19; 49:4; 59:5.

3. Eccl 1:2, 14; 2:1, 11, 15, 17, 19, 21, 23, 26; 3:19; 4:4, 7, 8, 16; 5:7, 10; 6:2, 4, 9, 11, 12; 7:6, 15; 8:10, 14; 9:9; 11:8; 10; 12:8.

4. Motyer, *Prophecy of Isaiah*, 385–89; Oswalt, *Book of Isaiah: Chapters 40–66*, 290–93.

5. I am grateful to Aaron Burt for his helpful groundwork (personal communication, April 2004).

6. R. N. Whybray, *Isaiah 40–66* (Grand Rapids: Eerdmans, 1981), 150. Whybray holds to the multiple authorship view of Isaiah and consequently believes Deutero-Isaiah was the focus of the servant passage in Isaiah 50.

7. See Heb 12:1–3, which challenges Christians to lay aside all sin to follow Jesus completely.

Chapter 17 The Suffering Servant

1. Oswalt, *Book of Isaiah: Chapters 40–66*, 378, makes the point that this word pairing occurs only in Isaiah, and the other three Isaianic uses of the expression (6:1; 33:10; 57:15) all describe God.

2. Later Syriac manuscripts, as well as the Targum, an early Aramaic witness to the Hebrew text, read "him."

3. A Hebrew cognate that comes from an Arabic root meaning "leap" has been suggested, but the word would occur only here in the Old Testament.

4. The word occurs twenty-four times in the Old Testament. Twenty of these occurrences are in Leviticus or Numbers, and outside Isaiah 52:15, all but two (2 Kgs 9:33; Is 63:3) are clearly cultic.

5. References to the expression "land of the living" include Jb 28:13; Pss 27:13; 52:5; 116:9; 142:5; Is 38:11; Jer 11:19; Ez 26:20.

6. The term *hamas* carries the meaning of "violence" today in both Hebrew and Arabic. Hamas is a militant Arab group that has often endorsed the use of violence (e.g., suicide bombings) to obtain its objectives.

7. See Lv 5–6 and J. C. Moyer, "Guilt; Guilty," in *The International Standard Bible Encyclopedia*, ed. Geoffrey W. Bromiley (Grand Rapids: Eerdmans, 1994), 2:580–81.

8. Whybray, *Isaiah 40–66*, 171; John L. McKenzie, *Second Isaiah*, The Anchor Bible 20 (Garden City, NY: Doubleday, 1968), xli.

9. Sawyer, *Isaiah*, 2:144, though he allows the messianic interpretation as well; Wright, *Book of Isaiah*, 130.

10. G. A. Smith, *Book of Isaiah*, 252–77, and Hanson, *Isaiah 40–66*, 166–69, adopt a development in the Servant Songs in which the nation is addressed first, then a smaller portion of the nation, and finally a single Messiah.

11. For an excellent defense of the New Testament's credibility, see F. F. Bruce, *The New Testament Documents: Are They Reliable?* 5th rev. ed. (Grand Rapids: Eerdmans, 1960).

12. Adolf Neubauer and S. R. Driver, *The Fifty-third Chapter of Isaiah according to the Jewish Interpreters* (New York: Ktav, 1969), 2:xxxix–lxv.

13. For an excellent discussion of Christian servant leadership, see Don N. Howell, *Servants of the Servant: A Biblical Theology of Leadership* (Eugene, OR: Wipf and Stock, 2003).

Chapter 18 Celebrating the Return

1. The Hebrew language distinguishes between singular and plural forms in commands. However, Isaiah sometimes used the singular form to refer to the nation as a whole.

2. Oswalt, *Book of Isaiah: Chapters 40–66*, 439.

3. Interestingly, Paul also cites Is 49:8 in this verse.

4. Heb. *shub*. The verb form also appears in the name of Isaiah's son Shear-Jashub, which means "a remnant will return/repent."

5. I wish to thank my colleague Steve Baarendse for pointing this out to me.

6. Matitiahu Tsevat, "The Basic Meaning of the Biblical Sabbath," *Zeitschrift für die Alttestamentliche Wissenschaft* 84 (1972): 447–59.

7. Oswalt, *Book of Isaiah: Chapters 40–66*, 529, agrees with Keil and Delitzsch, *Commentary on the Old Testament*, 7.2:404–5 on this point.

Chapter 19 The Grand Finale of God's Restoration

1. Claus Westermann, *Isaiah 40–66* (Philadelphia: Westminster, 1969), 367. The Hebrew word is *naqam*.

2. The Hebrew roots *hrb* and *smm*, which both describe desolation and devastation, occur twice.

3. The Masoretic Text reads literally "your sons," but an alteration of the vowels could make the reading "your maker."

4. Jer 49:7–22; Am 2:11–12; Ob 10–14.

5. See discussion of 61:2.

6. Oswalt, *Book of Isaiah: Chapters 40–66*, 689; Motyer, *Prophecy of Isaiah*, 542.

7. Cf. the terms in NIV and NASB, which are both possible renderings of the Hebrew, though they differ markedly.

8. Is 11:11; 20:6; 23:2, 6; 24:15; 40:15; 41:1, 5; 42:4, 10, 12, 15; 49:1; 51:5; 59:18; 60:9; 66:19.

9. Motyer, *Prophecy of Isaiah*, 542; for an opposing view, see Oswalt, *Book of Isaiah: Chapters 40–66*, 689–90.

Chapter 20 Isaiah and the Old Testament

1. The other six references are 2 Kgs 19:22 (parallel to Is 37:23); Pss 71:22; 78:41; 89:18; Jer 50:29; 51:5.

2. See earlier discussion (p. 142); Wolf, *Interpreting Isaiah*, 171.

3. See earlier discussion (pp. 142, 157); Walton, "New Observations," 129–32.

4. Motyer, *Prophecy of Isaiah*, 53, summarizes the possibilities.

Chapter 21 Isaiah and the New Testament

1. Of the approximately 1,300 verses in the New Testament, about seventy-five have either a direct quote from or an allusion to wording in Isaiah.

2. The text in Acts follows the Septuagint, though the Masoretic Text is very close.

3. In my discussion of Is 7–8, I argue that Mt 1:23 declares a secondary fulfillment of Is 7:14. Some argue that Mt 1:23 declares a direct fulfillment.

4. The Septuagint offers an even tighter parallel than the Masoretic Text.

Chapter 22 Isaiah and the Great Commission

1. Ferris L. "Chip" McDaniel, "Mission in the Old Testament," in *Mission in the New Testament: An Evangelical Approach*, ed. William J. Larkin and Joel F. Williams (Maryknoll: Orbis, 1998), 11, 16–19.

2. McDaniel, "Mission in the Old Testament," 11–12, suggests that the Jews of Jesus's day would have linked the action of God sending with the Old Testament word.

3. If Jesus's words in Mk 16:15–16 are original, then five examples of the Great Commission appear.

4. See Walter C. Kaiser, *Mission in the Old Testament: Israel as a Light to the Nations* (Grand Rapids: Baker Academic, 2000), 87–92, for a good bibliography on the issue.

5. Kaiser, *Mission in the Old Testament*, understands Israel's calling and the church's to be one and the same and believes that Israel largely failed to achieve God's call to evangelize the nations. Kaiser, however, holds the minority opinion.

6. Anson F. Rainey and R. Steven Notley, *The Sacred Bridge: Carta's Atlas of the Biblical World* (Jerusalem: Carta, 2006), 30–42; Arnold and Beyer, *Encountering the Old Testament*, 36; Yohanan Aharoni, *The Land of the Bible: A Historical Geography*, trans. Anson F. Rainey, 2nd ed. (London: Burns and Oates, 1979), 3–6.

7. See the earlier discussion of this passage.

Glossary

Akitu *festival* A Babylonian celebration in the month of Nisannu (March–April) marking the beginning of the New Year. During this festival it was believed Bel, head of the Babylonian pantheon, renewed a ruler's kingship for another year.

'almah A fairly uncommon Hebrew word that occurs in Isaiah 7:14 and has been translated either "virgin" or "young woman." The discussion of the term's meaning in its context is significantly influenced by the verse's citation in the New Testament (Mt 1:22–23) as ultimately fulfilled in the virgin birth of Jesus.

anointed one Heb. *mashiach* (sometimes translated Messiah). Anointing represented a visible setting apart of an individual for service to God. A priest might anoint someone with oil, while God typically anointed someone with the Holy Spirit. In the Bible, kings, priests, and prophets were anointed. Isaiah alluded to Cyrus, king of Persia, as God's anointed one (45:1). *See also* Cyrus.

apocalyptic A kind of writing with features similar to the book of Revelation—lots of symbolism and figurative language that describe a great future work of God. The word comes from the Greek word *apokalypto*, which means "to uncover or reveal something hidden."

Bel Chief deity of the Babylonian pantheon. His name appears in biblical names such as Belshazzar ("O Bel, guard the king!") and is related to the name of the Canaanite god Baal. In earlier times, Bel was known as Marduk, a form of which occurs in the name Merodach-Baladan ("Marduk has given a son!").

branch A prophetic term that denotes God's chosen instrument as being related to David's family line. Ultimately the branch motif is fulfilled in Christ (Is 4:2; 11:1; Jer 23:5–6; 33:15–16; Zec 3:8; 6:12–13).

call A special task or vocation to which an individual senses God's sacred commission (e.g., Isaiah's call, 6:8). The New Testament uses the term in the sense of a general call to salvation (Mt 22:14), a specific internal call accompanied by the Spirit's touch (Rom 8:29–30), and to God's service (Gal 1:1; Eph 4:1).

centrifugal witness The type of testimony to one's biblical faith that comes through verbal proclamation and attempts to persuade others. An intentional effort to speak to others is involved (Acts 1:8).

centripetal witness The type of testimony to one's biblical faith that comes through others observing believers living out their faith. In such cases, others may see believers' actions and glorify God or ask them about their faith (Dt 4:6; Mt 5:16).

Chaldeans A people group from central and southeastern Mesopotamia that formed the Chaldean dynasty in the eighth century BC. Their most famous king was Nebuchadnezzar II (605–562 BC), who conquered Jerusalem and Judah in 587 BC and took its people into exile. Because of the Chaldeans' location in Babylonia, the term "Babylonians" is also often used to describe them.

City of David The territory of Jerusalem under David's control during his reign (1010–970 BC)—mainly the southeastern hill the Jebusites originally occupied (2 Sm 5:6–10). Later kings such as Solomon and Hezekiah expanded the city's size significantly; Solomon added the temple mount area (1 Kgs 6), while Hezekiah fortified the city's walls (Is 22:10). The New Testament use of the term to refer to Bethlehem (Lk 2:4, 11) does not occur in Isaiah.

complacency An excessive feeling of self-sufficiency or self-satisfaction; in Isaiah, this feeling resulted in people forgetting or neglecting their relationship with God (56:10–12).

concordance A Bible study tool that lists words alphabetically and includes all the verse references where the words occur. Computerized concordance software can search groups of words or phrases simultaneously, thus creating the potential for even deeper study and understanding of the Bible.

co-regency A situation in which two kings (typically father and son) rule at the same time for various reasons of practicality. Many scholars understand co-regencies as helpful in explaining the chronology of the Israelite and Judean kings.

covenant A solemn agreement or promise wherein two parties agree to serve or bless each other in some way. God's covenant with Abraham (Gn 12:1–3) finds fuller expression in both God's covenant with Israel and with the church.

creation mandate God's command to humanity to fill the earth and exercise dominion over his creation as responsible stewards (Gn 1:28–30).

Cyrus King who established the Persian empire. Cyrus conquered Media, Lydia, and Babylon, the latter in 539 BC. In the first year of Cyrus's reign, he issued a proclamation allowing exiled Jews to return to Judah to rebuild Jerusalem and their cities (Ezr 1:1). Isaiah 45:1 actually spoke of him as God's "anointed one." *See also* anointed one.

daughter of Zion A poetic way of designating the women of Jerusalem (Is 3:16–17) or the city and population in general (Is 1:8; 37:22).

David Israel's second king (1010–970 BC), who established Israel's supremacy over its neighbors. He also received a promise from God concerning his throne (2 Sm 7).

day of the Lord A period of time (not a literal day) during which the Bible expects God will judge the sin of unbelievers, cleanse believers of their sin, and save his own. Different passages emphasize different aspects of the day; ultimately the expression designates the final judgment and salvation God brings to the world.

Decapolis The term literally means "ten cities" and designates a group of ten Greek cities east of the Sea of Galilee that were largely Gentile-populated. Jesus had some ministry in this area (Mk 7:31), including casting demons into a herd of swine (Mk 5:1–20).

Deutero-Isaiah In connection with the multiple authorship view of the book of Isaiah, a term used by scholars to denote a person or school of disciples responsible for the writing of Isaiah 40–66. *See also* Trito-Isaiah.

discipleship "Disciple" literally means "learner." Discipleship designates either the process of growing in one's relationship with the Lord or helping another do the same.

divination The practice of attempting to know the future and/or discern the will of God or the gods by magical practices or reading omens. Such practices were well-documented in ancient Egypt and Mesopotamia and even in ancient Israel, though the Bible condemned them (Is 8:19–20).

Edom The nation located south-southeast of the Dead Sea. The Edomites descended from Esau, Jacob's brother (Gn 36:1), and often fought with Israel and Judah (Jer 49:7–22).

Enuma Elish The Babylonian epic that describes how Marduk (also called Bel) became chief deity of the pantheon of gods. According to the epic, Marduk defeated the evil goddess Tiamat and made heaven and earth from her body. The gods then created humanity to serve them, and also, in gratitude to Marduk, built for him the city of Babylon.

eschatological, eschatology From the Greek word *eschatos* "last, final." Eschatology denotes the study of the last things, including the final judgment of humanity, the salvation of the faithful, and the creation of a new heaven and earth.

exodus The Hebrews' flight from Egypt under the leadership of Moses (Ex 12–14), culminating in the drowning of Pharaoh's army and rescue of Israel. The exodus constitutes the central salvation event of the Old Testament (Ps 136:10–15) and demonstrated God's covenant relationship with Israel.

fasting The intentional self-denial of food (and sometimes drink) for a period of time, for the purpose of focusing more completely on spiritual matters and one's relationship with God. Isaiah 58:3–12 stressed that God desired that fasting be accompanied by seeking God's face and ways, or it meant nothing.

foretelling A function of the prophetic office in which the prophet predicted future events for the purpose of encouraging present faithfulness to God.

forthtelling A function of the prophetic office in which the prophet proclaimed God's truth with primary application directly to his own generation.

Galilee of the Gentiles Galilee means "circle" or "region" and denotes the northern part of Israel's territory. Due to the crossing of major highway routes in Galilee, the area became much more international, and hence, much more susceptible to Gentile (usually pagan) influence. *See also* Gentiles.

Gentiles People of non-Jewish descent. The Hebrew word *goyim* is also translated "nations" and designates people groups rather than territories, as the Greek equivalent *ethne* (cf. "ethnic") suggests.

Gihon Spring Jerusalem's main water source, located at the east-southeast edge of the city along the lower slope of the Kidron Valley. King Hezekiah's tunnel diverted water from the spring to the Pool of Siloam farther inside the city (2 Chr 32:30).

gospel The term literally means "good news" and is the biblical term used to describe God's plan of salvation as accomplished by Jesus and announced by his followers. *See also* Gospels; Synoptic Gospels.

Gospels The first four books of the New Testament— Matthew, Mark, Luke, and John. *See also* gospel; Synoptic Gospels.

grace Theologically, the term denotes the undeserved favor people receive from God, especially with regard to salvation. The apostle Paul affirmed that grace is the foundation for salvation through faith in Jesus (Eph 2:8–9).

Great Commission, Great Commission mandate Jesus's command to his followers to proclaim the gospel of God's salvation through Jesus to the ends of the earth (Mt 28:18–20; Mk 16:15–16 [not in many early manuscripts]; Lk 24:45–49; Jn 20:21–22; Acts 1:8). The Great Commission mandate focuses primarily on the spiritual realm and on eternity. *See also* creation mandate.

guilt The responsibility an individual or group bears for its sin or wrongdoing. Sin is a violation of God's holy character and brings guilt on the sinner. Guilt in the Bible is always a condition, never a feeling.

guilt offering The guilt offering (Lv 5:14–6:7) appears closely related to the sin offering (Lv 4:1–5:13) and made restitution for a variety of offenses, including the profaning of sacred items and violations of a social nature. Isaiah 53:10 describes the servant (Jesus) as the ultimate guilt offering for God's people.

hesed Hebrew word variously translated "lovingkindness," "kindness," "faithfulness," "grace," "favor," "loyalty," and "covenant love." It generally describes all the blessing that comes to God's children because of their relationship with him.

Hezekiah Good king of Judah in the late eighth century BC who instituted many spiritual reforms. Hezekiah stood strong in his faith against Sennacherib, king of Assyria (Is 36–37), but showed poor judgment with the Babylonian delegation of Merodach-Baladan (Is 39). *See also* Merodach-Baladan II.

holiness God's separateness from his creation and his setting apart for himself certain things or people from his creation. Holiness is something God is and something he calls his children to be (Lv 19:2). Isaiah's encounter with God (6:1–8) profoundly shaped his sense of God's holiness and may have influenced his use of the name "Holy One of Israel" as a favorite title for the Lord. *See also* righteousness.

Holy One of Israel Isaiah's common designation for Yahweh, the God of Israel.

hope Confident assurance based on God's promise. Hope in the Bible is never wishful thinking; the Hebrew word is sometimes also translated "look" or "wait," but always with expectant anticipation.

Hoshea The northern kingdom of Israel's last king. Hoshea ruled nine years as Assyria's vassal king, but his rebellion led to the destruction of Samaria, Israel's capital, and the subsequent scattering of the people by the Assyrians.

Immanuel Hebrew term meaning "God is with us" (Is 7:14). The announcement of Immanuel's birth originally was to serve as a sign to Ahaz, Judah's faithless king. According to the Gospel writer Matthew, the prophecy of Immanuel's birth found its ultimate fulfillment in Jesus (Mt 1:22–23).

John the Baptist Also known as John the Baptizer, John was the forerunner to the Messiah and announced Jesus's coming (Jn 1:26–27). He described himself as the fulfillment of Isaiah's words (40:3; Jn 1:23).

justify, justification To declare righteous or count as righteous (not to be righteous or make righteous). Justification is a legal term describing a defendant receiving a verdict of "not guilty" (Is 53:11). In the New Testament, justification is that act of God wherein he forgives believing sinners of all their sin and credits to their account the righteousness of Jesus (Rom 3:21–28). However, the apostle Paul argued that justification by faith long preceded New Testament times by using Abraham as his supreme example (Gn 15:6; Rom 4:1–5).

kingdom The dynamic rule or reign of God. The sovereign God of history calls people to enter the kingdom through submission to his will, aligning themselves with his purpose.

Lachish An important city of Judah that guarded one of the valleys to the international coastal highway. Lachish suffered defeats at the hands of both Assyria and Babylon as its citizens sought to prevent the invaders from getting to Jerusalem.

lament A genre of poetry sometimes used in prophetic oracles. In a lament, the writer typically bemoans a sad condition either the individual or community is experiencing. He then expresses his trust in God to deal with the situation. Often a lament ends with praise as the writer ponders the truth that God is with him even if the circumstances don't suggest it.

Leviathan Some sort of sea creature mentioned by Isaiah as receiving God's judgment in the day of the Lord (Is 27:1). Some have tried to link Leviathan with Lotan, a Canaanite deity. While such a link may provide a general cultural backdrop, most scholars believe Isaiah's imagery represents God's final judgment of Satan in light of the language's similarity to Rv 12:9; 20:2. *See also* day of the Lord.

linear view of history The idea that history as we know it is going somewhere; that is, it has a starting point (Gn 1:1) and an ending point (Rv 21:1). Eastern religions (e.g., Buddhism, Hinduism), on the other hand, have a cyclical view of history that allows for an infinite number of cycles.

literary dependence Term that describes a writer borrowing or adapting material from an earlier source to some significant extent. In such cases, a relationship between the two texts is clearly observable, and one text is clearly primary. For example, 2 Kings 18–20 is dependent on Isaiah 36–39.

literary interdependence Term that describes a situation where two texts are connected in some clear way, but the direction of influence is unclear. An example would be Isaiah 2:1–4 and Micah 4:1–4.

Maher-Shalal-Hash-Baz Name of a child of Isaiah (8:1–4). The meaning of his name—"swift is the plunder, speedy is the prey"—pointed to the imminent defeat of Syria and Israel during the Syro-Ephraimite War (735–734 BC). *See also* Syro-Ephraimite War.

Manasseh Son of Hezekiah and evil king of Judah. Manasseh reigned 55 years, and his prolonged and extensive wickedness sent Judah into a downward spiritual spiral from which she was not able to recover (2 Kgs 21:1–18; Jer 15:4).

Marduk *See* Bel.

Masoretic Text One of the earliest and most reliable Hebrew texts of the Old Testament. Scholars believe it dates as early as the first century AD, and the scribes who oversaw its preparation (the Masoretes) carefully preserved the text's accuracy.

Medes A kingdom located south and southwest of the Caspian Sea, composed at first by nomadic tribes that later banded together. The Medes led a coalition force against the fading Assyrian empire and defeated Nineveh, Assyria's capital, in 612 BC. Even during the Persian empire, the Medes played an important role, as reflected in the references to both the Medes and the Persians in the book of Daniel (Dn 5:28, 31; 8:20; 9:1).

Merodach-Baladan II King of Babylon 721–710 and 703 BC. His attempts to assert Babylonian independence from Assyria included sending a delegation to King Hezekiah of Judah (Is 39:1–8) to assess possible future support. *See also* Hezekiah.

Mesha stela A monument prepared by order of King Mesha of Moab (2 Kgs 3:4–5) to commemorate his victory over Israel. In the stela, Mesha brags of how he threw off Israel's yoke of oppression, and claims "Israel has perished forever"—obviously a bit of an exaggeration! The text contains thirty-five lines of text written in Moabite, a Canaanite dialect closely related to Hebrew.

Messiah "Anointed one." From the Hebrew *mashiach*; prophets, priests, and kings were all anointed, but kings and priests were most often designated by this title. Isaiah used the term to describe Cyrus, whom God had anointed to bring his people home (45:1). Ultimately the concept of Messiah is fulfilled in Jesus; the Greek equivalent of *mashiach* is *christos*, from which the term "Christ" comes.

millennium A term used by some evangelicals to describe a thousand-year period begun by Jesus's Second Coming and during which Jesus reigns on earth with his saints (Rv 20:1–6). Other evangelicals understand the millennium in a figurative sense, referring to either the church age or to heaven. *See also* premillennial, premillennialism.

Nabu/Nebo Important god of the Babylonian pantheon (Is 46:1). Nabu was the son of Bel/Marduk, god of wisdom and the patron deity of the scribes. Nabu's name survives in the name Nebuchadnezzar, which means "O Nabu, protect my boundary."

Nebuchadnezzar II Second king of the Chaldean dynasty (605–562 BC) and conqueror of Judah and Jerusalem (2 Kgs 24:1, 10–17; 25:1–22). He is also mentioned commonly in the books of Jeremiah (39, 52) and Daniel (1–4).

onomatopoeic, onomatopoeia A convention of language in which the sound a word describes mimics the word itself (e.g., "bang," "fizz," "pop," "crunch," "squish," "snap").

paronomasia A play on words (e.g., see discussion of Is 5:7).

premillennial, premillennialism A view of eschatology held by many evangelicals purporting that Jesus's Second Coming will precede his establishment of a thousand-year reign on earth (Rv 19:11–20:6). *See also* eschatological, eschatology; millennium.

Rashi Influential medieval Jewish commentator who lived in the eleventh century BC. Rashi was the first Jewish scholar on record to suggest the suffering servant of Isaiah 53 was Israel. His extensive treatises on the Scriptures are still studied today by Jews and scholars of the medieval period.

redeem, redemption The paying of a price to secure the release of someone or something. Animals or property dedicated to the Lord could be redeemed, for example, if the owner paid an additional 20 percent beyond their established value (Lv 27:11–15, 27, 31). Isaiah describes God as his people's ultimate redeemer, who bought them back from exile (43:1, 14; 44:6). Likewise, the New Testament applies redemption language to Christ's work on the cross (Eph 1:7; Col 1:14).

remnant Something left over, a remainder. Theologically, the term often applies to a select group that plays a significant role of faith in the next step of God's salvation purposes (Is 10:20–21; 37:31–32; Rom 11:5).

repentance A conscious, willful turning away from sin. The Hebrew word (*shub*) literally means "to return," i.e., to return to one's spiritual roots. The Greek word *metanoeo* literally indicates a radical change of mind.

resurrection The act of coming back to life from the grave. Isaiah proclaimed this phenomenon would happen to God's people one day (26:19)—an event guaranteed by Jesus's resurrection (1 Cor 15:20–22).

righteousness Moral uprightness of heart and actions. In the prophets, righteousness is often related to socio-covenantal justice; indeed, justice and righteousness often appear together as something God brings to his people (Is 9:7; 33:5). At the same time, God is pleased when his people pursue righteousness (51:1, 7).

Sabbath The seventh day of the week, blessed by God because on that day he ceased from his creative activity (Gn 2:2–3). God therefore commanded his people to cease from their usual activities on the Sabbath to honor the day before him (Ex 20:8–11).

The book of Isaiah notes Sabbath observance as something that pleases God and demonstrates one's faithfulness (Is 56:2, 4, 6; 58:13–14).

sacrificial system The organized and detailed set of prescribed sacrifices in the Pentateuch (especially Leviticus) given to help people worship God on his terms. Sacrifices might be brought when a worshiper recognized a need for forgiveness, desired to express gratitude, wanted to show devotion, or needed to fulfill a vow.

Sennacherib Assyrian king (704–681 BC) who came against Hezekiah in 701 BC (Is 36–37). God's intervention led to Sennacherib's return to Assyria empty-handed.

Septuagint (LXX) An early Greek translation of the Old Testament (third century BC). The term comes from the tradition that seventy-two translators (six from each of Israel's twelve tribes) worked on the translation. The Septuagint provides an early and reliable witness to the Old Testament text and includes several apocryphal books as well—books that were an important part of Israel's heritage but were not on a level with Scripture.

seraph Angelic creatures of fiery-like appearance (Is 6:2). The term comes from the Hebrew verb *saraph*, which means "to burn."

servant A slave; someone who is the property of another. The term occurs over 800 times in the Old Testament to refer to common slaves as well as servants of the Lord such as Moses (Jos 1:2). Isaiah's use of the word servant is fluid, sometimes applying to Israel (41:8; 44:1), the remnant (49:6), or the Messiah (42:1–4; 52:13–53:12). The servant exists to do the master's will; paradoxically, Paul asserts that to be a slave of God is the only way to be truly free (Rom 6:22).

shalom The term is often translated "peace," but literally describes wholeness and completeness of life—life as God intended it to be in all its fullness.

social justice Living out the implications of our faith in society. Both Old and New Testaments are concerned that believers show their faith by godly living and just treatment of others. Social justice in and of itself is not the gospel, but it follows logically from a right relationship with God. Believers are to see others as God sees them and see issues as God sees them, and take appropriate action.

Sodom and Gomorrah Two cities in the Dead Sea region that God destroyed for their extreme wickedness (Gn 19:24–25). Sodom's arrogance and pride, coupled with its lack of concern for the poor and its sexual immorality, rendered it an appropriate point of comparison for biblical writers who warned the faithful of God's judgment of such evil (Ez 16:49–50; 2 Pt 2:6).

sovereignty of God The doctrine that God rules and guides all things, including creation, human history, and redemption according to his eternal purposes. God's sovereignty sometimes allows evil but ultimately will judge and end it, and also holds people accountable for their choices. The Bible also affirms that because God is sovereign, believers can pray with confidence.

Spirit God's Spirit is the Holy Spirit, the third person of the Trinity. Isaiah uses the expression "Spirit of the Lord" (11:2; 61:1) or simply "Spirit" (42:1; 48:16) to describe the divine Person who empowers believers to carry out God's purposes.

stewardship Biblical stewardship is our responsibility to manage life's resources well. A proper understanding of stewardship acknowledges that everything belongs to God; therefore, we are to manage and use these resources for his glory.

Synoptic Gospels A name that denotes the first three Gospels—Matthew, Mark, and Luke. The term "synoptic" means "with one eye," that is, expressing the same general perspective. The Gospel of John takes a significantly different approach as it narrates key events from Jesus's life.

Syro-Ephraimite War An event that occurred in 735–734 BC when a coalition of Syrian and Israelite forces moved to attack Judah to force Judah to join them against Assyria and its king, Tiglath-Pileser III (Is 7:1–16). Isaiah warned King Ahaz of Judah to trust God, but Ahaz chose to join forces with Assyria, leading to Israel's annexation by Assyria (2 Kgs 16:7–9; 17:3). *See also* Tiglath-Pileser III.

Targum Early Aramaic writings that contain (1) translations of the Old Testament into Aramaic and (2) commentary on the text of the Old Testament. The writings date largely to a few centuries prior to and after the ministry of Jesus and provide insights into early Jewish interpretation of the text.

theophany From the Greek words *theos* "God" and *phane* "manifestation," a term denoting an appearance of God (e.g., Is 6:1–8). Usually in such appearances the Lord temporarily assumed a human form (Gn 18:1–2).

theophoric From the Greek words *theos* "God" and *phero* "to bear, carry," a term meaning "God-bearing" or "god-bearing." Theophoric personal names are names that contain the name of a deity, for example, Isaiah (Heb. *Yisha'yahu* "Yahweh has saved"), Jerubbaal ("let Baal contend"), or Belshazzar ("O Bel, guard the king").

Tiglath-Pileser III Assyrian king who reigned from 745–727 BC and reestablished the Assyrians as the dominant power in the ancient world. *See also* Syro-Ephraimite War.

Trito-Isaiah In connection with the multiple authorship view of the book of Isaiah, a term used by scholars to denote a person or school of disciples responsible for the writing of Isaiah 56–66. *See also* Deutero-Isaiah.

vengeance The restitution or punishment that may follow wrongdoings or injustices against a particular party. Vengeance in Isaiah may involve punishment by God (34:8), but often designates a balancing of the scales of justice, a correction of unfair imbalances in society (61:2).

Via Maris An international road—also called the way of the sea—that runs along the Levant coast (Is 9:1). In later times the term designated the entire network of roads that ran from Mesopotamia through Syro-Palestine to Egypt.

Vulgate Latin translation of the Bible completed by Jerome about AD 400. The Western church used the Vulgate as its Bible of choice for over a thousand years.

way of the sea *See* Via Maris.

world evangelization The act of striving to accomplish the Great Commission prophesied by Isaiah (66:18–19) and commanded by Jesus (Mt 28:18–20). *See also* Great Commission.

Select Bibliography

Articles

Barber, Cyril J. "The Servant Songs: A Study in Isaiah." *Journal of Psychology and Theology* 14 (1986): 68–69.

Beuken, W. A. M. "The Emergence of the Shoot of Jesse: An Eschatological or a Now Event?" *Calvin Theological Journal* 39 (2004): 88–108.

———. "The Manifestation of Yahweh and the Commission of Isaiah: Isaiah 6 Read against the Background of Isaiah 1." *Calvin Theological Journal* 39 (2004): 72–87.

Croatto, J. S. "The 'Nations' in the Salvific Oracles of Isaiah." *Vetus Testamentum* 55 (2005): 143–61.

Dahms, John V. "Isaiah 55:11 and the Gospel of John." *Evangelical Quarterly* 53 (1981): 78–88.

Doohan, Helen. "Contrasts in Prophetic Leadership: Isaiah and Jeremiah." *Biblical Theology Bulletin* 13 (1983): 39–43.

Dumbrell, William J. "The Purpose of the Book of Isaiah." *Tyndale Bulletin* 36 (1985): 111–28.

Ellis, E. E. "Isaiah in the New Testament." *Southwestern Journal of Theology* 34 (1991): 31–35.

Erlandsson, Seth. "Burden of Babylon: A Study of Isaiah 13:2–14:23." *Springfielder* 38 (1974): 1–12.

Evans, Craig A. "The Function of Isaiah 6:9–10 in Mark and John." *Novum Testamentum* 24 (1982): 124–38.

Feinberg, Charles L. "The Virgin Birth in the Old Testament and Isaiah 7:14." *Bibliotheca Sacra* 119 (1962): 251–58.

France, R. T. "The Servant of the Lord in the Teaching of Jesus." *Tyndale Bulletin* 19 (1968): 26–52.

Grisanti, Michael A. "Israel's Mission to the Nations in Isaiah 40–55: An Update." *Master's Seminary Journal* 9 (1998): 39–61.

Hamborg, Graham R. "Reasons for Judgement in the Oracles against the Nations of the Prophet Isaiah." *Vetus Testamentum* 31 (1981): 145–59.

Jensen, Joseph. "Yahweh's Plan in Isaiah and in the Rest of the Old Testament." *Catholic Biblical Quarterly* 48 (1986): 443–55.

Johnson, Dennis E. "Jesus against the Idols: The Use of Isaianic Servant Songs in the Missiology of Acts." *Westminster Theological Journal* 52 (1990): 343–53.

Kaiser, Walter C., Jr. "The Great Commission in the Old Testament." *International Journal of Frontier Missions* 13 (1996): 3–7.

Lindsey, Duane. "Isaiah's Songs of the Servant." *Bibliotheca Sacra* 139 (1982): 12–31.

Litwak, Kenneth D. "The Use of Quotations from Isaiah 52:13–53:12 in the New Testament." *Journal of the Evangelical Theological Society* 26 (1983): 385–94.

Moore, John A. "The Light That Failed: Missions in the Old Testament." *Congregational Quarterly* 36 (1958): 36–43.

Neyrey, Jerome H. "The Thematic Use of Isaiah 42:1–4 in Matthew 12." *Biblica* 63 (1982): 457–73.

O'Kane, Martin. "Isaiah: A Prophet in the Footsteps of Moses." *Journal for the Study of the Old Testament* (1996): 29–51.

Payne, J. B. "The Unity of Isaiah: Evidence from Chapters 36–39." *Bulletin of the Evangelical Theological Society* 6 (1963): 50–56.

Person, Raymond F. "II Kings 18–20 and Isaiah 36–39: A Text Critical Case Study in the Redaction History of the Book of Isaiah." *Zeitschrift für die Alttestamentliche Wissenschaft* 111 (1999): 373–79.

Rimbach, James A. "Model Servant/Servant Model." *Concordia Journal* 10 (1984): 12–20.

Roberts, J. J. M. "Isaiah in Old Testament Theology." *Interpretation* 36 (1982): 130–43.

Rosenberg, Roy A. "The Slain Messiah in the Old Testament." *Zeitschrift für die Alttestamentliche Wissenschaft* 99 (1987): 259–61.

Rowley, Harold H. "The Servant Mission: The Servant Songs and Evangelism." *Interpretation* 8 (1954): 259–72.

Schibler, Daniel. "The Servant Songs: A Study in Isaiah." *Journal of the Evangelical Theological Society* 29 (1986): 472–74.

Snodgrass, Klyne. "Streams of Tradition Emerging from Isaiah 40:1–5 and Their Adaptation in the New Testament." *Journal for the Study of the New Testament* (1980): 24–45.

Thompson, Michael E. W. "Isaiah's Ideal King." *Journal for the Study of the Old Testament* (1982): 79–88.

Walton, John H. "Isa 7:14: What's in a Name?" *Journal of the Evangelical Theological Society* 30 (1987): 289–306.

———. "New Observations on the Date of Isaiah." *Journal of the Evangelical Theological Society* 28 (1985): 129–32.

Ward, James M. "Servant Songs in Isaiah." *Review & Expositor* 65 (1968): 433–46.

Watts, Rikki E. "Echoes from the Past: Israel's Ancient Traditions and the Destiny of the Nations in Isaiah 40–55." *Journal for the Study of the Old Testament* 28 (2004): 481–508.

Weren, Wilhelmus J. C. "The Use of Isaiah 5:1–7 in the Parable of the Tenants (Mark 12:1–12; Matthew 21:33–46)." *Biblica* 79 (1998): 1–26.

Books

Alexander, Joseph A. *Commentary on the Prophecies of Isaiah*. Grand Rapids: Zondervan, 1953.

Anderson, Bernhard W. *The Eighth Century Prophets: Amos, Hosea, Isaiah, Micah*. Philadelphia: Fortress, 1978.

Arnold, Bill T., and Bryan E. Beyer. *Encountering the Old Testament: A Christian Survey*. Grand Rapids: Baker Academic, 1999.

———. eds. *Readings from the Ancient Near East: Primary Sources for Old Testament Study*. Grand Rapids: Baker Academic, 2002.

Bartelt, Andrew H. *The Book around Immanuel: Style and Structure in Isaiah 2–12*. Winona Lake, IN: Eisenbrauns, 1996.

Beaton, Richard. *Isaiah's Christ in Matthew's Gospel*. New York: Cambridge University Press, 2002.

Blenkinsopp, Joseph. *Isaiah 56–66: A New Translation with Introduction and Commentary*. New York: Doubleday, 2003.

Brownlee, William H. *The Meaning of the Qumrân Scrolls for the Bible: With Special Attention to the Book of Isaiah*. New York: Oxford, 1964.

Brueggemann, Walter. *Isaiah 1–39*. Louisville: Westminster/John Knox, 1998.

———. *Isaiah 40–66*. Louisville: Westminster/John Knox, 1998.

———. *Using God's Resources Wisely: Isaiah and Urban Possibility*. Louisville: Westminster/John Knox, 1993.

Calvin, John. *Commentary on the Book of the Prophet Isaiah*. Translated by William Pringle. Grand Rapids: Eerdmans, 1948.

———. *The Gospel according to Isaiah*. Grand Rapids: Eerdmans, 1953.

Childs, Brevard S. *Isaiah: A Commentary*. Louisville: Westminster/John Knox, 2001.

Chisholm, Robert B. *Handbook on the Prophets: Isaiah, Jeremiah, Lamentations, Ezekiel, Daniel, Minor Prophets*. Grand Rapids: Baker Academic, 2002.

Clements, Ronald E. *Isaiah 1–39*. Grand Rapids: Eerdmans, 1980.

Conrad, Edgar W. *Reading Isaiah*. Minneapolis: Fortress, 1991.

Darr, Katheryn P. *Isaiah's Vision and the Family of God*. Louisville: Westminster/John Knox, 1994.

Erdman, Charles Rosenbury. *The Book of Isaiah: An Exposition*. Grand Rapids: Baker Academic, 1982.

Goldingay, John. *Isaiah*. Peabody, MA: Hendrickson; Carlisle, UK: Paternoster, 2001.

Gordon, Robert P. *"The Place Is Too Small for Us": The Israelite Prophets in Recent Scholarship*. Winona Lake, IN: Eisenbrauns, 1995.

Gross, Chaim. *The Book of Isaiah*. Philadelphia: Jewish Publication Society, 1972.

Hacking, Philip. *Isaiah: Free to Suffer and to Serve*. Grand Rapids: Baker Academic, 1995.

Hailey, Homer. *A Commentary on Isaiah: With Emphasis on the Messianic Hope*. Grand Rapids: Baker Academic, 1985.

Hallo, W. W., and K. Lawson Younger, eds., *The Context of Scripture*. 3 vols. Leiden: Brill, 1997–2002.

Hanson, Paul D. *Isaiah 40–66*. Louisville: Westminster/John Knox, 1996.

Hindson, Edward E. *Isaiah's Immanuel: A Sign of His Times or the Sign of the Ages?* Grand Rapids: Baker Academic, 1978.

Hoerth, Alfred J., Gerald L. Mattingly, and Edwin M. Yamauchi, eds. *Peoples of the Old Testament World*. Grand Rapids: Baker Academic, 1994.

Holladay, William L. *Unbound by Time: Isaiah Still Speaks*. Cambridge, MA: Cowley, 2002.

Hutton, Rodney R. *Fortress Introduction to the Prophets*. Minneapolis: Fortress, 2004.

Kaiser, Otto. *Isaiah 1–12: A Commentary*. Translated by John Bowden. 2nd ed. Philadelphia: Westminster, 1983.

———. *Isaiah 13–39: A Commentary*. Translated by R. A. Wilson. Philadelphia: Westminster, 1974.

Keil, Carl Friedrich, and Friedrich Delitzsch. *Commentary on the Old Testament*. 10 vols. Grand Rapids: Eerdmans, 1972.

Knight, George A. F. *The New Israel: A Commentary on the Book of Isaiah 56–66*. Edinburgh: Handsel, 1985.

———. *Servant Theology: A Commentary on the Book of Isaiah 40–55*. Edinburgh: Handsel, 1984.

Leupold, H. C. *Exposition of Isaiah*. 2 vols. Grand Rapids: Baker Academic, 1976.

Lindsey, F. D. *The Servant Songs: A Study in Isaiah*. Chicago: Moody, 1985.

MacRae, Allan A. *The Gospel of Isaiah*. Chicago: Moody, 1977.

Martin, Alfred, and John A. Martin. *Isaiah: The Glory of the Messiah*. Chicago: Moody, 1983.

Motyer, J. A. *Isaiah: An Introduction and Commentary*. Downers Grove, IL: InterVarsity, 1999.

———. *The Prophecy of Isaiah: An Introduction and Commentary*. Downers Grove, IL: InterVarsity, 1993.

Mouw, Richard J. *When the Kings Come Marching In: Isaiah and the New Jerusalem*. Rev. ed. Grand Rapids: Eerdmans, 2002.

Mullins, Terence Y. *Isaiah*. 2 vols. Minneapolis: Fortress, 1989.

Neubauer, Adolf, and S. R. Driver. *The Fifty-third Chapter of Isaiah: According to the Jewish Interpreters.* 2 vols. New York: Ktav, 1969.

North, Christopher R. *The Suffering Servant in Deutero-Isaiah: An Historical and Critical Study.* London: Oxford, 1956.

Oswalt, John. *The Book of Isaiah: Chapters 1–39.* Grand Rapids: Eerdmans, 1986.

———. *The Book of Isaiah: Chapters 40–66.* Grand Rapids: Eerdmans, 1998.

Pao, David W. *Acts and the Isaianic New Exodus.* Grand Rapids: Baker Academic, 2002.

Peterson, David. *Christ and His People in the Book of Isaiah.* Leicester, UK: Inter-Varsity, 2003.

Pritchard, James B., ed. *Ancient Near Eastern Texts Relating to the Old Testament.* 3rd ed. Princeton: Princeton University Press, 1969.

Quinn-Miscall, Peter D. *Reading Isaiah: Poetry and Vision.* Louisville: Westminster/John Knox, 2001.

Ridderbos, J. *Isaiah.* Translated by John Vriend. Grand Rapids: Zondervan, 1985.

Rosenbloom, Joseph R. *The Dead Sea Isaiah Scroll: A Literary Analysis.* Grand Rapids: Eerdmans, 1970.

Sawyer, John F. A. *The Fifth Gospel: Isaiah in the History of Christianity.* New York: Cambridge University Press, 1996.

———. *Isaiah.* 2 vols. Philadelphia: Westminster, 1986.

Seitz, Christopher R. *Isaiah 1–39.* Louisville: Westminster/John Knox, 1993.

———. *Reading and Preaching the Book of Isaiah.* Philadelphia: Fortress, 1988.

Shipp, R. M. *Of Dead Kings and Dirges: Myth and Meaning in Isaiah 14:4b–21.* Atlanta: SBL, 2002.

Sweeney, Marvin A. *Isaiah 1–39: With an Introduction to Prophetic Literature.* Grand Rapids: Eerdmans, 1996.

Thiele, Edwin R. *Chronology of the Hebrew Kings.* Grand Rapids: Zondervan, 1977.

———. *Mysterious Numbers of the Hebrew Kings.* Rev. ed. Grand Rapids: Kregel, 1994.

Watts, John D. W. *Isaiah 1–33.* Word Biblical Commentary 24. Waco: Word Books, 1985.

———. *Isaiah 34–66.* Word Biblical Commentary 25. Waco: Word Books, 1987.

Watts, Rikki E. *Isaiah's New Exodus and Mark.* Rev. ed. Grand Rapids: Baker Academic, 2000.

Westermann, Claus. *Isaiah 40–66.* Philadelphia: Westminster, 1969.

Whybray, Roger N. *Isaiah 40–66.* Grand Rapids: Eerdmans, 1981.

Widyapranawa, S. H. *The Lord Is Savior: Faith in National Crisis: A Commentary on the Book of Isaiah 1–39.* Grand Rapids: Eerdmans, 1990.

Wildberger, Hans. *Isaiah 1–12: A Commentary.* Minneapolis: Fortress, 1991.

———. *Isaiah 13–27: A Continental Commentary.* Minneapolis: Fortress, 1997.

———. *Isaiah 28–39: A Continental Commentary.* Minneapolis: Fortress, 2002.

Wolf, Herbert M. *Interpreting Isaiah: The Suffering and Glory of the Messiah.* Grand Rapids: Zondervan, 1985.

Wright, George E. *Book of Isaiah.* Richmond: John Knox, 1961.

Young, Edward J. *Book of Isaiah.* 3 vols. Grand Rapids: Eerdmans, 1972.

———. *Studies in Isaiah.* Grand Rapids: Eerdmans, 1954.

———. *Who Wrote Isaiah?* Grand Rapids: Eerdmans, 1958.

Youngblood, Ronald. *The Book of Isaiah: An Introductory Commentary.* 2nd ed. Grand Rapids: Baker Academic, 1993. Reprint, Wipf and Stack, 2000.

Scripture Index

Subject Index